Poetry for historia

Manchester University Press

Poetry for historians

Or, W. H. Auden and history

Carolyn Steedman

Manchester University Press

The right of Carolyn Steedman to be identified as the author of this work has been asserted
by her in accordance with the Copyright, Designs and Patents Act 1988.

Published by Manchester University Press
Altrincham Street, Manchester M1 7JA

www.manchesteruniversitypress.co.uk

John Ashbery, 'The Ridiculous Translator's Hopes', from *And the Stars Were Shining* by
John Ashbery. Copyright © 1994 by John Ashbery. Reprinted by permission of Georges
Borchardt, Inc., on behalf of the author, and by Carcanet Press, Manchester.

British Library Cataloguing-in-Publication Data
A catalogue record for this book is available from the British Library

ISBN   978 1 5261 2521 7 hardback

ISBN   978 1 5261 2523 1 paperback

First published 2018

The publisher has no responsibility for the persistence or accuracy of URLs for any
external or third-party internet websites referred to in this book, and does not guarantee
that any content on such websites is, or will remain, accurate or appropriate.

Typeset by
Servis Filmsetting Ltd, Stockport, Cheshire
Printed in Great Britain by
CPI Group (UK) Ltd, Croydon CR0 4YY

O lurcher-loving collier black as night,
Follow your love across the smokeless hill;
Your lamp is out, the cages are all still;
Course for heart and do not miss,
For Sunday soon is past and, Kate, fly not so fast,
For Monday comes when none may kiss:
Be marble to his soot, and to his black be white.

W. H. Auden, 'Madrigal', 1938.

The social revolution … can only create its poetry from the future, not from the past.

Karl Marx, 'The Eighteenth Brumaire of Louis Bonaparte', 1852.

I know – the fact is really not unnerving –
   That what is done is done, that no past dies,
That what we see depends on who's observing,
   And what we think[,] on our activities …

W. H. Auden, 'Letter to Lord Byron', July–October 1936.

Dakin How does stuff happen, do you think?
         People decide to do stuff.
         Make moves. Alter things.
Irwin I'm not sure what you're talking about.

Alan Bennett, *The History Boys*, 2004.

Contents

Introduction

All of this is only because I just wanted to *say* a poet's words, over and over again, to someone. Poetry may make nothing happen in the world – nothing at all, as W. H. Auden said; it may exist only in the place and time of its own creation, but it moves and matters because it maps onto other minds and experiences in ways quite unintended by the poet.[1] You may, if you're lucky, make something new out of it, as did Terry Frost in 1949 in his painting *Madrigal*. A student at Camberwell School of Art, he was at home for the vacation ('A Leamington Lad' is the title of a 2015 exhibition of his work). He had research to do for an assignment and in Leamington Spa Public Library came across Auden's poem 'Madrigal'.[2] The exhibition catalogue relates how 'Frost was attracted [to Auden's poem] because not only did he feel an empathy with the miners of the Midlands, but it described a miner leaving his work to meet his "Kate" and Frost's wife was always known as "Kate" in her family'.[3] 'It was pretty obvious he wasn't coming out of the bloody mine for a cup of tea', said Sir Terry, much later on.[4] The exhibition curator observed that *Madrigal* 'marks a significant point in Frost's career as it was his first abstract work'.[5] Lucky Sir Terry to

1 W. H. Auden, 'In Memory of W. B. Yeats (d. Jan 1939)', *Collected Shorter Poems, 1927–1957*, Faber and Faber, London, 1966, p. 142.
2 'Madrigal' was first published in *New Verse*, 30 (June 1938) as part of the documentary script 'Coalface'. See below, pp. 55, 150.
3 Chris Stephens, *Terry Frost*, Tate Publishing, London, 2004, p. 17, quoted Chloe Frost (ed.), *Sir Terry Frost R. A. (1915–2003). A Leamington Lad. Catalogue published to accompany the exhibition held at Leamington Spa Art Gallery and Museum, 24 July–11 October 2015*, Warwick District Council, 2015, p. 28.
4 Stephens, *Terry Frost*, p. 17.
5 Exhibition Notes, *Sir Terry Frost R. A. (1915–2003), A Leamington Lad*, Leamington Spa Art Gallery and Museum, 2015; *Madrigal*, 1949, Oil on Canvas, Leamington Spa Art Gallery & Museum.

have the chance to make something new out of something so beautiful; to make a new thing that is also beautiful in its turn. And have the ability to do so. Frost's *Madrigal* was a thing made in a future that hadn't happened yet when Auden made his; it is poetry, in its widest meaning, created in a future ten years on from the time of Auden's making.

This book isn't about history-poems, poems about historical events, or 'history-poetry': no 'Eve of Waterloo' or 'Charge of the Light Brigade' here; no *Battle of Minden, a Poem. In Three Books* (1769) by the entirely forgotten Sydney Swinney.[6] This book will discuss W. H. Auden's poetry, and other poetry of the modern era; some of it concerns Auden himself. Auden is so much present because I believed, for a very long time, that his poetry could teach me what kind of thing 'history' is, and what one is up to when doing it. ('Doing history' is an activity, a making of something; 'doing history' encompasses the whole activity: thinking about it, the work of imagination in knowing where to look for material, visualising it; researching it, writing it.) The distinction between 'history' and 'historiography' is important for what follows here; this book is organised by it. The questions put to Auden and other poets are historiographical rather than historical. Byron, for example, wrote historiographically when he versified about the *meaning* of an event already designated 'historical'. 'The Eve of Waterloo' is an extract from his semi-autobiographical poem *Childe Harold's Pilgrimage*, the first two cantos of which were published in 1812. Canto III, which includes 'The Eve', was written and published after Byron had visited the battle site as a tourist on his way to Switzerland in May 1816, so it was composed a year after the historical 'Waterloo' took place. It is not an account of the battle, or an act of personal testimony. It is a re-making of Byron's witnessing the desolate field of conflict, and about the sorrows of war. It presents an interpretation of the meaning of one particular battle, and war in general. It can be read as a historiographical discussion of a historical event in poetic form, though many other readings are possible – and made. For one historian, noting that in 1812, just before his trip to Europe, Byron delivered his famous speech defending Luddite activity to the House of Lords, it marks the passage of a man from politician to poet.[7]

---

6 Sydney Swinney, *The Battle of Minden, A Poem. In Three Books ... Enriched with Critical Notes by Two Friends, and with Explanatory Notes by the Author*, Dodsley, London, 1769–1772. The Battle of Minden (1 August 1759) was a decisive engagement of the Seven Years' War.

7 'The Eve of Waterloo' is part of Canto III, stanzas 21–28. It was not anthologised – did not exist as a separate entity – until the 1830s. Philip Shaw, *Waterloo and the Romantic*

So too may Tennyson's poem be read historiographically, as a cultural artefact produced by a poet who read a newspaper account of the Battle of Balaclava, in October 1854.[8] If patriotism were ever attributed to Tennyson, or praise bestowed on the common soldiers blindly following orders, it is no longer so; his poem is now almost universally understood as one of the ways in which mid-Victorian sensibility was taught to encompass the blind stupidity of war. W. H. Auden knew something of this history of reading when in 1943 he opined that Tennyson 'had the finest ear, perhaps of any English poet; he was also undoubtedly the stupidest; there was little about melancholia that he didn't know; there was little else that he did'.[9] As for poor Sydney Swinney, whom nobody reads, we might want to think of him as a poet writing testimonary history. He served as chaplain during the Seven Years' War (1756–1763) participating in the British army's campaigns in Germany; he was an eye witness to the Battle of Minden. He gained a contemporary reputation as a poet, published translations of classical poetry and occasional verse and song. His epic poem celebrating British victory over the French at Minden was never finished, as he explained in the 1772 edition.[10] The author himself and friends and colleagues did the work of annotating what there was of it; they provided historical context and setting in order to give the reader a more perfect account of an actual historical event, recorded by a witness to it. A reviewer (or perhaps Swinney himself) made apology for his use of the grandest form of all, the epic, but did not discuss its advantages and constraints.[11] To eighteenth-century writers and readers it was perfectly obvious that an elevated topic – a victory for the British in a European conflict – demanded the most elevated of all poetic forms. Had they had a discussion about the appropriate form for writing the history of victors (for 'History to the defeated/May say Alas but cannot help nor pardon') it would have been interestingly

---

Imagination, Palgrave Macmillan, Basingstoke, 2002, pp. 165–191; Carla Pomarè, *Byron and the Discourses of History*, Ashgate, Farnham, 2013; John Beckett, 'Politician or poet? The 6th Lord Byron in the House of Lords, 1809–13', *Parliamentary History*, 34:2 (2015), pp. 201–217.

8 Stefanie Markovits, *The Crimean War in the British Imagination*, Cambridge University Press, Cambridge, 2009.

9 W. H. Auden, 'Introduction to *A Selection from the Poems of Alfred, Lord Tennyson*' (1943), *Prose Volume II. 1939–1948*, Edward Mendelson (ed.), Princeton University Press, Princeton NJ, 2002, pp. 203–212.

10 M. John Cardwell, 'Swinney, Sidney (1721–1783)', *Oxford Dictionary of National Biography*, Oxford University Press, Oxford, 2004.

11 Swinney, *Battle of Minden*, p. 121.

historiographical.[12] As it was, Christopher Smart's puffery simply celebrated Swinney's 'EPIC ELEGANCE ... Sing on, BRIGHT BARD', at the poem's end.[13] Listening to a discussion that never took place among the poet and his friends, and once upon a time, I had a mind to call this book 'Poetry for Historiographers', but then I would have been read even less than the Revd Swinney has been.

Auden wrote a number of poems about historical events; two are famous for his later renunciation of their historiography. 'Spain 1937', quoted from above, was about an event – a civil war – that had already been designated 'historical'. He had spent time in Spain, was witness to violence perpetrated by both sides during the Civil War. The poem is an act of historical testimony *and* Auden's historiographical reflection on the events he described in 1937, and later, when he altered his account.[14] He said that his original last lines, in which History can only express pity for the sorrows she records, equated 'goodness with success' and that this was a 'wicked doctrine'. Auden also altered another' 'history' poem, 'September 1 1939', both before and after publication. The by-now American Auden sits in a bar on Fifty-second Street brooding on the long European history that has brought her to war. He thinks of Fascism and Martin Luther, of the erosion of the individual in mass society, of imperialism, state power, and psychopaths made masters of the universe: 'I and the public know/ What all schoolchildren learn,/Those to whom evil is done/Do evil in return'.[15] He contemplates History, not as a historian, nor indeed as a historiographer, but out of the habit which he told the young women readers of *Mademoiselle* they ought to cultivate: 'we were pretty much alike' he said of his own generation: 'we learned one thing then of value which we must not forget, namely, to take a serious interest in history instead of

12 Auden's first version of 'Spain' (1937) from which he later removed these lines. See below, p. 149.
13 Christopher Smart, 'VERSES TO THE AUTHOR on his POEM', Swinney, *Battle*, p. 129. There were only two books published, not the three of the title. Book 2 has a half-title and a preface dated 1772.
14 E. P. Thompson, 'Outside the Whale' (1960), *The Poverty of Theory and Other Essays*, Merlin, London, 1978, pp. 1–34; Edward Mendelson, *Early Auden* (1981), Faber and Faber, London, 1999, pp. 304–332; Humphrey Carpenter, *W. H. Auden. A Biography* (1981, 1983), Faber and Faber, London, 2010, pp. 217–218; Scott Hamilton, *The Crisis of Theory. E. P. Thompson, the New Left and Postwar British Politics*, Manchester University Press, Manchester, 2011, pp. 65–77.
15 Mendelson, *Early Auden*, pp. 324–330; Richard R. Bozorth, 'American Homosexuality, 1939–1972', Tony Sharpe (ed.), *W. H. Auden in Context*, Cambridge University Press, Cambridge, 2013, pp. 99–106.

thinking only about our own work and having a good time. We began to ask questions about how historical changes occur and to what extent we are each of us responsible, and the fact that our first answers were wrong matters very much less than the development of enough interest to go on asking'. Here, thinking about history – historical knowledge and historical understanding – was described as a kind of civic duty.[16] He had known for a long time (as in the second epigraph to this book) that 'no past dies', that (in a proposition that will be discussed in Chapters 8 and 9 of this book) nothing is capable of being dispersed, or going away. He also knew that how you *tell* the past, or write history, depends on what you're doing and thinking and making ('on our activities'), right now. The fictional sixth former Dakin in Alan Bennett's play *The History Boys* describes the historian's everyday activities and mode of thinking in a series of questions to his teacher that are acutely poetic: 'How does stuff happen, do you think? People decide to do stuff. Make moves. Alter things' – though his author did not put Dakin's last three in interrogative form.

Historiography is to history as poetics is to poetry. To modern students and scholars – to academics – in the West, 'history' means the study of past events and writing of them in narrative form; the narrative embodies an explanation of those events.[17] 'Historiography' on the other hand, embraces a study of the methodology historians have used in the development of history as an academic discipline *and* the whole set of works that have clustered around a historical topic. Historians ask: 'is there a historiography?' (how many books and articles and arguments are there about the English crowd in the early nineteenth century? On the gendered nature of harvest work in the early modern period? Whatever) rather as sociologists might ask what 'the literature' on a topic is. Students in British universities writing a dissertation are often advised to include a historiography chapter or section at the beginning of their work, laying out what has recently been published on their topic, the current state of

---

16 W. H. Auden, 'Then and Now: 1935–1950', *Prose Volume III. 1949–1955*, Edward Mendelson (ed.), Princeton University Press, Princeton NJ, 2008, pp. 164–168; orig. *Mademoiselle*, February 1950.

17 Hayden White, 'The Historical Text as Literary Artifact', Robert H. Canary and Henry Kozicki (eds), *The Writing of History. Literary Form and Historical Understanding*, University of Wisconsin Press, Madison WI, 1978, pp. 41–62; Paul A. Roth, 'Narrative explanations. The case of history', *History and Theory*, 27 (1988), pp. 1–13; David Carr, 'Narrative explanation and its malcontents', *History and Theory*, 47:1 (2008), pp. 19–30; Tobias Klauk, 'Is there such a thing as narrative explanation?', *JLT* 10:1 (2016), pp. 110–138.

the argument, and how they intend to advance the field. A second, much older meaning of 'historiography' is indicated by the title 'Historiographer Royal', which appointment pertained in England from 1660–1737. The Historian-laureate praised and lauded that which is already deemed to be historically significant and *worthy* of praise. The list of office holders includes two who held simultaneous appointment as Poet Laureate (John Dryden and Thomas Shadwell). It was a salaried appointment, held under royal patronage. A Scottish Historiographer Royal has been in place from 1681 to the present day, with a gap between 1709 and 1763.[18] Then, of late, 'historiography' has also come to mean something akin to the philosophy of history: there is interest in *historians'* own covert or overt philosophy of event, time, and causality; interest in the *meaning* they ascribe to what they put before you, usually in writing. Historiography is a way of thinking about and analysing a thing (a fairly recent development of the modern world) called History.

'Poetics' is the study of the linguistic techniques used by writers making poetry and other literature. Its aim is to disinter the way in which a text *works*: its internal operation. Sometimes, in accounting for 'poetics' as an intellectual activity, the third-century BCE philosopher Aristotle is quoted: 'I propose to treat of Poetry in itself and of its various kinds, noting the essential quality of each, to inquire into the structure of the plot as requisite to a good poem; into the number and nature of the parts of which a poem is composed; and similarly into whatever else falls within the same inquiry.'[19] With what stuff does poetics do its work? It does it with verse, of course, though here in this book by 'poetry' I sometimes mean what early modern writers and readers understood by poetry, that is 'usually verse, sometimes fiction'. Definitions and typologies of poetics emerged before the modern university system established separate disciplinary domains for literature (including poetry) and history, towards the end of the nineteenth century. In the earlier century, in schools, colleges, dissenting academies, and in some of the universities outside Oxford and Cambridge, English and History were commonly taught together.[20] Their separation, as forms of composition and understanding, and the traces of

18 See the illuminating interview with the Historiographer Royal of Scotland: Fiona Watson, 'Interview: Chris Smout (Historiographer Royal)', *History Scotland*, 1 (2001), pp. 61–66.
19 Aristotle, *The Poetics*, trans. S. H. Butcher, Section 1, Part I; The Internet Classics Archive, classics@classics.mit.edu (accessed 12 October 2017).
20 Blair Worden, 'Historians and poets', *Huntingdon Library Quarterly*, 68:1–2 (2005), pp. 71–93.

their indissoluble partnership, which has lasted from at least the seventeenth century until the present day, are the topics of this book. A poetics of history-writing is also possible, and has been discussed in the modern literature, though the 'poetics' in 'poetics of history' usually refers to the ideas and ideologies employed in a work of history rather than history *as a form* of expression or writing.[21] The *idea* of History is indeed beautiful – and poetic: that the past is irretrievably gone, yet still lives; that the written history is precipitated out of the Everything of the past, all of it, in a perpetual act of remaking.[22] This idea of history, which emerged in the long nineteenth century, is discussed throughout this book.

It is sometimes said that when historians do take any notice of the written artefacts produced by poets they are more likely to plunder them for content – for quotations to support the historical argument they are making – than they are to pay attention to them as forms of composition. In this way we 'detach the content of a poem ... from its properties of form and genre'. This is a naivety dressed up for misinterpretation, says Blair Worden.[23] We're *just asking for it*: the ensuing condescension of literary scholars. But, in fact, literary scholars are usually indulgent towards historians attempting to embed literary form and genre in the structure of their historical story. They even appear not to mind very much about historians speaking of poetry, for the 'history' in which their attempts are clothed is just more grist to their own critical mill. Historians have been kind as well, when I've done a literary turn in print: politely puzzled for example, at my spinning the yarn of Emily Bronte's *Wuthering Heights* in *Master and Servant. Love and Labour in the English Industrial Age*.[24] But Nelly Dean as narrator of capitalist modernity has obviously not done

---

21 Robert F. Berkhofer Jr, 'The challenge of poetics to (normal) historical practice', *Poetics Today*, 9:2 (1988), pp. 435–452; Philippe Carrard, *Poetics of the New History. French Historical Discourse from Braudel to Chartier*, Johns Hopkins University Press, Maryland MD, 1992; Jacques Rancière, *The Names of History. On the Poetics of Knowledge*, University of Minnesota Press, Minneapolis MN, 1994; Philippe Carrard, 'History as a kind of writing. Michael de Certeau and the poetics of historiography', *South Atlantic Quarterly*, 100:2 (2001), pp. 465–483. For history as a genre of writing, see Devoney Looser, *British Women Writers and the Writing of History, 1670–1820*, Johns Hopkins University Press, Baltimore MD, 2000; Anders Ingram, *Writing the Ottomans. Turkish History in Early Modern England*, Palgrave Macmillan, Basingstoke, 2015.

22 David Carr, *Narrative and History*, Indiana University Press, Bloomington IN, 1986; Carolyn Steedman, *Dust*, Manchester University Press, Manchester, 2001, pp. 142–170.

23 Worden, 'Historians and poets', p. 76.

24 Carolyn Steedman, *Master and Servant. Love and Labour in the English Industrial Age*, Cambridge University Press, Cambridge, 2007, pp. 193–216.

much for *their* reading of proto-industrialisation and domestic service in the Pennine region, c.1780 to 1810. This can only mean that *I* haven't done a very good job of making literature matter for the writing of history. The poetry that threads through this book is W. H. Auden's. I have loved Auden's poetry very much, though lately, and as shall be related, have learned that I must care for it in a new way, for the old one will no longer do. I *had* believed that Auden taught me about history as a written form and cultural activity; about the ways history gets written; about History's quiddity. But you love for the wrong reasons; or the shape of what you love dissolves as new knowledge washes over it. The poetry lessons remain, however; you go on reciting the Past as if there were one ('he merely told/the unhappy Present to recite the Past/like a poetry lesson'), which is why this book is about the poetics of history (the poetics of the written 'history') *and* about its poetry.[25] Often these thirty years past, I have thought that as a historian I needed permission for my love. It was a comfort, then, that Richard Hoggart appreciated and wrote about Auden and his poetry, for he conferred a kind of licence to do both. He had more right than me though, for he was appointed to Birmingham University's Centre for Contemporary Cultural Studies *as* an Auden scholar, and Auden himself appreciated – said he liked – Hoggart's 1951 study of his poetry, and Hoggart's own *Uses of Literacy*.[26] And, of course, Hoggart was not a historian. This one has plundered Auden's *Homage to Clio* (1960) for epigraphs more times than she cares to remember. 'Homage to Clio' – his homage to the Muse of History herself; the title of a poem and of a collection of history-poems – compels me. At the centre of *Homage to Clio* is Auden's eponymous twenty-thee stanza poem, conceived and written on the Italian island of Ischia in 1955, published in the same year, and collected together with many of his other 'history' poems of the post-War years in 1960.[27] Here, the poet reveals the Muse of History as a blank-faced girl, always, forever, present when anything happens – anything at all, at any time – *but with absolutely nothing to say*. At any moment '... we,

25 W. H. Auden, 'In Memory of Sigmund Freud (d. Sept. 1939)', *Collected Shorter Poems*, pp. 166–170.

26 Richard Hoggart, *Auden. An Introductory Essay*, Chatto and Windus, London, 1950; Richard Hoggart, *The Uses of Literacy. Aspects of Working Class Life*, Chatto and Windus, London, 1957; Simon Hoggart, 'Foreword', Sue Owen (ed.), *Rereading Richard Hoggart. Life, Literature, Language, Education*, Cambridge Scholars, Newcastle, 2008, pp. xii–xiii. Also Appendix 'Letter from W. H. Auden to Richard Hoggart, 7 January 1958', idem, pp. 175–177.

27 W. H. Auden, *Homage to Clio*, Faber and Faber, London, 1960.

at haphazard/And unseasonably, are brought face to face/By ones, Clio, with your silence. After that/Nothing is easy'. There are two mysteries here that I have long wanted to fathom. First there is Clio's silence: she has nothing to say. But in the iconography of the West over the 2000 years, Clio has quite often been depicted with a pen in her hand. When she transmogrified into Historia, the little emblem of history that every jobbing printer had in his shop ('I'll have a nice Dignita as a frontispiece, and finish with a Historia. Thank you, my man'), she invariably looked up from the book in which she was writing.[28] Is writing not a kind of saying? Is Auden's Historia silent on the page as well as mute in her person? It seems to be the case that she is. Then, in a striking reversal of the taken-for-granted chronological relationship between Memory and History, the poet entreats the Muse of History (briefly, for these lines of the poem, in guise as the Muse of Time, a conflation later to be discussed) to 'teach us our recollections'. And yet Western historiography teaches that History (professional, university-based history emerging during the long nineteenth century) usurped the functions of Memory. At the beginning of things, Mnemosyne was the mother of all the Muses (including Clio, History's own), at least according to some authorities of the Ancient World. Modern historians have believed the old authorities for the main part in giving various accounts of how History (as a way of thinking and as an academic discipline) came into the world, and what its relationship to Memory has been, over the last 300 years or so. Jacques Le Goff used the myth in order to begin his account of how History usurped the functions of Memory, over a very long period of time indeed, but accelerating at the end of the eighteenth century with the early development of history as a subject of inquiry in the academy, and later as information to be imparted to whole populations in European systems of mass education. Le Goff's 1977 account suggested that History in its modern mode is just one more technology of remembering.[29] Recently, the chronological relationship of memory to history has been less insisted on;[30] but Auden's suggestion that History – or Clio – or his expressionless girl – might *teach* us how to

---

28 As in various editions of Cesare Ripa's *Iconologia, or, Moral Emblems,* from 1603f.; *The English Emblem Book Project,* Penn State University Libraries, https://libraries.psu.edu/about/collections/english-emblem-book-project/ripa-toc (accessed 12 October 2017).

29 Jacques Le Goff, *History and Memory* (1977), Columbia University Press, New York NY, 1992, pp. 81–90.

30 Joan Tumblety (ed.), *Memory and History. Understanding Memory as Source and Subject,* Routledge, Abingdon, 2013.

perform the everyday cognitive activity of remembering has always struck as something to *understand*. Or to try to understand. The supplication to Clio to teach us our recollections – our memories – could as well be a description of history's function in the modern era, for formal, academic history does provide much of the material by which we *remember*, individually or collectively, things of which we have no direct experience: the Second World War for example, or the films our great-granny enjoyed in the 1930s; except that here, Auden addressed the Muse of Time, not Clio the Muse of History and subject of his poem; and Time, as he once famously observed, can do nothing but say *I told you so*.[31]

I thought Auden's poetry to be so historiographically acute and beautiful that sometimes I could see no way forward for my own writing but to carry on repeating his words, until the end of my days.[32] I knew that he never set foot in a local record office, never entered the portals of the National Archives (in his lifetime, the Public Record Office); but he understood, I believed, what history *was*, and what history *meant*. I read his fabulous and frequent musings of the post-War years as meditations on the meaning and philosophy of History, that is of history as a made and fashioned thing, rather than as historians' quotidian activities among documents, files, and registers.[33] I thought Auden's history-poems to be about Clio – History herself – asking questions about what she, herself, is: with his Clio I dimly made out 'history' as a way of thinking, and a way of writing; as a cognitive and literary form of the Western world that emerged on the long road to European modernity.[34]

Auden was particularly important for thinking about the relationship between the extraordinary and the everyday as experienced by historical actors and in the histories written about them. (*How does stuff happen, do you think? People decide to do stuff* ...). When social historians (like me) use the terms 'experience' and 'everyday life' they do so in order 'to side with the dominated against those who would dominate ... to invoke ... those lives that have traditionally been left out of historical

31 W. H. Auden, 'If I Could Tell You' (1940), *Collected Shorter Poems*, p. 201.

32 Carolyn Steedman, 'The Poetry of It (Writing History)', Angelika Bammer and Ruth-Ellen Joeres (eds), *The Future of Scholarly Writing. Critical Interventions*, Palgrave Macmillan, New York NY, 2015, pp. 215–226.

33 'Historical thought was an essential element of almost every poem Auden wrote in 1955'. Edward Mendelson, *Later Auden*, Faber and Faber, London, 1999, pp. 390–392.

34 The most succinct and resonant account of these processes, of heart and mind and writing, remains Franco Moretti's *Way of the World. The Bildungsroman in European Culture*, Verso, London, 1987, pp. 3–75.

accounts, swept aside by the onslaught of events instigated by elites', says Ben Highmore.[35] 'Everyday' has been my shorthand. How else could I read Auden's 'Makers of History' (1955), but as an exegesis on Clio's affection for the workers of the world? The poem tells that she loves 'those who bred them better horses,/Found answers to their questions, made their things'. You must emphasise *them* and *their* as you recite: they are the owners and exploiters, the high-ups; 'the cold advisors of yet colder kings ... who scheme, regardless of the poor man's pang'; those for whom others labour.[36] And it is so *satisfying* to see poets – house-poets, minstrels, balladeers, and *laureates* in royal households – kept like servants for the task of writing: to see 'Even those fulsome/Bards they boarded' as the workers.[37]

Auden's poetry shadowed my most recent book about one of those workers, a Nottinghamshire stockingmaker in the era of Luddism. Writing *An Everyday Life*, I made a memo to myself: whatever happened, I *must not* do a 'Musée des Beaux Arts' with the framework knitter Joseph Woolley on whose diaries the book is based. Auden's poem of that title inscribes a particular relationship between grand, large-scale historical events and the everyday. In 'Musée', in an art gallery, someone (perhaps the poet himself) muses on how the old masters always got the relationship between the ordinary and extraordinary *just right*. Ordinary life carries on whilst the extraordinary (a boy falling out of the sky) is a scarcely noticed backdrop. Meals are eaten, roads are walked, windows are opened and shut by people who, if they knew what History was being made just out of their line of vision, might not want it to happen at all. Whatever happens – whatever disaster, failure, suffering, astonishing event occurs – there always must be some 'who did not specially want it to happen'.[38] It is a poem you want to put before every undergraduate student of history, to demonstrate the idea of historical contingency. Practically, as a writer – a

---

35 Ben Highmore (ed.), *The Everyday Life Reader*, Routledge, London and New York NY, 2002, p. 1; Carolyn Steedman, *An Everyday Life of the English Working Class. Work, Self and Sociability in the Early Nineteenth Century*, Cambridge University Press, Cambridge, 2013, pp. 265–266.

36 W. H. Auden, 'Makers of History', *Collected Shorter Poems*, pp. 297–298; probably written a few weeks before 'Homage to Clio', says Edward Mendelson, *Later Auden*, p. 397. For the 'cold advisors', Percy Bysshe Shelley, *Political Essay on the Existing State of Things* (1811), p. 11; http://poeticalessay.bodleian.ox.ac.uk/# (accessed 12 October 2017).

37 W. H. Auden, 'Makers of History', *Homage to Clio*, Faber and Faber, London, 1960, pp. 30–31.

38 W. H. Auden, 'Musée des Beaux Arts', *Collected Shorter Poems*, p. 123.

historian – I did not want to say that Joseph Woolley the stockingmaker wanted or did not want the Luddite rebellion 'to happen', for I simply did not have enough information about him to come to a conclusion either way. More philosophically, I thought that to 'do a Musée' would be to place the extraordinary thing (Luddism in a time of state-sponsored terror; a boy falling out of the sky) at the centre of the frame, with the small, unconsidered, less important lives and happenings enacted at the periphery of the grand narrative centre of a History. To have done that would be to say that Luddism was historically significant but that Joseph Woolley was not. To have written in that way would have been to do a 'Musée des Beaux Arts'.

In modern social theory the Everyday is: 'someone walking dully along', opening a window, having their tea, or setting up a knitting frame: performing a routine of some kind that has been done a thousand times before. It is not reflected on, or subjected to analysis by the performer or historical subject, because it is a conceptual framework in the observer's mind, not the mind of those walking, or putting the kettle on, or drinking with Joseph Woolley down the Coach and Horses public house, Clifton, Nottinghamshire in 1801. But there is a corrective to the social-theory 'everyday', in historian Michel de Certeau's description of the way in which ordinary people (all of us) theorise everyday life. He said they were and we are 'unrecognized producers, poets of their own acts, silent discoverers of their own paths in the jungle of functionalist rationality'.[39] Just noticing it, thinking about it, day dreaming, perhaps writing about it, is a poetic act.

In the 1770s, philosopher and language-theorist James Beattie described the relationship between the everyday, the extraordinary, and the writing of them both (which he called 'poetic arrangement') in the following way:

> I hear a sudden noise in the street and run to see what is the matter. An insurrection has happened, a great multitude is brought together, and something very important is going forward. The scene before me ... is in itself so interesting, that for a moment or two I look in silence and wonder. By and by, when I get time for reflection, I begin to inquire into the cause of all this tumult, and what it is that people would be at; and one who is better informed than I, explains the affair ... or perhaps I make it out for myself, from the words

---

39 Michel de Certeau, *The Practice of Everyday Life*, University of California Press, Berkeley CA, 1984, p. xviii.

and actions of the persons principally concerned. – This is a sort of picture of poetical arrangement ...[40]

He did not mean that he wrote verse, or poetry, out of what he saw, heard tell, and thought about (though you might, and some of the examples used in his essay were epic poems). 'Poetical arrangement' described the intentional organisation of the experience of an event. It suited the 'order and manner in which the actions of other men strike ones senses' and was thus 'a more exact imitation of human affairs' than the historical arrangement he then went on to discuss. The formal organisation of his poetic telling was a product of thinking about it; his active 'reflection' on it. He made (in this instance) no distinction between *telling* and *writing* (though writing is strongly implied throughout these passages). 'Just noticing' is the poetic act; the event takes on meaning by the observer working out 'what it is that people would be at' as they *do stuff ... make moves. Alter things.*

When Beattie had finished describing the extraction of the extraordinary from the everyday as a primary poetic act, he went on to speculate about how a historian might write up the disturbance in the street. A historian, said Beattie, would behave differently; she would provide a different kind of explanation. He would begin his narrative not with the noise in the street, but with context, perhaps 'the manners of ... [the] age' and a description of the political constitution of whatever country he or she was writing about. Then he would introduce a 'particular person': birth, parents, social circumstances – a full biography of the life events that shaped his subject as someone of particular viewpoint and opinion. The historian will have in mind a cumulative event (the thing to be explained), like the revolution which was Beattie's implied example. The historian (unlike the poet) has stepped away from the window, focused in imagination on one particular person, one 'turbulent spirit', one rebel or revolutionary. She will then provide an account of how her historical subject got acquainted with 'other turbulent spirits like himself', and how later found himself rioting in the street. And so the narrative will proceed, 'unfolding, according to the order of time, the causes, principles, and progress of' – whatever was being described. The purpose of it all would be to explain the already-given event or person. History-writing like this, said Beattie, is 'more favourable to calm information'; but the poetical

---

40 James Beattie, 'On Poetry', *Essays. On Poetry and Music, as they affect the Mind. On Laughter, and Ludicrous Composition. On the Utility of Classical Learning*, William Creech, Edinburgh and E. & C. Dilly, London, 1776, p. 104.

method has the advantage as far as the pleasures of 'the passions and imagination' are concerned.[41]

By invoking the Aristotlean distinction between historical and literary composition, Beattie indicated how very much the differences between them preoccupied eighteenth-century commentators. One recent translation of Aristotle's *Poetics* (c.330 BCE) describes the differences between poet and historian like this:

> The distinction between historian and poet is not in the one writing prose and the other verse. You might put the work of Herodotus into verse, and it would still be a species of history; it consists really in this, that the one describes the thing that has been, and the other a kind of thing that might be. Hence poetry is something more philosophic and of graver import than history.[42]

For the eighteenth-century critic, the distinction between prose and poetic composition was the least interesting difference between a historian and a poet.[43] They concentrated on the lessons about time and futurity that the distinction provided: 'the object of the poet is not to relate what has actually happened, but what may possibly happen, either with probability, or from necessity ... [the historian] relates what actually has been done', said one.[44] In Beattie's 'picture of poetical arrangement' all is hustle and bustle; in his story of what is happening, the rioters in the street are inseparable from the poet at the window, who is perpetually on the edge of telling about what is going on, or busy asking questions about what he will, any moment now, make into the story of it. The poetical arrangement teeters on the edge of a future in which it will already *have been told* (perhaps it never will be; perhaps the not-being-told is equally the future). The historian, on the other hand, already *knows* what is to be told, for he has in mind explaining something that *has happened*. So Beattie differed from his contemporaries in the quiet conviction that the

41 Beattie, *Essays*, p. 105.
42 *The Poetics of Aristotle*, translated by Ingram Bywater, with a preface by Gilbert Murray, is in the public domain: www.authorama.com/the-poetics-10.html (accessed 12 October 2017). Also Aristotle, *Poetics*, trans. and intro. Kenneth McLeish, Nick Hern Books, London, 1998, pp. 13–14.
43 Henry James Pye, *A Commentary Illustrating the Poetic of Aristotle, by Examples taken chiefly from the Modern Poets. To which is prefixed, a new and corrected edition of the translation of the Poetics*, John Stockdale, London, 1792, pp. 25–28 ('The Object of Poetry and How It Differs from History').
44 Pye, *A Commentary*, p. 25.

questions he addressed were about writing, and in his concern for actual poets and actual historians doing the writing (or the telling).

By the end of the eighteenth century, the comparison between poetry and history was a commonplace of magazine and educational literature: the allure of one, the dullness of the other were laid out for many readerships: 'their difference, according to [Aristotle] ... is not in the *form*, or *stile, but in the very nature of the things. But how so? History only paints what has* happened, poetry what *might* have happened.'[45] But the line between the two was there to be traversed: some contemporary songsters were delighted to contemplate mash-up history and poetry.[46] No mash-up, though, for 1813 readers of *The Lady's Magazine*: for them, the independent provinces of History and Poetry had been demarcated so clearly that they could hear Clio being told that

> 'tis thine to bid us be historical,
> And write of wars, and plagues, and queens, and kings;
> Not in poetic style, or allegorical,
> As the fond Love-Muse sings,
> But in plain prose: – then bid me be a proser;
> Else to write history would be a poser.

The ladies should aim to do better than the eighteenth-century historians: 'Teach me to beat Hume, Smollet, Belsham, Rapin,/Or even him who wrote the "Cheats of Scapin"'. The last, Thomas Otway, whose farce was first staged in 1676, was really not-a-historian ('him Thalia taught the farce to scribble') but the ladies and the Muse were meant to know enough of poesie 'for the rhime's sake, to raise no quibble' at his inclusion on the list.[47] These eighteenth-century perspectives on history and poetry are useful for understanding Auden as a poet and as a historical thinker.

45 'It is the end of oratory to persuade, of poetry to please, and history to instruct by the recital of true events', *The Freemasons' Magazine; or, General and Complete Library*, Vol. 5, London, 1793; Vicesimus Knox, *Essays Moral and Literary*, 13th edn, Vol. 1, London, 1793, p. 211.

46 Or to 'Jumble together music, poetry, and history', as in *The Apollo. Being An Elegant Selection of Approved Modern Songs, Favourite Airs From Celebrated Operas, &C. To Which Are Prefixed, Twelve New and Original Songs (Never Before Published) Written to Beautiful & Familiar Tunes*, for the author, Bath, 1791, p. 167.

47 Mr. J. M. Lacey, 'Invocations, Serious and Comic', *The Lady's Magazine; Or Entertaining Companion for the Fair Sex, Appropriated Solely to Their Use and Amusement*, 44 (1813), pp. 192–193. For Rapin, below, pp. 224–225. William Belsham was a contemporary political historian. Thalia is the Muse of Comic Poetry.

In the following account of Auden's history-poems, you have to do all three of the things suggested by Auden and Beattie: put the kettle on and ignore the boy falling out of the sky; go to the window and involve yourself, if only in imagination, in what is happening in the street; turn away and meditate on *how stuff happens*: how, and out of what earlier histories, Auden wrote his history-poems. You will be neither historian nor poet as you do these things; rather just somebody or other trying to make something else – something new – out of the material of the world.

As a historical thinker, Auden worked within the framework of Christianity. I had not known, until very recently, how much there is to understand of the Christianity he returned to in the 1940s, and the eschatological, or at least, grand-theory, histories he read before the production of the 'history-poetry' discussed here.[48] The long and short of it was that my earlier belief that Auden taught me about history as a literary form, as a form of understanding and about the ways history gets written, had to be abandoned. Auden *actually* said that the Clio to whom he paid homage was, in fact, not Clio or Historia *at all*. He told several friends – it's on the record and repeated in several handbooks and guides to his poetry – that she was, in fact, the Virgin Mary, and had been so since 1955.[49] I'd read *that* ten years ago, and insouciantly dismissed it: what did I care about the intentions of poets? That's the intentionalist fallacy, isn't it? – an error I was warned at school against committing. The point was, surely, that the poem existed as a statement about the meaning of history: that Clio was a historiographical statement of W. H. Auden? And even if she wasn't the Muse of History, I could write about her as if she were. That was before I had encountered Auden's return to Anglicanism at the end of the 1930s (in its Episcopal form, for he was now resident in the New York, though not yet a US citizen). In October 1940, while he was still recommending secular orthodoxies in his prose, says Edward Mendelson, he quietly began attending the local Episcopal church and rejoined the Anglican Communion he had left at 15.[50]

Auden read so *very much* grand-theory history, popular in the 1920s, 1930s, and then again in the 1950s, that I had to do so as well. He does not appear to have cared very much for Spengler and Toynbee, which

48 Susannah Young-ah Gottlieb, 'Auden in History', Tony Sharpe (ed.), *W. H. Auden in Context*, Cambridge University Press, Cambridge, 2013, pp. 181–192.

49 Stan Smith (ed.), *The Cambridge Companion to W. H. Auden*, Cambridge University Press, Cambridge, 2004, p. 62.

50 W. H. Auden, 'Introduction', *Prose Volume II*, p. xx.

would at least have given me a foothold; the 'big' historians he cared about were equally grand but less well-known philosophers of Western history.[51] Now – my duty as a historian! – I must attempt to understand Auden as a Christian, a Christian poet, and a Christian philosopher of time and history. Edward Mendelson provides a brilliant means for relating Auden's Christian history to the Marxist history and related teleological and purposive historical thinking he appeared to espouse in the 1930s. I had first learned of Auden's apostasy in this regard from E. P. Thompson, had accepted Thompson's figuring of Christianity as the cause and culprit of Auden's defection; I had been able to go blithely on my way, quoting the bits of Auden that suited my purposes, as I always had.[52] But the realisation that I was actually going to have to *read* Eugen Rosenstock-Huessy's *Out of Revolution* (1938) and Denis de Rougement's *Love in the Western World* (1940), Charles Cochrane's *Christianity and Classical Culture. A Study of Thought and Action from Augustus to Augustine* (1940), and Reinhold Niebuhr's *The Nature and Destiny of Man* (1941), provoked much anxiety. It was not knowing *what kind of thing they are* that troubled me. It was different with Auden's influences from Kierkergaard or indeed from *The Confessions* of St Augustine. Mendelson tells us that in 1954, just before the *Homage to Clio* cycle of poems was composed, Auden was reading Augustine; Auden wrote about Augustine undertaking the first serious analysis of the experience of time, and about Augustine's distinction between natural and historical time 'which Christianity encouraged if it did not invent'.[53] I had read – been taught to read – *Being and Nothingness* and *The City of God* as *historical* texts, examples of Western thought, aspects of cultural history. But Auden's was so very *Christian* a historiography; the reading list inscribed theology *as* historiography; and because it is theology as historiography, it is so resolutely Western–Occidental in its understanding of the past, that my spirit … withered and died. It wasn't that I had no experience of making this kind of attempt. I worked *very hard* (and willingly so) at understanding what the Revd John Murgatroyd (1719–1806), of Slaithwaite, West Yorkshire, understood of his Anglican God, so that I might tell how he was able to give houseroom and love and care to his household servant's little bastard daughter (*how that stuff happened*). And he loved little Eliza's mother Phoebe Beatson too, and *not* in a different register, but out of the love God had inscribed

51 Gottlieb, 'Auden in History', pp. 181–182.
52 Thompson, 'Outside the Whale', pp. 1–34.
53 Mendelson, *Later Auden*, p. 309.

on all his Creatures.[54] Murgatroyd's motions of the heart were a product
of Christian *caritas* and the West Riding Enlightenment. But one reviewer
at least of *Master and Servants* thought I didn't do a very good job; that
an unbeliever couldn't possibly *have done* a good job of understanding a
broadly latitudinal Anglican in the early Age of Atonement. (I tried to put
John Murgatroyd's theology in place for the period from about 1740 to the
early years of the new century.)

Edward Mendelson uses the term 'purposive' for the kind of Marxist
history he says that Auden stopped reading c.1940, and also for the
grand-theory history, like Rosenstock-Huessy's, that he took to after
that.[55] 'Purposive' is an apposite term for the last, for in much Christian
thought, the course of past events is seen as goal- directed: they are events
with somewhere to go, and some final meaning to demonstrate. More
generally, 'purposive' is a term quite widely used by literary critics discussing historical work, but is generally avoided by historians unless they
are having a good laugh at the ridiculousness of states and governments
seeking to manipulate 'the lessons of the past' for their own purposes.[56]
The grand-theory, purposive histories that Auden read and enjoyed from
the late 1930s onwards were so demanding of my understanding – I was so
inadequate a reader of them – that I failed to notice, for a very long time,
that he also possessed the ordinary, everyday political and social history of
anyone educated beyond elementary school level in the twentieth-century
UK. He had the same historical story of the industrial revolution, the
scientific and French revolutions; of Romanticism in relation those revolutions in manners, thought, and politics; of the Decline of Feudalism; of
the English Civil War, the Rise of the Gentry; the transmission of culture
in English society by the eighteenth-century Church of England ... as
me; or as anyone who sat through history lessons between about 1900
and 1980, in school or university. He learned of new work in social and
political history through the books he reviewed. In 1952, for example,
using a taken-for-granted knowledge of the historical past in Britain, he
told his overseas readers about the debt social reform in England owed to
religion: 'the British Labour Party for example ... [is] closely associated
with the Evangelical movement'. To support this argument he discussed

54 Steedman, *Master and Servant*.
55 Mendelson, *Early Auden*, pp. 306–314, 324; *Later Auden*, pp. 306–307, 390–392, 420.
56 'Purposive history of this kind is as beguiling as necromancy and as about as reliable,
    too', says Anthony Hopkins, 'The Real American Empire', James Belich, John Darwin,
    Margret Frenz, and Chris Wickham (eds), *The Prospect of Global History*, Oxford
    University Press, Oxford, 2016, pp. 146–159.

Britain's and Europe's different conceptions of 'revolution', and conducted a brisk survey of political history from the Tudors to the execution of Charles I.[57] He bemoaned those undergraduates ('and not stupid ones') who insisted that '*Pickwick Papers* was written in the 1890s ... lack of any sense of historical order is just as great an obstacle to the enjoyment and understanding of literature as a tiny vocabulary'.[58] He also discussed the methodologies of cultural, social and literary historians, as shall be later discussed; but it is true that this was done in his prose writing, not in his poetry, and that most critics have disinterred Auden's 'big' history rather than his commentary on the social and the cultural variety – or the small.

Auden's disavowal of Marxist history and historiography has been emphasised, but he retained one of its fundamental perspectives right through to the 1960s, in his discussions of *poiesis*. *Poiesis* (Ancient Greek) derives from the term 'to make'. The verb signifies an action that both transforms and continues the world in and out of which things are made. It is what Karl Marx had in mind when he declared in 1852 (as in one of the epigraphs to this book) that 'the social revolution ... can only create its poetry from the future, not from the past', and in the same work, that 'Men make their own history...'. In 1939, Auden wrote about the immense contribution Marxism had made 'to our understanding of history, in its emphasis on Man the Maker, the producer of wealth, as opposed to the obsession of earlier historians with Man the Politician, the consumer. It has made us realise that history is made up of an immense number of individual acts of which by far the greater number are not acts of warfare or diplomacy, but acts of physical work with physical materials, earth, stone, metal, etc., and that it is Man the Maker who is the prime cause of historical change, for he creates wealth for the consumption of which Man the Politician struggles.'[59]

This account of Auden's history poetry – of Auden as a theorist of history; of Auden the historiographer – avoids biography for the main part. There is *so much* brilliant accounting for Auden's life, his poetry, and his sexuality, that it would be stupid to attempt to add to it. I have tried to

57 W. H. Auden, 'Portrait of a Whig', *Prose Volume III*, pp. 273–285. This first appeared in British Council, *English Miscellany. A Symposium of History, Literature and the Arts*, Edizioni di Storia e Letteratura for the British Council, Rome, 1952.
58 W. H. Auden, 'Speaking of Books', *Prose Volume III*, pp. 571–573, orig. *New York Times Book Review*, 15 May 1955.
59 W. H. Auden, 'Appendices. Appendix I. "The Prolific and Devourer"', *Prose Volume II*, pp. 411–458.

keep myself on the straight and narrow of my quest: to understand what theory of history is expressed in his poetry; and *why* it is so expressed. I am interested in his conventional historical education as a child and adolescent, not just because I'm a historian bound to think 'context' in the way James Beattie described in the 1770s, but because it may add something to new accounts of how the common historical imagination is made in different times and places. These are questions put in Alison Landsberg's *Engaging the Past*. As in much recent public history, Landsberg follows history to the places where it is made outside the academy: in film and among film audiences and in television docudrama (though not to primary school classrooms, or to poetry writing, which in this book *are* sites of history's making). When Mendelson said that historical thought was an essential element of nearly everything Auden wrote during the mid 1950s, he raised the same kind of questions as Landsberg, though he never thought of Auden as an ordinary historical thinker, nor of Auden doing everyday 'history-in-society' as described by Jorma Kalela.[60] And then, as she must, and right now, Clio makes her entry, stage right, points to her book in which she writes everything down; all of it; everything; draws my attention to the time line there inscribed (she may or may not be the Queen of Heaven but she is certainly Queen of the Time Line) and then points – still mute – to the words: 'Cold War'. Auden has to be considered as a poet of the Cold War, in double exile, from England and from the US, writing in his Ischian and Kirschstetten summers, all the way through the 1950s and 1960s.

There is a ghost of the history that Auden did not live through – of what he missed – that may haunt this book as it has haunted the writing of it. The ghost is all that frames a common post-War experience in the UK. He left in 1939. Conscription, the site of battle, the home front, bombing, Blitz, and rationing; all of these are frequently mentioned in the literature as what he did *not* experience. He was never a citizen of the British Welfare State; his Cold War was a US Cold War, not a British one. But far more significant for the Auden story of history and poetry, are the absent battles of the books, the bitter wranglings of the clerisy in 1950s and 1960s Britain. He may have read the excoriating attacks from the Old World, and from the old and new left, and new-New Left, on the revisions he made to his political poetry of the late 1930s.[61] But he never had to sit

---

60 Mendelson, *Later Auden*, pp. 390–392; Jorma Kalela, *Making History. The Historian and the Uses of the Past*, Palgrave Macmillan, Basingstoke, 2012, pp. 24–49.

61 Lin Chun, *The British New Left*, Edinburgh University Press, Edinburgh, 1993; Dennis

in a small claustrophobic room (university seminar room, one for public meetings hired out by the hour, the private function room of some pub or other) and listen to the Boy Marxists explain to him, in patient and exhaustive detail, exactly why his position was so very incorrect. But I think he did not read the charge list drawn up against him, by E. P. Thompson, for example, in regard to 'Spain'.[62] I wish he had written another 'Letter to Lord Byron', thirty years on from the first, in 1966, say, to tell how later experiences rewrote his earlier autobiographical and political entry in Clio's book.

This book is about poets who have written (historiographically speaking) about history, about the poetics of the very idea of 'history' itself, the long persistence of the philosophy that separates one from the other; and about the choices there have been, in different times and places, of 'telling what had been'.[63] In the end, we might discover more about what it is we do when we write history, and read it, too. But before the utility of the ancient opposition of poetry to history is discussed, we shall consider some *really useful knowledge* about poetry, for historians.

Dworkin, *Cultural Marxism in Postwar Britain. History, the New Left, and the Origins of Cultural Studies*, Duke University Press, Durham SC, 1997.

62 Above, Note 52.

63 George Eliot draws attention to ways of telling the past in Book I, Chapter 11 of *Middlemarch* (1871–1872): 'Herodotus, who also, in telling what had been, thought it well to take a woman's lot for his starting-point.' The 'also' signals herself, the author, who took several women's lot as starting point for her historical novel, set 'forty years since' (in the novel 'lot' signifies both destiny and dowry). Written in the late 1860s, *Middlemarch* concerns 1820s Coventry and Warwickshire in the lead-up to the Great Reform Act of 1832. Passage of the reform bill through Parliament structures the text. See Carolyn Steedman, 'Going to Middlemarch: History and the novel', *Michigan Quarterly Review*, 40:3 (2001), http://hdl.handle.net/2027/spo.act2080.0040.310 (accessed 12 October 2017). Sir Walter Scott thought sixty years a more appropriate distance than forty from which to write about the past. He discussed this in the Introduction to *Waverley; or, 'Tis Sixty Years Since* (1814).

PART I

History

1

Servant poets: An Ode on a Dishclout

'A servant write verses!' says Madam Du Bloom:
'Pray what is the subject – a Mop, or a Broom?'
'He, he, he,' says Miss Flounce: 'I suppose we shall see
An ode on a Dishclout – what else can it be?' …
'I once had a servant myself', says Miss Pines
'That wrote on a wedding some very good lines'.
Says Mrs Domestic, 'And when they done,
I can't see for my part what use they were *on*;
Had she wrote a receipt, to've instructed you how
To warm a cold breast of veal, like a ragout,
Or to make cowslip wine, that would pass for Champagne,
It might have been useful, again and again'.

> Elizabeth Hands, 'A Poem, On the Supposition of an Advertisement
> appearing in a Morning Paper, of the Publication of a Volume of
> Poems, by a Servant-Maid', 1789.

Christian Tousey his My Naime and England his My Naishan
and Solsbury my Dwelling plas and Christ His My Salvaton

> Mrs Christian Tousey, Hir Book, 1748.

Christian Tousey's Book, deposited in Wiltshire County Record Office,
is folded and hand-sewn, about 10 cm square, probably put together in
the kitchen out of some kind of wrapping paper; it contains undated lists
of spending on foodstuffs day by day.[1] Discussing the twentieth-century
development of recording and writing systems among the Vai people

---

1 Wiltshire Country Record Office, 776/922A. Household Account Book, kept by
Christian Tousey of Salisbury, a cook or housekeeper.

of Liberia, the anthropologist Jack Goody noted that several of the Vai records he consulted had been compiled by men who had worked as cooks at some point in their life, and who had thus, like Mrs Tousey, become familiar with elementary forms of bookkeeping.[2] In eighteenth-century England, if you wanted writing abilities ('graphic-linguistic abilities' is Goody's term) that *had some use* in a household servant, then it was the cook you wanted them in, as Elizabeth Hands' Mrs Domestic points out in the first epigraph to this chapter. In modest households, in a cash-short economy, the kitchen door was egress for most small coin; it needed to be accounted for on a daily basis. Your cook was likely to *be* your one domestic servant, a multi-tasking young woman, who took charge of the kitchen and the household cleaning, milked the house cow if there was one, and washed the baby's nappies.[3] Tousey's Book was compiled by two hands, the second probably the mistress's (or master's) detailing payment to unspecified others, probably charwomen, or bought-in work-boys. The way in which a single-servant household was managed and maintained by the supplementary employment of a steady stream of casual domestic workers or 'helpers', the calculations necessary for paying them, as well as records of daily marketing, meant that an account book like Tousey's was likely to come under regular scrutiny by the employer.[4]

Someone else had access to Christian Tousey's Book; but she called it her own. Once, there was a disparaging little note on its catalogue card in the record office at Trowbridge, in a hand nearly as faded as Tousey's own (but which must have been made in the 1950s or 1960s), wondering why such triviality had ever been thought worth preserving. But the inside cover of 'Hir Book' belies inconsequentiality: she places herself within a history of literacy and many accounts of the social and psychological consequences of writing.[5] This woman knew what a book was and how

2 Jack Goody, *The Interface Between the Written and the Oral*, Cambridge University Press, Cambridge, 1987, p. 212.

3 Carolyn Steedman, *Labours Lost. Domestic Service and the Making of Modern England*, Cambridge University Press, Cambridge, 2009.

4 Ann Walker, *A Complete Guide for a Servant Maid; or, the Sure Means of Gaining Love and Esteem*, T. Sabine, London, 1787, pp. 26–27; John Trusler, *Trusler's Domestic Management; or, the Art of Conducting a Family, with Economy, Frugality and Method*, J. Souter, London, 1819, p. 88.

5 James Gee, *Social Linguistics and Literacies. Ideology in Discourses*, Falmer, Basingstoke, 1998, p. 59; Goody, *Interface*, pp. 191–208; Harvey J. Graff, *The Legacies of Literacy. Continuities and Contradictions in Western Culture*, Indiana University Press, Bloomington IN, 1987, p. 264; David R. Olson, 'Literate Mentalities: Literacy, Consciousness of Language, and Modes of Thought', Olson, Nancy Torrance, and Angela Hilyard (eds),

organised, with cover, title, and epigraph. Her inscription suggests the form of schooling she experienced: limited though it may have been, it was in all likelihood conducted in a parochial school, where first steps in reading were to do with the God-given identity the Catechism inquires into ('What is your Name?' 'Who gave you this Name?').[6] This inferred experience suggests that she could read simple literature of the faith, and probably a great deal more besides. By whatever method she had been taught to read (the syllabic method and its implications for prosody will be discussed shortly) she had been given the means to make the discovery that letters, syllables, and words represent the sounds of spoken language, and so had the resources to spell some of the words she used ('his' for 'is', 'Solsbury' for 'Salisbury') from speech, as well as from (sometimes imperfect) visual recall of the words on page or slate. Her little verse inscribes a geography and a cosmology. The writer knows that Salisbury is smaller than England. She knows that both of them exist in a much vaster order of things.[7] The inscription also registers a particular form of Protestant Christianity, which many histories of its educational project from the sixteenth century onwards, tell of the construction of particular kinds of social and religious subject shaped by access to the written word.[8] The

   Modes of Thought: Explorations in Culture and Cognition, Cambridge University Press, Cambridge, 1996, pp. 141–151; *The World on Paper: The Conceptual and Cognitive Implications of Writing and Reading*, Cambridge University Press, Cambridge, 1994; Walter J. Ong, *Orality and Literacy. The Technologising of the Word*, Methuen, London, 1982; 'Writing is a Technology that Restructures Thought', Gerd Bauman (ed.), *The Written Word: Literacy in Transition*, Clarendon Press, Oxford, 1986; Sylvia Scribner and Michael Cole, *The Psychology of Literacy*, Harvard University Press, Cambridge MA, 1981; David Vincent, *The Rise of Mass Literacy. Reading and Writing in Modern Europe*, Polity, Cambridge, 2000, pp. 92–94.

6 W. H. Auden remembered his childhood rehearsal of the Catechism when in 1961 he wrote that 'The purpose of all educational institutions, public or private, is utilitarian and can never be anything else; their duty is to prepare young persons for that station in life to which it shall please society to call them.' W. H. Auden, 'The Poet as Professor', *Prose Volume IV. 1956–1962*, Edward Mendelson (ed.), Princeton University Press, Princeton NJ, 2010, pp. 317–319; orig. pub. *Observer*, 5 February 1961. He substituted 'society' for the 'God' of *The Book of Common Prayer*: 'What is thy duty towards thy Neighbour? ... [T]o learn and labour truly to get mine own living, and to do my duty in that state if life, unto which it shall please God to call me.'

7 Anthropologists and psychologists suggest (or until very recently suggested) that she would not have known these things in the way she did, had she not been literate. Olson, *World*, pp. 20–44; Goody, *Interface*, pp. 191–195, 209–257; Vincent, *Rise of Mass Literacy*, pp. 20–25; Graff, *Legacies of Literacy*.

8 Paul Delaney, *British Autobiography in the Seventeenth Century*, Routledge and Kegan Paul, London, 1969; Dean Ebner, *Autobiography in the Seventeenth Century*, Mouton,

inscription is also in doggerel, which no child is or ever has been *taught* in school, but which the exercise books of even modern schoolchildren show is acquired there.

Poetical maids were fashionable in the second half of the eighteenth century, their popularity sometimes attributed to a proto-Romantic taste for humble genius – for plebeian literary creativity – and to the edifying consequences of contemplating talents that might, without your charitable donation to the subscription list of a Mary Leapor or an Ann Yearsley, be doomed to disperse themselves upon the desert air of a provincial village or a gentleman's back kitchen.[9] Some have more unkindly said that 'natural poets' made 'splendid household pets who could fawn in words', usually having in mind the long half-career of the thresher poet Stephen Duck (1705–1756) whose talents were thought to have flourished in inverse proportion to his climb up the ladder of patronage.[10]

Mary Leapor (1722–1746) served in at least two Northamptonshire gentry households during her brief life, producing there a corpus of poetry which was first published posthumously in 1748 and which achieved its first critical edition some 250 years later.[11] *The Works of Mary Leapor* (2003) was heralded by a flurry of articles, provoked as her modern editors suggest, by a feminism that 'created an environment in which writers like [her] could be re-examined'.[12] The relationship between the servant poet and her patroness Bridget Fremantle has been particularly well described,

The Hague, 1971; Margaret P. Hannay (ed.), *Silent But for the Word. Tudor Women as Patrons, Translators and Writers of Religious Works*, Kent State University Press, Ohio OH, 1985; Carmen Luke, *Pedagogy, Printing and Protestantism. The Discourse on Childhood*, SUNY Press, New York NY, 1989; Elspeth Graham, Elaine Hobby, Hilary Hind, and Helen Wilcox, *Her Own Life. Autobiographical Writings by Seventeenth-Century English Women*, Routledge, London, 1989; Felicity Nussbaum, *The Autobiographical Subject*, Johns Hopkins University Press, Baltimore MD, 1989; Effie Botonaki, 'Seventeenth-century Englishwomen's spiritual diaries. Self-examination, covenanting, and account keeping', *Sixteenth Century Journal*, 30 (1999), pp. 3–21; Linda Olson, 'Did Medieval English Women Read Augustine's *Confessiones*? Constructing Feminine Interiority and Literacy in the Eleventh and Twelfth Centuries', Sarah Rees Jones (ed.), *Learning and Literacy in Medieval England and Abroad*, Brepols, Turnhout, 2003, pp. 69–96.

9 William J. Christmas, *The Lab'ring Muse: Work, Writing and the Social Order in English Plebeian Poetry, 1730–1830*, University of Delaware Press, Newark NJ, 2001.

10 Betty Rizzo, 'The patron as poet maker. The politics of benefaction', *Studies in Eighteenth-Century Culture*, 20 (1990), pp. 241–266.

11 Mary Leapor, *Poems on Several Occasions*, 2 vols, for the author, London, 1748–1751, in Richard Greene and Ann Messenger (eds), *The Works of Mary Leapor*, Oxford University Press, Oxford, 2003.

12 Leapor, *Works*, p. xxix.

leaving room for modern scholars to imagine the recognition by a rector's daughter of true poetic talent in a subordinate and the development of an Enlightened friendship around the making of poetry – as well as the tensions and impossibilities of one attempted across a vast social divide. It is for those impossibilities that the relationship between the philanthropist Hannah More and Ann Yearsley ('Lactilla'–'The Milkwoman of Bristol') is now usually discussed. The record of Yearsley's creative independence and More's anxieties about it are well preserved.[13] Even in More's fraught correspondence with friends about Yearsley's insistence on writing the poetry *she* wanted to write, reaping the financial rewards of its publication, and spending the money on what *she* wanted, not on what More thought proper for a milkwoman, her patroness' acknowledgment of Lactilla's talents and abilities is discernable.

Ann Yearsley was not More's servant, though she had much to do with More's cook and kitchen: her poetry came into More's life through the kitchen door. Collecting kitchen waste for her pigs from More's cook, Yearsley showed the woman her poetry, and she showed it to her mistress. The pigswill was in fact the most difficult and perplexing factor in the relationship between poet and patron, for Lactilla had an arrangement for it with the cook. More attempted to override what Yearsley called a 'contract' at the high point of one of their quarrels about the subscription money and as a way of punishing Yearsley for her ingratitude and insubordination.[14] Both cook and milkwoman knew that in doing so More had transgressed the boundaries of customary practice and the law that 'everyone' knew. As Yearsley pointed out, at length and in print, More had no grounds on which to be offended by the kitchen-door arrangement, for the pigswill was the perquisite of the cook, and the whole world knew it.[15]

Mary Leapor *was* a cook among a household retinue of servants (or part of a 'menial Train', as she put it); not a jobbing girl in a single-servant household turning her hand to dusting and the dinner; but, rather, hired

---

13 Madeleine Kahn, 'Hannah More and Ann Yearsley. A collaboration across the class Divide', *Studies in Eighteenth Century Culture*, 25 (1996), pp. 203–223; Anne Stott, *Hannah More. The First Victorian*. Oxford University Press, Oxford, 2003, pp. 73–74; Charles Howard Ford, *Hannah More. A Critical Biography*, Peter Lang, New York NY, 1996, pp. 71–100.

14 For ordinary people's understanding and use of the law in this period, Carolyn Steedman, 'A lawyer's letter. Everyday uses of the law in early nineteenth century England', *History Workshop Journal*, 80 (2016), pp. 62–83.

15 Kahn, 'Hannah More', p. 216. Ann Yearsley, 'Narrative', *Poems on Various Subjects. A Second Book of Poems … by Ann Yearsley*, G. G. J. & J. Robinson, London, 1787.

in the capacity of cook to a gentry family, and in no other.[16] In 'Crumble Hall' the servant-poet wanders the corridors and grounds of the country house (at sun-up it appears, truly the servant's hour) for the purposes of nostalgia (its 'hospitable Door/Has fed the Stranger, and reliev'd the Poor') and for the purposes of aesthetic judgement, for the grounds are being cleared for a new landscape garden – ancient oaks uprooted 'to clear the Way for Slopes and modern Whims'.[17] The poet spends longest in the kitchen, visiting it twice in the course of her tour. She describes its larder store of 'good old *English* Fare', sketches out a recipe (for cheese cakes), admires the skill (her own) that went into the 'soft Jellies' stored in the larder, and gives the menu for the servants' dinner (boiled beef and cabbage).

Jeannie Dalporto has suggested how disconcerting it might be for a member of the employing classes to see depicted 'servants who have lost sight of their servitude', behaving as if their place in the big house is assured by affective relationships – not by contract or hiring agreement, or by the system of landownership, rent, and investment that the country estate represented.[18] But there is more to it – to the affront – than this. The servants carry on their complex lives as if the family of the house simply does not exist; affective relationships are between themselves, not between servant and employer. The kitchen is a social universe presented as completely independent of the economic structures actually inscribed in 'Crumble Hall'. In this poem, labour, and the objects and products of labour, belong entirely to the workers. The ploughman resting by the kitchen fire dreams of '*his* Oxen', and when rain threatens worries for '*his* new-mown Hay'. Urs'la the kitchen maid, in love with the unresponsive Roger, works entirely for him, not for the Family on the other side of the door. 'For you *my* Pigs resign their morning due', she cries to his snoring form slumped across the kitchen table (emphases except for *Roger*'s name added):

> *My* hungry Chickens lose their Meat for *you*:
> And was it not, Ah! Was it not for *thee*,
> No goodly Pottage would be dress'd by *me*.

16 Leapor, 'Crumble Hall', *Works*, pp. 206–211, l.110.
17 Leapor, 'Crumble Hall', l.176.
18 Jeannie Dalporto, 'Landscape, labor and the ideology of improvement in Mary Leapor's "Crumble Hall"', *The Eighteenth Century. Theory and Interpretation*, 42 (2001), pp. 228–244.

For *thee* these Hands wind up the whirling Jack,
Or place the Spit across the sloping Rack.
I baste the Mutton with a chearful Heart,
Because *I* know *my Roger* will have a part.

To employ a poetical maid was a fashionable thing to do and literacy in a cook was certainly a useful commodity; but perhaps these factors did not outweigh the discomfort of realising that the servants might live an autonomous life in your kitchen, quite independent of what law and legal theory said they were: mere aspects of your own personality, exercising your own (unused) capacity to turn spits and collect eggs, as kinds of proxy.[19] And as for the cultural clout associated with the possession of a literary servant, perhaps many less-elevated employers than Lady Kingsborough discovered that it was all very well sending to London for a glamorous and recently published philosophical governess to tutor her daughters on the Irish estates; you might indeed be doing your best by the girls in employing Mary Wollstonecraft; but she would turn out to be obdurately and infuriatingly her Self, alienating the affections of the children, unassailably disapproving of your fondness for pugdogs, flirtatious with the gentlemen in the drawing-room, and possessed of a large and (to the gentlemen) alluring bosom and a demandingly overdeveloped sensibility. If we may attribute to Lady Kingsborough a sentiment she could not have voiced – certainly did not voice in this manner – *Impossible! Not what I pay her for!*[20] But in a smaller, far more modest household a mistress might welcome a literary – or at least a literate – servant. Writing skills were particularly useful in a cookmaid, for the purposes of reckoning and accounting, as already mentioned, but also because they were a means by which – when she left, as she surely would – you could get to keep some of the skills and abilities you had acquired access to at the hiring.[21] She might leave you a recipe for Banbury Cheese, for example, instructing you in writing that 'Madam the Season for making Bambory Chess is from Lamos to all Holontids Let your veats be A bout A inch & a hf Dress

---

19　Carolyn Steedman, 'Servants and their relationship to the unconscious', *Journal of British Studies*, 42 (2003), pp. 316–350.

20　Janet Todd, *Mary Wollstonecraft. A Revolutionary Life*, Weidenfeld and Nicholson, London, 2000, pp. 84–109 for Wollstonecraft's time on the Kingsborough estate, Mitchelstown, County Cork.

21　Steedman, 'Servant's labour'; Michael Symons, *A History of Cooks and Cooking*, Prospect Books, Totnes, 2001, pp. 27–188; Jack Goody, *Cooking, Cuisine and Class. A Study in Comparative Sociology*, Cambridge University Press, Cambridge, 1982, p. 99.

and Scald with whay and water mixed from Lamos to mickelmas ...',
going over the finer points of the instructions several times in tagged-on
afterthoughts.[22] A writing maid might be able to exercise your skills in
managing farm and other outdoor servants during your absence, as Molly
Wood did for her mistress Frances Hamilton, when the latter departed
for six weeks holiday in Wells at Christmastide 1786. Molly started as
she had been instructed to go on, in Mrs Hamilton's day book: '1786
Dec 31 meer went For Coal to Taunton Thos clove wood & Cleand best
nives Edward pick sticks brought down Saw dust From the Sapit'.[23] Full
written instructions had been left on the previous pages. Now, all through
January 1787, Molly Wood exercised her mistress's capacities in literacy
and household management, which is what the law said her position as
servant embodied: she was Mrs Hamilton's proxy, or prosthesis, during
this month, in writing.

It is not known whether or not Elizabeth Hands, whose poetry is the
focus of this chapter, worked as a cook, only that before her marriage
and the birth of her daughter in 1785 she was a servant to at least one
Warwickshire family, in the north of the county between Coventry and
Rugby.[24] And yet her reading of the professional cookery manuals is
inscribed in her poem 'On the Supposition of an Advertisement appearing in a Morning Paper, of the Publication of a Volume of Poems, by
a Servant-Maid', with the ability to make the 'ragou' that Miss Pines
thinks would be *really useful knowledge* in a maid.[25] An assertion of plain

22 Somerset Archives (SA), DD/GB, 148–149, Gore Family Papers. Volume 1, DD/
    GB/148: 264, nd (probably 1771).
23 SA, DD/SF, Bishop Lydeard Farming Accounts and Household Accounts, Mrs.
    Frances Hamilton. Box 7. 2: 63–72.
24 W. K. Riland Bedford, *Three Hundred Years of a Family Living, Being a History of the
    Rilands of Sutton Coldfield*, Cornish, Birmingham, 1889, pp. 112–114; Tim Burke (ed.),
    Eighteenth-Century Labouring Class Poets, Volume III, 1700–1800, Pickering and Chatto,
    London, 2003, pp. 153–155; Cynthia Dereli, 'In search of a poet. The life and work of
    Elizabeth Hands', *Women's Writing*, 8 (2001), pp. 169–182; Caroline Franklin (ed.), *The
    Romantics. Women Poets 1770–1830*, Routledge, London, 1996, pp. i–xiii; Donna Landry,
    The Muses of Resistance. Laboring Class Women's Poetry in Britain, 1739–1796, Cambridge
    University Press, Cambridge, 1990, pp. 186–209; Jan Fergus, 'Provincial Servants's
    Reading in the late Eighteenth Century', James Raven, Helen Small, and Naomi Tadmor
    (eds), *The Practice and Representation of Reading in England*, Cambridge University Press,
    Cambridge, 1996, pp. 202–225; Cynthia Dereli, 'Hands, Elizabeth (bap. 1746, d.1815)',
    Oxford Dictionary of National Biography, Oxford University Press, Oxford, 2004.
25 For cookery manuals as used by servants, Carolyn Steedman, 'Poetical maids and cooks
    who wrote', *Eighteenth-Century Studies*, 39:1 (2005), pp. 1–27. This chapter is a rewrit-
    ing and revision of 'Poetical maids'.

English taste has been discerned in the work of authorial women cooks of this period, an endorsement of simple, clear flavours, and of cookbooks 'not stuffed with a nauseous hodge-podge of French kickshaws', as Ann Peckham assured readers hers was not.[26] As English cooking style moved away from debased versions of court cuisine, to production of the French sort *à la mode* and on the cheap, many cooks (the shock-troops of culinary change) contemplated the *ragout*.[27] Martha Bradley, like Ann Peckham, thought that it typified the French way of mixing together so many ingredients that purity of flavour was lost. And yet she had several recipes for *ragoux* and perhaps her 'To Ragoo a Breast of Veal' had penetrated the poetic imagination if not the kitchens of central Warwickshire by 1789. Bradley gave detailed instructions for ragoo-ing a cut of fresh meat, a recipe written in the teeth of her opinion that 'the French, who never know when to stop, serve up a Capon [for example] ... with a rich Raggoo about it, but this is a Confusion, and the Taste of one Thing destroys another'.[28] It is economical *English* home cooking that the fictional Mrs Domestic is after, the using-up of leftovers and the making of ersatz champagne, not fully Frenchified dishes; Elizabeth Hands makes sure you know this, just as she makes sure the reader knows that the servant 'who wrote on a Wedding some very good lines' is herself, for six verses 'On a Wedding' are to be found some thirty pages on, in the real volume that the ladies and gentlemen in the drawing room have just seen advertised (in the real *Coventry Mercury*), and that you, now, hold in your hands.[29] Hands knows that you – the reader – will know that the bean dish on which Mrs. Domestic is complimented ('"Your haricots, ma'am, are the best I e'er eat ... may I venture to beg a receipt?"') was actually cooked by her maid, though you may have doubts about her production of poetry. Hands does not need to labour either of these points (Supposition II, l.60–71). It is Hands' knowingness and her control of it, for fashioning into a good

---

26 Ann Peckham, *The Complete English Cook, or, Prudent Housewife*, Griffith Wright, Leeds, 1773, Preface.
27 Gilly Lehmann, Women's cookery in eighteenth-century England. Authors, attitudes, culinary styles', *Studies on Voltaire and the Eighteenth Century*, 305 (1992), pp. 1737–1739; *Martha Bradley: The British Housewife: or, the Cook, Housekeeper's and Gardiner's Companion*, Prospect, Totnes, 1996, 'Introduction'.
28 Lehmann, *British Housewife*, pp. 37–38, 55–56, 97–98.
29 Elizabeth Hands, *The Death of Amnon. A Poem, with an Appendix, containing Pastorals, and other Poetical Pieces*, N. Rollason, Coventry, 1789, pp. 47–49 for Supposition I; pp. 50–56 for 'A Poem, on the Supposition of the Book Having Been Published and Read' (Supposition II).

joke, that astonishes. Modern critics have scarce got the measure of the insubordination – the barefaced cheek, the nerve of it – that the two 'Suppositions' imply (at least to social historians whose understanding of female domestic service in this period is framed by the pathos and melodrama – the knowledge of gender and labour exploitation – taught us by the last half century of labour and women's history). There is simply not a way of concluding that these two poems were 'offensive to none'; they are – surely – intentionally offensive, and wonderfully so.[30] Hands appears to have got away with a sustained satire on bourgeois and gentry manners and to have laughed heartily at her employers' pretensions to literary taste as well as at the mean-mindedness of their cuisine. The maidservant watching them *knows* more than they do.

Roger Lonsdale, who first brought Hands to modern critical attention by including the 'Death of Amnon' and other pieces from her volume in his *Eighteenth-Century Women Poets* (1989), remarked that Hands expected 'Amnon' to disconcert her social superiors.[31] Of the two much more discomforting 'Suppositions', Clifford Siskin – he calls them 'extraordinary' – has convincingly argued that the sublime trick of the second ('on … the Book Having Been Published and Read') works precisely because the two 'Suppositions' were *not* read, just as 'Amnon' was not read. Hands shows the gentlemen and ladies in the parlour discussing at length 'precisely those books – from the Bible to "Poems" by a "poor servant maid" [which] they have never read' and never will read.[32] Hands' textual control appeared to extend to her reviewers, and Richard Clough in the *Gentleman's Magazine* opened his assessment by recalling 'A Wag of our acquaintance' who, 'coming into a bookseller's shop in the country, where subscriptions were taken in for the benefit of this poetess, burst out [with] … "The Death of Ammon"! Who the devil is this Ammon? Hah! I have read a great many books, but never met with the "Death of Ammon" before" '.[33] 'Amnon' is spelled incorrectly in the heading to the review as well, a gloriously accidental joke by the compositor, probably.

30 Dereli, 'In search', pp. 169–182, 180; Fergus, 'Provincial Servants', p. 224.
31 Roger Lonsdale (ed.), *Eighteenth-Century Women Poets*, Oxford University Press, Oxford, 1990, pp. 422–429.
32 Clifford Siskin, *The Work of Writing. Literature and Social Change in Britain, 1700–1830*, Johns Hopkins University Press, Baltimore MD and London, 1998, p. 221. Landry, *Muses*, pp. 188–189.
33 'Review of New Publications. *The Death of Ammon* [sic] *A Poem; with an Appendix, containing Pastorals and other Poetical Pieces. By Elizabeth Hands*', *Gentleman's Magazine*, 60 (1790), p. 540.

Hands did indeed give her reviewers most of their lines. 'Let Mrs. Hands be the judge in her own cause' said the *Monthly Review*; 'in the words of Miss Rhymer and the honest old Rector … "There are various subjects indeed:/With some little pleasure I read all the rest,/But the Murder of Amnon's the longest and best".'[34]

Amnon was reviewed not so much for the novelty of a servant's writing, but because a woman – perhaps because a plebeian woman – treated of a subject so portentous and elevated (and on 'a delicate theme', observes Captain Bonair in Supposition II). '"Tis a Scripture tale, ma'am – he's the son of King David"', explains the old Rector:

> Quoth Madam, 'I have it;
> A Scripture tale? – ay – I remember it true;
> Pray, is it I' th' Old Testament or the New?
> If I thought I could readily find it, I'd borrow
> My housekeeper's Bible, and read it tomorrow'.
> ''Tis in Samuel, ma'am', says the Rector: – Miss Gaiety
> Bowed, and the Reverend blushed for the laity.
>
> Supposition II, 1.45–9.

Hands transmuted Amnon's desire for his sister Tamar, his rape of her, and his consequent death at the hands of their vengeful half-brother Absalom (2 Sam. 13) into blank verse, considered to be the noblest of metrical forms by contemporary literary theorists.[35] Her theme was important (as well as delicate): 169 of her 1,200 subscribers were clerical gentlemen, including members of Oxford and Cambridge colleges and two Bishops, though this high proportion may have had more to do with the networking skills of Hands' sponsor Philip Bracebridge Homer than with their interest. (Yet Hands anticipated interest, in the shape of her 'Reverend old Rector'.) Homer was classics master at Rugby school, had studied at Oxford, and maintained an extensive clerical and literary acquaintance – 'a community of interest' in John Brewer's terms.[36] To subscribe to

---

34 'Monthly Catalogue for November 1790', *Monthly Review*, 179 (1790), pp. 345–346.

35 Franklin, *Romantics*, p. ix; *Encyclopaedia Britannica; or, a Dictionary of Arts and Sciences, Compiled Upon a New Plan*, Bell and C. Macfarquhar, Edinburgh, 1771, 'Poetry'; Anne Janowitz, *Lyric and Labour in the Romantic Tradition*, Cambridge University Press, Cambridge, 1998, p. 7.

36 Birmingham University Library, Special Collections, 1956/V27–27A. Philip Bracebridge Homer, Letters, Papers, Copy of *The Garland* &c. Birmingham Central Library, Archives Department, Homer425; 'Accounts of the Births, Deaths and

such a publishing enterprise was in the first place a charitable act: the *Gentleman's Magazine* hoped that monetary homage to the poetical talents of a blacksmith's wife might 'make the remainder of her life comfortable to herself and family'.

This was indeed how Elizabeth Hands had first been presented to the reading public, as a deserving – and talented – case: 'Had the poetical Fancy derived any Assistance from Education, She would probably have stood high in the Rank of female Writing ... but She has had no opportunities of Improvement, except for the careful Perusal of Books, which she was permitted to make Use of in the Families to which she was a Servant, and from the gradual Purchase of a Few, as her Finances could afford it.'[37] Recognition of her talent was also an act of approbation – this was evident to all reviewers – of character and merit in Mrs Hands, measured by the 'uncommonly numerous list of subscribers', and the 'extraordinary patronage' of 'persons of rank and consideration' that it showed.[38] Thirty-one members of the nobility subscribed (including the former Lord Chief Justice, William Earl of Mansfield and his family of legitimate and illegitimate nieces at Ken Wood);[39] and seven members of parliament, including Edmund Burke and Charles James Fox, bishops as already enumerated (plus the Dean of Canterbury), the Poet Laureate, the President of the Royal Society, the 'Swan of Lichfield', Anna Seward. Over 400 subscribers came from Warwickshire (about 600 from the Midlands counties including its major towns and cities), but it sold in London as well (90 subscribers) and extraordinarily well in Oxford and Cambridge. It was popular in Norfolk, and got as far north as Leeds.

It is not very likely that Edmund Burke or Lord Mansfield read the volume when it was sent out to subscribers in September 1789.[40] The Newdigates of Arbury, Warwickshire (Sir Roger and his wife sent in five shillings for the larger, superior version), kept a careful log of their library

Other Circumstances of the Children of the Rd. Henry Secheverell Homer, Rector of Birdingbury, & Vicar of Willoughby, Warwickshire'; Eric Benjamin Branwell, *The Ludford Journals of Ansley Hall*, privately printed, 1988, pp. 78–85; Fergus, 'Provincial Servants', p. 223; John Brewer, *The Pleasures of the Imagination. English Culture in the Eighteenth Century*, Harper Collins, London, 1997, pp. 182–183.

37 'Proposals for printing by Subscription for the Benefit of the Author', *Jopson's Coventry Mercury*, 24 November 1788, p. 3.
38 Rizzo, 'Patron as poet maker'; Stott, *Hannah More*, p. 73; Jonathan Bate, *John Clare. A Biography*, Pan Macmillan, Basingstoke, 2004, pp. 143–192 and passim. Fergus, 'Provincial Servants', pp. 223–224.
39 Carolyn Steedman, 'Lord Mansfield's women', *Past and Present*, 176 (2002), pp. 105–143.
40 *Jopson's Coventry Mercury*, 14 September 1789, p. 3.

during these years, recording books as they came in and those lent out to friends; *The Death of Amnon* does not appear on their lists.[41] They had perhaps merely received the object by which they supported a deserving case of 'elevated genius' in a 'poor serving maid'.[42] Homer had told the *Gentleman's Magazine* reviewer (he was assiduous in getting her noticed as well as in recruiting subscribers) that there was 'no woman poet, in this age, from whom he [had] received so much entertainment', and he certainly had read it. (Though one wonders about how much space and opportunity there was for Hands to slip off to the *Mercury* offices and have material inserted that Homer had not seen. We simply do not know how far his editorial grasp reached.) Homer was a poet himself and keenly interested in prosody. In his published work and private poetic musings he never attempted the heroic, Miltonic metre, and produced no blank verse on topics tragic and elevated. In *The Garland* he apostrophised many a flower, but scarce looked at one, contenting himself with listing their attributes and associations.[43] Privately, for some 'sweet maiden of the Leame' (the River Leam runs through what was then Leamington Priors and is now Leamington Spa), he struck 'again, the golden wire'. But he *cared* about poetry and spent much time translating Latin verse into English and composing his own. We should at least entertain the notion that he knew that Elizabeth Hands could do something that he could not do himself; that he recognised poetic talent where he saw it.[44] The *Gentleman's Magazine* thought him generous in precisely this way, 'not jealous or envious of any who aim to attend the Heliconian hill, and particularly attentive to female merit'. Bertie Greathead, to whom *Amnon* was dedicated, may have promoted Hands for the same reasons, certainly among his very grand family: seven members of its Midlands branches subscribed to it, and he purchased a further seven volumes for himself. His mother was a daughter of the Duke of Ancaster, his wife an Ancaster

41 Warwickshire County Record Office, Newdigate of Arbury, CR 136/A [565]. Notebook of books received and sent out from Arbury; CR 136/A [621] Appointment and Memorandum Diaries.

42 *Jopson's Coventry Mercury*, 23 November 1788.

43 Mary Wollstonecraft noted that Homer's *The Garland* 'contains ... common sense, and a few lines which may be termed pretty. We shall select a few verses from the poem addressed to the Crocus.' Janet Todd and Marilyn Butler (eds), *The Works of Mary Wollstonecraft. Vol. 7. On Poetry. Contributions to the Analytical Review, 1788–1797*, Pickering, London, 1989, p. 98.

44 Birmingham Central Library, Special Collection, 1956/V27–27A. Philip Bracebridge Homer, letters, papers &c. Philip Bracebridge Homer, *The Garland; A Collection of Poems*, C. S. Rann, Oxford, nd [1783]).

niece; he wrote plays and poetry and the family had promoted talent in the serving class before.[45] In the 1770s, a very young Sarah Siddons (Sally Kemble as was) had been his mother's maid, and continued to visit the Greatheed family at the Guy's Cliffe estate just outside Warwick well into the nineteenth century.[46] Dramatic and poetic talent might exist in a plebeian woman, as far as he was concerned.

Why might a woman like Elizabeth Hands choose to write poetry rather than prose narrative? Our assumption as historians is still that someone like her would more likely first inscribe some version of 'I' upon the page, accounting for a hard-won individuality by reference to a range of available religious models for a life-story.[47] 'Why poetry?' is not a question asked about the working-class writers whose work continues to be discovered. Modern scholars properly acknowledge the compulsion to write poetry: Donna Landry says that Mary Leapor appears to have written not because she *could* make verses but because she could not *not* write verse.[48] But even Jonathan Bate's biography of John Clare, extraordinary testimony to the extraordinary difficulties facing a working man who wanted to write, does not ask 'why write poetry?' For Clare there was lack of time, of space, of a surface on which to rest a scrap of paper, of the paper itself, and of writing implements. An unannounced call from an interested reader (and social superior) eager to discuss the lyric form had to be attended and might cost him a day's wages. Clare wrote when and where he could, in fields, resting by roadsides, and on what he could; before his madhouse years, paper was much harder for him to come by than it was in Elizabeth Hands' or Christian Tousey's kitchens.

Poetry itself, from the Bible, and in the language of the hymnal and the psalter, shaped a basic instruction in literacy, certainly for the poorer sort, though children of all ranks and stations encountered it when learning to read. Presenting a child who is having difficulty learning to read with verse was a strategy of instruction discovered by educators and psycholinguists

45 Corinna Russell, 'Greatheed, Bertie (1759–1826)', *Oxford Dictionary of National Biography*, Oxford University Press, Oxford, 2004.

46 Warwickshire County Record Office, CR1707, Heber-Percy of Guys Cliffe, 1759–1826. Diaries of Bertie Greatheed. CR 1707/116, entry for 10 September 1805; CR 1707/122, entries for 14 and 17 July and 17 November 1818.

47 Michael Mascuch, *Origins of the Individualist Self. Autobiography and Self-Identity in England, 1591–1791*, Cambridge University Press, Cambridge, 1997.

48 Donna Landry, 'The Labouring Class Women Poets. "Hard Labour we most chearfully pursue"', Sarah Prescott and David E. Shuttleton (eds), *Women and Poetry, 1660–1750*, Palgrave Macmillan, Basingstoke, 2003, pp. 223–243.

of the 1970s.[49] Many unrecorded and inventive – or despairing – teachers may have made this discovery from the seventeenth century onwards, when printed verse in the vernacular became widely available. Verse looks easy on the page, unlike intimidating blocks of densely set prose. Wide margins, relatively short lines, space for the eye to rest between stanzas, all help an initial reader in the visual processing necessary for understanding that in some way, letter-marks relate to what can be voiced. Verse is *short* and semantically self-contained; its form is much less socially ramified than the novel – though for the later eighteenth century the novel cannot be our point of comparison. Neo-literates may have held in their hands a chapbook almanac or fortune teller, a Protestant conversion narrative, a ghost story, or the latest *Seven Champions of Christendom*, hot off the Banbury press in 1771; but not a triple-decker proto-gothic novel, which in any case operated by social and textual conventions that were probably incomprehensible to uncertain early readers. Poetry usually inscribes smaller and more independent units of thought than does fictional prose narrative. This point applies to six lines from, or indeed, the whole twelve books of *Paradise Lost* (or to a Canto of *The Death of Amnon*) as much as it does to 'The Death of Cock Robin': rhyme, metre, assonance, and figurative devices hold groups of lines together, as units of perception and understanding. Above all, rhyme (to a lesser extent, alliteration and assonance) provides a powerful regularity to support the good guessing by which any young (or inexperienced) reader proceeds. But it is highly unlikely that John Clare, or Christian Tousey, or Mary Leapor – that any eighteenth-century child – was formally instructed in reading by means of poetry. Rather, what we know about much later reading acquisition in English society alerts us to the resource a child might have found in the mass circulation of verse in the eighteenth century. After the printed sermon-collection, poetry was probably the most widely available genre of writing.[50] For those who held a volume of poetry or ballad sheet in their hands, it was a bridge between the world of the book and a resonant oral culture in which newly invented poetry, oral and written, served to celebrate and affirm many social occasions and cultural connections (she

49 Marlene and Robert McCracken, *Stories, Songs and Poetry to Teach Reading and Writing*, American Library Association, London, 1986. W. H. Auden thought the same: 'Verse, owning to its ... mnemonic power, is the superior medium to prose for didactic instruction.' 'Introduction to Poets of the English Language' (orig. W. H. Auden and Norman Holmes Pearson (eds), 1950), in *Prose Volume III. 1949–1955*, Edward Mendelson (ed.), Princeton University Press, Princeton NJ, 2008, pp. 103–154; 128–129.

50 Brewer, *Pleasures of the Imagination*, p. 172.

'wrote on a Wedding some very good lines').[51] Many a recently discovered plebeian poet of the eighteenth century was a *really useful* social item, in the way of Elizabeth Hands' writing a carillon for a wedding. Christopher Jones, the announcement of whose *Miscellaneous Attempts* (1782) in *Jopson's Coventry Mercury* may have set Elizabeth Hands a-thinking about how she might make some money (or simply, that she could do it too) produced verse on national events (war, naval victories, responses to 'Parliamentary Intelligence' in the press) and local ones 'On the Death of ...' many a provincial notable, productions that must in their own way have been 'useful again and again', for they were what was required at a wake and the funeral bard's metrical blueprint was infinitely re-usable.[52] Poetry was a form of language available to the literate, the non-literate, and the vastly complex set of abilities between the two that pertained in any English community: it has been noted that Alexander Pope, who was only really cruel about the thresher-poet Stephen Duck on one occasion (and that when Queen Caroline had suggested him for the laureateship), said that his published verse was only what you could find in any country village.[53] For children and other literacy learners in those communities, poetry provided an immediate form to work with, in the written language.

We do not know for certain how these plebeian poets were taught to read; but we can say that when it was formally done it was by some version of the syllabic method. A child – or young adult learner – was expected to learn the alphabet (how not? The alphabet was sublime and/ or God-given, the key to unlock all understanding),[54] that is, they must get by heart the letter *names*, rather than the sounds the letters represent. Rather rapidly (and sometimes, if nineteenth-century evidence is anything to go by, in parallel, for you could recite the alphabet on a daily basis for years in a village school, whilst doing quite other and sophisticated things with the written word) the learner was introduced to the phonetic

51 Vincent, *Rise of Mass Literacy*, pp. 92–94.
52 Charles Jones, *The Miscellaneous Poetic Attempts of C. Jones, An Uneducated Journeyman-Woolcomber*, for the author by R. Trewman, London, 1781; announced *Jopson's Coventry Mercury*, 25 August 1783, p. 3; Bridget Keegan (ed.), *Eighteenth-Century Laboring Class Poets, 1700–1800. Volume II, 1740–1780*, Pickering and Chatto, London, 2003, pp. 303–332.
53 Rizzo, 'Patron as poet maker', p. 245.
54 James Beattie, *The Theory of Language. In Two Parts: Of the Origin and General Nature of Speech*, Strahan, Cadell & Creech, Edinburgh, 1788, p. 16; Thomas Astle, *The Origin and Progress of Writing, as Well Hieroglyphic as Elementary, &c*, for the author, London, 1784, p. 6.

qualities of the twenty-six letters by articulating strings (primers usually printed them in rows) of syllables: *ba–ca–da–fa–* ... building these up into units that conveyed meaning as do *bat–cat–dash–fat* ... and then gaining further experience of letter sounds (and the variety of sounds that might be conveyed by the same letter) by combining syllables.[55] After this, as might be supposed, the primers took wildly divergent approaches, for as contemporary language theorists were at pains to point out, English is not organised at the structural level by syllabification, but rather by stress, that is by the irregularly falling emphasis of the human (English) voice in articulation.[56] Poetic rhythm encapsulates the essential features of any particular language. The suggestion here is that the syllabic method of literacy teaching may have allowed children and other learners a direct access to understanding the rhythmic structure of English, by allowing them to play with its sound system.

The repeated reading aloud and chanting of syllables provided a key to unlock the reading process, or at least James Beattie thought so; he was very keen that children should be made to pronounce each syllable distinctly (but naturally! a hard combination indeed!) when reading aloud.[57] All of this method involved voicing: the runs of syllables (and, sometimes, the wild nonsense of their conjunction) were said out loud, often – we must presume this – in chorus with other children. This may be seen as a kind of formalised speech-play, or echo of a baby's first babbling, mapping what many learners knew already (albeit unconsciously) about the organisation of their spoken language.[58] In some refinements of the syllabic method (it seems in some early nineteenth-century Lancastrian-inspired

55 Ian Michael, *The Teaching of English from the Sixteenth Century to the Present Day*, Cambridge University Press, Cambridge, 1987, pp. 72–130.

56 Beattie, *Theory of Language*, pp. 62–64, 66–67; Anon., *The Art of Poetry on a New Plan. Illustrated with a great Variety of Examples from the best English Poets, and of Translations from the Ancients*, 2 vols, Newbery, London, 1762, Vol. 1, p. 813; Edmund Waller, *Ballads and Songs chiefly taken from Dr Percy's Reliques of Ancient Poetry ... with Prolegomena Notes and a Glossary. The Whole collected and published by Theophilis Miller*, Kuemmel, Halle, 1793, pp. 32–33.

57 Beattie, *Theory of Language*, p. 61.

58 Courtney B. Cazden, 'Play with language and metalinguistic awareness. One dimension of language experience', *International Journal of Early Childhood*, 6 (1974), pp. 12–23; Mary Sanches and Barbara Kirshenblatt-Gimblett, 'Children's Traditional Speech Play and Child Language', Kirshenblatt-Gimblett (ed.), *Speech Play*, University of Pennsylvania Press, Philadelpha PA, 1976; Catherine Garvey, 'Play with Language and Speech', Susan Ervin-Tripp and Claudia Mitchell-Kernan (eds), *Child Discourse*, Academic Press, New York NY, 1977.

schools for poor children) other sensory support for playing about with syllables (of finding out more about what you already knew about language) was offered, pupils being asked to repeat them again and again whilst tracing *ba–ab*, *bat–tab* … in trays of sand with a finger.[59]

What can be said about the syllabic method (which has to be assumed for the main part, from printed instructional and fragmentary autobiographical material) is that a method of literacy teaching may have affected thinking about poetry, not least because it connected with oral culture and a child's individual experience of language through early speech development. Syllabic methods of literacy instruction may influence a child to play with rhyme and rhythm (*ba–bat–batch–bachelor/run fast to catch her*). Much later phonic methods of teaching the child to recognise sounds first may possibly have favoured alliteration and the avoidance of rhyme. But this is truly uncharted territory. It's worth observing, however, that syllables are perceptually salient; how very much a syllabic method of teaching may have underscored the *thinginess*, the real existence of *bat* and *cat* and *mat*, as entities in the world and of language, in a way that learning that 'buh' is the sound with which *bat* begins, is not to learn of something perceptually real, in the same way. We can also note the very great opportunity for play (some would say for prosody, and some would say for parody) that the method allowed; and then we should look at the poetry that was – perhaps – produced out of it.

A working-class poet, writing at the very end of the eighteenth century, offers an answer to the question: 'Why poetry?' The answer was detailed, spelling out the poetic form, the metre, and the rhyme scheme that Robert Bloomfield (1766–1823) chose, as well as reasons for his choice. He described a spell of shoemaking in London in the 1790s, away from his Suffolk home and family. In May 1796, he started to compose what would be published as *The Farmer's Boy* whilst he worked at his bench, completing it in November 1797.[60] He composed all of it and committed it to memory before writing it down between May and November of that

---

59 Ronald Morris, *Success and Failure in Learning to Read*, Penguin, Harmondsworth, 1973, pp. 41–46.

60 Robert Bloomfield, *The Farmer's Boy. A Rural Poem*, Vernor and Hood, London, 1800; B. C. Bloomfield, 'The publication of *The Farmer's Boy* by Robert Bloomfield', *The Library*, Sixth Series, 15 (1993), pp. 75–94; Robert Bloomfield, *Selected Poems*, John Goodridge and John Lucas (eds), Nottingham Trent University, Nottingham, 1998. For shoemaker poets, Bridget Keegan, 'Cobbling verse. Shoemaker poets of the long eighteenth century', *The Eighteenth Century: Theory and Interpretation*, 42 (2001), pp. 195–217.

year. The final version was dated 22 April 1798.[61] Why poetry? Why rhyming couplets, in fact, of mainly iambic pentameters? 'Nine tenths of it was put together as I sat at work', he wrote in September 1798, 'where there were usually six of us':

> No one in the house has any knowledge of what I have employed my thoughts about when I did not talk I chose to do it in rhime for this reason; because I found allways that when I put two or three lines together in blank verse, or something that sounded like it, it was a great chance if it stood right when it came to be wrote down, for blank verse has ten-syllables in a line, and this particular I could not adjust nor bear in memory as I could rhimes.[62]

Of course, had Bloomfield read Beattie's *Theory of Language* or one of the many technical guides to English prosody available, he would have known that whilst the five-stress line of English blank verse *may* have ten syllables, that is not the correct way of analysing it, which is by stress: five strong stresses make an iambic line, each strong stress preceded by a weak one.[63] (W. H. Aden had much to say about these historic matters of syllable, stress, metre, and meaning, as we shall see.) The iambic pentameter is, as many an eighteenth-century theorist pointed out, a highly encapsulated item of information about the way in which English works as a system of sound and articulation – the 'most natural' to it, in their terms (or in the modern scholar's terms: 'Poetic rhythm is a heightening and exploitation of the rhythm of a particular language').[64] Yet Bloomfield concentrated on rhyme and on syllables; he valued them because both allowed him to remember what he had composed, in a way that blank verse (unrhymed iambic pentameters) did not.[65] Commenting on a much later *aficionada* of syllabic verse, Auden speculated on the childhood sources of her poetics, thought her similar 'mistake' about the iambic pentameter to be glorious. 'No questioning of how ... [Marianne Moore] came to write her syllabic verse has yet succeeded in eliciting ... an explanation which does not mystify still further ... I strongly suspect that she owes her discovery

61 Bloomfield, 'Publication of *The Farmer's Boy*', p. 78.
62 British Library, BL Add MS 28.266: 83–84, 85–86, quoted Bloomfield, 'Publication'.
63 Thomas Carper and Derek Attridge, *Meter and Meaning. An Introduction to Rhythm in Poetry*, Routledge, London, 2003, pp. 102–103.
64 Derek Attridge, *Poetic Rhythm. An Introduction*, Cambridge University Press, Cambridge, 1995, p. 3.
65 Ruth Finnegan, *Oral Poetry. Its Nature, Significance and Social Context*, Cambridge University Press, Cambridge, 1977, pp. 72, 90–102.

to providential ignorance, that, when as a child she first read traditional English verse, she noticed that metrically equivalent lines contained, normally, the same number of syllables, but did not notice (and was never told) that they also contained the same number and same kind of [metric] feet. O blessed mistake!'[66] 'The blessed mistake' was Bloomfield's too. We should also note that it evidently never occurred to him to compose prose narrative. For an autobiography, any kind of fictional narrative, a diary entry, a recipe – whatever – you really do need to have a writing implement in hand and something to write on, there and then. When you do not have these tools, you cannot really write.

Most proletarian poets 'wrote' like Robert Bloomfield. John Clare did not take paper and portable ink-pot to the field or the limekiln (though he once, memorably, wrote a fragment on his hat-band – with a pencil we must presume – whilst in a field).[67] Labour occupies hands; you must compose in your head, using aural rather than visual memory; this is what Bloomfield said. And it was the same for the ploughman, the thresher, the journeyman weaver, the young woman sweeping out the parlour, the cook making a *ragout* of veal. But in the kitchen there were surfaces to rest on; there was paper of a sort around, and perhaps something to write with (anyway, you could always whip up a little ersatz ink, from soot, and scrapings from an iron pot and some very strong tea) alongside the elderflower champagne. And the gall bladder of a recently eviscerated chicken would have been useful for fixing your ink ... Cooking processes are irregularly timed and leave moments for composition. No wonder that the cook it was who wrote.

When Robert Bloomfield's first editor saw the manuscript of *The Farmer's Boy* he was worried that 'seeing it divided into the four Seasons' the author was attempting – as so many 'so injudiciously and unhappily' had – to transmute James Thomson's best-seller, 'that noble Poem [*The Seasons*] from Blank Verse into Rhime; ... from its own pure native Gold into an alloyed metal of incomparably less splendour, permanence and worth'.[68] Blank verse had very high status in eighteenth-century English prosody; when its splendours were extolled it was usual to remind readers that it was the form of choice for Shakespeare and Milton. Elizabeth Hands' 'Death of Amnon' commanded attention because the unrhymed

---

66 W. H. Auden, 'A Marianne Moore Reader', *Prose Volume IV*, pp. 392–395, orig. review of *A Marianne Moore Reader*, *Mid-century*, February 1962.

67 Bate, *John Clare*, pp. 89–109, 451–458.

68 Bloomfield, *Farmer's Boy*, p. ii. James Thompson's *The Seasons* (1726–1730) was the century's most influential poem series.

pentameters suggested – as *Jopson's Coventry Mercury* pointed out – 'elevated genius' in one so low, and it was on her ability to sustain the heroick style that her reviewers judged her: 'if here and there an unequal line has insinuated itself into the five cantos of this heroic poem ... we must pardon the inexperienced Muse, and consider it as more than compensated by the sentiments conveyed in the whole'.[69] The rest of the volume, its 'miscellaneous articles' and the two 'Suppositions', would be read by Mrs Hands' subscribers 'without the severity of criticism' – meaning exactly the opposite. In more judgemental mode, *The Analytical Review* designated all the pieces, including *Amnon*, 'singsong'.[70] Most of them actually *are* singsong, a less elevated way of describing the iambic tetrameter than did Beattie, but in line with modern accounts of metre and meaning in English prosody. Discussing Chartist and other nineteenth-century poetry of labour, Anne Janowitz has revealed 'a dialectic within English poetry of a fundamentally oral stress (four-beat) metre and the syllable stress (five-beat) metre of artifice, that is, print culture'.[71] For Derek Attridge, English poetics, all of it, is determined by a division into four-beat and five-beat systems: 'five-stress poetics is determined by its difference from the plurality of four-stress metres'. Four-stress metres in written poetry provide 'the simplest and strongest rhythmic patterns', infinitely open to speech-like rhymes. The five-beat line's special character is due to the way it resists the four-beat line: this 'helps explain its widespread use in literary verse ... and its virtual absence in popular verse which tends to prefer more salient rhythms'.[72] Rhythm in poetry 'works', says Attridge, not because of any inherent quality, but because of the literary culture in which it poetry gets written and read and the modes of understanding the society provides.[73] As we have seen, eighteenth-century society provided hierarchies of knowledge about the rhythmic patterns and rhyme schemes

---

69 *Gentleman's Magazine*, p. 540.

70 This review was by Mary Wollstonecraft who declined to 'lend a hand to support a humble muse, whose chief merit is a *desire* to please' because there was quite enough support for her shown by 'the respectable number of subscribers' to the volume: 'if we cannot praise the attempt of a servant-maid of low-degree, to catch a poetical wreath, even after making due allowance of her situation, we will let her sing-song die in peace'. 'Article 43', *The Analytical Review or History of Literature, Domestic or Foreign*, 6 (January–April 1790), p. 98: *Works of Mary Wollstonecraft. Vol. 7*, p. 203. But this was kinder than she had been to Phillip Bracebridge Homer; Note 43, above.

71 Janowitz, *Lyric and Labour*, p. 7.

72 Attridge, *Poetic Rhythm*, p. 159; Goodridge and Lucas, *Selected Poems*, pp. xvi–xvii; Finnegan, *Oral Poetry*, pp. 90–102.

73 Attridge, *Poetic Rhythm*, p. 11; Finnegan, *Oral Poetry*, pp. 90–102.

chosen by its poets, labouring or otherwise. This was information transmitted in a highly codified technical language, which needed instruction
to be understood (tetrameter, pentameter, trimeter, and so on; trochee,
dactyl ... and so on).[74] Some scholars writing recipes for poetry still
think, as they did in the eighteenth century, that these descriptive terms
are necessary (or perhaps actually useful) for conveying knowledge about
poetic techniques; or at least did so until the revolutionary proposals
of *Meter and Meaning* that 'rhythm in English poetry is realized by the
alternation of beats and offbeat', and that this is how we should describe it,
abandoning the hallowed terms derived from Classical poetics.[75]

From 1771 onwards there was a hymn of praise to the rhythmic resources
of the English language to be found in the *Encyclopaedia Britannica* and
many other handbooks and guides: there is just *so much* cadence, rhythm,
stress, *so many* words and sounds available to English-language poets. The
availability of emphasis (stress) in English was the means 'whereof ... a
necessary union between sounds and sense ... in versification, unknown
to the ancients' was effected.[76] There was the very high cultural status of
blank verse, as we have seen, and a certain sneering at the four-beat
('singsong') line. In fact, Elizabeth Hands' use of the iambic tetrameter
reveals that not all of the gentry gathered in the drawing room are quite
up to date in their literary criticism (or that the old Rector retains his own
strong links with oral poetry and commonsense critical principles):

> 'That "Amnon", you can't call it poetry neither,
> There's no flights of fancy, nor imagery either;
> You may style it prosaic, blank verse at the best;
> Some pointed reflections, indeed, are expressed;
> The narrative lines are exceedingly poor.'

                                          Supposition II, l. 102–107.

---

74 See Glyn Maxwell, *On Poetry*, Oberon, London, 2012, pp. 84–107, on this point: 'I
    don't teach prosody. Iambs, dactyls, spondees, trochees ... If you need to know what an
    anapaest is in a hurry, use Google.'

75 Carper and Attridge, *Meter and Meaning*.

76 *Encyclopaedia Britannica*, 'Poetry'. The celebration continued into the twentieth cen-
    tury: 'By comparison with French, English seems an anarchic language, but this very
    anarchy, if it stimulates the proper revolt against it, can give rise to new and living struc-
    tures. Would Valery, I sometimes patriotically wonder, have finished his poetic career
    so soon if he had had the vast resources of *our* tongue, with all the prosodic possibilities
    which its common syllables permit, to play with?' W. H. Auden, 'L'Homme d'Esprit.
    Introduction to *Analects* by Paul Valery', *Prose Volume III*, pp. 590–596; review written
    1955, published *Hudson Review*, Autumn 1969.

This is indeed clever, in its punning on 'prosaic' in order briefly to say exactly what is meant in regard to poetics, prosody, and want of knowledge of both in the Rector and the general company. And we are obliged to ask whether or not the Rector knew about the high literary and cultural value of blank verse, for this is not the critical response of a well-educated gentleman. Had he not read his Beattie? Nor Joseph Priestley, on the theory of language? Perhaps it was unlikely that a Church of England clergyman would read a Unitarian. But then, Priestley was but 20 miles away in Birmingham, active nerve centre of propositional scientific knowledge and propositional and prescriptive knowledge about poetry.[77] Elizabeth Hands' characterisation of the Rector allows her readers (still) to *think these things*. It is very clever indeed. The eruption into printed and published verse of a resonant and still largely shared oral culture by the socially despised tetrameter was commented on thus by Elizabeth Hands:

> 'Who', says Lady Pedigree, 'can this girl be?
> Perhaps she's descended from some Family – ' ...
> 'I know something of her', says Mrs Devoir;
> 'She lived with my friend Jack Faddle, Esq.
> ''Tis some time ago, though; her mistress said then
> The girl was excessively fond of a pen;
> I saw her, but never conversed with her, *though*:
> One can't make acquaintance with servants, you know'.
> ''Tis a pity the girl was not bred to high life',
> Says Mr Fribello. – 'Yes, – then', says his wife,
> 'She doubtless might have wrote something worth notice'.
> ''Tis pity,' says one – says another, 'and so 'tis'.
> 'O law!' says young Seagram, 'I've seen the book, now
> I remember; there's something about a mad cow'.
> 'A mad cow! – ha, ha, ha', returned half the room.
> 'What can y'expect better?', says Madam du Bloom.

> Supposition I, l. 72–9; and 'Written, originally extempore, on seeing a
> Mad Heifer run through the Village where the Author lives.'

---

77 Joel Mokyr has proposed a new history of the industrial enlightenment, fuelled by the spread of philosophical propositions about new technology and the 'how-to-do' (prescriptive) knowledge that taught workers and their employers how to make, build, and construct. *The Gifts of Athena. Historical Origins of the Knowledge Economy*, Princeton University Press, Princeton NJ, 2002, pp. 28–77; Jenny Uglow, *The Lunar Men: The Friends Who Made the Future*, Faber, London, 2002, pp. 319–323 for Birmingham's literary and scientific culture.

There is no scandal here in Elizabeth Hands *living with* Jack Faddle, Esq. This was the conventional way of describing the contract to serve clinched at the hiring, as in 'NB Jonathan if he lives wth me to June 1796 is to have £2 2s 0d'.[78] However, there *is* possibly a frisson of misbehaviour among the better sort, hinted at by Hands. Why is Jacky Faddle Mrs Devoir's 'friend'? Why does she slip – so effortlessly that you have to pay it attention – from Mr to Mrs Faddle, as if trying to cover something up? *Why is Jacky Faddle called Faddle in the first place?* (To faddle: *v. tr.*, *v. intr.* – To pet, to fondle, to make much of; to play about with [1755].)

In the later eighteenth century, the organisation and agencies of literacy affected the most far-flung parts of the British Isles. Knowledge travelled fast, often by the movement of skilled artisans, by print communication and newly developed transportation systems; the cost of moving around Britain decreased in this period. By the 1760s, most of Britain received mail daily, and much of what the mail delivered was newspapers. The mid century also saw the end of law Latin, and a more general end to Latin's dominance as a mode of communication. Descriptive and taxonomic systems were standardised over a wide range of print products. Many a worker was provided with the means to visualise methods and techniques of *making something* by handbooks and manuals – and we should include here the cook in the kitchen perusing the latest how-to information on the *ragout*.[79] Poetry and knowledge about poetry spread in the same way, allowing people to become familiar with the way it looked on the page. This *seeing* altered prosody, says Attridge. This observation inscribes a history for eighteenth-century writing in general, and poetry in particular, because the 'gradually increasing importance of the visual dimension' accelerated wildly for new audiences along the lines of communication laid down by an expanding book trade.[80] Technical knowledge about poetry was available to those (like Robert Bloomfield and Elizabeth Hands) who probably did not read the manuals and guides provided by high literary culture. The suggestion here has been that these poets 'discovered' or intuited this knowledge for themselves, out of their experiences in literacy learning, and that the syllabic method of teaching drew their attention to the rhythmic potentialities of language in a highly specific way. In describing the spread of technical and scientific knowledge during the Industrial Revolution in Britain, Joel Mokyr has said that it does not

---

78 Somerset Archives, DD/FS 5/8. Bishops Lydeard Farm Accounts, 1791–1799.
79 Mokyr, *Gifts*, pp. 56–76.
80 Attridge, *Poetic Rhythm*, p. 2; Brewer, *Pleasures*, pp. 125–166.

matter if propositional knowledge is incorrect by later standards: if you can japan a piece of metal, lustre the motif on a teacup – or write a poem; not his example – with that knowledge, then it is good enough to be going on with. And Elizabeth Hands' knowledge about poetry as a technology of language *may* have come from her reading: she and several commentators mentioned the free access she had been given to household libraries in her various places. But her knowledge (her technical know-how) also came from her own reflection on the language system she employed and the heightened cognitive means that a poetic system (oral or written) provides.

From the time of classical antiquity, commentators have bemoaned the inadequacies of writing for expressing meaning.[81] A piece of written language may be a reasonable model of what a speaker said, but it is pretty useless for conveying what the speaker *meant*. Writing systems have great difficulty in capturing the prosodic features of speech: intonation, loudness or softness of volume, or voice quality. Spoken utterances imply, hint, insinuate; they also assert and define. Written language can do the last two; it cannot easily do the first three. It cannot readily indicate its hidden and intended meanings, as speech can. Writing, to say it at its most definitive and forceful, lacks illocutionary force.[82] Or does it?

> 'Some whimsical trollop most like', says Miss Prim,
> 'Has been scribbling of nonsense, just out of a whim,
> And, conscious it neither is witty or pretty,
> Conceals her true name, and ascribes it to Betty'.
>
> Supposition I, l.41–4.

The illocutionary force here comes from the device of irony, to be sure; but also from the present-ness, the now-ness, that the rhythmic structure (the four-beats) forces out of this utterance. David Olson describes the slow and gradual evolution of punctuation marks, the way in which, across many writing systems, punctuation attempts to give writing the illocutionary force it lacks.[83] Printers' type draws attention to the phrasing and emphasis of spoken language, to its syntactic structure, and to its sound

---

81 Olson, *World*, pp. 89–92. Jean-Jacques Rousseau, *On the Origin of Language: Two Essays. Jean Jacques Rousseau and Johann Gottfried Herder* (Rousseau orig. pub. 1781), University of Chicago Press, Chicago IL, 1966; *A Discourse on Inequality* (1755), Penguin, Harmondsworth, 1984; Jacques Derrida, *Of Grammatology*, Johns Hopkins University Press, Baltimore MD, 1974, pp. 30–37, 101–140, 302–113.

82 Olson, *World*, pp. 92, 154–155.

83 Olson, *World*, pp. 190–195.

system; it is a device for making meaning (or the intention of the speaker) plainer, by drawing attention to the rhythmic and phonetic structure of the language, by simply showing what the voice did, where it paused, stopped, trailed away, or made emphasis. Poetry – metrical composition – certainly in the few poets we have considered here, allowed a writer to do the same thing as punctuation. That is to say, poetic composition brought into writing the pauses and emphases of spoken language, tone and timbre of voice: the means to hear or reckon meaning.[84]

Elizabeth Hands' poetry gives the historian access to a ferment of inquiry and investigation into language and the question of *how it worked*. Hands may have had access to this knowledge, by reading or by overhearing, but her verse is also highly articulate evidence of the ways in which craftsmen and women, exercising their skills (in weaving, cooking, and versification), could increase their own knowledge and make technical discoveries that they were not actively prevented from trying out. Indeed, Hands received a good deal of encouragement to do what she did, though we do not know what that encouragement *meant*. What *were* they up to, the Warwickshire *bon ton*, the Midlands *tout monde*, in letting her get away with it? When Hands wanted us to know something of what she really meant, she chose the iambic tetrameter, and everything it implied about a language and a social system. And some members of the Warwickshire bourgeoisie appear to have known exactly what Hands was up to, and what gentry encouragement of her insubordination *meant*, albeit fifty years on, albeit in a novel. In her 1833 *Constance*, Katherine Thomson performed the comic turn – the comic strategy – of having her readers laugh at the servants before they could laugh at their employers (at you and her) with a 'warning' scene, encapsulating the belief of employers that their domestics teetered perpetually on the brink of handing in their notice (of giving warning). Thomson set *Constance* fifty years back in 1780s Warwickshire, in the county town of Warwick – bang slap in the middle of Hands territory – opening with the tea-time ejaculation of a mistress to her servant: '"Thomas ... this water don't boil, Thomas".' The narrator continues:

> The words conveyed no very important meaning, but they were uttered in a tone so different to the apathetic manner habitual to Mrs Cattell, that her consequential domestic, humoured, as servants were wont to be fifty years ago,

84 John Barrell, *Poetry, Language and Politics*, Manchester University Press, Manchester, 1988, pp. 120–121; Bate, *John Clare*, pp. 563–578.

did condescend, as he was quitting the room, to turn round and look at her. 'She is in a fuss – a miff about something', was Thomas's internal ejaculation, while his audible expostulation consisted of this laconic reply, 'This here water *do* boil, ma'am' ...

' "Thomas won't stand it long, I can tell you, my dear; he's not a man to be run after, nor interfered with" ' says her husband a few minutes later, to which she replies ' "Bless me, Mr. Cattell, he's stood it these fifteen years" ... "And if I don't give you satisfaction, – ma'am –" said Thomas, re-entering the room. Thomas well knew that those words always brought his mistress to reason; and setting down the toast at the same time, he retreated, having said, he thought, just enough.'[85]

W. H. Auden was surely correct when he noted (in 1963) that satire, like Hands' satire (and maybe Thomson's historical satire), 'flourishes in a homogenous society where satirist and audience share the same view as to how normal people can be expected to behave, and in times of relative stability and contentment, for satire cannot deal with serious evil and suffering'.[86] Even in the *annus horribilis* of 1789, the Great Year of Revolution, the curtain sliding open on terrifying social instability, things were homogenous enough for parties on both sides of the drawing-room door to know what the other was up to, to laugh knowingly and pointedly at each other, tittering behind a fan in the parlour, or sniggering up a sleeve in the kitchen. It *was* cruel, though; a cruelty silently witnessed by the servant's satire, her rebellious gesture at inequity and condescension; for she knows that if she writes, there maybe someone (maybe, someone like Katherine Thomson) who will read her later, and know what *her* laughter, at least, actually meant.

A poem, then, was and is a really useful item of social and psychological information. It allows historians to see, just a little bit, what was *in the head* of their historical subjects, to measure by a small degree their knowledge of the world and the book. To gain some grip on *their* technical knowledge of writing in general and poetry in particular is at least as useful as knowing about the worker's performance of the eighteen stages of manufacture that produced Adam Smith's famous pin, or about

85 Katherine Thomson, *Constance. A Novel. In Three Volumes*, Richard Bentley, London, 1833, Vol. 1, pp. 1–3. Rosemary Mitchell, 'Thomson, Katherine (1797–1862)', *Oxford Dictionary of National Biography*, Oxford University Press, Oxford, 2004.
86 W. H. Auden, 'Notes on the Comic', *The Dyer's Hand and Other Essays*, Faber and Faber, London, 1963, pp. 371–385; this quote p. 384.

the complex, coordinated movement of hands and feet, with cross bar, sinkers, and jack strings that produced the stocking shapes made by a framework knitter, over a fourteen-hour day, and a lifetime. And just as useful as knowing what the cookmaid had to go through to *ragout* a breast of veal. But W. H. Auden thought that poetic form – 'Rhymes, meters, stanza forms, etc.'– were like enough to the poet's servant as to actually *be* one.[87] We shall now turn to the topic of the poet and his (many) servants.

87 Auden, *Dyer's Hand*, p. 22.

2

W. H. Auden and the servants

But artists, though, are human; and for man
    To be a scivvy is not nice at all:
So everyone will do the best he can
    To get a patch of ground which he can call
    His own. He doesn't really care how small.
So long as he can style himself the master:
Unluckily for art, it's a disaster.
          W. H. Auden, 'Letter to Lord Byron', July–October 1936.

British biographers of W. H Auden make something of the Auden family as members of the servant-employing class (those from the US, less so): listing a household's domestics delivers an encapsulated item of social and historical information, as it has done since at least the early eighteenth century. Your readers will know a lot about your historical subject if you list the coachman, two maids, and the cook employed by George Augustus Auden (1872–1957), general physician of York, and his wife Constance Bicknell Auden (1869–1941) at the time of the birth of their third and youngest son Wystan Hugh, in 1907.[1] The biographer may have a lot more to say about the rank, status, and background of the family, but it is not necessary to do so, if you mention the servants.[2] Your subject may himself have written, quite frequently, about his father the doctor, his mother with a university degree, a 'study full of books on medicine, archeology, the classics ... a rain gauge on the lawn and a family dog ... family

---

1 Humphrey Carpenter, *W. H. Auden. A Biography*, Faber and Faber, London (1981, 1983), 2010, p. 4.
2 Richard Davenport-Hines, *Auden*, Heinemann, London, 1995, pp. 6–33; Carpenter, *W. H. Auden*, pp. 1–12.

prayers before breakfast, bicycle rides to collect fossils or rub church brasses, reading aloud in the evenings ...' without once mentioning the servants who supported their way of life; but you know the servants are there, dusting the study and preparing breakfast (in some accounts of the Auden household routine, they are required to attend morning prayers, so they would have been up betimes to get it ready for the family).[3] They may have mown the lawn, though the Audens would have been usual in employing a bought-in gardener to do that, and in 1933 Dr Auden was doing his own winter garden tidy.[4] The maids of Auden's early childhood home were remembered by their categorical opposites, the servants working at his public school, Gresham's at Holt in Norfolk, which he attended between 1920 and 1925: 'the cooking, if undistinguished – no one seems ever to have solved the problem of school maids who are almost invariably slatternly and inefficient – was quite adequate'.[5] He remembered one servant's name from his childhood home, that of the presumably tidy and efficient 'old cook Ada, [who] surely knew her stuff'.[6] The servants were also present by default in the same essay when he contemplated the lessons taught to middle-class children of the era about relationships with working-class people. He wrote, he said, as 'the son of book-loving, Anglo-Catholic parents of the professional class, the youngest of three brothers'. From 'the monied classes' he thought he was like all the other boys at Gresham's, unable 'to see the world picture of ... [the working] class objectively'. 'The public school boy's attitude to the working-class

---

3 For a similar 'Childhood', lived some twenty years before Auden's and which also never once accounts for the servants, see R. G. Collingwood, *Autobiography*, Oxford University Press, London, 1939, pp. 1–5. For Auden's reading of Collingwood and a notably similar fondness for gasometers and industrial machinery inculcated in both little boys, below, pp. 164–167. 'The Childhood' was a post-romantic literary form, much used in the later nineteenth century. Richard N. Coe, *When the Grass Was Taller. Autobiography and the Experience of Childhood*, Yale University Press, New Haven CT, 1984.

4 W. H. Auden, *The Prolific and the Devourer* (1976, 1981), Ecco Press, Hopewell NJ, 1994, p. 9, quoted by Davenport-Hines, *Auden*, p. 14; for the servants at morning prayers, Adrian Caesar, 'Auden and the Class System', Tony Sharpe (ed.), *W. H. Auden in Context*, Cambridge University Press, Cambridge, 2013, pp. 69–78; 69. For the winter tidy – 'My father down the garden in his gaiters' – 'the enormous comic ..., drawn from life;/My father as an Airedale and a gardener ...', W. H. Auden, 'Poem', *New Verse*, 7 (February 1934), pp. 6–7.

5 W. H. Auden, 'Honour [Gresham's School, Holt]', Graham Greene (ed.), *The Old School. Essays by Divers Hands*, Jonathan Cape (1934), Oxford University Press, Oxford, 1984, pp. 1–12.

6 W. H. Auden, 'Letter to Lord Byron' (1936), W. H. Auden, *Collected Poems*, Faber and Faber, London, 1991, pp. 81–113; 106.

and the not-quite-quite has altered very little since the war,' he said in 1934. 'He is taught to be fairly kind and polite, provided of course, they return the compliment, but their lives and needs remain as remote to him as those of another species.'[7] Edward Mendelson discusses Auden's thinking on social class in either sexual terms – 'The erotic objects in his earlier poems were generally from the working classes, rarely his social or intellectual equals. They earned their living with their bodies' – or as a twentieth-century writer's problem of representation.[8] But here is an analogous proposition: that any upper middle-class boy born in the early decades of the twentieth century learned how to think of the lower orders by means of his family's domestic servants.

Auden's upbringing had taught him lessons about social class; so too had a family history, which for him inscribed the eighteenth-century rise of the middling sort, the early industrial revolution, the growth of the professional bourgeoisie, and the opportunities offered to their class by rentier capitalism: 'My father's forbears were all Midland yeoman/ Till royalties from coalmines did them good', he told the departed Lord Byron – though did not appear to know that Byron was a fellow, though much grander, Midlander, who had also derived some of his Newstead Abbey revenues from coal.[9] But then, as he said when attempting explain changes in the creative arts and their markets between Byron's lifetime (1788–1824) and 1936, 'I've simplified the facts to be emphatic,/ Playing Macaulay's favourite little trick/Of lighting that's contrasted and dramatic'. This is the only indication, anywhere, that Auden had read Thomas Babbington Macaulay's works of history and, interestingly, had a critical stance on Macaulay's prose style. It's far less interesting that *Byron*

7 Auden, 'Honour', p. 3.
8 Of Auden's time working with John Grierson at the GPO Film Unit, with a film maker who made strenuous attempts to discard comic stereotypes of the working class, to portray 'fishermen and miners in a dignified and realistic light', Mendelson says that Auden had real doubts about whether it was possible to portray anyone outside one's own class. Edward Mendelson, *Early Auden* (1981), Faber and Faber, London, 1999, pp. 211, 282–283; Donald Mitchell, *Britten and Auden in the Thirties. The Year 1936* (1981), Boydell Press, Woodbridge, 2000, p. 57; Ian Aitken, 'Grierson, John (1898–1972)', *Oxford Dictionary of National Biography*, Oxford University Press, Oxford 2004; online edn, January 2015. Also Jonathan Foltz, 'Vehicles of the Ordinary. W. H. Auden and Cinematic Address', Bonnie Costello and Rachel Galvin (eds), *Auden at Work*, Palgrave Macmillan, Basingstoke, 2015, pp. 49–68.
9 Auden, 'Letter to Lord Byron', p. 105; John Beckett with Sheila Aley, *Byron and Newstead. The Aristocrat and the Abbey*, University of Delaware Press, Newark NJ and Associated University Presses, London, 2001, pp. 55, 156, 165.

could not possibly have read a historian whose first works were published in the 1840s; but Macaulay's judgement on Byron, that 'he was himself the beginning, the middle, and the end of his own poetry – the hero of every tale – the chief object of every landscape', is the ironic undertow to *Letters from Iceland* which contain the one to Byron.[10]

None of these lessons – about class, sex, and history – were taught in York. Wystan Auden was born in the city in February 1907, but in 1908, when he was eighteen months old, the family moved to Solihull, Warwickshire: Dr Auden had been appointed School Medical Officer for Birmingham. Solihull was then a large village some six miles south east of the city centre where the Birmingham Education Offices were located. It was served by the Great Western Railway, which offered a ten-minute journey into the city. The opening of Solihull Station in 1852 had prompted families with comfortable incomes from industry and investment and the professional bourgeoisie to purchase substantial villas within striking distance of the railway station; many of these were located in Lode Lane, the new Auden address. Perhaps the Lode Lane house was chosen with Dr Auden's daily commute into Birmingham in mind; but 24 Lode Lane (or where No. 24 was; 'Apsley' or 'Apsley House' has been demolished) is a fair stretch to Solihull Station: half an hour at a brisk pace. Another reason for the choice of Solihull over other Warwickshire villages bordering Birmingham, or one of the city's several salubrious suburbs, may have been its reputation as a strongly Anglican parish, though several biographical accounts suggest that Solihull churches were not high church enough for Mrs Auden.[11] Up until 1905, Solihull had been under the diocese of Coventry and Lichfield, but was then moved to the newly formed Diocese of Birmingham.[12] Auden remembered discussion of the low-church proclivities of the Bishop of Birmingham ('doctrinal

---

10 Auden, 'Letter', p. 103; Catherine Hall, *Macaulay and Son. Architects of Imperial Britain*, Yale University Press, London, 2012, pp. 259–329; Fiona MacCarthy, *Byron. Life and Legend*, John Murray, London, 2002, pp. 211–212, citing Macaulay's review of Thomas Moore, *Life of Lord Byron, Edinburgh Review*, June 1831.

11 Michael John Protheroe, 'The Development of Elementary Education in a Voluntary School, 1862–1992. A Study of Change and Continuity in the National Elementary School, Solihull, between the Revised Code and the Geddes Axe', thesis submitted for the Diploma in Education, University College, 1974, p. 30; John Burman, *Solihull and Its Schools*, Cornish, Birmingham, 1939, passim; Robert Pemberton, *Solihull and Its Church*, for the author, Exeter, 1905. For Mrs Auden's Anglicanism, Carpenter, *W. H. Auden*, pp. 5–6.

12 Pemberton, *Solihull and Its Church*, p. 28.

and liturgical controversy') in the two Solihull homes of his childhood.[13] After 1911 and the appointment of the low-church Bishop Wakefield to the office, there was nowhere in the diocese that was liturgically very comfortable for high-church Anglicans. When the Audens relocated again in 1913 (little Wystan now 6 years old) it was to Homer Road, a mere five minutes from Solihull Station and very close to the parish church of St Alphege. In the year after the move, Dr Auden acted as sidesman and as parish lay representative to the Ruraldecanal Conference and the Diocesan Conference.[14]

But perhaps Dr Auden did not take the train, but used a horse and trap for his commute and for his inspection of sanitary arrangements in Birmingham schools.[15] There is no coachman recorded living-in at 24 Lode Lane; the employment of a live-out coachman, or one hired from a local livery company, would not have been recorded under servant tax

13 W. H. Auden, 'W. H. Auden', Dean of New York (ed.), *Modern Canterbury Pilgrims. The Story of Twenty-three Coverts and Why they chose the Anglican Communion*, Mowbray, London, 1956, pp. 32–43; p. 33. 'The bishop of our diocese [who] was an extreme modernist [and] who refused to visit the church we attended' was Henry Wakefield (Bishop 1911–1924). His predecessor Charles Gore (Bishop 1905–1911) had been a key figure in the Anglican high-church movement. There is no mention of Bishop Wakefield in the *Solihull Parish Magazine* from 1911 to 1919, when the Audens moved from Solihull into Birmingham: Solihull's St Alphege's was the high church the low-church Bishop did not visit.

14 *Solihull Parish Magazine*, 33:2 (February 1913); 38:16 (April 1914).

15 Richard R Trail, 'George Augustus Auden, b.27 August 1872 d.3 May 1957 MB Cantab (1897) MD Cantab (1900) DPH Cantab (1910) MRCS LRCP (1896) FSA (1920) MRCP (1909) FRCP (1919)', Royal College of Physicians, *Lives of the Fellows*, http://munksroll. rcplondon.ac.uk/Biography/Details/155 (accessed 12 October 2017). Dr Auden's work for the Birmingham Education Committee was varied and innovative. See, for example, Richie Nimmo, *Milk, Modernity and the Making of the Human. Purifying the Social*, Routledge, Abingdon, 2010, pp. 62–63; Birmingham Central Library, Birmingham Archives Heritage and Photography, BCC/1/BH/1/1/1, Education Committee and Its Related Sub-committees, 1903–1937, Annual Reports to the City of Birmingham Education Committee of the School Medical Officer; George Augustus Auden, 'Height and weight of Birmingham school children in relation to infant mortality', *School Hygiene*, 1:5 (1910), pp. 290–291; 'The open-air school and its place in educational organization', *Public Health*, 7 (1912), p. 253; 'The Local Authority and the Health of the Child', Charles William Kimmins (ed.), *The Mental and Physical Welfare of the Child*, Partridge, London, 1927, pp. 171–178. Dr Auden's involvement with *School Hygiene* suggests acquaintance with luminaries of child health, mental and physical, Margaret McMillan, David Eder, Ernest Jones, and with James Kerr, the famous schools medical officer of Bradford and, later, the LCC. Carolyn Steedman, *Childhood, Culture and Class in Britain. Margaret McMillan, 1860–1931*, Virago, London, 1990, pp. 97, 204, 210.

legislation, or in the 1911 census.[16] But in 1911 there *were* servants in the Lode Lane house. Ada Elizabeth Lowly was returned as the Audens' cook. Her age (31 years, so not old at all) and her birthplace in West Hartlepool suggest that she may have come with the family from York. The housemaid Flora Munday, 17 years old and born in Rudge, Staffordshire was a West Midlands girl. There was also the exotic-sounding Emma Lucie Heiniger, 20 years old, of Swiss nationality though born in Colombia, South America, who was returned as governess.[17] This was a smaller household staff than the Audens had supported in York. Both Carpenter and Davenport-Hines point out that George Auden had taken a drop in salary when he moved to the Birmingham post. It would be unusual, however, for the family not to have employed bought-in cleaners, charwomen, and jobbing gardeners to supplement their staff of three.[18] W. H. Auden does not appear to have remembered the Swiss governess (he was 4 years old when she was enumerated). His older brother (John Bicknell Auden, 1903–1991) did, recalling her presence in the household from 1908 onwards, and that he had been 'jealous no doubt of affection and attention being transferred to a new arrival'. He was happiest, he said, 'between 1908–1911 while staying with my two aunts and an uncle who lived during vacation time in three houses at Wyesham, near Monmouth. I had been escorted there by a Swiss nanny. Wystan ... was too young to remember that I was the only one of the three brothers who had a friend of my own, and all the way from Switzerland. Alas, sixty years later even her name is forgotten ...'[19]

I have come to think of W. H. Auden as a servant-reared child; or if not reared by servants (for by all accounts Constance Auden was a *very* hands-on mother) as a typical product of the Edwardian three-servant

---

16 Male servants 'within the meaning' of eighteenth-century legislation were a taxable item for their employers up until 1937. Carolyn Steedman, *Labours Lost. Domestic Service and the Making of Modern England*, Cambridge University Press, Cambridge, 2009, pp. 129–171.

17 There were Heinigers in York (and all over the UK) in the 1890s. A York Heiniger married a woman who became purveyor of provisions; but none of their daughters were of the right age to be Emma. There may have been Swiss geological and other scientific expeditions to Colombia before the famous Helevetic Expedition of 1910, and a child born to a Swiss father in 1891 or 1892, her birth registered in Switzerland.

18 Lucy Delap, *Knowing their Place. Domestic Service in Twentieth-century Britain*, Oxford University Press, Oxford, 2011, pp. 35–41.

19 John Auden, 'A Brother's Viewpoint', Stephen Spender (ed.), *W. H. Auden. A Tribute*, Weidenfeld and Nicholson, London, 1975, pp. 25–26.

household.[20] One could see his rigid work routine, his insistence on early rising, his habit of leaving all social occasions at 9 pm, sometimes in mid-conversation, so that he might be tucked up in bed by 10, the punctual serving of meals at his table, the certain and absolute cocktail hour, on the dot … as legacies of highly organised household procedures in Lode Lane and Homer Road, Solihull. Humphrey Carpenter is particularly informative on the poet's domestic routine and attributes it to 'a deep nostalgic affection for the manners and rules of … [his] childhood'; it was partly an attempt to recreate a 'strict Edwardian upbringing', and 'as his years in exile in America went by he began more and more to model his domestic life … according to a pattern of nursery strictness'.[21] Of course, many bourgeois children served by maid and cook grow up without any such routine; some children of the poorer sort have routines quite as strict as Auden's when they are grown: I really appreciate a day that starts with an alarm at 6, believing that if I haven't begun work by 8 or, at the very latest, 9, I might as well give up and go shopping, for nothing can come of a late start. I am edgy if not tucked up by 10. Auden 'never wrote at night – "Only the Hitlers of the world work at night; no honest artist does"'.[22] I know many who do write at night, who produce good prose and excellent history, and who are nothing like Hitler; but I have never done it myself. But working in a room with curtains drawn against the daylight (Harborne Birmingham, New York, Ischia; anywhere Auden wrote between 1930 and his death in 1973) I cannot fathom. Once when it was suggested that Auden accompany colleagues on a walk, he replied 'What on earth *for?*'; I understand that no more than I do the Benzedrine and the downers that fuelled the working machine (I do understand the dissipation of the writing day in a stiff drink).[23] But there is great satisfaction in reading

---

20 For the historical resonance of the three-servant household, Sally Mitchell, *Daily Life in Victorian England*, Greenwood Press, Westport CT, 1996, p. 52.
21 Carpenter, *W. H. Auden*, p. 305; also pp. 203, 265, 299, 320, 325, 364, 392, 412, 424, 434; also Thekla Clark (with an Introduction by James Fenton), *Wystan and Chester. A Personal Memoir of W. H. Auden and Chester Kallman*, Faber and Faber, London, 1995, pp. 9–18.
22 Orlan Fox, 'Friday Nights', Spender, *W. H. Auden*, pp. 173–181; p. 174, quoted Carpenter, *W. H. Auden*, p. 279.
23 Carpenter, *W. H. Auden*, p. 391; James Stern, 'The Indispensable Presence', Spender, *W. H. Auden*, pp. 123–127. 'What on earth for?' was from his later years when, according to Thekla Clark, he suffered terribly from his feet. When living in Forio, Ischia, and despite the feet, he appears to have walked into town daily for the shopping. And he had a dog to walk as well. Clark, *Wystan and Chester*, p. 18 and passim. He was a good walker ('I like to walk, but not to walk too far', he told Lord Byron); Carpenter's pages are full of walks.

about a working routine that was so productive of so very much poetry and prose (there is pleasure, as Auden said, in just reading about a writer's working habits). His proclamation that 'no genuine writer cares about popularity as such. He needs approval of his work by others in order to be reassured that the vision of life he believes he has is a true vision and not a self-delusion, but he can only be reassured by those whose judgement he respects', is a fine motto for all writers, poetical or otherwise.[24] Such practices of mind and everyday life may have had nothing at all to do with the habits and manners inculcated in a small child in a servant-keeping household of Edwardian Warwickshire. But it is a different matter with the housekeeping question, which is raised in all accounts of Auden's middle and later years.

Auden once exclaimed to Edmund Wilson 'I hate living in squalor – I detest it! – but I can't do the work I want to do and live any other way.'[25] The squalor has been endlessly displayed by biographers, journalists, playwrights, and literary critics high and low, contemporaneously and posthumously, these sixty years past. Many find the story of Vera Stravinsky, the chamber pot, and the chocolate pudding irresistible; it is certainly the most recycled dirty story told about Auden.[26] I find the repeated stories of domestic dirt and disorder extremely depressing to read. In those moments of readerly imagination, as I get out my mop and pail and bottle of bleach and in a dour and resigned sort of way

---

24 W. H. Auden, *The Dyer's Hand and Other Essays*, Faber and Faber, London, 1963, p. 14.

25 Edmund Wilson, *The Fifties. From Notebooks and Diaries of the Period*, Leon Edel (ed.), Farrar, Straus and Giroux, New York, 1986, pp. 292–293, quoted by Davenport-Hines, *Auden*, p. 284. Also Rebecca Mead, 'Ink A Home-EC Bible and W. H. Auden', *The New Yorker*, 20 March 2000, p. 46.

26 1952 – Christmas dinner at Auden's and Chester Kallman's loft apartment – greasy plates and cutlery, immense quantities of booze –Vera Stravinsky visits the grubby lavatory, finds a basin of dirty fluid on the floor, helpfully empties it down the pan – come dessert the company discovers that she has flushed away Chester's chocolate pudding, put down to set in a chamber pot. This version from Davenport-Hines, *Auden*, pp. 284–285, citing several other accounts. The fashion for using Victorian chamber pots (and washstand basins and ewers) as tableware developed in the UK in the 1970s in its long Laura-Ashley moment of home decor, and this was New York in the early 1950s. But a chamber pot is a good receptacle for pudding-for-crowds, and a bathroom floor probably the coolest place to set it, it being too big for the refrigerator. Alan Bennett told the pudding story in his review of Dorothy Farnan's *Auden in Love* (1985): 'The Wrong Blond', *London Review of Books*, 7:9 (23 May 1985), pp. 3–5. I am disappointed to find no reference to chamber pots in Katharine Whitehorne's *Cooking in a Bedsitter* (1961), Penguin, Harmondsworth, 1963, for I had believed that's where I first learned of culinary uses for china bedroom ware.

go about giving the place (wherever) a good going over, I am bound to think that Auden just didn't know *how*; that he may have hated dirt and disorganisation, but that as a child of a servant-keeping household, had never learned *how* to put things right. I do not object to the dirt *in itself*, for I have my little Brillo pad to tackle the encrusted stove in some Auden kitchen, somewhere or other; it's the retelling of the *story* of the dirt that offends and depresses. Even Alan Bennett cannot make me laugh at its recycling. This is perhaps because Bennett's play *The Habit of Art*, which confronts Auden, his past, and his biographer Humphrey Carpenter, uses the most time-worn literary vehicle of the Western world for assessing character: Bennett employs the servants to do it.[27] It's 1972; we're in Oxford, in Christ Church's minimally converted old Brewhouse, which had been provided as 'lodgings for one of its most distinguished sons'.[28]

> *Auden's scout, Mr Boyle, in shirtsleeves and apron, though with collar and tie, is making ritual and ineffectual attempts to tidy the room, which is both messy and bleak ... [He] is expressionless, emptying ash from various receptacles into a bucket ... May, a middle-aged woman, has come on in outdoor coat and shopping bag. Boyle picks up a mouldy soup bowl and shows it to May. She picks up a cloth.*
>
> **May**   Dishcloth?
> **Boyle** His vest ...
> **May**   I'll rinse that out.
> **Boyle** I wouldn't. Where do you think he pees?

The servants then discuss Auden's notorious habit of peeing in wash basins, his stinginess with lavatory paper, his habit of going without underwear.[29] The servant's voice elides criticism of the bourgeois employer as it has done in all kinds of literary production for (at least) the last 500 years. In their interminable recycling of the Auden dirt stories, few commentators make a distinction between household and personal squalor. Auden appears to have been (to this reader) pretty clean in his person; in many biographical accounts he is often in the bath. It seems to me rude beyond

27 Bruce Robbins, *The Servant's Hand. English Fiction from Below* (1986), Duke University Press, Durham and London, 1993, pp. 27–32. For the servant as Fate, passim.
28 Alan Bennett, *The Habit of Art*, Faber and Faber, London, 2009, p. viii.
29 Bennett, *Habit*, pp. 11–14. Also for Auden's last days in Oxford, Edward Mendelson, *Later Auden*, Faber and Faber, London, 1999, pp. 509–511; Carpenter, *W. H. Auden*, pp. 441–447; Davenport-Hine, *Auden*, pp. 337–340. Auden himself wrote about the 'very nice cleaning woman' who did the Brewhouse. Carpenter, *W. H. Auden*, p. 445.

all measure for Nicolas Nabokov to have recalled his 'astonishment at seeing the dirt of his fingernails', and in a memorial volume to boot! How very inappropriate![30] It was just that Auden couldn't be doing with the kitchen floor or the washing up. The practice of peeing in the washbasin (avoidance of flushing) is supposed to have been his response to a Californian water crisis, shortly after he moved to the US. But any child far from a lavatory, with knowledge of the nanny's, or housemaster's, or mother's ears peeled for night time movement (*any* mother's ears peeled, not just the bourgeois ones of Edwardian Solihull), learns to pee where and in what they can.

Auden's was a life lived with servants. There were servants in the Solihull and Harborne households; maids and cooks, cleaners, gardeners, and odd-job men at his preparatory and public schools, and at his Oxford college. Households like the Audens' were structured by the servant's labour, or by its absence: at Constance Auden's end in 1941 Dr Auden told the story of her death (in a letter to a friend) in terms of domestic service: 'She had been in failing health for some time & had a bad heart attack on Whit Tuesday, but ... was soon active. We have had no maid since Maggie married eighteen months ago & later only a woman coming in for 3 hours more or less daily ...'[31] Auden employed servants during his US years, from 1940 onwards. 'Oh, my Negro maid has left me', he told Alan Ansen, of his Cornelia Street apartment in December 1947. 'She didn't show up after the day she cursed me.' He contrasted his current establishment with the one he grew up in: 'It's a disgrace I have to live like this. It's so hard to get accommodation in this country. I make as much money as my father did when he was my age, and he had a wife and three children to support, and he was able to afford a house and an adequate staff of servants while I have to live in two rooms and keep my bed in a working room, something I dislike extremely.'[32] There were servants of a sort in the Ischian household throughout the 1950s up until the retreat to Kirchstetten, Austria, in 1958, where he also employed domestic help. The presence of servants in the Christ Church College Brewhouse has been noted, though college scouts and cleaners were not in Auden's pay. All the others were. The woman with a Brillo pad in her hand feels sorry

30 Nicolas Nabokov, 'Excerpts from Memories', Spender (ed.), *W. H. Auden*, pp. 133–148; 133.
31 Davenport-Hines, *Auden*, p. 215.
32 Alan Ansen, *The Table Talk of W. H. Auden* (1989), Nicholas Jenkins (ed.), intro. Richard Howard, Faber and Faber, London, 1990, pp. 93–94. Also, Davenport-Hines, *Auden*, pp. 243–261.

for the two nameless black servants 'who cleaned and cooked the meals –
formal heavy meals, which were eaten in the basement with plush-covered
furniture' of the bohemian – commune, you have to call it, *avant la lettre*
– run by Auden in Brooklyn in the early 1940s.[33] They are not named;
but English literary history teaches how unlikely it would be if they were;
and whilst they may not have had murder in their heart (how can we tell
their heart, when they have no name?) as they plunged the greasy dishes
into the sink, 'the barest expository mention of a servant's existence is suf-
ficient to place ... [Auden's] life in problematic relation to the labouring
community'.[34]

The servant stories from Ischia are more amusing than the dirty ones.
Auden and Chester Kallman spent their summers on the island between
1947 and 1957, wintering in New York. One of the houses they inhabited
came with Giocondo; he is called a houseboy, or majordomo, depending
on the disposition of the biographer, some of whom remark that the
name was improbable, whilst not caring to discover what was his last,
or family, name.[35] In the Forio house, Giocondo lived in, gardened,
tidied up around the place, laid the table, and cooked when Kallman was
away. Carpenter thinks that he was also (possibly) employed 'to provide
sexual services'.[36] Edward Mendelson says that the poems Auden wrote
in Italy 'were the first that noticed the daily ordinariness of a place where
he actually lived', and there is more written evidence of the couple's
domestic routine from Ischia than from anywhere else Auden lived.[37]
Auden also appears as an Ischian householder involved with the provi-
sioning and maintenance of a domestic sphere – much more so than in
the stories told of New York and Kirschstetten, though in Kirschstetten
he was reported as happy with 'the absurdities of Frau Emma, his housekeeper ... Her death was one of the factors which darkened the last

33 And very sorry indeed for the poor agency maid who came in one a week to clean the St
    Mark's Place apartment in New York in the 1960s; Carpenter *W. H. Auden*, pp. 408–409.
    For the 1940s Middagh Street household, Davenport-Hines, *Auden*, pp. 207–208, here
    quoting Golo Mann, 'A Memoir', Spender (ed.), *W. H. Auden*, pp. 98–103. Also Bonnie
    Costello, 'Setting Out for "Atlantis"', Costello and Rachel Galvin (eds), *Auden at Work*,
    Palgrave Macmillan, Basingstoke, 2015, pp. 133–155; 133–134.
34 Robbins, *Servant's Hand*, p. 123, for 'the silent messenger ... with murder on his face as
    he takes orders for tea'.
35 But James V. Hatch, *Sorrow Is the Only Faithful One. The Life of Owen Dodson*, University
    of Illinois Press, Urbana and Chicago IL, pp. 190–194, notes that he was Giocondo
    Sacchetti.
36 Carpenter, *W. H. Auden*, p. 363.
37 Edward Mendelson, *Later Auden*, p. 291; Clark, *Wystan and Chester*, pp. 1–36.

years of his life' – happy with a servant in a way he had not been since his childhood.[38]

Maybe 'amusing' is the wrong word for the Giocondo story (none of this is to say anything *at all* about the actually-existing Signor Sacchetti). But it is about something less sad than the ghosts of numberless young men and women in the back kitchens of Western modernity, up to their elbows in filthy water whilst *they* (the high-ups, the appropriators, the masters and mistresses) get on with their incomprehensible but clearly more satisfying lives – elsewhere; on the other side of the kitchen door.[39] The Giocondo story is a good one because it repeats the ur-story of English state and social formation, as first expounded by Samuel Richardson in *Pamela*, in 1740. Auden was not likely to have recognised this, as not only had he not read *Pamela*, but said he never would.[40] Pamela, the eponymous 15-year-old servant of Richardson's epistolary fiction, not only has a highly articulate and well thought-through discourse on the idea of doing the dishes (an empirical political philosophy, derived from John Locke, to say why she shouldn't be asked to do the washing up),[41] but she also constitutes a major reference point for eighteenth- and nineteenth-century employers supplying their domestics with rules and regulations: 'Never tell the affairs of the family you belong to; for that is

38 Basil Boothby, 'An Unofficial Visitor', Spender, *W. H. Auden*, pp. 93–97. Lots of lighting up and wreaths of cigarette smoke when journalist Polly Platt interviewed Auden and Kallman in their 'Austrian peasant's house' in 1966 – but no overflowing ashtrays. This picture of perfect domestic order and cleanliness is rarely mentioned when describing Auden's household arrangements. Polly Platt and W. H. Auden, 'Interview: W. H. Auden', *The American Scholar*, 36:2 (1967), pp. 266–270.

39 Steedman, *Labours Lost*, passim and pp. 65–100, 228–254.

40 'I shall never read *Kalevala* [nineteenth-century epic poem composed by Elias Lönnrot from Finnish folklore and oral sources], *The Anatomy of Melancholy*, or *Pamela*'. W. H. Auden, 'The World that Books Have Made', *Prose Volume III. 1949–1955*, Edward Mendelson (ed.), Princeton University Press, Princeton NJ, 2008, pp. 270–272; orig. *New York Times* book review, 2 December 1951.

41 When the Comical Girl (Pamela is very funny, and intended to be so) believes she has been dismissed her place, she combines John Locke's empirical philosophy of experience with some misremembered chapbook Story of the Protestant Martyrs, to declaim that: 'I have read of a good bishop that was to be burnt for his religion; and he tried how he could bear it, by putting his fingers into the lighted candle: So I, t'other day, tried, when Rachel's back was turned, if I could not scour a pewter plate she had begun. I see I could do't by degrees: It only blistered my hand in two places. All the matter is, if I could get plain-work enough, I need not spoil my fingers. But if I can't, I hope to make my hands as red as a blood-pudding, and as hard as a beechen trencher, to accommodate them to my condition.' *Pamela, or, Virtue Rewarded* (1740), Vol. 1, Letter XXIV.

a sort of treachery … but kept their secrets and have none of your own'; 'Whatsoever happens in your master's house is never to be spoken out of your master's doors. A tale-bearing servant is always an unfaithful servant.'"[42] 'This', says Bruce Robbins, 'is the servant's original sin: the making known outside the dialogue of what goes on within [a household].'[43] Pamela made Mr B.'s gentry household open to all by means of her letters home; Giocondo did not *write* his stories of the goings-on in the Auden household.[44] But after a fatal embezzlement of his employers' money, or the forging or cashing of a cheque he shouldn't have cashed (or … there are multiple variants of the tale), he was dismissed his service by Auden and Kallman, set himself up in a café-bar in town, and reaped a modest living by supplying journalists and other interested inquirers with stories of their household, 'told out of doors', well after the couple had left for Austria.[45]

So Auden had servants, and servant troubles, not so very different from those of the employing classes of the Atlantic world from the early modern period through to the mid-twentieth century.[46] He also possessed a theology of service – or a theology of servants – believing that in literature, at least, a figure like Jeeves in P. J. Wodehouse's cycle of novels expressed

---

42 Anon., *Domestic Management, or the Art of Conducting a Family with Instructions to Servants in General, Addressed to Young Housekeepers*, H. D. Symonds at the Literary Press, London, 1800, p. 92; Charles Jones, *The History of Charles Jones, the Footman. Written by Himself*, J. Marshall (Printer to the Cheap Repository for Religious and Moral Tracts), London, 1796, pp. 4–5.

43 Robbins, *Servants Hand*, p. 83.

44 'I can't let her stay, I'll assure you', says the master to his house-steward; 'not only for her own freedom of speech, but her letter-writing of all the secrets of my family.' *Pamela, or, Virtue Rewarded* (1740), Vol. 1, Letter XXVIII.

45 Carpenter, *W. H. Auden*, pp. 386–387; Clark, *Wystan and Chester*, p. 35; Davenport-Hines, *Auden*, p. 295. For those interested in analogies between the Pamela-figure and the Giocondo-figure in the story of domestic service in the West, it is interesting to note that every word Mr B. utters about or addresses to Pamela, every move he makes (on her), is occasioned by the passion that grips him for her pretty little person, her clever little mind. For some, the always unequal sexual relationship between employer and servant *is* the narrative of service. See Kristina Straub, *Domestic Affairs. Intimacy, Eroticism, and Violence Between Servants and Masters in Eighteenth-Century Britain*, Johns Hopkins University Press, Baltimore MD, 2008.

46 But Robert J. Steinfeld, *The Invention of Free Labor. The Employment Relation in English and American Law and Culture, 1350–1870*, University of North Carolina Press, Chapel Hill NC and London, 1991, for the differences between British and US servant-employing cultures, and the preference, from the seventeenth century to the present day, of US domestic workers to be called 'help' rather than 'servant'.

Christianity's highest form of love: charity, or *caritas*; the love of God for man and of man for God: 'So speaks comically – and in what other mode ... could it on earth truthfully speak? – the voice of Agape, of Holy Love', he wrote of butler Jeeves.[47] Then, in 1963, 'to illustrate the use of the master-servant relationship as a parable of agape' he took examples from 'books which present the parable in a clear simplified form, *Around the World in Eighty Days* by Jules Verne and the Jeeves series'.[48] He also explored the psychology of the relationship – and of the servant – by means of Dickens' Sam Weller from *The Pickwick Papers*. (Here was one of the [fictional] 'working-class and the not-quite-quite' whose life and needs were not utterly remote to him.)[49]

Not *every* aspect of Auden's theology of service would have been recognised by English gentlemen of the employing classes during the long English eighteenth century; but many would. There were powerful Christian narratives to promote the thesis that master and servant were really relations; that the one was part of the other and that they were bound together in a love that recognised – some said, inscribed – hierarchy and subordination. Religious tract material repeated the injunction that the servant was bound in obedience and subordination to a master who was also a kind of father; it promoted the Biblical texts that carried this message well into the nineteenth century. High court judges sometimes appeared to aver this principle too, for was not the perfection of the English common law that it embodied the tenets of the reformed faith? But despite all the repeated prescriptions for godly relations within a household, as far as I can discover, the anonymous author of *Laws Concerning Master and Servants* of 1785 was the last *legal* voice to aver that 'Master and Servants are Relatives'; and in any case his declaration was accompanied by a brisk affirmation of modern contractual relations: 'And a Servant in the Intendment of our Law seems to be such a one

---

47 W. H. Auden, 'Balaam and the Ass. The Master-Servant Relationship in Literature', *Prose Volume III*, pp. 445–472; orig. *Thought*, Summer 1954; *Encounter*, July 1954.

48 Auden, *The Dyer's Hand*, p. 139.

49 W. H. Auden, 'Dingley Dell and the Fleet', *Dyer's Hand*, pp. 407–428; p. 419. For other reflections on the psychology of the employer, W. H. Auden, 'Am I That I Am?', *Prose Volume III*, pp. 527–532. This was a review of Nigel Dennis' 1955 novel, *Cards of Identity*, orig. *Encounter*, April 1955. 'I have read no novel published in the last fifteen years with greater pleasure and admiration', wrote Auden of this satire on psychologists and their 'Identity Club', which meets once a year to promote various theories of identity. The story line also involves local townspeople coerced into becoming the Club's servants.

as by Agreement and retainer oweth Duty and Service to another, who therefore is called Master'.[50] Even Anon's first proclamation, from a much older religious and political world, confirmed the modern legal commentator's brisk view that 'servitude is nothing else but plain Contract, and to be guided by the Rules and Conditions of that Bargain Invariably'.[51]

But the late eighteenth-century assertion of contractual over godly relations may not have made much sense to Auden, had he ever come across it, for he appeared to believe that 'contract' was a different thing from 'law' and that the service relationship came into being through the 'conscious volition' of two equal parties. 'A contractual relationship ... is ... asymmetric', he conceded: 'What the master contributes e.g., shelter, food and wages, and what the servant contributes, e.g., looking after the master's clothes and house, are qualitatively different and there is no objective standard by which one can decide whether the one is or is not equivalent to the other.' That is why contract was different from law, he said: in law 'all sovereignty lies with the law or with those who impose it and the individual has no sovereignty ... the relationship of all individuals to a law is symmetric; it commands or prohibits the same thing to all who come under it ... Of a contract, on the other hand, one can only ask the historical question, "Did both parties pledge their word to do it?"' He quotes Sam Weller asserting these things to Mr Pickwick, and Sancho Panza to Don Quixote, to underscore his point about the relative freedom of the individual in a relationship in which he is bound to serve, and in which all four of his examples express the implacable hierarchies of Christian love.[52] A gentleman of the late eighteenth- century might have had trouble following this argument, for several reasons. First, contract *was* law in eighteenth-century England (and still is) and the law of service in relation to the Poor and Settlement laws was widely accessed across the society.[53] Second, legal commentators and theorists had worked hard throughout the century to place law (rather that God) at the heart of the service relationship. Reiterating the century-old political philosophy of John Locke, John Barry Bird told magistrates and masters in 1799 that, really, 'in strictness everybody ought to transact his own affairs' – wash

50 Gentleman of the Inner Temple, *Law Concerning Master and Servants, Viz Clerks to Attornies and Solicitors ... Apprentices ... Menial Servants ... Labourers, Journeymen, Artificers, Handicraftmen and other Workmen*, His Majesty's Law Printer, London, 1785, p. 1.

51 John Taylor, *Elements of the Civil Law*, privately printed, Cambridge, 1767, p. 413.

52 Auden, 'Balaam and His Ass', pp. 107–109.

53 Steedman, *Labours Lost*, pp. 10–26; 172–198.

his own dishes, get rid of his own fag ends, though these were not his examples; it was only 'by the favour and indulgences of the law that he can delegate the power of acting for him to another'.[54] This was a lesson that you taught small children at the century's end: servants were there to do what was actually the employers job, by virtue of the legal relationship between them. '*I pay her wages to do my business for me*' insists one fictional mother in 1783 to a horribly behaved fictional child who has just slapped her nursemaid. She never wants the servants to do anything for the child 'unless they are desired in a pretty manner'.[55]

By virtue of contract, the servant might be understood as a prosthesis, or extra limb of the master or mistress.[56] It was the retainer, the monetary (or equivalent) handing over of some*thing* to the servant *and* the understanding or agreement or contract enacted in the moment of hiring that made him or her one under the Laws of Master and Servant, which governed labour relations in Britain and her colonies up until the 1950s.[57] But there is no reason at all why a poet should not construct a theology – or philosophy of service – disconnected from the history of service in the societies he inhabited and from his own experience of it. Indeed, some say that the *whole point* of the serving class, when depicted in novel or stage play, is to allow the masters and mistresses to remove themselves from the social and legal reality that ties them to their servants –and from the meaning of those servants – in a class society.[58] But the work of literature is not one a master or mistress can delegate to paid subordinates, though there was a good laugh to be had in the eighteenth century at the idea of those who tried.[59]

54 James Barry Bird, *The Laws Respecting Masters and Servants, Articled Clerks, Apprentices, Manufacturers, Labourers and Journeymen*, W. Clarke, London, 1799, p. 6.

55 Steedman, *Labours Lost*, pp. 48, 232–233. Dorothy Kilner, *Life and Perambulations of a Mouse*, John Marshall, London, 1781, pp. 18–19, 28–32.

56 Carolyn Steedman, 'The servant's labour. The business of life, England 1760–1820', *Social History*, 29:1 (2004), pp. 1–29; *Labours Lost*, 46–50.

57 Douglas Hay and Paul Craven (eds), *Masters, Servants, and Magistrates in Britain and the Empire, 1562–1955*, University of North Carolina Press, Chapel Hill NC and London, 2004.

58 Carolyn Steedman, 'Servants and their relationship to the unconscious', *Journal of British Studies*, 42 (2003), pp. 316–350.

59 Steedman, 'Servants', pp. 316–318. And there's still fun to be had by reading the nineteenth- and twentieth-century novel so that it turns out to be the servant who wrote it. Carolyn Steedman, *Master and Servant. Love and Labour in the English Industrial Age*, Cambridge University Press, Cambridge, 2007, pp. 193–216; *Labours Lost*, pp. 22–23. Also Jean Fernandez, *Victorian Servants, Class, and the Politics of Literacy*, Routledge, London and New York NY, 2010. All servants who, in the fictional realm, write as their employer's or author's prosthetic hand, are Pamela's daughters (and sons). Robert

Given Auden's personal and historical relationship with servants and the Christian idea of service as *agape*, as holy love; given his frequently expressed philosophy of service; what do we make of his assertion that the poet's devices of language are his servants? 'Rhymes, meters, stanza forms, etc., are like servants. If the master is fair enough to win their affection and firm enough to command their respect, the result is an orderly happy household. If he is too tyrannical, they give notice; if he lacks authority, they become slovenly, impertinent, drunk and dishonest,' he wrote as one of a series of *aperçus* about writing.[60] Are the servants just a figure of speech? It wouldn't be the last time they were employed in this way; advice to inexperienced writers still instructs how to make writing their servant by not being a servant to the words, even though modern student readers of internet composition advice sites may not find much experiential resonance in the servant simile. But the advice to master words comes easier in the modern era; early modern counsel to students was to master *writing* (correct posture; proper wielding of the pen; the pen itself to be correctly cut, so as to leave no blot, the paper placed at a precise angle on the table, etc.), not words. Students were taught how to become skilled at *writing*, not so much to master words, which bore an edgy relationship to the Word, over which God's creatures could not have dominion.[61]

That Auden enjoyed the comparison between rhymes and metre and the drunken servant of English literary culture (the Solihull servants of his childhood – we must presume this – were not drunkards) is suggested by his contemplation of the servantless man in the shape of 'the poet who writes "free verse"'. He who is not catered to by rhyme scheme and stanza form 'is like Robinson Crusoe on his desert island: he must do all his cooking, laundry and darning for himself'. To be sure, 'manly independence' may be the result of doing without servants; it may sometimes 'produce something original and impressive, but more often the result is squalor – dirty sheets on the unmade bed and empty bottles on the unswept floor'. The poet John Berryman thought that the 'showpiece' of the essays published in *The Dyer's Hand* was the 'study of the Master-Servant relation in literature, "Balaam and his Ass"': Quixote-Sancho,

Palfrey Utter and Gwendolyn Bridges Needham, *Pamela's Daughters* (1936), Russell and Russell, London, 1972.

60 Auden, 'Writing', *Dyer's Hand*, pp. 13–27; p. 22.

61 Roger Chartier, 'The Practical Impact of Writing', Chartier (ed.), *A History of Private Life. III. Passions of the Renaissance*, Harvard University Press, Cambridge MA and London, 1989, pp. 111–159; James Jerome Murphy (ed.), *A Short History of Writing Instruction. From Ancient Greece to Contemporary America*, Routledge, New York NY, 2012.

Lear-Fool, Giovanni-Leporello, others'.[62] But the servants were on
Auden's mind throughout. If the 'Prologue' to the book, which includes
'Reading' and 'Writing', was written in the early 1960s, it was done in a
serviced apartment in New York, or in the not un-serviced calm of the
Kirchstetten house. In Alan Bennett's imagination, in another serviced
scene of writing, as we have seen, a college servant, 'expressionless', empties fag ash into a bucket, into all eternity: once you have the servants on
your mind, as both Bennett and Auden had, they do not leave.[63]

Just as servants, imagined and real, did the work of exposing social
contradiction throughout the long transition to Western modernity, so
'the barest expository mention of a servant's existence' in a poet's prose
writing is enough to expose his. For Auden *was* contradictory in his statements about words, poetry, and poetics. In writing poetry, words were
sometimes the master, and he freely admitted it. Words could not be dominated; they could not be ordered about: 'It is both the glory and the shame
of poetry that its medium is not its private property, that a poet cannot
invent his words and that words are products, not of nature, but of human
society, which uses them for a thousand different purposes.'[64] They are
multi-purpose things, but they keep to their own edges.[65] 'A sentence
uttered makes a world appear', he observed in a sonnet included in the
collection *Homage to Clio*. In the poetic utterance – the words, arranged
as they are by rhyme and metre – 'all things happen as it says they do;/
We doubt the speaker, not the tongue we hear:/ … Syntactically, though
it must be clear;/One cannot change the subject half way through,/Nor
alter tenses to appease the ear'.[66] You cannot order them about to do
things they cannot do. And then there were the inhibitions and resources
of a poet's first language. Auden frequently compared French and English
poetry in regard to their sound structure, the one syllable-timed, the other
timed by stress, or accent.

> If French poets have been more prone than English to fall into the heresy of
> thinking that poetry ought to be as much like music as possible, one reason may

62 John Berryman, 'Auden's Prose', *New York Review of Books*, 1 February, 1963.
63 Platt, 'Interview. W. H. Auden', pp. 266–270; Mendelson, *Later Auden*, pp. 452–453;
    Alan Levy, *W. H. Auden. In the Autumn of the Age of Anxiety*, Permanent Press, Sag
    Harbor NY, 1983.
64 Auden, 'Writing', p. 23.
65 The phrase is from 'Objects', *Collected Shorter Poems*, p. 412.
66 W. H. Auden, 'Words', *Homage to Clio*, Faber and Faber, 1960, p. 28. 'Objects' is the
    preceding sonnet. On both of them, Mendelson, *Later Auden*, pp. 412–413.

be that, in traditional French verse, sound effects have always played a much more important role than they have in English verse. The English-speaking peoples have always felt that the difference between poetic speech and the conversational speech of everyday should be kept small, and, whenever English poets have felt the gap ... was growing too wide, there has been a stylistic revolution to bring them closer again. In English verse, even in Shakespeare's grandest rhetorical passages, the ear is always aware of its relation to everyday speech.[67]

Later, in the *Dyer's Hand*, he suggested that 'Accent has always played so important a role in English prosody that no Englishman, even if he has been brought up on the poetry written according to the traditional English prosodic convention in which lines are scanned by accentual feet, iambics, trochees, anapaests, etc., has any difficulty in recognizing ... a formal and rhythmical ... poem ... which is written in an accentual meter.'[68] As discussed later in this book, and in his later life, Auden laboured hard to make syllabic poetry fully English (in language terms), though not necessarily more like French poetry, for there was always the irreducible quiddity of a stress-timed language, lurking in the kitchen, drinking by the fire in a slovenly kind of way, ignoring the increasingly frantic ringing of the bell: an unmastered servant, blind drunk.

'By comparison with French, English seems an anarchic language', wrote Auden when he started to write poetry by syllable rather than stress. 'But this very anarchy, if it stimulates the proper revolt against it, can give rise to new and living structures.' He wondered if Valery, for example, would 'have finished his poetic career so soon if he had had the vast resources of *our* tongue, with all the prosodic possibilities which its common syllables permit, to play with?'[69] His appreciation of the syllabic poetry of Marianne Moore has already been mentioned. He conceded that her poetry wasn't for those looking for something as 'far removed as possible from ... prose';

67 Auden, *Dyer's Hand*, p. 24. See Mendelson, *Later Auden*, pp. 85–86 for these differences in the timing and stress of different European languages.

68 Auden, *Dyer's Hand*, pp. 296–297.

69 W. H. Auden, 'L'Homme d'Esprit. Introduction to *Analects* by Paul Valery', *Prose Volume III*, pp. 590–596. Written 1955; orig. *Hudson Review*, Autumn 1969. He was funnier in his irritation at French verse when out of print: Basil Boothby remembered many conversations which 'included angry repetitions of French alexandrines with English stresses, making ... [them] sound like "The Assyrian came down like a wolf on the fold ... " to show that "Frogs" ... didn't understand poetry'. 'Unofficial Visitor', p. 96.

that 'the syllabic verse employed by Miss Moore, which disregards accents
and permits rhyming on unaccented syllables, is far harder to grasp at first
hearing'. Moore's 'must be uttered in a conversational tone with only the
slightest line-end pauses', he wrote in 1959.[70] 'A syllabic verse, like Miss
Moore's ... is very difficult for the English ear to grasp', he reiterated in
1963.[71] What distinguished it from ordinary conversation was 'not so much
rhythm or tone as the articulation of the thoughts expressed, the sequence
of ideas', he said.[72] We shall return to this point.

Edward Mendelson says that Auden 'transformed syllabic verse into
one of the great permanent resources of English poetry'.[73] His use of the
syllabic line had started before the 1950s; he used it for the thinking he
most cared to do and the ideas that earned his attention. It is used in 'In
Memory of Sigmund Freud', as Mendelson further points out, as a 'rejec-
tion of his [the poet's?] assertive power'. In a syllabic structure (Mendelson
calls it a 'syllabic metre') each line has a fixed number of syllables, but no
recurring pattern of stressed and unstressed syllables. Auden is quoted as
saying that he had become 'interested in the possibilities of syllabic metre
as one way of achieving a balance between freedom and order'; that he
'wanted to get away from conventional patterns of iambics and trochees,
and, at the same time, not to lose the sense of pattern'.[74] The verse forms
favoured by a poet 'indicate the kind of coherence and order he sees, or
wants to see, in the world outside', Mendelson further remarks. But as
he also points out, 'there is no getting away from the fact that English is
inherently accentual, like all Germanic languages, and Auden's syllabic
verse was the product of more complex and difficult negotiations than he
implied'. Later discoveries about the rhythmic structure of the English
language – the peculiarity of English stress-timing – and the relatively
new view that its distinctiveness as a language lies in the 'coexistence, in
some degree of tension, of *two* series of energy pulses in speech – those
that produce the syllables, and those that augment the certain syllables
with stress', owes much to Auden's earlier discoveries.[75]

---

70 W. H. Auden, 'Miss Marianne Moore, Bless Her!', *Prose Volume IV. 1956–1962*, Edward
      Mendelson (ed.), Princeton University Press, Princeton NJ, 2010, pp. 226–229. Review
      of Moore, *How to Be a Dragon*; orig. *Mid-Century*, Fall 1959.
71 Auden, 'Marianne Moore', *Dyer's Hand*, pp. 296–305; 296–297.
72 Auden, 'Miss Marianne Moore', *Prose Volume IV*, p. 227.
73 Mendelson, *Later Auden*, pp. 85–86.
74 Mendelson, *Later Auden*, pp. 85–86.
75 Thomas Carper and Derek Attridge, *Meter and Meaning. An Introduction to Rhythm in
      Poetry*, Routledge, New York NY and London, 2003.

The thing is, elaborate workings out of Auden's evolution from a poet who employed stress-timing to a poet using syllable-timing makes things harder for a reader of his poetry, and raises the questions you don't want to ask, for they seem so very naive: is his syllabic verse to be read silently, voiced in the head, or spoken out loud? English readers tend not to hear the syllables in verse organised syllabically, so attuned are they to stress. It is said that in his later poetry, Auden exploited this tendency of readers by various technical means, so that the pattern on the page diverged from its audible expression.[76] We already have the testimony of a nineteenth-century working-class poet who argued that if you were not a master yourself, but a worker who had to compose poetry in your head because your hands were busy all day at your shoemaker's bench, lines timed by syllables rather than stress were much easier to remember when it came to writing them down. But Robert Bloomfield didn't actually *write* syllabic verse; he wrote five-beat lines; he *remembered* by syllable-count, he didn't compose by it. But with Auden's great, late poetry, once you know that its organisation is syllabic rather than by metric feet, you constantly hover in some liminal space between seeing and hearing the poetry. In reading aloud you cannot force syllabification on the English language, as it is generally spoken.

You might, as a reader of the 1950s, and had your parents provided you with Naomi Mitchison's *An Outline for Boys and Girls* way back in 1932, be even more stranded between two systems for describing versification, one learned in childhood, one now (in the 1950s and 1960s) promulgated by the poet. Auden made a contribution on 'Writing' (including 'Verse Form') to this encyclopaedia for children.[77] (At the time of writing, Auden had been teaching at Larchfield Academy, Helensburgh for two years, moving to the Downs School, Herefordshire in 1932.) To explain metre to children, he proceeded by analogy: 'Metre is group excitement among words', he told them; it is 'a series of repeated movements ... Rhythm is what is expected by one word of another ... There is always some degree of rhythm in all language. The degree depends on the power of feeling.' He went on to explain stress, or 'accents', which he also described as 'long and short syllables'. They were really 'quite simple', he said. As

---

76 Susannah Young-ah Gottlieb, 'Auden in History', Sharpe (ed.), *W. H. Auden in Context*, pp. 181–192; p. 187: his syllabic verse employed what he called 'the fullest elision', that is, he always elided 'between the contiguous vowels or through *h*'.

77 Naomi Mitchison, *An Outline for Boys and Girls and Their Parents*, Victor Gollancz, London, 1932.

in a dance 'the motion or metre of a line of poetry can be described in different ways according to how you choose to look at it. In English poetry ... we generally describe it by accents – light and heavy steps – because that is the most obvious feature about the movements of English speech. But remember always that such a description of movements is only a description; it isn't the movement itself.'[78] Understanding a line of poetry was the same as understanding its meaning: 'You will always read a line of poetry right if you know its meaning.' Which of course, is another rather severe problem with the later poetry (in its ambiguity of meaning, also is its glory. Of course).

Later, 'rhymes, meters, stanza forms' would cavort away in his kitchen, at their own private servants' ball, as the employer took up with the syllable, and started to rely on its services. A late eighteenth-century employer would have been discomforted if he ever found out about their autonomous life, quite independent of what law and legal theory said they were: mere aspects of the master's personality, exercising his own (unused) capacity to wash floors and empty the ashtrays (or, produce poetry), as kinds of proxy.[79] Hovering at the kitchen door, you can't quite see them, or make out what they're saying. Perhaps the Muse may tell us more of how Auden wanted the words to serve him. The Muse we put our questions to right now must be Calliope, Muse of epic poetry, or Terpsichore, she of chorus and dancing, for as we already know, his Clio's defining characteristic was her silence. Auden did not master the Muses, or even try. He said he was in love with them (or her), telling the Indian Congress for Cultural Freedom in 1951 that a poet is 'somebody who makes something and who therefore has a duty to see that what is made is well, and not shoddily made ... [as] what I make are verses which say something, it is my duty to see that so far as I know and as far it goes, what they say is true and not false ... Why do I do this? ... because ... [I am] in love ... with the muse of poetry.'[80] But she wasn't that reliable a girl, for she 'is always whispering to you, and fifty percent of what the Muse says is rubbish and has to be rejected. What you wait for is for the Muse to speak

78 W. H. Auden, *Prose Volume I. 1926–1938*, Edward Mendelson (ed.), Faber and Faber, London, 1996, pp. 12–24, reproduces 'Writing'.

79 Carolyn Steedman, 'Servants', pp. 316–350. See above, p. 31.

80 W. H. Auden, 'Address to the Indian Congress for Cultural Freedom', *Prose Volume III*, pp. 246–250. Congress held 28–31 March 1951. For the (now) sinister connotations of the Congress and its fellow-travellers (including Auden) as Cold War warriors, Matthew Spender, *A House in St John's Wood. In Search of My Parents* (2015), Collins, London, 2016, pp. 44–48, 87–101, and passim.

with authority ...'[81] Then he grows in confidence with her, as a kind of equal: 'the Muse, like Beatrice in *Much Ado*, is a spirited girl who has little use for an abject suitor as she has for a vulgar brute'.[82] Perhaps she allows you to forget the servants, whom you cannot master; he certainly never wanted Clio to be a servant to him.

81 W. H. Auden, 'A Symposium on Art and Morals', Appendix III, Public Lectures and Courses, *Prose Volume III*, pp. 663–670; Smith College 23–24 April 1953.

82 Auden, *Dyer's Hand*, p. 16.

3

The uses of Clio

THE MUSES, daughters of Jupiter and Mnemosyne, goddess of memory,
were the reputed goddesses of the several arts and sciences ... They are represented young and very handsome, and are nine in number. Their names are,
*CLIO, CALLIOPE, ERATO, THALIA, MELPOMENE, TERPSICHORE,
EUTERPE, POLYHYMNIA, and URANIA.* Clio presides over history ...
> *The Elements of Useful Knowledge ... Short Systems of Astronomy,*
> *Mythology, Chronology, and Rhetoric; with a Brief Account of the Trial*
> *and Execution of Louis XVI ... by the Rev. J. Adams, London, 1793.*

... for the purposes I have in view
The English eighteenth century will do.
> W. H. Auden, 'Letter to Lord Byron', 1936.

What did Auden pay homage to in 'Homage to Clio'? Why might a poet
evoke the Muse of History? Who is she, and where does she come from?
Answers to these questions come later, except to the very last, for we can
demonstrate that she had been in these islands for a very long time and
had by the end of the eighteenth century arrived in the Atlantic sea-board
of the Americas, as both history and poetry. The Muse helps map the
coming of History to the modern world, in the forms of it that Auden
understood, used, and eschewed.

A name, or a chapter heading – 'Clio' – arrived with Herodotus. As
'Herodotus most excelleth, both for the pleasaunt course of the story,
and the plentifull knowledge conteyned therein, I thought him not unfit
at his first entry into Englande' said an English translator of 1584.[1] He

---

1 *The Famous Hystory of Herodotus Conteyning the Discourse of Dyvers Countreys, the*
Succession of Theyr Kyngs, the Actes and Exploytes Atchieved by Them. The Lawes and

explained that he had followed the convention of the ancients in dividing the text according to the names of the nine muses, and here presented the first two, Clio and Euterpe (by this time designated the Muse of lyric poetry).[2] This convention was retained by translators and printers throughout the eighteenth century. One Greek and Latin text of 1715 consisted entirely of the first book, *Kleio*, which gave the publication its title.[3] Eight eighteenth-century imprints of Herodotus' work used the Muses as chapter headings, the last of 1792 getting as far as the third, Thalia (Muse of comedy). Many more elite readers besides the Earl of Hardwicke may have known the work as 'the Clio of Herodotus'; occasionally Herodotus himself was referred to *as* Clio.[4] 'Herodotus, in Clio tells us ...' was a common formulation derived from translations of Montesquieu's *L'Esprit des lois*.[5] 'Herodotus, Clio' appeared in the footnotes to Biblical exegesis, in travel writing, and in emergent anthropology produced by writers exploring the habits and manners of the ancients and newly encountered Others; they used the *Histories* as a great storehouse of social and cultural detail. Even a knowledge that only encompassed the first book, which largely concerned the origins and progress of the Greco-Persian Wars (499–449 BCE), provided a wealth of detail on 'customs of the Lydians ... the Massagetae', their history, dress, food, sexual conventions, and religious beliefs.

But Herodotus' work was a minor port of entry for Clio; the commonplace knowledge was that 'the first of the Muses takes her name from glory, [and] renown. Her province was to preside over history' came from many other sources.[6] Only scholars were in a position to learn that the

Customes of Every Nation with the True Description and Antiquitie of the Same. Devided Into Nine Bookes, Entituled with the Names of the Nine Muses, Thomas Marsh, London, 1584.

2 Jessica Priestley, *Herodotus and Hellenistic Culture. Literary Studies in the Reception of the Histories*, Oxford University Press, Oxford, 2014, p. 192. The divisions of Herodotus' work acquired the Muses' names in the late Hellenistic period (last century BCE).

3 Herodotus, *Herodotou Kleio, in Usum Regiæ Scholæ Cantuariensis*, R. Knaplock, London, 1715.

4 Philip Yorke Earl of Hardwicke, *Athenian Letters; Or, the Epistolary Correspondence of an Agent of the King of Persia, Residing at Athens during the Peloponnesian War. Containing the History of the Times, in Dispatches to the Ministers of State at the Persian Court*, J. Walker, London, 1792.

5 Charles de Secondat, baron de Montesquieu, *The Spirit of Laws ... With Corrections and Additions Communicated by the Author*, trans. Thomas Nugent, J. Nourse and P. Vaillant, London, 1750, Vol. 2, p. 70.

6 L'Abbé de Tressan, *Mythology Compared with History; Or, the Fables of the Ancients*

'history' ascribed to Herodotus was no such thing; that the word meant rather 'careful inquiries', or 'careful researches'; that it acquired the signification of 'history' only with writers much later than Herodotus, and that *The Histories* themselves do not mention Clio or any other of the Muses.[7]

How do I know these things? I, who like Nelly Dean can make out only the odd Latin phrase and have no Greek?[8] Clio's modern research procedure is to enter 'Clio' into databases of digitised texts from the seventeenth and eighteenth centuries, specifically Early English Books Online and Eighteenth Century Collections Online (ECCO).[9] In ECCO you will find 5,774 *clio*s (you cannot search using an initial capital letter) from the eighteenth century. When you've discarded *Cleo* (short for Cleopatra in play-texts), the common *clione* (sea angel; pelagic sea slug), the number of naval ships and racing horses named *Clio*, and all the other enthusiasms of the search engine, about a thousand of these constitute some reference to, some teaching about, Clio the Muse. Using these procedures and then doing what it's possible to do with EEBO (locate every English text mentioning Clio, or the Clio of Herodotus from 1534–1700; about 200), and BL 19th Century (a much more hit and miss affair, containing a mere 65,000 books from the British Library), I examined 305 appearances of Clio (I did not count reprints of texts). Clio appears exclusively as History in 65 of them, as Poetry in 55, and is both History *and* Poetry, or some other aspect of human endeavour in the arts and sciences, in the rest. Clio was both History *and* Heroick Poetry, *and* the narration of heroes and heroism for much of the eighteenth century, at the same time as

Elucidated From Historical Records. ... to Which is Now First Added, An Enquiry into the Religion of the First Inhabitants of Great Britain. Together with Some Account of the Ancient Druids. ... Translated From the French by H. North, T. Cadell and W. Davies, London, 1797.

7 William Desborough Coolley (ed.), *Comments on the History of Herodotus ... from the French of P. H. Larcher ... in Two Volumes*, Whitaker and three others, London, 1844, Vol. 1, p. 1: 'Herodotus has no appeal to the Muses. And consequently informs his audience of the restricted parameters of his knowledge, often expressing uncertainty, conjecture'. Or outright ignorance: Jon Marincola, 'Herodotus and the Poetry of the Past', Carolyn Dewald and John Marincola (eds), *The Cambridge Companion to Herodotus*, Cambridge University Press, Cambridge, 2006, pp. 13–28; 15.

8 Carolyn Steedman, *Master and Servant. Love and Labour in the English Industrial Age*, Cambridge University Press, Cambridge, 2007, p. 128. Nelly Dean in *Wuthering Heights* (1847) is able to read any book that takes her fancy, she says, 'unless it be that range of Latin and Greek and that of French – and these I know one from another, it is much as you can expect of a poor man's daughter'.

9 https://historicaltexts.jisc.ac.uk/home.

she emerged as modern History. 'The Goddess Clio will her Trumpet sound,/And loud Calliope Inspire her Sons,/In Numbers Mighty as the Theam to sing', proclaimed a funeral idyll for that of William III.[10] Or she was just a Muse without portfolio, as when Ovid was quoted to say that 'Nor Clio nor her sisters have I seen,/As Hesiod saw them on the shady green'.[11] She was transmitted with and without function or attribute in Dryden's Virgil and the Virgils of others (after Dryden, her dress – to be discussed – was a focus of attention); by Pindar as he appeared in the many 'lyric repositories' of the century ('OH; Clio, warm me now to sing,/In strains sublime, heroic fire:/Oh, now from Helicon take wing,/With Pindar's flame my soul inspire'); and by much quotation of Horace's lines: 'Quem virum, aut heroa, lyrâ, acri/Tibia sumes celebrare, Clio?'. This was translated as 'What man, what hero, wilt thou chuse, to celebrate his rising fame, And consecrate in verse his name?' in 1742, and as 'What man, what hero, wilt thou chuse,/Theme of thy lyre, immortal muse?/What god shall Clio praise?' in 1793.[12] (There was always a bit of amnesia about the fact that Clio and her sisters *were* gods.) Ausonius' version of Clio was referred to in passing (his text was deemed responsible for the cither she holds, or the guitar she invented – for the lower end of the market, as we shall see), but no translation was published.[13] Clio was

10 John Oldmixon, *A Funeral-idyll, Sacred to the Glorious Memory of K. William III*, Nicholas Cox, London, 1702.

11 *Ovid's Art of Love. In Three Books. Together with His Remedy of Love. Translated Into English Verse, by Several Eminent Hands. To Which Are Added, the Court of Love and the History of Love. With Copperplates*, for the booksellers, London, 1793.

12 Virgil, *The Works of Virgil. Containing His Pastorals, Georgics and Æneis. Translated into English Verse; by Mr. Dryden. In Three Volumes*, J. and R. Tonson and S. Draper, London, 1748; John Dryden, *The Poetical Works of John Dryden, Esq. In Three Volumes. With the Life of the Author*, Apollo Press, Edinburgh, 1794; Virgil, *Virgilii Maronis Opera. Interpretatione et Notis Illustravit Carolus Ruæus, ... Jussu Christianissimi Regis, Ad Usum Serenissimi Delphini. Juxta Editionem Novissimam Parisiensem. Huic Editioni Accessit Index Accuratissimus, Antè Editis Longè Locupletior*, C. Bathurst and twelve others, London, 1777; *The Lyric Repository: A Selection of Original, Ancient, and Modern, Songs, Duets, Catches, Glees, and Cantatas, Distinguished for Poetical and Literary Merit; Many of Which are Written by Dr. Johnson, Peter Pindar*, J. Johnson, London, 1788; James Brown, *Odes, Elegies, Songs, &c*, for the author, Bristol, 1786; Thomas Broughton, *An Historical Dictionary of All Religions from the Creation of the World to this Present Time. ... Compiled from the Best Authorities*, C. Davis and T. Harris, London 1742; Horace, *The Odes, Epodes, and Carmen Seculare of Horace. Translated Into English Verse by William Boscawen, Esq*, John Stockdale, London, 1793.

13 Joseph Spence, *A Guide to Classical Learning; Or, Polymetis Abridged. In Three Parts ... Being a Work, Necessary, not only for Classical Instruction, but for All Those who wish*

usually named as 'the first and chief Sister of the nine Muses', or at least at the head of the list provided, though from the late seventeenth century onwards a significant minority of authorities put Calliope (epic poetry; eloquence) on top, for the sweetness of her voice.[14] A schoolbook from 1799 had Clio and Calliope equal at the head of the line.[15] In 1800, a text for young military men in training suggested that Clio was always triumphant in any contest between the Sisters because she possessed the power of writing: 'When e'er Calliope recites,/Hoping to wear the Crown;/ Clio takes her pen and writes/Her fine Ideas down'.[16] Clio was literate, or mostly literate, throughout the century; it is not clear from any of the literature through which the Muses flit during the long eighteenth century that any of them but Clio could write.[17] Eighteenth-century children, other neo-literates, and those wishing to acquire polite learning, were told the meaning of her name: 'Her name is derived from the Greek ... glory, or ... to celebrate' (1742); 'named from Glory ... from the Famousness of

to have a True Taste for the Beauties of Poetry, Sculpture and Painting. By N. Tindal, Translator of Rapin, J. Dodsley, and R. Horsfield, London, 1764.

14 Horace, *The Odes, Epodes, and Carmen Seculare of Horace, Translated into English Prose ... Together with the Original Latin from the Best Editions*, by David Watson MA, J. Oswald, London, 1712; Alexander Adam, *A Summary of Geography and History, Both Ancient and Modern ... with an Abridgement of the Fabulous History or Mythology of the Greeks ... the Second Edition, Corrected, to Which is Added, A Geographical Index, Containing the Latin Names of the Principal Countries, Cities, ... Illustrated with Maps*, A. Strahan and T. Cadell jun. and W. Davies, London and W. Creech, Edinburgh, 1797. For Calliope on top, François Pomey, *The Pantheon, Representing the Fabulous Histories of the Heathen Gods, and Most Illustrious Heroes; in a Short, Plain, and Familiar Method, by Way of Dialogue. The Sixteenth Edition. Revised, Corrected, Amended, and Illustrated with New Copper Cuts ... for the Use of Schools. By Andrew Tooke*, A. Ward and four others, London, 1747 (further edn 1778); *The Universal Pocket-book; Being the Most Comprehensive, Useful, and Compleat Book of the Kind, Ever Yet Publish'd. Containing ... A Map of the World ... A List of Places At Court, with Their Salaries and in Whose Gift ...*, T. Cooper, London, 1740; *Glossographia Anglicana nova: or, a dictionary, interpreting such hard words of whatever language, as are at present used in the English tongue, with their etymologies, definitions, &c*, Daniel Brown and seven others, London, 1707.

15 'Calliope and Clio are first in the train,/And Euterpe, Erato o'er harmony reign./Behold Melpomene next; and then, hand in hand,/Polyhymnia, Terpsichore grace the fair band.' Harriet English, *Conversations and Amusing Tales. Offered to the Publick for the Youth of Great Britain*, Hatchard, London, 1799.

16 Samuel Nash, *Juvenile Epigrams, and Poems, Written by Samuel John Nash, LLD and Addressed to the Gentlemen of the Army, and the Navy*, for the author, London, 1800.

17 For writing in the training of late eighteenth-century naval officers, Elodie Marie Duché, 'A Passage to Imprisonment. The British Prisoners of War in Verdun under the First French Empire', PhD thesis, University of Warwick, 2014.

the Things that she records' (1747); the 'particular Names of the Muses are also very significant, as Clio, from Clerou [Glory] – because great is the Glory of Learning' (1766); 'Clio which means glory' (1780); 'CLIO, so called from the glory which she gives to those heroes and great men, whose actions are described in History, over which she presides' (1790).[18] She provided a useful lesson for those learning their Latin, and for some few, their Greek: the name explained uses of Greek nouns of the feminine gender ending in 'o' in 1710, and the pronunciation of Latin words ending in 'o' in 1743, and at the end of the century.[19]

Those consulting dictionaries were told simple truths about Clio's provenance and province: she was the first, the chief, the 'mistress of history, and the patroness of heroic poets'. Those who adopted her name as a pseudonym (Addison for the *Spectator* was the most famous of these, and his use of 'Clio' to declare his faithful report of things, endlessly repeated) associated themselves and the reader with truth and truthfulness. Definitions became more nuanced and anthropologically informed, even for schoolchildren, towards the end of the century. In antiquity, explained the *New Royal and Universal Dictionary of Arts and Sciences* in 1772, the Muses 'were the fabulous divinities of the heathens, who were

18 Broughton, *An Historical Dictionary of all Religions*; François Pomey, *The Pantheon*; D. Gordon, *The Young Man's Universal Companion. Containing, among many other Necessary and Entertaining Particulars. I. A Geographical Description of the World; the Fourth Edition … With An Accurate Map of the Whole World*, P. Hill, S. Payne, and D. Davidson, London, 1766; Charles Marriott, *The New Royal English Dictionary; Or, Complete Library of Grammatical Knowledge. Containing a Full and Copious Explanation of all the Words in the English Language. … to Which is Prefixed, A Copious Grammar of the English Language*, J. Wenman, London, 1780; *Mythology Made Easy; Or, A New History of the Heathen Gods and Goddesses, Demi-gods, and Other Fabulous Deities of the Ancients, … Designed to Facilitate the Study of History, Poetry … &c.*, G. Riley, London, 1790.

19 Robert Blau, *The Accidences of the Parts of Speech; Or, the Rudiments of Etymology. After a New and Easie Method. Containing, 1. The Alphabet with its Division, and the Definitions of the Eight Parts of Speech most Intelligible by Youth; … 2. The Accidences of Noun and Pronoun with their Examples and all that Relates to Them; … 3. Verb & its Accidences, with Four Regular Examples & Some Irregular. … 4. Participle with all that Relates Thereto, Adverbs, Prepositions, Interjections and Conjunctions, with their English*, for the author, Edinburgh, 1710; John Milner, *An Abstract of Latin Syntax; Together with Directions for Construing, Parsing; and Making Latin by the Signs of Cases. To Which is added, Prosody, … for the Use of Schools*, John Noon, London, 1743; F. Decan, *The Quantity; Or, Measure of Latin Syllables, Interspersed with Useful and Familiar Rules, to Assist Young Poets in the Composition of Pentameters and Hexameters*, F. & C. Rivington, London, 1795; John Carey, *Latin Prosody Made Easy; Or, Rules and Authorities for the Quantity of Final Syllables in General, and of the Increments of Nouns and Verbs*, for the author, London, 1800.

thought to preside over the arts and sciences ... Under the name of Muse the poets only pray for the genius of poetry, and all the talents and circumstances necessary for the happy execution of their undertaking. So that the muses are of all ages, countries, and religions.'[20] The history of the Muses is 'only filled with absurd traditions' claimed the third edition of *The Travels of Anacharsis* in 1800; but their name indicated their origins: 'It seems as if the first poets, enchanted with the beauties of nature, were led to invoke the nymphs of the woods, hills, and fountains; and that yielding to the prevailing taste of allegory, they gave them names relative to the influence they might be supposed to have over the productions of the mind.'[21] '*Feigned* to inhabit Parnassus', the fictional mistress of a boarding school says firmly to her girls in a text of 1790. Nevertheless, the task was to learn the names and spheres 'of all the imaginary beings'. 'Being blessed with an exceeding good memory', one of the students completes the task quickly and repeats them the next day to Mrs Steward; 'and then enquired of her, if she thought it possible for reasonable creatures ever to give credit to all that abominable nonsense?'. The mistress's reply is judicious and thoughtful: 'I will not ... pretend to say that what you have now been learning about Pegasus and Helicon were ever really believed by any one, for the Graces, the Furies, and the Nine [Muses] were beings purely of the Poets [sic] imagination ...'.[22]

The translator who first brought Clio to the British Isles – so he said, in 1584 – dwelt on her sex. 'Right courteous Gentlemen,' he wrote, 'we have brought out of Greece into England two of the Muses, Clio and Euterpe, as desirous to see the lande as to learne the language; whome I trust you will use well because they be women, and you can not abuse them because you be Gentlemen ...'[23] Clio was not generally ill-used by the poets, gentlemanly or otherwise, who had need of her favours: '– O Clio! these

20 *A New Royal and Universal Dictionary of Arts and Sciences: Or, Complete System of Human Knowledge. Containing ... A Very Great Variety of Useful Discoveries, ... the Anatomical, Chemical, and Medicinal Parts by M. Hinde, ... the Mathematical Parts by W. Squire, ... Gardening and Botany by J. Marshall, ... Criticism, Grammar, Poetry, Theology, &c. By the Rev. Thomas Cooke ... and the Other Parts by Gentlemen of Eminence*, J. Cooke, London, 1772.

21 Jean-Jacques Barthélemy, *The Travels of Anacharsis the Younger, in Greece, during the middle of the fourth century before the Christian æra. Abridged from the original work of the Abbé Barthelemi. Illustrated with plates, designed and engraved by H. Richter*, Vernor and Hood and five others, London, 1800.

22 Dorothy Kilner, *Anecdotes of a Boarding-school; or, An Antidote to the Vices of those Useful Seminaries ... in Two Volumes*, for the author, London, 1790, Vol. 2, p. 92.

23 *Famous Hystory of Herodotus*, 'To the Gentlemen Readers'.

are Golden Times;/I shall get Money for my Rhymes,/And thou no more go tatter'd', wrote one in 1742.[24] The tatters (and in some cases Clio's begging in the courtyards of the wealthy) were explained by reference to several translations of Juvenal: Clio stood in for the 'starving poet, who is forced by his poverty, to leave the regions of poetry, and would fain beg at great men's doors'.[25] As stories emerged about her being handmaiden to Apollo in his aspect as law-giver, lawyers entreated her aid, sometimes in a peremptory way: 'INDITE, my Muse! – indict! Subpoaen'd thy lyre!/ The praises to record, which rules of Court require!/'Tis thou, Oh Clio! Muse divine,/And best of all the Council Nine, Muse, plead my cause!' She was also useful in court because of her supposed connection (who *wasn't* she connected to?) with Hermes/Mercury, the lawyer's special friend: 'In keen iambics, and heroic verse,/Clio will all the traitor's crimes rehearse;/Will, to posterity, the fact transmit;/ With all the dignity of buskin'd wit', in the stage play *Poetical Justice* of 1768.[26] Poets were equally demanding: 'Madam CLIO! no resistance,/Come quickly, lend your best assistance'.[27] Historians, as they existed in the eighteenth century, were quiet about her; though towards its end, military men writing history appeared to prefer her in the aspect of Historia; those celebrating a victory in verse did not wish to

> slight the Bard's aspiring Lays,
> But, 'tis to History they trust for Praise.
> The Muse, alone, who the Historian guides,
> Who shuns all Fiction, and o'er Facts presides,

24 *The Summer Miscellany; or, A Present for the Country. Containing the Pin, An Epigram. Physick and Cards*, T. Cooper, London, 1742.

25 Juvenal, *A New and Literal Translation of the I, II, IV, VII, VIII, XIII, XIV Satires of Juvenal, with Copious Explanatory Notes; ... by the Rev. M. Madan*, for the author, Dublin, 1791; also edn 1789; Juvenal, *The Original Text of Juvenal and Persius, Printed for the Most Part, According to Henninius's Edition; Cleared of All the Most Exceptionable Passages; ... by Edward Owen, MA*, Rivington and three others, London, 1786.

26 François de Callières, *Characters and Criticisms Upon the Ancient and Modern Orators, Poets, Painters, Musicians, Statuaries, & Other Arts and Sciences. With An Heroick Poem (in Blank Verse) Intituled the Age of Lewis the Great. Written Originally in French by the Archbishop of Cambray, and made English by J. G.*, Richard Smith, London, 1714; 'ODE, BY THE ATTORNEY-GENERAL', John Hawkins, *Probationary Odes for the Laureatship: with A Preliminary Discourse, by Sir John Hawkins, Knt*, James Ridgway, London, 1791.

27 Samuel Whyte, *Poems on Various Subjects, Ornamented with Plates, and Illustrated with Notes, Original Letters and Curious Incidental Anecdotes*, for the author, Dublin, 1795.

The Record-Muse, alone, can best display,
Their multitudinous Names in bright Array.[28]

For old generals remembering battles long ago, Clio *was* a kind of truth.[29]
Some thought that Clio could not – would not – visit a modern battle
field 'Where thund'ring cannon vomit smoke and fire,/And balls and
shells fly whistling o'er my head;/Say, will the muse her votary inspire?/
Will Clio deign midst scenes like these to tread?' – so that particular
soldier was really writing about the impossibility of *his* writing a scene of
carnage.[30] On occasion, when the motives and intentions of combatants
were deemed ignoble, Clio was made to tear the pages of military success
from her book.[31] A prisoner of war incarcerated on a British ship during
the American Wars of Independence pleaded 'ASSIST me, CLIO!/while
in verse I tell/The dire misfortunes that a ship befell/'.[32] High-ranking
military and naval men were an exception to the general population:
throughout the century, in numerous dictionaries, guides to life and literature, and school texts, Clio was History for the low much more than
she was for the elite. And the word 'historian' was only rarely associated
with Clio, and certainly not in the way that had been conventionalised
by the mid nineteenth century when, describing statuary surviving in

28 George Twisleton Ridsdale, *An Ode, Congratulatory, Monitory, and Epistolary, on the
   Ever-memorable Victory Obtained by Lieut. General Johnson, at Ross, Over the Rebels,
   on the 5th of June, 1798. Composed for the Anniversary Rejoicing on the Ensuing Fifth of
   June, 1799*, for the author, London, 1799. Risdale was celebrating the Battle of New
   Ross, County Wexford, during the Irish Rebellion of 1798, fought between the United
   Irishmen and British Crown forces.

29 Sydney Swinney, *The Battle of Minden, A Poem. In Three Books ... Enriched with Critical
   Notes by Two Friends, and with Explanatory Notes by the Author*, Dodsley and four others
   in London, Merril, Cambridge, Tessaman, and York, 1769–1772.

30 'Written in the Trenches Before Valenciennes, and Enclosed in the Preceding Letter',
   *A Sketch of the Campaign of 1793. Part I. Letters From an Officer of the Guards, on the
   Continent, to a Friend in Devonshire*, T. Cadell and W. Davies, London, 1795.

31 Abbé Jean Baptiste du Bois, *Critical Reflections on Poetry, Painting and Music. With an
   Inquiry into the Rise and Progress of the Theatrical Entertainments of the Ancients. Written
   in French by the Abbé du Bois ... Translated Into English by Thomas Nugent, Gent. From the
   Fifth Edition Revised, Corrected, and Inlarged by the Author*, John Nourse, London, 1748.

32 'THE BRITISH PRISON SHIP. Written 1780. CANTO I. The CAPTURE', Philip
   Moron Freneau, *The Poems of Philip Freneau. Written Chiefly During the Late War*, for
   the author, Philadelphia, 1786. Guides to ancient mythology and handy pocket compan-
   ions to the classics were published in New York in the 1790s; for example, John Fellows,
   The Lady & Gentleman's Pocket Magazine of Literary and Polite Amusement, J. Lyon &
   Co, New York NY, 1796.

Rome, a scholar insists that Clio is a lesson in the historian's adherence to honesty and factuality: 'To the right of Apollo is Clio, who presides over history, and holds in her hand a trumpet, the symbol of historic fame: she is clothed in white, the emblem of truth, which should ever guide the pen of the historian.'[33]

Sometimes she was denigrated, or caught in an attitude unbecoming to her high function (though for the main part dignity attached to her name). She was Satire, or at least satiric in 1714, when she was invoked to attack medical quackery ('Dame CLIO! be glorious, draw/Out of thy Magazine, a Satyr's Claw:/Thy sharpest Quills of Porcupines let fly,/With staining ink, against the insulting Fry/Of Emp'ricks, Quacks, and Charlatans, that kill/The Mob with Jargon').[34] She's a snuff-taking madam who must have pissed on the tongue of a failed poet in a rather rude one-sheet satire of 1725.[35] She smokes and drinks: in a mock tragedy of 1763 *all* the Muses take to drink when they hear that mortals are going to try writing without them; 'CLIO smoking by the Fire side,/Let drop her Pipe, fell back, and almost dy'd'.[36] Far from being lovely and glacial in her dignity, she's a sunburnt and ordinary girl in 1751; or maybe that's just the 'unpolite and plain' – and witty – woman the poet can love when he does *not* look at her with Clio's eyes.[37] In the mid century she could have a pithy turn of phrase, as when a Poet calls out:

> MUSES ... descend your hill,
> Assist my greatly daring quill!
> That first attempts a Pudding's praise,
> Ye muses aid the novel lays.

---

33 Jeremiah Donovan, *Rome, Ancient and Modern, and its Environs*, 4 vols, for the author, Rome, 1842–1844, Vol. 2, p. 478; Stephen Bann, *The Clothing of Clio. A Study of the Representation of History in Nineteenth-century Britain and France*, Cambridge University Press, Cambridge, 1984. Donovan was describing a statue of Clio. Most of *Clothing of Clio* considers the plastic arts, rather than textual representation.

34 Thomas Boydell, *Medicaster Exenteratus; Or, the Quack's Pourtrait. A Poem*, for the author, London, 1714.

35 *Elegy on the Much Lamented Death of Ch—les Co—ey, the Poet*, [A satire on Charles Coffey, one sheet], Dublin, 1725.

36 George Downing, *The Temple of Taste; Or, A Dish of All Sorts. Consisting of Prologues, Epilogues, Songs ... &c. ... to Which is Annex'd a New Farce, Call'd Newmarket; Or, the Humours of the Turf. With A Sketch of One Year's Account of the Life of the Author*, for the author, London, 1763.

37 *Vocal Melody; Or the Songster's Magazine in Three Parts. Being A Collection of Two Thousand of the Most Celebrated English and Scotch Songs*, R. Baldwin, London, 1751.

A Pudding! sister, Clio cries,
He might as well have talk'd of pyes ...
        No, no, says she, with sneering look,
        Invoke not us; consult the cook.[38]

In *Love of Fame* (1753) 'Daphnis, says Clio, has a charming eye:/What a pity 'tis her shoulder is awry'.[39] Satiric – or maybe sarcastic is a better word – on occasions then; but she was never *funny*. With incompetent poets she can be impatient, as when in 1776 she jeers that the poet may 'Wish to recall a certain vow,/Which late you rashly made,/When, in a pettish mood, you swore/To leave off rhyming, and no more/Invoke the muses aid'. This is a polite way for the poet to tell the lady who requires him to write, that he doesn't want to.[40] (The year before, a different poet had firmly stated that Clio had nothing to do with poetry: 'Clio the Great, the celebrated Chief, Triumphant reigns in the historick Leaf;/In History alone does Clio shine, Exalted, fair, and eminently fine'.)[41]

She's a practical girl – she's a useful, handy Muse (after Swift, *Cadenus and Vanessa*, 1726), and much of her usefulness lies in her literacy. She writes, or indites, as early as 1710, using a quill (as noted) in 1714 and (anachronistically in 1794 – for you are looking at an ancient representation) a pen. She writes in both senses of the word, by indicting and composing. She is connected to books. How-to instructions for drawing her in 1701 insist on 'a Coronet of Bays; in her right hand a Trumpet, in her left a Book, upon which may be written Historia her name is from Praise or Glory'; '*always* represented under the form of a young girl, crowned with laurel, holding a trumpet in the right hand, and a book in the left', insisted Anne Fisher in 1788.[42] She appears to be particularly connected

---

38 Thomas Hudson, of Blakiston, *Poems on Several Occasions. In Two Parts. By Mr Hudson*, Thompson, Newcastle-upon-Tyne, 1752.
39 Edward Young, *Love of Fame, the Universal Passion. In Seven Characteristical Satires*, for the author, London, 1753, p. 62.
40 Though he does: 'On Being Desired by Lady Camden to Write Verses on Bayham Abby, the Seat of John Pratt, Esq., Near Tunbridge Wells. By the Same', John Almon, *An Asylum for Fugitives. Published Occasionally*, Vol. I, for the author, London, 1776 (later called *An Asylum for Fugitive Pieces*).
41 Robert Hill, *Poems on Several Occasions, Chiefly Miscellaneous; Calculated to Please the Admirers of Taste, … to Which are Added Some Pastorals*, for the author, London, 1775.
42 William Salmon, *Polygraphice; Or, the Arts of Drawing, Engraving, Etching, Limning, Painting, Varnishing, Japaning, Gilding, &c in Two Volumns* [Sic]. … *the Eighth Edition. Enlarged*, A. and J. Churchill and J. Nicholson, London, 1701; Anne Fisher, *An Accurate New Spelling Dictionary, and Expositor of the English Language. Containing a Much Larger*

to the kitchen (acquainted with puddings and pies, smoking by the fire ...)
certainly more so than the other Muses. This may be seen as an attempt to
domesticate the Muse; one woman who invoked her in 1799 noted that *her*
Clio had given way to Country Joan, and gave the reasons why:

> I live at home, and only ask
> More leisure for life's active task.
> My numbers are impeded oft
> By peeping in the apple loft.
> A chicken by the kite is taken;
> The felon rats despoil the bacon;
> The blackbirds on the cherries seize;
> The pigs have rooted up the peas;
> Away the unfinish'd ode is thrown,
> And Clio yields to country Joan.

But still: though in housewifry she is 'no pattern,/I scorn the name of
rhyming slattern'.[43] Clio had been a bit of a feminist since 1754 – or at
least allowed a man to celebrate a notable woman in feminist terms – when
John Duncombe asked her to bear him to the Kentish strand, where stood
'Miss Eiza C – ... equal'd by few of either sex for strength of imagination,
soundness of judgment, and extensive knowledge. Tho' mistress of the
ancient and modern languages, an excellent poet, and a natural and moral
philosopher; so great is her unaffected modesty, 'tis to be fear'd that even
this impartial praise will offend her. She has translated, from the Italian,
Algarotti's *Dialogues on Light and Colours*, and has an admirable nocturnal
ode to Wisdom, in Dodley's *Miscellanies*.'[44] Only Clio can take him to the
side of this paragon. Learned and literate, her 'tow'ring mind' was evoked
at the same time as the inadequacies of her education (but only when Apollo

---

Collection of Modern Words than Any Book of the Kind and Price Extant, for the author,
London, 1788.

43 Jane West, *Poems and Plays*, Longman and Rees, London, 1799. In 1739, Clio polishes
the sea like glass, in order that some beauty or other may see her own face. But this was
not housework as Jane West knew it. Charles Carthy, 'A Poem Inscribed to the Right
Honourable Lord *Howth*, On the Birth of a Son', *A Translation of the Second Book of
Horace's Epistles, Together with Some of the Most Select in the First, with Notes. A Pastoral
Courtship, from Theocritus. One Original Poem in English, and a Latin Ode Spoken Before
the Government on His Majesty's Birth-day*, for the author, Dublin, 1730.

44 John Duncombe, *The Feminiad. A Poem*, M. Cooper, London, 1754.

had been in charge of it).[45] Or she is just a name: for a beloved woman, for a child in her christening ode, or for a 3-year-old in a stage play.[46]

Some laughed at the uncertain *politesse* acquired by getting the Muses' names by heart from the almanacs and schoolbooks. ' "Mr. Tickle," said Mr. Mawworm, "I am assured ... will sing nothing to stimulate the pruriency of the passions, to exacerbate resentment, or make the understanding tollutate, or titu-bate. I love, as my learned brother says, the divine Polyhymnia as much as I do Clio, Terpsichore, or Urania." – "So, so," said Aaron, "wine will let out the secret. – You love Polly Plymsy, do you? O you are an arch one!" '.[47] As an entity who had grown as earthly children do, she was given the birthday of 1 May.[48] Who has departed, in *The Charmer. A Collection of Songs* from 1782? – 'AH whither, my Clio! ah whither hast fled?/What grove dost thou visit, what vale dost thou tread?/ Ah! return; no more from your fond poet stray./My lyre is quite tuneless, when Clio's away.' Is it a woman who's dun gone? – a Muse? – the poet's talent? All three of them is the answer.[49]

Contradictory, then, is the word for Clio's attributes and aspects in eighteenth-century England: wife, virgin, spinster, girl, dame; she is often imagined along with her sisters as a schoolgirl; sharp-tongued *and* dulcet-toned; cares for nothing but the truth, and only cares for fame; learned and a bit dim; loquacious *and* silent; strict, mournful, serious, grave; makes men famous in poetry *and* prose – though there was a commentary on Sappho translated in 1789 that settled that one, if anyone

---

45 Beni. Hederici, *Lexicon Manuale Graecum, Omnibus Sui Generis Lexicis Longe Locupletius: in Duas Partes Divisum: Quarum Prior Vocum Graecarum Ordine Alphabetico Digestarum ... Interpretationem Latinam Continet. Altera Vocum Phrasiumque Latinarum ... Interpretationem Graecam Exhibet*, H. Woodfall and thirty-one others, London, 1756; George Colman, *The Connoisseur. By Mr. Town, Critic and Censor-general*, George Faulkner, Dublin, 1756.

46 Samuel Bentley, *Poems on Various Occasions; Consisting of Original Pieces and Translations*, for the author, London, 1774, p. 181; 'The Register Office', in *A Collection of the Most Esteemed Farces and Entertainments Performed on the British Stage*, W. Thompson, North Shields, 1786–1787, p. 240.

47 Anon., *Berkeley Hall; or, the Pupil of Experience. A Novel. In Three Volumes*, J. Tindal, London, 1796, Vol. 2.

48 'Three thousand years ago, on this sweet day,/ ... Clio, whom contending nations praise,/Embloom'd, by her sweet birth, the first of May'. Aaron Hill, *The Works of the Late Aaron Hill, Esq.; in Four Volumes*, for the author's family, London, 1753, Vol. III; Christine Gerrard, *Aaron Hill, The Muses' Projector, 1685–1750*, Oxford University Press, Oxford, 2003.

49 *The Charmer: A Collection of Songs, Chiefly Such As Are Eminent for Poetical Merit; ... in Two Volumes*, J. Sibbald, Edinburgh, 1782, Vol. 1.

cared to read it: should any one wonder about the author's invocation of Clio in a work about a poet, he should reflect that 'that the whole literary discipline belongs to these virgins, amongst whom Clio is the especial protectress of historic writers'. Clio *wrote*; her writing transcended the divisions between history and poetry.[50]

There was a little flurry of complaints from gentleman scholars in the 1760s about the very great difficulty of seeing – imagining – Clio. 'As to [all] the muses, it is remarkable that the poets say but little of them in a descriptive way, though they invoke them so often', said Joseph Spence in 1764. Thomas Blackwell agreed: 'They seem in themselves wild and incoherent – rambling from image to image, taking the marque of Fable, and shewing their real Face but by starts' – until Horace got hold of them, he thought, and composed 'those striking Odes to CLIO, and the Sister-Muses that are Master-pieces of Lyric Poetry'.[51] Things were not much better when you looked to theatrical representation, or to the plastic arts. There were the robes, the laurel crown, she was usually young; she carried a book and/or a lyre/plectrum (for her guitar) or a trumpet (for purposes of proclamation) or a pen/quill. She was young, but not particularly lovely; always 'a little grave' – serious certainly: Clio does not laugh.[52] Even when scholars explored her representation in earlier eras, her image remained occluded, as in 'The Magnificent Entertainment: Giuen to King James, Queene Anne his Wife … Upon the day of his Maiejeties Tryumphant Passage … through his Honourable Citie … 15 of March I603', from which the 1795 scholar learned only that 'at one end [were] the Nine Muses, at the other, the Seven Liberal Arts'.[53] There were complaints about her clothing: the leopard-print onesie acquired from Dryden's translation of Virgil ('girt with Gold, and clad in particolour'd cloth') had become leopard print robes in 1754, 'spotted skins and radiant gold' in a play script of 1764, 'variegated skins' in a new translation

50 Alessandro Verri, *The Adventures of Sappho, Poetess of Mitylene. Translation from the Greek Original, Newly Discovered*, T. Cadell, London, 1789.

51 Joseph Spence, *A Guide to Classical Learning; Or, Polymetis Abridged. In Three Parts … Being a Work, Necessary, Not Only for Classical Instruction, but for all Those who Wish to Have a True Taste for the Beauties of Poetry, Sculpture and Painting. By N. Tindal, Translator of Rapin*, J. Dodsley, and R. Horsfield, London, 1764; Thomas Blackwell, *Memoirs of the Court of Augustus*, A. Millar, London, 1764.

52 Oliver Goldsmith, *The Bee. A Select Collection of Essays, on the Most Interesting and Entertaining Subjects, by Dr. Goldsmith*, W. Lane, London, 1790.

53 *A Collection of Scarce and Interesting Tracts, Tending to Elucidate Detached Parts of the History of Great Britain; Selected From the Sommers-collections, and Arranged in Chronological Order*, R. Edwards, London, 1795.

of Virgil in 1784.[54] On stage she usually wore buskins (quasi-historical knee-high boots), so showed some leg, though covered well enough.[55] Buskins were often associated with the performance of tragedy, so when 'all the dignity of [Clio's] buskin'd wit' was referred to in 1768 (in poetry, not playscript) there may have been some allusion to the Tragedy of History, only full realised a century later in a fiction of the law: 'Would that I were Light as air' says a Clio in 1887; 'But the burden that I bear Would break a merry heart in twain. I am Clio, Muse of History. Ah, the gods know why Mine eyes are ever wet with gathering mist: For mine it is to chronicle events ...'[56]

Who knows what she looked like in a pantomimic ballet of 1791? No details of costume are given and the only thing to distinguish Clio from her sisters is her book, 'the page of History glowing with the fame of her heroes'.[57] And who, watching a street pageant in Coventry or Birmingham, would know that the white robed girls with leaves in their hair *were* the Muses? – for all of them bore a remarkable resemblance to the Queen of the May.[58] 'They were a frequent ornament for libraries of old, and are often

54 Virgil, *The Works of Virgil, Containing His Pastorals, Georgics and Æneis. Translated into English Verse; by Mr. Dryden. In Three Volumes*, J. and R. Tonson and S. Draper, London, 1748; Virgil, *The Works of Virgil, in Latin and English ... The Æneid Translated by ... Christopher Pitt, the Eclogues and Georgics, with Notes ... by ... Joseph Warton. With Several New Observations by Mr. Holdsworth, Mr. Spence, and Others. Also, A Dissertation on the Sixth Book of the Æneid, by Mr. Warburton. On the Shield of Æneas, by Mr. W. Whitehead. On the Character of Japis, by ... Dr. Atterbury, ... And, Three Essays ... by the Editor. In Four Volumes*, Dodsley, London, 1753; Samuel Foote, *The Patron. A Comedy. In Three Acts. As it is Performed at the Theatre in the Hay-market. By Samuel Foote, Esq.*, P. Wilson and four others, London, 1764; William Mills, *The Georgics of Virgil, translated into English blank verse by William Mills*, for the author, London 1780,
55 Valerie Cumming, C. W. and P. E. Cunnington, *The Dictionary of Fashion History*, Berg, Oxford and New York NY, 2010. It had, however, been long established that Clio usually went in barefoot: Sir John Harington, *Nugæ Antiquæ. Being a Miscellaneous Collection of Original Papers in Prose and Verse. Written in the Reigns of Henry VIII, ... James I, &c. By Sir John Harington, ... with An Original Plate of the Princess Elizabeth*, W. Frederick, Bath, Vol. 2, 1775.
56 *Poetical Justice; or, The Trial of A Noble Lord, in the Court of Parnassus, for An Offence, Lately Found Bailable in the Court of King's Bench*, J. Murdoch, London, 1768; F. Herondo, *The World's Argument; Or, Justice and the Stage. A Dramatic Debate*, Selwyn, London, 1887.
57 Jean Bercher Dauberval, *Amphion and Thalia; Or, Amphion, the Pupil of the Muses: A Pantomimic Ballet, in One Act. Composed by M. d'Auberval, ... Represented for the First Time At the King's Theatre in the Pantheon, the Seventeenth of February, MDCCXCI*, Reynell, London, 1791.
58 James Potts, *The Historical, Political, and Literary Register. Containing An Account of*

seen, and very properly, on the tombs, either of poets, or philosophers, or musicians, or astronomers', observed Joseph Spence. 'On these you often meet with all the nine muses, with some deity, particularly Apollo, in the midst of them.' The gentleman scholars who surveyed the antiquities of the ancient world, from their writing table or in person, those who visited the monuments and antiquities of the British Isles, said much the same. Arthur Young was muted in his praise of a Clio he viewed in Oxford ('Statue of Clio sitting. Turn of the head and neck fine; and the attitude good'), having just waxed lyrical about a partially draped, 'exquisite' Venus.[59] Eighteenth-century commentators were not as much concerned with her nakedness as the nineteenth-century historians and readers who pondered her exposed bosom: what did it *mean*? The naked truth? Maternal succour?[60] The eighteenth-century textual Clio always had her clothes on.

Difficult to make out; of versatile function (verse? heroic verse? history? the narratives of the renowned only?); most of her commentators were, nevertheless, convinced of her long residence in Albion. Perhaps, a poet mused in 1795, her entry had been the first stopover in the making of a vast empire:

When Calliope and Clio to Britain's rude isle
Perchance on a visiting came,
All then was confusion, till they deigned to smile,

Every Public Transaction. ... of the Year, printed by the author, London, 1796, also for a delicate sneer at young provincial women attempting to display their learning and *politesse* by bringing Shakespeare and the Muses into their conversation.

59 Spence, *Guide to Classical Learning*. This had been the opinion in 1745: 'It is indeed surprising, how confus'd and indistinct the Dress, Symbols, Instruments, and often even the very Characters, of many of the Muses appear, wherever they are either introduc'd by the old Poets, or treated of by the Mythologists, or represented by their Statues ...', Samuel Madden, *Boulter's Monument. A Panegyrical Poem, Sacred to the Memory of That Great and Excellent Prelate and Patriot, the Most Reverend Dr. Hugh Boulter*, for the author, London, 1745; J. Salmon, *A Description of the Works of Art of Ancient and Modern Rome, Particularly in Architecture, Sculpture & Painting. To Which is Added, A Tour Through the Cities and Towns in the Environs of That Metropolis*, London, 1800; Edward Burch, *A Catalogue of One Hundred Proofs From Gems, Engraved in England, by E. Burch*, for the author, London, 1795; Richard Gough, *British Topography. Or, An Historical Account of What Has Been Done for Illustrating the Topographical Antiquities of Great Britain and Ireland*, T. Payne and J. Nichols, London, 1780; Arthur Young, *A Six Months Tour Through the North of England. Containing, An Account of the Present State of Agriculture, Manufactures and Population, ... in Four Volumes*, W. Strahan and three others, London, J. Balfour, Edinburgh, London, 1774, Vol. 3.

60 Bann, *Clothing of Clio*, pp. 1–7, 11–13.

And hoist here the standard of fame.
In process of time, by the muses grand aid,
Our i'land extended her sway
O'er empires and kingdoms; no land ever made
Of commerce and arts such display.[61]

She was in Albion to celebrate victory and mourn the fallen in 1760.[62] A practical girl, she had usually disembarked in Kent, the closest shore line to Helicon, was glimpsed in Fulham and Chelsea, expected in Oxford and Cambridge, and a lady once asked Clio to come and sit by her on a mountainside, presumably not in Norfolk where she dwelled, perhaps in Wales, where lived the gentleman to whom she addressed her poem.[63] She had been bid hasten to Suffolk in 1747 to view architectural and artistic delights in the environs of Bury St. Edmund's.[64]

Most interesting was her entry into Scotland and Wales, where one of her uses was to inscribe local dialects and languages, as Thomas Chatterton did, discreetly, in 1770.[65] A retrieval of Dunbar's poetry in 1775 entreated 'Juno, Latona, and Proserpina,/Diana the Goddess of Chest and Wods grene,/My Lady Clio, that Help of Makers bene,/Thetis se grene and prudent Minerva …', in a kind of Middle Scots.[66] In 'Jamie and Willie.

61 *The Charms of Melody; Or, Siren Medley. Being the Most Extensive Collection of Love … Political Songs, Old English, Irish, Scotch and German Ballads, Legendaries, &c. Ever Brought Together in a Single Publication, Selected from the Best Poets and Most Admired Writers*, for the author, Dublin, 1795.

62 Robert Lloyd, *The Tears and Triump[hs] of Parnassus. An Ode for Musick, As It is Perform'd at the Theatre-royal in Drury-lane*, Vaillant, London, 1760; Gentleman of the University of Oxford, *An Agreeable Companion for a Few Hours, Either on the Road or at Home. In Several Fugitive Pieces*, F. Newbery and two others, London, 1773.

63 G. Pearch, *A Collection of Poems, in Four Volumes by Several Hands*, for the author, London, 1775, Vol. 4; Hederici, *Lexicon Manuale Graecum*, for the author, London, 1756; *A Classical Arrangement of Fugitive Poetry. Vol. XVI*, for the author, London, 1797; Anne Francis, *Miscellaneous Poems, by A Lady*, printed for the author, and sold by the booksellers in Norwich and Norfolk, Norwich, 1790.

64 John Winter, *Bury, and its Environs, A Poem, Written in the Year MDCCXLVI*, W. Owen, London, 1747.

65 'For Clio, the historic muse,/Two authors bid with equal views;/The one in female vestments clad,/The other wrapped around in plaid;/Long they contended for the field,/Too headstrong both and proud to yield;/At length exclaimed the bonny Scot,/Suppose, Fair lass! We share the lot?' Thomas Chatterton, *The Auction A Poem: A Familiar Epistle to a Friend*, George Kearsley, London, 1770.

66 *The Caledoniad. A Collection of Poems, Written Chiefly by Scottish Authors*, 3 vols, William Hay, London, 1775, Vol. 2.

A Pastoral' (1797) two lads (probably shepherds, though nobody says) discourse upon reading, for Jamie is 'Unskill'd in beuks, I kennae whilk to read'. Willie recommends a few 'fav'rite anes' of his own 'an' o' a favour'd muse' ('Clio, lovely maid'), including Shakespeare, Cowley, 'Arbuthnot, Swift, Rowe, Young, Steele, Garth, an' Gray', and 'Homer, Virgil, Ovid, and ... Chaucer'. This way will Jamie learn how all the 'shepherds e'er Arcadia own'd,/Kend how to gie the past'ral pipe to sound'. (They *have* to be shepherds.)[67] She was used as the pseudonym for a lover, as by Thomas Blacklock who wrote several epistles to Clio, including the most pedestrian 'answer to one in which she informed me of her departure from Dumfries'.[68] She could be used in Scotland as in England (and in strict Southern English) to regret having *not* become a poet: ''Tis true, we're torn from the harmonious maid,/To whom our youth its first devotions paid', wrote Lord John Maclaurin Dreghorn to a friend in 1798;

> But had we still continued her to woo,
> Should we have been as happy as we're now?
> Had I still haunted the Parnassian rills?
> Could I have liv'd so near to Pentland hills?
> And, did you still to Clio pay your vows,
> You would not, trust me, keep so good a house.
> Let us be happy rather, that, in time,
> We left the captivating love of rhyme.[69]

Mainly, she stood in for an augury of the poet's success, whichever riverbank he was wandering along: 'If CLIO smile, while at her shrine I bow,/In happier notes succeeding lines shall flow'.[70] In Wales, however, and towards the close of the eighteenth century when Historia operated so powerfully in her antiquarian mode, Clio was asked to perform a more distant and scholarly role:

> Recording Clio, leave the classic climes,
> Where war and havoc swell the roll of crimes;

67 Robert Buchanan, *Poems on Several Occasions*, for the author, Edinburgh, 1797.
68 Thomas Blacklock, *Poems on Several Occasions*, for the author, Edinburgh, 1754.
69 *The Works of the Late John Maclaurin, Esq. of Dreghorn: One of the Senators of the College of Justice, ... in Two Volumes*, for the author, Edinburgh, 1798, Vol. 1.
70 James Alves, *The Banks of Esk; Or, A Saunter from Roslin to Smeaton. A Poem, Descriptive, Historical, & Moral; with An Introductory Canto, ... to Which is Added, Drummond Castle; A Poem of the Same Kind. With an Address to Impudence*, for the author, Edinburgh, 1800.

Where Mecca triumphs in a barb'rous reign
And Learning shuns the desolated plain
Come, where the Arts illume th' alluring way …
Here the thoughtful Clio stops the gay,
And shews the little place where greatness lay.[71]

How Clio was imagined, seen, and understood depended almost
entirely on a gentleman's (or lady's, or Caledonian shepherd's) schooling:
on the version of Clio's parentage and province that had been transmitted
in their dual Latin/English text, or the compendium of useful knowledge
purchased; on the translator their particular dictionary or compendium
had relied upon. There was no *conflict* between poetry and history in these
representations: Clio could represent both forms of thinking and writing,
and one or the other. The difference was that poets and aspiring poetasters
courted Clio, invoked her to help with their endeavours; those writing
about past events (we will call them historians for the moment) declared
her name as a guarantee of truth, and to signal the high seriousness of their
narrative, whether it be in prose or poetry; whether it concerned victory
or defeat, or simply the endeavours of the local hunt, as in 'Record their
Actions, and preserve their Praise./What Clio sings … shall last,/In spite
of Jove, or Fire, or Envy's Blast'. This was a praise song to Albion, with
Dorset hunting country as its guise.[72] Or, for the narration of tragedy,
you could invite another of the Sisters to accompany her, as at the death
of General Wolf:

Haste, CLIO, to thy native plains,
Which now victorious blood distains,
Where MARS, undaunted god of war,
With fury drives his rattling car,

---

71 Richard Llwyd, *Beaumaris Bay. A Poem; with Notes, Descriptive and Explanatory;
Particulars of the Druids, Founders of Some of the Fifteen Tribes of North Wales, the
Families Descended From Them, … with An Appendix*, for the author, London, 1800. A
long footnote explains the lost history of Joan, Princess of Wales, who mediated between
her husband and father in the quarrel that divided the Welsh forces fighting King John.
This happened in 1212. Joan was another discrete and accomplished woman – like Clio.
For the eighteenth-century antiquaries who laid the foundations of modern historical
method, Rosemary Sweet, *Antiquaries. The Discovery of the Past in Eighteenth-Century
Britain*, Hambledon, London, 2004.

72 William Churchill, Officer in General How's Regiment, *October; A Poem. Inscrib'd to the
Fox-hunters of Great Britain. In Two Books*, for the author, London, 1717, Book I.

Where ALBION'S glorious ensign courts the gale,
And ALBION'S thunders shake th'affrighted vale;
And with thee bring the sadly-sighing maid
MELPOMONE – for she must close the song.

(Melpomene was originally the Muse of song, later of tragedy.) Military men were the most likely to employ Clio to record recent history, whether of battles lost or won.

No historian – what, after the long nineteenth-century professionalisation of the discipline, we now understand by 'historian' – evoked Clio. David Hume's *History of England* (1754–1761) did not; Gibbon, in *The Decline and Fall of the Roman Empire* (1776–1789) did not mention Clio, though he discussed the religious beliefs of the ancients. Adam Ferguson, John Millar, William Robertson – not a word about her in their works of history. Devoted admirers and family commissioned a vast statue of Catharine Macaulay wearing Clio's robes, and she was often referred to as a modern Clio; but a recent assessment is that such identification served to silence Macaulay; 'her fame as the Muse of History trivialised the history she wrote, making her more of a novelty and less of a serious historian than her male contemporaries'.[73] Under such circumstances you'd not mention Clio; and Macaulay never did. As a recognisably academic history emerged from the late eighteenth century onwards, Clio lost her usefulness for those writing about the past, for the past became the historian's terrain, not hers.

Why do this? Spend so much time on what we all really, somehow, knew anyway? That it was good fun, and that it's pretty easy to do for the eighteenth century, are not answers. The point is this: that towards the end of the eighteenth century, the curriculum was put in place for those who would study the classics in the public schools (and in some other less-elite settings) for the next century and a half.[74] During the course of

73 Cecile Maccuzzo-Than, ' "Easier than a Chimney Pot to Blacken". Catharine Macaulay, "the celebrated female historian" ', Paula R. Backscheider and Timothy Dykstal (eds), *The Intersections of the Public and Private Spheres in Early Modern England* (1996), Routledge, Abingdon, 2013, pp. 78–104.

74 Steedman, *Master and Servant*, pp. 110–130 for the classics curriculum in one West Riding parochial school in the later eighteenth century. Also Martin Lowther Clarke, *Classical Education in Britain, 1500–1900*, Cambridge University Press, Cambridge, 1959; Richard S. Tompson, *Classics or Charity? The Dilemma of the 18-century Grammar School*, Manchester University Press, Manchester, 1971; Ian Michael, *The Teaching of English from the Sixteenth Century to 1870*, Cambridge University Press, Cambridge,

the nineteenth century, a cultural regime of Hellenism favoured Greek over Latin in the universities and elite schools; towards its end, Latin came to be understood as mind-training and mental discipline for middling-sort children; Auden acquired the classical languages at a time when it had become relatively unusual to be taught Greek. New translations (of Homer, Virgil, and Horace, of Juvenal and Perseus, of Livy and Lucian) were available for use in the preparatory and public schools by 1915, when Auden went off to his. More classical writers were added to the school reading lists. But an introduction to the Ancient World and its culture of thinking and feeling was effected by the same texts, for schoolboys of the late eighteenth century and the early twentieth century, when W. H. Auden was introduced to Greek and Latin. This was not done for the main part at his resolutely 'modern' public school, but at his preparatory school in Sussex. All of this, then, is a staging post on the long road to understanding who Auden's Clio *was*, and what his History may have been. And a point to note in this excursion along Clio's by-ways is that it was far less likely that ordinary aspiring readers of the early twentieth century encountered Clio (the word; the name for Fame; the 'history' she never really was) in the course of everyday life, as earlier readers might have done by consulting the guides to polite learning which had flourished in the eighteenth-century book market; now, learning and the acquisition of knowledge was the school's province, in a system of increasingly compulsory education.[75]

Herodotus, who did not deal with Clio, was referred to often in the eighteenth century because 'Clio' (as the first book of his *Histories* was named) was an invaluable source for ethnographers and historians. Thucydides (c.460–c.400 BCE) was not so well known: there were fewer translations and much less distribution of his work than that of Herodotus. *The History of the Peloponnesian War* was done into Latin in the mid-fifteenth century and a Greek text appeared in 1502. Thomas Hobbes translated

---

1984, pp. 317–320; Christopher Stray, *Classics Transformed: Schools, Universities, and Society in England, 1830–1960*, Clarendon Press, Oxford, 1998; Norman Vance and Jennifer Wallace (eds), *The Oxford History of Classical Reception in English Literature (Volume 4, 1790–1880)*, Oxford University Press, Oxford, 2015.

75 Clarke, *Classical Education*; Stray, *Classics Transformed*. For nineteenth-century enthusiasm for the culture of Ancient Greece – Hellenism – Richard Jenkyns, *The Victorians and Ancient Greece*, Basil Blackwell, Oxford, 1980; Frank Miller Turner, *The Greek Heritage in Victorian Britain*, Yale University Press, New Haven CT and London, 1981; Isobel Hurst, *Victorian Women Writers and the Classics. The Feminine of Homer*, Oxford University Press, London, 2006.

his writings into English directly from the Greek in 1628 (2nd edn 1676). There had been a translation from the French *Histories* in 1550. Hobbes' was reissued several times; and then in 1753, William Smith, Rector of Holy Trinity, Chester, made a new one (by subscription). 'It will be ... needless to tell the English Reader, how many versions have been made of Thucydides into Latin', he said. Those translations had been designed to 'bring the author more under the observation of what is generally stiled the learned world'. What the Revd Smith wanted to do was not so much what translators into the European languages had done (introduce him 'into general acquaintance, as an historian capable of innocently amusing most ranks of men'), but rather to 'usefully instruct ... the persons, who from duty and from passion would guard the rights or secure the welfare of public communities. The grand business of History is to make men wiser in themselves and better members of society.' He really was not against other ranks or innocent amusement; but he thought that readers must go beyond their own experience; History could do this: not only open 'past ages to their view' but also provide individuals with 'a more extensive scope to reflexion than any personal experience can'.[76] Clio had never been asked to make men and women better creatures, or give them a view of culture and society beyond their immediate context. Smith's appears to have be the last new translation of Thucydides into English for more than a century. Yet Clio *was* occasionally introduced to Thucydides. In 1742, Thomas Broughton high-handedly insisted that 'She is usually represented under the form of a young woman, crowned with laurels, holding a trumpet in her right hand, and a book in her left, with the name of Thucydides written in it.'[77] In her 1792 book for the girls' educational market, Mrs Taylor of Manchester said the same.[78] Taylor had done well, thought the *Critical Review*, in providing 'a general knowledge of objects subservient to liberal education ... particularly useful to young ladies,

---

76 Thucydides, *The History of the Peloponnesian War, Translated From the Greek of Thucydides ... by William Smith*, for the author, London, 1753. In making one reference to Herodotus, Clio did enter the text, in a note: 'Herodotus relates this remarkable piece of history, in Clio.'

77 Broughton, *An Historical Dictionary*.

78 'CLIO, goddess of history, drawn young, crowned with laurel, with a trumpet in the right, and a book with Thucydides' name in the left'; Mrs Taylor of Strangeways Hall, Manchester, *An Easy Introduction to General Knowledge and Liberal Education ... for the Use of the Young Ladies, at Strangeways Hall, Manchester*, for the author, Warrington, 1791. See Carol Percy, 'Learning and Virtue. English Grammar and the Eighteenth-Century Girls' School', Mary Hilton and Jill Shefrin (eds), *Educating the Child in Enlightenment Britain. Beliefs, Cultures, Practices*, Ashgate, Farnham, 2009, pp. 77–98.

by saving them the trouble of having recourse for information to other books'.[79]

We modern historians love Herodotus, for his engaging interest in the world, the wealth of ethnographic detail he provides, the attention he pays to women, and for his careful, cheerful insistence, that though he was *told* the strange things he recounts, that does not mean he *believes* they happened that way, or that there ever were giant ants roaming India. For example, in Argos, at the beginning – not of things, but of his *History* – there was a quarrel between the Greeks and the barbarians, which arose from the abduction of Io. There followed a half a century of response, revenge, repercussion, to- and fro-ing, and small wars, which involve much more famous abductions than that of Io. Herodotus tells us, now, as he begins, that this is the Persian account. There is at least one other version of these events, but Herodotus is quite clear that they are not the ones he is recounting here. It is for textual strategies like this in the writing of his *Histories* – his admission that his account is not a definitive one; that things may have happened another way – that Herodotus has become a (fairly new) hero of modern cultural history.

The antiquaries of eighteenth-century England probably provided us with more of our modern concerns and methodologies than did the likes of Hume and Robertson. Their preoccupation with coins and pottery shards and other material artefacts, with field systems, archaeological traces, and ancient documents as evidence of the habits and manners of the past, their deep devotion to the footnote (or the endnote; but the profound importance of *having* notes as the mark of honesty and traceability) is entirely congenial to modern academic historical researchers. 'One cannot account for changes in historical knowledge, methodology and interpretation between the early modern period and the nineteenth century without recognising the enormous importance of "antiquarian" research', says Rosemary Sweet; but the antiquarians did not evoke Clio, or use Herodotus as epigraph or emblem, though very occasionally a symbolic History or Historia sat hard by some ruin, preserving the monuments of antiquity with her book and pen, in illustrations inserted by the printer/ bookseller. In the frontispiece to George Raymond's *New, Universal and Impartial History of England* (1787), a pleasant-looking young woman in contemporary dress is supplied by Genius and Industry with the records of antiquity, to transcribe in her book. As she writes, Britannia bends

79 *The Critical Review, or Annals of Literature*, Vol. 6, London, 1792, p. 480.

from her throne to crown History – for it is she – with a laurel wreath.[80] Thucydides, on the other hand, became the choice of the newly professionalised historians of the nineteenth century. Leopold von Ranke and other positivist historians praised his high seriousness, his 'scientific' objectivity in the handling of documentary evidence. 'Thucydides' evoked a world in which power was played out between generals and senators; a world of high politics and very important battles; there are no women, no children, no weird habits and manners of ordinary or extraordinary people in Thucydides. It has been said that his *History* was favoured in the US during the Cold War era: his 'terse skeptical manner ... deep cynicism about political, rhetorical, and ideological hypocrisy, with its all too recognizable protagonists ... engaged in a war of attrition fought by proxy at the remote fringes of empire' confirmed readers to themselves as hardheaded realists in global politics.[81] Clio as a Cold War Muse – strange daughter attributed to severe father – will return in the second part of this book.

80 Sweet, *Antiquaries*, pp. xv–xvi; George Frederick Raymond Esq., *A New, Universal and Impartial History of England, From the Earliest Authentic Records, and Most Genuine Historical Evidence, to the Summer of the Year 1786 ... Embellished ... with Upwards of One Hundred and Twenty Beautiful Copper Plate Engravings ... Raymond ... assisted by Alexander Gordon and Hugh Owen, Esqrs. and others*, J. Cooke, London, 1787. Historia appears (unnamed) on the front cover (before binding) of an abridgement of Hume's six volumes made for the educational market: *Parson's Genuine Pocket Edition of Hume's History of England, with a Continuation to the Death of George II by Dr Smollett & a further Continuation to the Present Time by J. Barlow Esq. Embellished with Historical Engravings & Delicate Portraits of all the English Monarchs, & most Eminent Characters of the Present Reign*, Vol 5, J. Parsons, London, 1793.

81 Daniel Mendelsohn, 'Arms and the Man', *New Yorker*, 28 April 2008; Katherine Harloe and Neville Morley (eds), *Thucydides and the Modern World: Reception, Reinterpretation and Influence from the Renaissance to the Present*, Cambridge University Press, Cambridge, 2012, pp. 10–12; Richard Ned Lebow, 'International Relations and Thucydides', idem, pp. 197–213.

4

An education

The purpose of all educational institutions, public or private, is utilitarian and can never be anything else; their duty is to prepare young persons for that station in life to which it shall please society to call them.

W. H. Auden, 'The Poet as Professor', *Prose Volume IV. 1956–1962*, Edward Mendelson (ed.), 2010, pp. 317–319; *Observer*, 5 February 1961.[1]

... Savoury and Newcomen and Watt
And all those names that I was told to get up
In history preparation and forgot

W. H. Auden, 'Letter to Lord Byron', 1936.

Under Clio's former regime – the old one, the eighteenth-century one – in which the modes of classical antiquity were interpreted for the cultural and educational purposes of audiences who had not a word of Greek or Latin, she did not have much interest in where things came from, what their meaning was, and what had made them what they were. The idea that our perspective on the past 'depends on who's observing', that how we interpret it depends 'on our activities' (what we're doing and thinking in the world, right now) was quite alien to her. Then, in the old dispensation, some things happened in the world; Clio's task was to proclaim those which were notable and deserving of fame. She made a limited number of heroic events and people – men – famous. She did not, as did the young

---

1 'What is thy duty towards thy Neighbour? ... [T]o learn to live and labour truly to get mine own living, and to do my duty in that state of life, unto which it shall please God to call me.' 'A Catechism. That Is to Say, an Instruction to be Learned of Every Person, Before He be Brought to Be Confirmed by the Bishop', *Book of Common Prayer*.

1787 Historia of the last chapter, consult documentary evidence of these happenings in order to tell her story of famous deeds. She did not, in this way, *make* history, though she was sometimes depicted with a pen in her hand, and even writing things down in her book; what she told was a story of something that *had already been*: she recorded and proclaimed events; she doesn't *write* them, in the creative or compositional meaning of 'write'. If she had a voice – other than that of a sarky pipe smoking harridan in some stage-play or other – she used the detached, distant language of a Thucydides; sometimes, because of the kind of event narrated, the tone of voice could suggest to a reader that irony was implied. She did not cry, or weep, at all in her eighteenth-century English manifestations; after the eighteenth century, you would have to be a poet, or at least, *not-a-historian*, to have Clio weep in your text.

Clio was deserted, abandoned, or went to ground, throughout the long emergence of modern history (history as a way of writing and thinking). The modern muse, if there is one, is named Historia, or History, and she consists of the knowledge that the writing of it is not the same thing as the event described; that History is precipitated out of the Everything of the past, to make a particular kind of narrative and form of analysis, usually in writing. The thing (event, happening, person) is not the same as its narrative. The narrative, which is a History, is something that never *was*, as it was told, or is told now, in the history book you're reading.[2]

The only way to ask questions about a modern manifestation of Clio – about where Auden's Clio came from – is to use modern Historia's protocols. The poet will not – certainly did not – tell us where she came from. We (really I mean 'I') have to investigate the education of the poet; that is, the ways in which he was taught to understand the world of his childhood and adulthood, the ideas and beliefs provided by the social system he inhabited, and the literature though which these were conveyed. This chapter will investigate Auden's Clio in the light of the teaching – secular, Christian, and profane – that he experienced, through his own schooling and the schoolteaching he did. It will pay particular attention to his education in the classics and in protestant Christianity, and to the forms of literature, language, and historical writing to which he was introduced. Or to which he may have been introduced. The pursuit ends up at the historian's usual *just-can't-be-sure*. His preparatory and public schools have not preserved curriculum and reading material from the early twentieth century. There has to be the social historian's usual

2 See below, pp. 239–244.

resort to context: to what preparatory schools *in general* taught of Greek and God and history and poetry in the first decades of the new century. Auden himself recorded a great deal of his experience of being taught and of teaching, but the modern social history procedure – this isn't a biography, after all – is to find that information useful only when it can be considered in the light of a more general experience. Perhaps, with only these rackety tools at her disposal, a historian really has no right to ask the questions about Clio and Auden's Clio, and the poetry and history that make up this book. But she does.

'I've taught everything', said Auden to one interlocutor in 1947, including arithmetic ('I once thought of doing a series of arithmetic textbooks') and 'Drawing, French, Latin, History ... Twelve-year-old boys are the best people to talk to. They're so intelligent. They get tremendously interested for about five minutes, then forget all about it.'[3] Before leaving for the US in 1939 he had taught in two British private schools, Larchfield Academy, Helensburgh (1930–1932), and The Downs School, Malvern (1932–1935); both were independent preparatory schools for boys. He returned to The Downs briefly in 1937 to cover for an absent teacher.[4] Sometime during that last summer term he wrote the haunting first-hand testimony to confinement in the classroom – the prison house for teachers and taught – that is 'Schoolchildren'.[5] He published for children during his schoolmastering years; *The Poet's Tongue* is still praised as the best of all poetry anthologies for schools. Auden and his co-editor John Garrett arranged the poems they had selected alphabetically by first line; poets' names were omitted from the main text. This was an arrangement which allowed prayers and limericks, lyrics, and lampoons, Shakespeare and

3 Alan Ansen, *The Table Talk of W. H. Auden* (1989), Nicholas Jenkins (ed.), Faber and Faber, London, 1990, p. 19.
4 In Naomi Mitchison's encyclopedia for children (see above, p. 73), Auden provided the briefest of contributor identities – a line and a half as opposed to the others' average of 25: 'Wystan Auden (born 1907) writes poetry and teaches at a school in Scotland.' A very nice line portrait was provided by the editor. *An Outline for Boys and Girls and Their Parents*, Gollancz, London, 1932, p. 851. 'I have written biographies of most them,' said Mitchison, 'but some of them would not let me do that, and others made me cut out what I thought were the best and funniest bits' (p. 13).
5 For Auden as schoolteacher, Humphrey Carpenter, *W. H. Auden. A Biography* (1981, 1983), Faber and Faber, London, 2010, pp. 111–178. For a student's view of his time at the Downs School, John Duguid, 'Mr Auden, Schoolmaster', *The American Scholar*, 69:3 (2000), pp. 81–86. For 'Schoolchildren', below pp. 138–139. W. H. Auden, 'Schoolchildren', *Collected Shorter Poems, 1927–1957*, Faber and Faber, London, 1966, pp. 78–79; Carolyn Steedman, 'Prisonhouses', *Feminist Review*, 20 (1985), pp. 7–21.

T. S. Eliot, to jostle anonymously for the child's attention. Auden and Garrett were very clear that as an anthology for the schools, teachers must be addressed first: 'the study of the classics is diminishing, much of the training in the discipline of language which used to fall to Latin and Greek devolves on the English teacher, and works which make serious demands on understanding or afford material for the study of prosody should be included'.[6]

The editors' eschewal of context, historical and authorial, was ped-agogically fashionable in the 1930s, under a regime of progressive education that held sway in many state schools until the 1970s.[7] I. A. Richards described an originating practice of progressive poetry teaching in *Practical Criticism* (1929). For some years during the 1920s, in the Cambridge University English School, he had 'made the experiment of issuing printed sheets of poems – ranging in character from a poem by Shakespeare to a poem by Ella Wheeler Wilcox – to audiences who were requested to comment freely in writing upon them. The authorship of the poems was not revealed ...' This was done to provide a new tech-nique for 'those who wish to discover for themselves what they think and feel about poetry'.[8] Much later, Denys Thompson attested to the very great influence Richards' teaching method had had on the curriculum in state schools; in many of them, 'knowledge of history, social back-ground, linguistic origins of and Aristotle ... ceased to be tested'.[9] When at Cambridge himself, Thompson had been a student of F. R. Leavis; together they collaborated on *Culture and Environment* (1933), a critique of 'mass' culture. When Auden reviewed it in 1933, he described it succinctly as 'a practical text book for assisting children to defeat propaganda of all

---

6 Wystan Hugh Auden and John Garrett, *The Poet's Tongue*, Bell, London, 1935; Stephen Burt 'Wake all the dead!', *LRB* Blog, 19 July 2010 www.lrb.co.uk/blog/2010/07/19/ stephen-burt/wake-all-the-dead/ (accessed 12 October 2017); W. H. Auden, *Prose Volume I. 1926–1938*, Edward Mendelson (ed.), Faber and Faber, London, 1996, pp. 109, 195–199, 759.

7 Ronald King, *All Things Bright and Beautiful? A Sociological Study of Infants' Classrooms*, Wiley, Chichester, 1979; William Edward Marsden, 'Contradictions in progressive pri-mary school ideologies and curricula in England. Some historical perspectives', *Historical Studies in Education*, 9:2 (1997), pp. 224–236; William G. Raga, 'Condescension and critical sympathy. Historians of education on progressive education in the United States and England', *Paedagogica Historica*, 50:1–2 (2014), pp. 59–75.

8 I. A. Richards, *Practical Criticism*, Kegan Paul, London, 1929, p. 3.

9 Denys Thompson, 'The relevance of I. A. Richards', *Use of English*, 23:1 (1971), pp. 3–31.

kinds by making them aware of which buttons are being pressed'.[10] He enjoyed all the accompanying books he'd been sent for review, including Leavis' *How to Teach Reading. A Primer for Ezra Pound* (1932); 'our school teaching is far too bookish', he concluded.

In 1939, in another collaboration, Auden produced the pamphlet *Education Today and Tomorrow*, a short, well-researched report on the state of the schools (state and private), teachers and teacher training, and the curriculum. Auden and his collaborator, Thomas Worsley, could not think of a 'worse course than segregating teachers by themselves in those training colleges which are not attached to a university. The teacher should know more about life than other people; his pupils always do.' A good teacher was made 'by friendship with all sorts of people, by love affairs, by an active life'. As far as the elementary school curriculum was concerned, one suggestion the authors made was that foreign languages and history were probably unsuitable for 7–11-year-olds, 'as having no relation with the child's experience'.[11]

In 1936, Auden was 'very much in two minds as to what to do. Whether to go on teaching or not. If I do, I think a secondary day school.' He told another friend that he was thinking about tutorial work for the Yorkshire Workers Educational Association;[12] but he did not teach young adults until the 1940s, when he was employed by several US colleges and universities. His pre-US theories of schooling and learning were based on the experience of young children, including himself, in the preparatory school system from 1915 onwards (1915 was when he started at St Edmund's preparatory boarding school at Hindhead, Surrey). At the end of his schoolmastering career in 1939 he concluded that:

> A teacher soon discovers that there are only a few pupils whom he can help, many for whom he can do nothing except teach a few examination tricks, and a

10 F. R. Leavis and Denys Thompson, *Culture and Environment*, Chatto and Windus, London, 1933; Auden, *Prose Volume I*, pp. 125–127; orig. 'A Review of *Culture and Environment*, by F. R. Leavis and Denys Thompson, and Other Books', *Twentieth Century*, May 1933.

11 Wystan Hugh Auden and Thomas Cuthbert Worsley, *Education Today and Tomorrow. Day to Day Pamphlets*, Hogarth Press, London, 1939; W. H. Auden, 'Education. By W. H. Auden and T. C. Worsley', *Prose Volume I*, pp. 389–424; 416, 417. For the classic statement of the value of the learner's experience in education, John Dewey, *Experience and Education*, Collier, New York NY, 1938. Also Evan Kindley, 'Auden's Preoccupations. Education and *The Orators*', Bonnie Costello and Rachel Galvin (eds), *Auden at Work*, Palgrave Macmillan, Basingstoke, 2015, pp. 216–230.

12 Carpenter, *W. H. Auden*, pp. 175, 206.

few to whom he can do nothing but harm. The children who interested me were either the backward i.e. those who had not yet discovered their real nature, the bright with similar interests to my own, or those who, like myself at their age, were school-hating anarchists. To these last I tried, while encouraging their rebellion, to teach a technique of camouflage, of how to avoid martyrdom.[13]

In the US his encounters with young adults in the college classroom were of a different kind, for he did not have his own experience of the British private school or university system as a reference point for the students he encountered. They were, however, constantly present in his mind as he gauged his own reactions to them. In 1941, at Ann Arbor (University of Michigan), he was 'lonelier and more lost than first days at boarding school'.[14] Davenport-Hines reports that at Swarthmore college in 1942 he was very tired of 'reading "creative" mss, each more infantile than the last'.[15] In his poetry teaching at Ann Arbor and Swarthmore College he developed a kind of cloze-procedure for studying poetry: he gave students copies of mimeographed poems unknown to them, with blanks for certain words. They were to fill in rhymes and words of particular stress in order to think about the metrical structure and meaning of the anonymous poem.[16] 'Cloze testing' or 'cloze deletion procedure' was not given a name until the 1950s, but it was a popular literacy technique among English primary schoolteachers in the 1970s, and appears to have been developed as early as the 1820s by the British radical educationalist Samuel Wilderspin.[17] Auden may have encountered the technique during his own childhood acquisition of literacy, but his US poetry-teaching

---

13 W. H. Auden, 'Appendices. The Prolific and Devourer', *Prose Volume II, 1939–1948*, Edward Mendelson (ed.), Princeton University Press, Princeton NJ, 2002, pp. 411–458.
14 Carpenter, *W. H. Auden*, p. 318. The chapter 'Teacher Again' (pp. 318–361) is a full account of his US teaching years.
15 Richard Davenport-Hines, *Auden*, Heinemann, London, 1995, p. 221.
16 Carpenter says that he first used this technique at St Marks College, Southborough, a private Massachusetts school where he was guest teacher in 1939; Carpenter, *W. H. Auden*, pp. 264, 326.
17 Gail Cohen Weaver, 'Using the cloze procedure as a teaching technique', *The Reading Teacher*, 32:5 (1979), pp. 632–636; Samuel Wilderspin, *The Importance of Educating the Infant Poor From the Age of Eighteen Months to Seven Years. Containing An Account of the Spitalfields Infant School, and of the New System of Instruction There Adopted ... Second edition, with considerable additions*, for the author, London, 1824; Phillip McCann and Francis A. Young, *Samuel Wilderspin and the Infant School Movement*, Croom Helm, London, 1982; John Howlett, *Progressive Education. A Critical Introduction*, Bloomsbury, London, 2013, pp. 103–140.

procedure also seems to owe much to the pedagogical theory of I. A.
Richards, developed in the 1920s.

'Courses, Syllabi, Examinations, and a Curriculum' for his teaching at
US colleges and at the New School for Social Research, New York, are
an appendix to the second volume of Auden's *Prose*. At the New School
in the fall of 1940, he taught a fifteen-week course on 'The Language
and Technique of Poetry'; syllabus questions included 'What is the real
difference between poetry and prose?' and 'How does form contribute to
meaning?'. The final examination paper for the 'Analysis of Poetry' course
taught at Michigan in spring 1942 included '19th Century Controversial
Prose' with a quotation from Andersen's 'Snow Queen' ('little Kay was
quite blue with cold'), and the instruction to 'Write a debate between
J. S. Mill, T. Huxley, Matthew Arnold, Carlyle and Cardinal Newman as to
the meaning and truth of … [a] parable'.[18] 'The Meaning and Techniques
of Poetry', a course taught at the New School in fall 1948, asked students
to 'Explain the stanza structure of [Auden's own] "Warm are the still and
lucky miles"'.[19] To answer questions about British nineteenth-century
intellectual life (or at Swarthmore, to be examined on 'The History of
Ideas 1660–1760' or 'Romanticism from Rousseau to Hitler') students
must perforce have acquired some knowledge of European history; but
discussion of the historiographical paradigms and theory of history Auden
took with him to the US, and what he there acquired, will wait until later
in this chapter.

His own school education had provided him with little poetry and less
history; what he took with him to St Edmund's preparatory school in
1915 (8 years) and to Gresham's public school in 1920 (13 years) has been
exhaustively described by Auden's biographers: fairytales (the nineteenth-
century literary artefact it seems, rather than the folktale), the legends of
Greece and Rome, the Norse and Icelandic sagas, and poetry (though
he once claimed that 'until my sixteenth year I read no poetry'). 'Norse
mythology always appealed to me infinitely more than Greek', he recalled
in 1947; 'Hans Andersen's *The Snow Queen* and George Macdonald's *The*

18 Hans Christian Andersen's 'The Snow Queen' (1844) haunts Auden's memories of
his childhood, though sometimes he said Andersen's 'Ice Maiden' (1861) was his
favourite. Finding the frozen little self in these fairytales was not uncommon among
twentieth-century British children. See Carolyn Steedman, *Landscape for a Good
Woman*, Virago, London, 1986, for little Kay, quite blue with cold.

19 Auden, 'Appendices. Appendix III. Courses, Syllabi, Examinations, and a Curriculum',
Prose Volume II, pp. 464–480; 465, 479; 'Twelve Songs … III', Auden, *Collected Shorter
Poems*, p. 159.

Princess and the Goblins were my favourite fairy stories, and years before I ever went there, the North of England was the Never-Never Land of my dreams.'[20] Asked to describe his ideal nursery library in 1952 ('the books read with passion before acquiring critical notions'), he listed the complete works of Beatrix Potter, Lewis Carroll (both *Alice*s), Andersen ('The Little Mermaid' [1837] this time around), some *Icelandic Legends* or other, Macdonald Fraser's *The Princess and the Goblin*, Thackeray's *The Rose and the Ring*, Verne's *Child of the Cavern*, Ballantyne's *The Cruise of the Cachalot*, and Conan Doyle's Sherlock Holmes series. Hoffman's *Struwwelpeter* was mentioned with caution; and then *Hymns Ancient and Modern* and the mnemonic sonnets from Kennedy's *Latin Primer*.[21] His fondness for books about mine-working, geology, the internal combustion and other engines, featured in his description of a typical home education provided by a liberal, professional upper middle-class family.[22] In his 'Valediction' of 1975, Stephen Spender connected 'the intricate, complex, hand-made engines of language he produced' to the small-scale machinery Auden so loved, as found in Yorkshire mines; or, his poems were like 'the limestone landscapes of that northern countryside of hills and caves and freshets where he spent his childhood'.[23] He actually spent his childhood in Warwickshire suburbia between Birmingham and all 'these broken things' of the industrial West Midlands, as his 'By the Gasworks,

20 Auden, 'I Like It Cold', *Prose Volume II*, pp. 332–336; orig. *House and Garden*, December 1947.

21 W. H. Auden, 'Hic et Ille', *Prose Volume III, 1949–1955*, Edward Mendelson (ed.), Princeton University Press, Princeton NJ, 2008, pp. 323–334; orig. *Preuves*, May 1952. He certainly did retain the mnemonic verses, all his life: 'I enjoy rhymes, almost any rhymes', he told Polly Platt in 1966: 'He put his head back and closed his eyes, then recited: "Dies in the singular/Common we define/But its plural cases/Are always mascu-line." He spread his hands out and smiled. "We used to say that in school".' Polly Platt and W. H. Auden, 'Interview: W. H. Auden', *The American Scholar*, 36:2 (1967), pp. 266–270; 269. The verse has been repeated in Maurice Bowra, *New Bats in Old Belfries. Some Loose Tiles*, Wolfson College, Oxford, 2005, p. 54.

22 W. H. Auden, 'A Literary Transference', *Prose Volume II*, p. 42; orig. *Southern Review*, Summer 1940. For Auden's childhood reading, Carpenter, *Auden*, pp. 3–15; Davenport-Hines, *W. H. Auden*, pp. 6–33. See R. G. Collingwood, *Autobiography*, Oxford University Press, London, 1939, for a very similar (in class terms) little boy reading everything he could find about 'the natural sciences, especially geology, astronomy, and physics; [learning] to recognize rocks, to know the stars, and to understand the working of pumps and locks and other mechanical appliances up and down the house', about ten years earlier than Auden.

23 Stephen Spender, 'Valediction', Stephen Spender (ed.), *W.H. Auden. A Tribute*, Weidenfeld and Nicholson, London, 1975, pp. 224–248.

Solihull'(1924) attests; but the notion of a poem as a small machinery of language and perception first apprehended in childhood still holds good.[24] How he was taught to read, we do not know. As with other middle-class boys of the era, we have to assume it was done at home, by parents or governess, though there is a hint in his brother's 'Wystan and I were at the same two preparatory schools' that they may both have attended, briefly, one of the many small Solihull private schools available to parents like theirs. (They both attended Greshams, but that was a public, not a preparatory, school.)[25] There were also the rich resources of Dr Auden's cultural life available to his children. He belonged to the Solihull Arts and Sciences Association; one of the Audens' neighbours in Lode Lane was its secretary, and its enticing programme between 1909 and 1911 included a talk on the history of aviation, another by one who had been 'by pony through Iceland', and many given by Birmingham University academics, on topics from phonology to the fairytale. But it is unlikely that a father took a 4-year old to any of these.[26]

Perhaps he was introduced to Kennedy's *Latin Primer* in Solihull before he went to preparatory school; according to the few extant accounts of St Edmund's School curriculum, it certainly preoccupied him once he got there. But much later, editing his *Portable Greek Reader* (1948), he suggested that stories from classical antiquity accompanied him to school: 'Once upon a time there was a little boy. Before he could read, his father told him stories about the War between the Greeks and the Trojans. Hector and Achilles were as familiar to him as his brothers ... At seven

---

24 W. H. Auden, *Juvenilia. Poems 1922–1928*, Katherine Bucknell (ed.), Faber and Faber, London, 1994, p. 55. In his address to the dead poet, he told Lord Byron that 'We lived at Solihull, a village then;/Those at the gasworks were my favourite men'; and that 'my heart has stamped on/The view from Birmingham to Wolverhampton./ ... Tramlines and slagheaps, pieces of machinery,/That was, and still is, my ideal scenery'. W. H. Auden, 'Letter to Lord Byron' (1936), *Collected Poems*, Edward Mendelson (ed.), 1976, Faber and Faber, London, 1991, pp. 81–133; 106, 88–89.

25 John Auden, 'A Brother's Viewpoint', Spender (ed.), *W. H. Auden*, pp. 25–30.

26 *Solihull Parish Magazine*, 31:1 (January 1909); 32:9 (September 1912). For George Auden's wide interests, Minutes of Evidence given before the Royal Commission on Ancient Monuments in Wales and Monmouthshire, Vol. 1 [Cd. 6549], HMSO, London, 1912, p. 119: 'Mr George Augustus Auden, Apsley, Solihull, Birmingham; M. A., M.D., B.C. Cantab., M.R.C.P., London [Member of the Royal College of Physicians]; Fellow of the Society of Antiquaries, Copenhagen; Member of the British Association for the Advancement of Science (Secretary of the Committee for Consideration and Registration of Megalithic Remains in the British Isles), and Member of the Committee for distinguishing the Age of Stone Circles.'

he went to school and most of the next seven years were spent in translating Greek into Latin and English and vice-versa.' He knew that readers would find it hard to believe that he recounted here, not a fairytale, 'but a historical account of middle-class education in England thirty-five years ago'.[27] Very heavy on the classical languages was St Edmund's preparatory school, all of Auden's contemporaries agreed, even those eager to laud the eccentricity of its arrangements and the comings-and-goings of its more than eccentric teaching staff in time of war. There was a Literary Society and briefly a 'St Edmund's School Literary Journal'; there were prizes for maths, French, history, scripture, drawing, 'and even poetry', though very little curriculum time was devoted to these subjects.[28] 'English, it is interesting to note,' remembered the headmaster's daughter, 'was only represented by two hours of geography and two hours of history a week, out of which a few minutes were devoted to spelling, derivations and synonyms.'[29] Auden's first exposure to the Greek language and Greek verse was between 1915 and 1920, for Gresham's School, to which he moved in 1920, was 'a new kind of public school … it had modern ideals and was based on modern curricula; very little Latin was taught and no Greek … progressive but not cranky, it was exactly designed to appeal to cultured parents of the liberal professional classes'.[30] Auden described 'a Classical Side and a Modern side' at Gresham's. 'The latter was regarded by boys and masters alike in much the same way as, in a militaristic country, civilians are regarded by officers, and with the same degrees of inferiority: history and mathematics were, like professional men, possible; the natural sciences … like tradesmen, were not. The Classical Side, too, had its nice distinctions: Greek, like the Navy, was the senior, the aristocratic service.'[31] (So Auden *did* remember being taught some Greek there.)

Auden wrote of the endless translation task of his early school years.

---

27 W. H. Auden (ed.), *The Portable Greek Reader*, Viking Penguin, New York NY, 1948, 'Editor's Introduction'.

28 Bernard Palmer, *Willingly to School. A History of St Edmund's, Hindhead*, The Governing Body of the St Edmund's School Trust, Hindhead, 2000, pp. 187–195; 74–75; 133, 213, 232.

29 Rosamira Bulley, 'A Prep School Reminiscence', Spender (ed.), *W. H. Auden*, pp. 31–36.

30 Robert Medley, 'Gresham's School, Holt', Spender (ed.) *W. H. Auden*, pp. 37–43; W. H. Auden, 'Honour [Gresham's School, Holt]', Graham Greene (ed.), *The Old School. Essays by Divers Hands* (1934), Oxford University Press, London, 1984, pp. 1–12; John Walsh, 'Auden. The Lost Poems', *Independent*, 4 September 2007, www.independent.co.uk/arts-entertainment/books/features/auden-the-lost-poems-463874.html (accessed 12 October 2017) for poetry, including Auden's, at Gresham's.

31 Auden, *Portable Greek Reader*, p. 1.

It would be useful to know how much Latin and Greek *poetry* he was required to translate, and what kind of verse forms and metrical systems he may have become familiar with. He remembered with fondness the mnemonic verse of his Latin primer, but for any further insight into his acquisition of poetic technique, we have to rely on what was generally available for teaching purposes, and what was usually taught in the private school system. A catalogue of Latin and Greek textbooks of the period 1800–1970 suggests that between 1841 and 1930 at least (for this a catalogue of *extant* books only) 110 school readers were available to schools, 22 of which concerned poetry, including the composition of poetry in Greek. In the same period 40 guides to Latin Verse Composition were available, and 224 Latin Readers, 18 of which contained poetry, or poetry and prose.[32] There was more information available to a small boy at school about the syllabic arrangement of Latin verse than the stress-timed arrangement of Greek poetry. But it's almost not worth saying that – as we have little idea of the texts used at Auden's schools, and whether or not versification was taught. And the important titles available to a school like St Edmund's School at the beginning of the twentieth century, including W. H. D. Rouse's *Demonstrations in Greek Iambic Verse* (1899), T. Y. Sargent's *Models and Materials for Greek Iambic Verse* (1899), A. Sidgwick and F. D. Morice's *Introduction to Greek Verse Composition* (1906), E. Squire and J. H. Williams' *Exercises for Greek Verse*, 1906, and Rouse's *Damon – A Manual of Greek Iambic Composition* (1906), all appear to me not to be what you would put before a 10-year-old, then or now. But what do I know, Nelly Dean that I am? Though of course, they may have been used as the master's (or mistress's) method book and never handed over to the children.[33] Nevertheless, the recipes for writing Latin verse of the period look to be more accessible to young children. And for Latin there was more material available to promote what the cataloguers said

---

32 William B. Thompson and J. D. Ridge, *Catalogue of Greek and Latin School Text Books (1800 onwards). Part One, Dictionaries Grammars Vocabularies Notes and Miscellanea Composition Manuals (Prose and Verse) Readers Selections*, University of Leeds, School of Education 1970. *Part Two Greek Texts, Notes, Vocabularies, Translations ...* 1974 (bound as one, separate pagination).

33 As was the case with the Revd Murgatroyd's teaching of the classics in Slaithwaite school in the second half of the eighteenth century. One text was quite expensive enough for the instruction of generations of children. In fact, Murgatroyd purchased very few and mainly relied on the primers he had acquired in his own youth. Carolyn Steedman, *Master and Servant. Love and Labour in the English Industrial Age*, Cambridge University Press, Cambridge, 2007, pp. 110–130.

was the historical point of their compilation: 'the very sentences used for translation often reflect, and sometimes foreshadow, the changing social attitudes in which people were learning their Latin or Greek'.[34] For Latin acquisition, there was more supporting material about social life than there was for Greek, such as in S. E. Winbolt's *Dialogues of Roman Life* (1913, repr. 1930) and Winbolt's and F. H. Mark's *Roman Life Reader* (1910). But poetry in any language was not part of the official curriculum at either of Auden's schools, and neither was literature in general. This did not prevent its consumption and creation and among the children: 'I remember the planning of an ambitious historical novel between Auden, Isherwood and myself', said Harold Llewellyn Smith in 1975. 'It was to have been in the manner of Harrison-Ainsworth, and its "Gothic" scenario was shamelessly derived from Marple Hall, the ancestral seat of the Bardshaw-Isherwoods.'[35] Auden found himself in a new educational world when he came to teach 8–13-year-olds in the 1930s, with the study of the classics much diminished from the time of his own education in them.[36]

'I'm going to do am anthology of Greek literature. What do you think I should put in it?', he asked Alan Ansen in 1947.[37] I had hoped to find some trace of what passed through his head as a child, or was inculcated in him by study of the classics between 1915 and 1925, in the choices Auden made for *The Portable Greek Reader*. He said that for anyone brought up in the way he had been brought up, 'Greece and Rome are so mixed up with his personal memories of childhood and classroom that it is extremely difficult to look at these civilisations objectively. This is particularly so, perhaps, in the case of Greece ...'[38] But what he planned for the anthology was different from what it turned out to be. In 1947, he paused not for an answer from Ansen, but continued:

I'm having the sixth and twentieth book of the *Iliad*, the whole *Oresteia* (for tragedy), either the *Clouds*, the *Birds*, or the *Frogs* (for comedy), the Sicilian

34 Thompson and Ridge, *Catalogue*, p. iii.
35 Harold Llewellyn Smith, 'At St Edmund's 1915–1920'; Spender (ed.), *W. H. Auden*, pp. 34–36. William Harrison Ainsworth (1805–1882) was a historical novelist. Among the forty-two novels he published was *The Lancashire Witches* (1849). *Rookwood* (1834) was his best-known transposition of gothic conventions into English social history.
36 'Introduction to *The Poet's Tongue*, by W. H. Auden and John Garrett', Auden, *Prose Volume I*, pp. 195–199.
37 Ansen, *Table Talk*, pp. 74–75.
38 Auden, *Portable Greek Reader*, p. 1.

expedition and the Melian dialogue from Thucydides – oh, did Hobbes do a translation? – the story of Polycrates from Herodotus, all the fragments of Heraclitus, Hippocrates' *Airs, Waters, and Places*, parallel passages from the *Physics* and *Metaphysics* about the unmoved mover, the *Timeaus* and *Symposium* of Plato and the *Poetics*, I think. I don't know what to do about political ideas. Yes, maybe the *Laws* would be a good idea. Then I want a short Christian section: the beginnings of John ... the Romans, the thirteenth Corinthians and finish up with the Athanasian Creed ... I shall have some Euclid, I guess ... I'd like to put in a little Oppian.

Alexander Pope's verse translation of a section of the *Iliad* appeared in the published text, as did 'The Book of the Dead' from the *Odyssey*. The whole of the *Oresteia* (in modern translation by George Thomson) was there, as was Aristophanes' *The Birds*. He got what he wanted in the case of Thucydides (*not* Thomas Hobbes' seventeenth-century translation), but there was no Herodotus in the *Reader*. The Heraclitus made it as far as 'The Word' from an 1892 UK translation, as did the Hippocrates he planned, and the selections from Aristotle. Plato appeared with *Timaeus*, *Phaedo*, the *Symposium*, and the *Laws*. There was no *Poetics* included, but selections from Aristotle's *Politics*, the *Nicomachean Ethics*, the *Physics*, and *Metaphysics*. Euclid's *Elements* came from a 1941 *Greek Mathematical Works*. There was no Oppian, and no New Testament or other Christian material at all. Extracts from twenty-six authors not mentioned at the planning stage were also included, including Hesiod, Pindar, and Epictetus. Counting the Christian material as one item, only seven of the thirty-seven authors extracted from were named in his original plans.

The *Reader* is divided thematically into 'Cosmologies', 'The Hero', 'Nature', 'Man', and 'Society', across which sixty-one extracts are distributed (some authors – Plato, Aristotle, Homer – appear in more than one section). Copyright permissions detailed at the beginning of the *Reader* suggest that of all the extracts anthologised, only thirteen came from works published after Auden's school and university days. Only five of the *editions* of texts for which permission to reproduce was sought are detailed in Thompson and Ridge's *Catalogue*, but the vast majority of the authors and works from which Auden extracted had been available in UK editions as textbooks and class readers during his childhood and adolescence. Whether they *were* so used at St Edmund's School, or at home in Solihull, we do not know, but all of Auden's 'Editor's Introduction' displays a long and detailed acquaintance with Greek literature and poetry. He was (still is) highly informative on the irreducible factors of semantics and speech in turning the poetry of one language into the poetry of another. He informs about word order and diction in Greek; he explains that Greek is an inflected language, in which sense does not depend on word position as it does in English. Prosodic difficulties of translation were explained: quantitative unrhymed verse like the Greek was patterned by the 'weight' of syllables; in qualitative (English) verse stressed syllables come at regular intervals. He did not say it here, but did elsewhere: that the Old Norse and Old English verse he had been familiar with from early childhood was also based on the patterns of stress-timed everyday language. Here, introducing *The Reader*, he emphasised translation of poetry of one language into another as 'an invaluable training for a poet'. He thought that 'the better a translation is as English poetry, the less like Greek poetry it is (e.g. Pope's *Iliad*)'.

His explanation of the little engine of language that is a poem – how it is made and how it works – is, however, a very small part of a long exegesis of Greek culture: the mental habits and social manners of classical antiquity. Statements like 'Greek poetry is primitive ... primitive poetry says simple things in a roundabout way', and their 'kind of thinking is as extraordinary to us as any habits of an African tribe', are read now under the shadow of *Orientalism* and Orientalism; but Auden believed he was anticipating the reactions of readers in 'feeling that they were a very odd people indeed'; but '[i]t is the unlikeness of the Greeks to ourselves, the gulf between the kind of assumptions they made, the kind of questions they asked', in which lay the value of attempting to understand. He did not discuss the incommensurability that it is the modern historian's task to work on and with: that you cannot know the past and that history is something written out of that unknowing. But his assertion that a culture revealed questions asked long ago by people about their own thought – how thinking *worked*, how there were always other ways of doing that thinking – is a fine poetics of incommensurability. However, the work in which R. G. Collingwood formulated the idea that the historian must strive to re-create the parameters in which past thought occurred had not yet been published.[39]

By the time Auden entered Christ Church College, Oxford, in 1925, Greek was no longer a university entry requirement.[40] He was studying

39 Auden was familiar with Collingwood's pre-1948 work; Collingwood had discussed one of Auden's stage-plays in *The Principles of Art* (1938). Edward Mendelson, *Later Auden*, Faber and Faber, London, 1939, pp. 140–141, 144–145.
40 Robert Currie, 'The Arts and Social Studies, 1914–1939', Brian Harrison (ed.), *The History of the University of Oxford, Vol. VIII. The Twentieth Century*, Clarendon Press, Oxford, 1994, pp. 109–138.

English by the autumn of 1926 and there are very full accounts of his first encounters with Old English poetry, by now a cornerstone of the Oxford English degree.[41] It appears that his childhood reading of Northern European literature had been in Norse mythology and collections of Icelandic stories – in prose, not poetry.[42] Chris Jones points out that Auden was 'the first Saxonizing poet to receive a university education which would have been familiar to most British students of English during the twentieth century'.[43] Jones also points out that Auden's enthusiasm for Old English poetry did not translate into the student's examination success in examination papers that emphasised phonology, spelling form, and dialectal variation. However, as Auden spent so much creative energy in experimenting with its forms and techniques in his own verse, it is relatively easy to trace Old English stress patterns in his work, certainly in the verse-plays he wrote in collaboration in the 1930s. Chris Jones also argues that it was in the 1930s that he learned to use Old English as a resource for his later poetry, 'discarding it where thin and meagre and preserving it where efficacious'.[44] It is possible, thanks to Jones' work, to see and hear those resources in Auden's use of alliteration, assonance, and particular stress patterns and rhyme structures associated with Old English. Jones suggests that the strange near-yet-farness of Old English for modern English speakers allows them to experience the full anxiety of estrangement from their 'Anglo-Saxon, linguistic homeland' (quite apart from Auden's anxious inscription of queer estrangement from himself,

---

41 Chris Jones, 'W. H. Auden and "The 'Barbaric' Poetry of the North". Unchaining one's daimon', *The Review of English Studies*, 53 (2002), pp. 167–185; also 'Anglo-Saxon Anxieties. Auden and "The Barbaric Poetry of the North"', Jones (ed.) *Strange Likeness: The Use of Old English in Twentieth-Century Poetry*, Oxford University Press, Oxford, 2006, pp. 68–121.

42 But Auden described his enchanted meeting with the essays of W. P. Ker, in Oxford, in 1925: 'what good angel lured me into Blackwell's one afternoon and, from such a wilderness ... picked out for me the essays of W. P. Ker ... a kind of literary All Souls Night in which the dead, the living and the unborn writers of every age and in every tongue were seen as engaged upon a common, noble and civilizing task. No other could have so instantaneously aroused in me a fascination with prosody, which I have never lost.' W. H. Auden, *The Dyer's Hand and Other Essays*, Faber and Faber, London, 1963, pp. 42–43. Ker provided much information on Danish ballads, Viking culture, and the early historians of Norway: *Collected Essays. In Two Volumes*, Macmillan, London, 1925, Vol. 2, pp. 63–221. Ten years on, Auden may have remembered Ker's essay on Byron (Vol. 1, pp. 207–223) and thought the dead poet a suitable recipient of a 'letter from Iceland'.

43 Jones, 'W. H. Auden', p. 1.

44 Jones, *Strange Likeness*, p. 88.

which is a main theme of Jones's exegesis). Auden himself commented on these questions of poetics in terms of technique: 'In general the further away from you in time or feeling that poets are, the more you can get out of them for your own use. Often some piece of technique thus learnt really unchains one's own Daemon quite suddenly.'[45]

I have not the tools to ask Jones' marvellous questions about Latin and Greek influences on Auden's poetry (or about the Anglo-Saxon, for that matter). My questions are about poetry made as a form of history and a type of historiography. Questions of language and written composition are important for understanding the making and structure of any work of history (where it comes from; out of what philosophies and beliefs the written artefact is made), and I think we do know enough from Auden's early education in the classics to give his Clio a sharper focus in a wider perspective (though we have not yet exhausted these questions about her origins, or Auden's understanding of history). The poet appears to contemplate all of this in the beautiful fragment 'Venus Will Now Say a Few Words' (1929), which may well be about 'dead' languages in general, including Old English, as Jones says; but the striking idea provoked here is the nature of the traces that different languages (and invasions) leave behind: that Latin had to die, that Clio was never in England in the first place, for so very few English place-names reflect the Roman occupation. Jack is English (if not Olde Englishe) in this poem, as is a countryside full of rusting agricultural machinery:

> Think – Romans had a language in their day
> And ordered roads with it, but it had to die:
> Your culture can but leave – forgot as sure
> As place-name origins in favourite shire –
> Jottings for stories, some often-mentioned Jack,
> And references in letters to a private joke,
> Equipment rusting in unweeded lanes ... [46]

But neither the Greek nor the Old English acquired in his youth can be said to have provided the unique tonal quality of the poetry Auden produced

45 Jones, *Strange Likeness*, cites 'Letter from W. H. Auden to John Pudney, dated 28 April 1931. Berg Collection, MSS Auden, 902054'. The letter also included a recommendation that Anglo-Saxon be studied for 'word order and sentence structure'.
46 Edward Mendelson, *Early Auden*, Faber and Faber, London, 1981, pp. 81–82; Auden, *Collected Poems*, p. 44.

in the 1930s. Many of his early poems suggested 'fatality', said Geoffrey Grigson: 'assonances and alliterations coming together to make a new verbal actuality as it might be of rock of quartz, a milieu of the profound Midlands, half aboriginal, half soiled or damaged, half abandoned'.[47]

Uncovering Auden's education in history is a simpler task, mainly because there was so little taught at his schools. Two hours a week between 1915 and 1920 at St Edmunds, as Rosamira Bulley recalled, and some of those devoted to English language. St Edmund's appears to have been a typical preparatory school in this regard: 'The time spent on historical teaching varies but little in the different schools' (120 were surveyed), reported A. M. Curteis to the Board of Education in 1900. 'English history is very properly the starting point', he said, though half the schools he visited added Greek or Roman history, especially for older boys. In most classrooms a textbook formed the basis of instruction ('Usually Gardiner's *Outline of English History*'). This was supplemented 'by the use of wall maps and blackboards, sometimes by lantern slides, relief maps and models, in one case even of the rubbing of brasses'. Perhaps each boy in some classes was provided with a copy of the text; but Curteis' report suggests that many teachers used the class's sole copy as a method book, dictating sections, or telling 'stories' from it to the children. He reported approvingly on oral teaching, and thought it commendable that the majority of schools he visited 'confined textbooks to "reference" and "revision"'. The questions he had seen teachers put to the boys were 'any sane teacher's method'; nothing wrong with that.[48] He had seen satisfactory and innovative work in the history hour: children had been encouraged to 'think ... for themselves'; he had seen debates, lantern slide shows (sometimes connecting history to art or current events); time lines displayed on classroom walls ('Calendar[s] of Great Events'); some classes investigated a historical 'event of the day'.

These 'modern' interactive methods developed during the early twentieth century; Auden attended school during a great flowering of published social history for children, most of it targeted at teachers of primary-age children in the state system. William Claxton's *Peeps into the Past, or, History without History Books* recommended itself to ele-

---

47 Geoffrey Grigson, 'A Meaning of Auden', Spender (ed.), *W. H. Auden*, pp. 13–25; 16.

48 A. M. Curteis, 'The Teaching of History in Preparatory Schools', Board of Education, *Special Reports on Educational Subjects Vol. 6. Preparatory Schools for Boys. Their Place in Secondary Education*, HMSO, London, 1900, pp. 207–219; Samuel Rawson Gardiner, *Outline of English History, B. C. 55–A. D.-1880, first published in 1881 and brought up to the current year in 1895 and 1899*, Longman, London, 1901.

mentary school teachers by reminding them of the HMI who had opined that 'history as commonly taught therein, of very little value'. Claxton recommended the use of historical artefacts and photographs in the classroom, and museum visits and visits to 'ancient dwellings' even if only in the imagination.[49] There were at least two dozen reissues of the *Piers Ploughman Histories* between 1913 and 1937. All of the new history readers were illustrated; some catered for children in the very early stages of literacy acquisition.[50] E. M. Tappen's *In Feudal Times. Social Life in the Middle Ages*, about the 'life and habits of thought of the people who lived between the eighth and fifteenth centuries', had, among other section headings, 'How to Capture a Castle', 'Daily Life in a Castle', 'Life in Town', and 'Schools and Literature'. 'Mohammed', 'Mohammedans', and 'Romance languages' were to be found in the index.[51] *Chambers's Periodic Histories* enticed children into the role of researcher with 'An Unwritten Story' – a little discourse on historical and archaeological method, and the poetry of 'a little shoe or a battered toy [found] whilst digging in the sand'.[52] Nancy Neimeyer produced *Stories for the History Hour* in 1917, written for telling, not reading aloud; it was important 'to put the most important historic truth a child can comprehend into a form which a child can understand'. Although 'a history story must be as much history as story', Neimeyer had sometimes thought it best 'to trust to a suggestion, based on evidence, than to spoil the story for lack of it'.[53] For ordinary twentieth-century children in the elementary schools of England, these history primers were no invitation *at all* to feel that the citizens of ancient Rome or the inhabitants of a Saxon village 'were a very odd people indeed'.[54] Viking warriors and

49 William J. Claxton, *Peeps into the Past, or, History without History Books*, Pitman, London, 1911; Mary Sarson and Mary E. Paine, *Piers Plowman Histories, Junior Book II. Greek, Roman, and Old English History* (1913), 3rd edn, Philip, London, 1937.

50 Nancy Smith, Hilda Booth, and E. H. Spalding, *Piers Plowman Histories, Junior Book I. Stories of Hebrew, Trojan, Early Teutonic, and Medieval Life*, Philip, London, 1913, was, said its authors, a book of pictures for the child 'who cannot easily read to himself'; 'The explanatory letterpress is simple enough to be read to children by an older person until they are able to read it unaided'; 'The stories which they illustrate are told in Junior Book 1 of the Piers Plowman Histories'.

51 E. M. Tappen, *In Feudal Times. Social Life in the Middle Ages. Told Through the Ages Series*, Harrap, London, 1913.

52 Marie Bain, *Chambers's Periodic Histories. Book III. England in the Making (To 1066 AD)*, Chambers, Edinburgh, 1915.

53 Nancy Niemeyer, *Stories for the History Hour. From Augustus to Rolf*, Harrap, London, 1917, pp. 6–7.

54 Auden, *Portable Greek Reader*, p. 1.

medieval housewives (and there *were* housewives) were depicted as doing the equivalent of putting the kettle on for a nice cup of tea, or getting up in the morning and looking out of the window (or the aperture screened by pieces of linen soaked in linseed oil; the primers were nothing if not correct in historical detail), or even just walking dully along, showing off their jerkins and cross garters and wimples and aprons.

Reporting on the teaching of history for the Preparatory Schools Association in 1930, E. K. Milliken did not mention teaching material like this. His 'sturdy friends' among textbooks were Warner and Martin, *The Groundwork of British History* and Ransom's *An Elementary History of England*, he was fond of Lay's *The Pupil's Classbook of English History*; but he knew that this remote 'bird's eye view' of past events was not so much in favour with present-day educationalists. The choice for preparatory school history must be either British History BC 55–1939, or World History to 1600. As he pointed out, British History had been favoured in the past, 'and ensures satisfactory results in the History Paper of the Common Entrance Exam'. Still, World History offered 'a much wider view of a vast field of knowledge', especially if you didn't go beyond 1600. He had been touched by the new social history ('when Social History marches side by side with the most dramatic episodes of Political History, a fascinating combination can be effected'). 'Legend should be told as legend and myth as myth', he thought, while 'the Little Arthurian approach, which even in these times, is dying a hard death with its stories about Alfred's culinary misadventures and Cnut's paddling activities, should be utterly eschewed'. And, above all, there was practicality: 'taking the narrowest and least worthy view of the subject's value, it is fairly safe to say that even if the History paper in the Common Entrance retains its present requirements, the normal Preparatory school boy can comfortably obtain, by the process of wise selection, forty to fifty per cent in the subject without venturing beyond the Tudor period'.[55]

There are traces of the history teaching Auden was likely to have expe-

---

55 E. K. Milliken, *The Teaching of History*, Incorporated Association of Preparatory Schools, Pamphlet No. 3, 1930. Here is a disparaging little comment about Lady Maria Calcott's *Little Arthur's History of …* series, which had first appeared in 1835. The last edition held by the British Library appeared in 1904. For state school history teaching 1900–1944, see David Cannadine, Jenny Keating, and Nicola Sheldon, *The Right Kind of History. Teaching the Past in Twentieth-Century England*, Palgrave Macmillan, Basingstoke, 2011, pp. 18–101. For women as producers of history for children and school history readers, Bonnie G. Smith, *The Gender of History: Men, Women, and Historical Practice*, Harvard University Press, Harvard MA, 2000.

rienced. He impressed his friends at St Edmund's (or they were impressed in later life) by his parodic discourse on an event in medieval religious history: two forms accustomed to sharing a room for prep were housed separately; 'he dubbed the event "The Great Schism"', making comparison with division of the Roman Catholic Church (1378–1415) during which period rival popes sat in both Rome and Avignon.[56] It appears that for the main part he studied medieval and what is now called 'early modern' history. He remembered an item of what looks to be the 'Little Arthurian' history disapproved of by Milliken, in the story of King John gnawing a rush mat in his rage. It seemed to the child that this is just how a St Edmund's schoolmaster might, unpredictably, behave. There were several history readers available to preparatory schools in which he may have read about The Rage of King John and encountered this bit of ersatz history. York and Tout's *History of England* (1910) is a likely source. But though King John is enraged in many readers, and gnaws the floor rushes in some, he never gnaws a rush *mat*, a form of floor covering promoted to institutions like schools for its hygienic qualities in the early twentieth century.[57] And as much as I would like to find the genesis, for example, of Auden's 'Roman Wall Blues' in the miserable voice of Kipling's 1911 'Roman Centurion'–

Legate, I come to you in tears – My cohort ordered home!
I've served in Britain forty years. What should I do in Rome?
Here is my heart, my soul, my mind – the only life I know. –
I cannot leave it all behind. Command me not to go!

– the document forbids me to do so; there is no evidence of St Edmund's school, or of the Auden parents purchasing Fletcher and Kipling's *A School History of England*, or that their youngest son ever read it.[58]

56 Llewellyn Smith, 'At St Edmund's', p. 35. Or he could have been referring to The Great Schism of 1054 when the Eastern and Western Christian Churches divided from each other.

57 Carpenter, *W. H. Auden*, p. 17; F. Powell York and T. F. Tout, *History of England*, Longman, Green, London, 1910. Also G. F. Bosworth (ed.), *Cambridge Historical Readers, Intermediate*, Cambridge University Press, Cambridge, 1914. King John's Rage is all over the internet; see, for example, www.magnacharta.com/bomc/king-john-the-genesis-of-a-sinister-reputation/ (accessed 12 October 2017).

58 C. R. L. Fletcher and Rudyard Kipling, *A School History of England*, Clarendon Press, Oxford, 1911, pp. 19–20, 'The Roman Centurion Speaks'. There are lovely illustrations here of 'The Cave People', 'The Landing of the Danes', and twenty-three poems in which historical subjects speak. Of course the Centurion in Auden's 'Roman Wall

At Oxford, Auden made it clear that he was not interested in modern social and labour history. At some point, between the Natural Sciences degree course he had been admitted to and his settling in the English School, he considered PPE, but 'to an introvert like myself, the social conditions of the poor in the 19th century as expounded by G. D. H Cole do not click'.[59] His own social and political history of the modern period in Britain, frequently expressed in the reviewing work he did, may have been acquired during preparation for the courses he taught at Swarthmore, or other North American colleges, or from the very book that was under review, as with Joseph Bronowski's book on Blake, of which he wrote in December 1947 that 'Blake's lifetime coincided with a period of intense political and economic crisis; weakened from within by the strains of a transition from a mercantile to an industrial economy, and without by the strain of the American and French wars, its social and political beliefs threatened by the ideology of the French Revolution, the social structure of England was nearer collapse than at any time since 1640.'[60]

More open to view is the religious education Auden experienced. We do not know the form of family prayers conducted by Dr Auden in the family home but there is much information in various biographies of Auden about the religious instruction provided by his mother. We know that however many types of Anglican service Constance Auden sought out for her children in Solihull and the wider county of Warwickshire and in Birmingham, all the liturgy the children were exposed to remained within the Church of England's very broad parameters. We know that John and

Blues' is miserable because he *wants* to go home, but both poems employ the same rhythmic structure, in (mainly) four-beat lines. Auden, 'Twelve Songs ... XI', *Collected Shorter Poems 1927–1957*, pp. 93–94. For Auden's account of Kipling as historian, W. H. Auden, 'The Poet of Encirclement', *Prose Volume II*, pp. 198–203; orig. 'Review. *A Choice of Kipling's Verse. Made by T. S. Eliot with an Essay on Rudyard Kipling*', *New Republic*, 24 October 1943. See also Susannah Young-ah Gottlieb, 'The Fallen Empire', Costello and Galvin (eds), *Auden at Work*, pp. 156–178.

59 Davenport-Hines, *Auden*, pp. 52–53; this cites here a letter written in 1928, long after Auden has settled to English. Marc Stears, 'Cole, George Douglas Howard (1889–1959)', *Oxford Dictionary of National Biography*, Oxford University Press, Oxford, 2004. Cole arrived in Oxford in 1925, but it does not appear that Auden heard him lecture when he was making his choice between PPE and English. However, Cole published a great deal and spoke frequently at public meetings between 1925 and 1928. University of Oxford, Nuffield College Library, MSS.GDHC, Papers of G. D. H. Cole in Nuffield College Library, www.nuffield.ox.ac.uk/media/2016/gdhcole.pdf (accessed 12 October 2017).

60 W. H. Auden, 'Mystic – and Prophet', *Prose Volume II*, pp. 337–339; orig. review of J. Bronowski, *A Man Without a Mask, New York Times Book Review*, 14 December 1947. See also Mendelson, *Early Auden*, p. 184; Auden, *Prose Volume I*, pp. 744–745.

Wystan Auden were prepared for confirmation – and the younger boy actually confirmed – at St Edmund's School, at the age of 14. St Edmund's advertised its insistence on chapel attendance; the programme of religious training it provided may have been a factor in the Audens' choice of it for their two younger sons. From its foundation in the 1890s, 'religion, and in particular a regular pattern of chapel services ... underpin[ned] all the school's other activities ... The climax of the chapel year from 1898 until 1986 was the annual visit of the diocesan bishop or his nominee to conduct a confirmation. This was very much a state occasion, with the parents and maybe godparents of the candidates swelling the congregation.'[61] John and Wystan and their classmates preparing for confirmation followed the religious curriculum laid down in *The Book of Common Prayer*: 'So soon as Children are come to a competent age, and can say, in their Mother Tongue, the Creed, the Lord's Prayer and the Ten Commandments; and can answer the questions of [a] short Catechism: they shall be brought to the Bishop ...'.[62] Through the centuries ministers and parents have proceeded with this training in different ways, but most used the question and answer format that the Catechism employs to ensure that a child, out of his or her own heart, understands the articles of faith declared at baptism by its godparents.[63] The child committed to heart, probably not the Athanasian Creed (which Auden later wanted for his *Greek Reader*) but the more commonly used Nicene Creed, though the Athanasian Creed was to be found in the *Book of Common Prayer* in an authorised form that

---

61 Palmer, *Willingly to School*, pp. 215–22. Before the formation of the diocese of Guildford in 1927, Hindhead lay in the diocese of Winchester, possessed of a bishop who was perhaps confessionally closer to Constance Auden's taste than the Bishop of Birmingham. See above, p. 56–57.

62 *Book of Common Prayer*, '19. The Order of Confirmation'.

63 For the confirmation teaching of schoolmaster and cleric John Murgatroyd in West Yorkshire c.1750–1800, Steedman, *Master and Servant*, pp. 110–130. Had Auden attended the Sunday School attached to St Alphege's, Solihull, he would have experienced a bang-up-to-the minute question-and-answer teaching method: 'Instead of the ordinary Children's Service on Sunday afternoons we shall adopt the method of teaching known as "the method of the Catechism" ... three exercises of questioning, instruction, and homily, appealing to the will, mind and heart of the child. I hope that parents will encourage their children to write an analysis of the instruction, as children remember best what they put down in writing for themselves.' *Solihull Parish Magazine*, 32:1 (1912), p. 5. He was too young for confirmation instruction in 1912; he may, however, have belonged to the Church Choir before he left St Edmund's: *Solihull Parish Magazine*, 33:4 (April 1913), p. 3 thanks Mrs Auden (and three others) for their kind gifts of books for the Choir Boys Library. But little Wystan was only 6 years old; Constance Auden was more likely clearing out for the move to Homer Road.

might be used in churches at the service of Holy Communion. There is extraordinary insight here, into the forms of language, the cadences, and speech rhythms committed to memory by generations of children from the sixteenth century onwards. But we are not to know *how* this language was remembered and used; all that can be said of the particular child under consideration, is that it does not appear (to me) to provide the phonological and syntactic basis of his poetry. The legacy of all teaching in childhood depends in some degree on the affective relationship between teacher and taught. The eighteenth-century Church of England thought hard about the ways in which its children might be confirmed in their faith, and there were instructions for parents and ministers that were not available in the nineteenth and twentieth centuries. So how Geoffrey Gunnell Newman, Curate of Farnham (1913–1917), Chaplain and Assistant Master at St Edmunds School, Hindhead (1920–1921), proceeded with his small class of boys we cannot tell – only know that Auden loved him, because he said so, and remembered loving him for a very long time.[64]

When Auden's understanding of history is discussed by modern scholars, he emerges as a proponent of 'big' history; of history's *meaning* and the philosophy derived from it.[65] When we come to his Clio, we shall have to consider his reading of the grand, sweeping teleologies of Western thought that preoccupied him in the 1940s and 1950s. They are, as we shall see, legible in his thought because they were connected to his childhood experience – 'An Education' – but more particularly to his thorough grounding in church history. What he knew of the early church, its fathers, teachers, and apostles and of the many great schisms of Western Christianity, allowed him to claim that 'Christianity, of all religions, attaches a unique importance to history'. He quoted the Apostles' (Nicene) Creed to make his point: 'I believe in Jesus Christ who suffered under Pontius Pilate, was crucified, dead and buried.' This, he said, 'expresses the belief that, for God, a particular moment in history when the Jews had reached a certain point in their development ... and the gentiles in theirs, was "the fullness of time," the right moment for

64 'Newman, Geoffrey Gunnel', *Crockford's Clerical Directory, 1888–1932*; UK Crockford's Clerical Directory online, www.crockford.org.uk/ (accessed 12 October 2017). Tony Sharpe, *W. H. Auden*, Routledge, Abingdon, 2007, p. 31; Davenport-Hines, *Auden*, p. 39. Christopher Isherwood, three years older than Auden and also a pupil at St Edmund's was confirmed not there, but at his public school. *Lions and Shadows. An Education in the Twenties* (1938), Vintage, London, 2013, p. 8.
65 Susannah Young-ah Gottlieb, 'Auden in History', Tony Sharpe (ed.), *W. H. Auden in Context*, Cambridge University Press, Cambridge, 2013, pp. 181–192.

the eternal vow to be made Flesh and the Divine Sacrifice to take place'. Little doubt here that there is such a god; but he raised the question: 'If such a god does exist, then all the historical realities of that time ... must have been known to Him as characteristics of the fullness of time.'[66] He knew that as a historical creature man experiences needs as desires 'which are historically conditioned'.[67] He could relate church history to social history, as when disapproving of T. S. Eliot's view of culture: Eliot was wrong to associate its transmission with specific social classes, because since the eighteenth century, in Britain, culture had been transmitted by the church.[68] But the modern social historian is wary – warier than she was when Auden was only a poet – for we have learned, after Vico, that sacred history belongs to God; is unknowable, and not our business; that only what's left over is ours:

> In the light of thick darkness enveloping the earliest antiquity, so remote from ourselves, there shines the eternal and never failing light of a truth beyond all question: that the world of civil society has certainly been made by men, and that its principles are therefore to be found within the modifications of our own human mind.[69]

This is the creed of social historians, if they have one.[70] I proceed with some anxiety now, knowing that Auden's Christian God is very close to Clio. And She to Him. And I must so proceed, for as Sean O'Brien says, in a situation where religious belief is impossible or inconceivable for those who might form Auden's contemporary constituency of readers, 'it would be a serious loss if it also became impossible to grasp how much his religious thought is bound up with his apprehension of the sometimes ungovernable power of poetic language'.[71]

66 W. H. Auden, 'Religion and the Intellectuals. A Symposium', *Prose Volume III*, pp. 170–176; orig. *Partisan Review*, February 1950; Tony Sharpe, 'The Church of England. Auden's Anglicanism', Sharpe (ed.), *W. H. Auden in Context*, pp. 69–78.

67 W. H. Auden, 'The Things Which Are Caesar's', *Prose Volume III*, pp. 196–210; orig. *Theology*, November and December 1950; Mendelson, *Later Auden*, pp. 275–294; 310–392; Teresa Bru, 'Essaying in autobiography: Wystan Hugh Auden's and Walter Benjamin's faces', *Biography*, 33:2 (2010), pp. 333–349.

68 Mendelson, *Later Auden*, p. 302.

69 Giambattista Vico, *The New Science of Giambattista Vico* (1744), trans. Thomas Goddard Bergin and Max Harold Fisch, Doubleday, New York NY, 1961, pp. 52–53. See below, pp. 204–205.

70 Joseph Mali, *The Legacy of Vico in Modern Cultural History. From Jules Michelet to Isaiah Berlin*, Cambridge University Press, Cambridge, 2012, p. 234.

71 Sean O'Brien, 'Auden in Prose', Sharpe (ed.), *W. H. Auden in Context*, pp. 329–336.

5

W. H. Auden and me

　　　　　　　　… we go back
to 'Consider this and in our time';
it's a key text, no doubt about it:
the first garden party of the year,
the leisurely conversation in the bar,
the fact that it is later
than we think. I set an essay

on what exactly Auden meant –
and in one month's time in this small room
one way or other I will write 'See me'
And in one way or another she will.
　　　　　　Peter Sansom, 'Teaching Auden', *Everything You've Heard is True*,
　　　　　　　　　　　　　　　　　　　　　　　Carcanet, 1990.

I never taught Auden; or maybe a bit, in a tangential kind of way, to be
later described. I do not believe I have ever wanted to know, or to find out,
or even to think about, *what exactly Auden meant*; I *have* been puzzled;
I haven't *got* his poetry; I have longed to know where it came from and
where he was coming from; I want to know *how it works*. But I was taught,
somehow, from my earliest days, that 'what does it really mean?', 'what
did the author mean?', were not proper questions to put to texts. And
after many a long internal struggle, historians know that there really is no
orginary 'how it happened', no real 'once upon a time'; that things only
happened as they have been told.

　　I was introduced to Auden's poetry – to one of his poems – in my
O-level English literature class, South London, in the 1962–1963 school
year. One of the set texts was an anthology of narrative poetry and ballads,
from which were selected for examination some Child and Border ballads

('Edward', 'The Twa Corbies'), 'The Rime of the Ancient Mariner', 'The Journey of the Magi', and Auden's 'O what is that sound?', simply called 'Ballad' here.[1] The last came, somehow, with the absolute certainty of knowledge that the point of poetry was its ambiguity; that you just *couldn't* know what it meant. This I must have been taught, though possibly not in that particular classroom. Is it a man or woman who speaks? Who, in answer to the question about the sound of drumming coming closer from down in the valley, says: 'Only the scarlet soldiers, dear,/The soldiers coming.'? Who has betrayed whom? Who cries out 'O where are you going? Stay with me here!/ Were the vows you swore deceiving, deceiving?'? Who replies: 'No, I promised to love you, dear,/But I must be leaving'? These questions were discussed; we knew that there wasn't an answer to any of them; that indeterminacy was the point of asking them. We wouldn't have put it like that. We were 15 years old. But we – probably – played about with the questions after class, just as a year later under the influence of our A-level French set-texts we devised a wet-your-knickers comic routine in which the romantic poets Hugo and de Musset ('Huggo and Mussett') were a seedy, down-at-heel music hall duo, doomed to play the Bingley Hippodrome, c.1909 and into all eternity, with sad, pathetic hopes of one day making the Bradford Empire.[2] With hindsight, it's clear that we knew

1 A. A. Evans (ed.), *The Poet's Tale. An Anthology of Narrative Verse (London English Literature)*, London University Press, London, 1957. Q. 10 of the Summer 1963 O-level paper asked us to 'Give an account of the ballad *Edward*. What similarities do you find between this poem and W. H. Auden's *Ballad* beginning 'O what is that sound …': 'University of London, General Certificate of Education, Summer, 1963. Ordinary Level English Literature (Syllabus A). Two and a half hours'. This anthology is not discussed by Lionel Warner, 'Teaching Poetry to Teenagers', Michael Lockwood (ed.) *Bringing Poetry Alive. A Guide to Classroom Practice*, Sage, London, 2011, pp. 99–112; 108, though 'difficult and possibly inappropriate' poems by Auden in other school anthologies are.

2 Oh yes. Just as Auden and his school and university friends made their imaginary world 'Mortmere', we made ours, complete with funny voices in role and each part with character and genealogy. Ours, however, did not continue into our 20s for then we no longer knew each other; but there were new friends with whom to make new Mortmeres; a lifelong activity. A 'self-indulgence' lay behind 'every attitude that … [was] held and used for the sake of its rhetoric and with the consciousness of this use', says Frederick Buell of Mortmere: *W. H. Auden as a Social Poet*, Cornell University Press, Ithaca NY and London, 1973, pp. 33–76. It was the world that Christopher Isherwood and his friend Edward Upward lived during their Cambridge years and after. Isherwood recalled an earlier 'school-saga world' which he had shared with Auden during their time at St Edmund's: 'a kind of Mortmere – a Mortmere founded upon our preparatory school lives'. He was three years older than Auden. Christopher Isherwood, *Lions and Shadows*.

a lot – of things, ideas, history. We enjoyed bathos (and might have even known it by that name, for a list of figures of speech was committed to memory, sometime between 1960 and 1965). But we couldn't have made comedy out of 'Oh what is that sound', for it was a poem in the tragic mode, as we were shortly about to learn in our A-level class by reference to Aristotle's theory of the drama. The pictures in your head, the redcoats' boots thundering on the cottage floor, were your own private business, but in class you said: *It's Culloden isn't it? It's 1746.* Those two had something to do with the Jacobite Rebellion, simply because you could. The Fifteen and The Forty-five (the two Jacobite Rebellions) had been studied sometime before History O-level.[3] Sometime before 1962 I had written on the front cover of my history notebook, 'I refuse to learn any more English history until our rightful monarch is restored'. Me the Republican? Wrote that? Expressed allegiance to an exiled king? Yes; and I am ashamed. I have never before written this down. I *knew* I was a republican; it was more a joke than a statement of political principle; an ironic bit of snidery directed at what we thought of as an incompetent history teacher; we thought we knew more than she did, about democracy and popular feeling expressed in the face of aristocratic state power. Horrid girls! How unfortunate those who had to teach us! Though I'm sure they said we were a joy, what with our smart questions about states and governments, rebellion and revolution, the iambic tetrameter and the French alexandrine.

We *did* know what a tetrameter was. We might even have said of Auden's ballad: *ABCB quatrains with alternating four-stress and three-stress lines*; we

An Education in the Twenties (1938), Vintage, London, 2013, pp. 144–145. For 'funny voices' in everyday social interaction and in print, Jonathan Rée, 'Funny voices. Stories, punctuation and personal identity', *New Literary History*, 21:4 (1990), pp. 1039–1060.

3   The ballad was published in 1934, two years after Auden's Scottish time at Larchfield Academy; Andrew Thacker, 'Auden and the Little Magazines', Tony Sharpe (ed.), *W. H. Auden in Context*, Cambridge University Press, Cambridge, 2013, p. 337. He knew R. L. Stevenson's *Kidnapped*, in which the Jacobite uprising is presented in something of the same way. But as every internet blogger analysing the poem says, it's about what may happen to personal relationships in any situation of political oppression. Isn't it? Or: it's about what Auden said it was in a 1971 lecture: 'a painting of the Agony in the Garden, where the soldiers in the background appear harmless', and "it is only because one has read the Gospel story, that one knows that, in fact, they are coming to arrest Jesus'; Katherine Bucknell, 'Phantasy and Reality in Poetry', Bucknell and Nicholas Jenkins (eds), *'In Solitude, for Company'. W. H. Auden after 1940*, Oxford University Press, Oxford, 1995, pp. 177–196; 193; quoted Edward Mendelson, 'Auden and God', *New York Review of Books*, 6 December 2007. Mendelson's piece is a review of Arthur Kirsch, *Auden and Christianity*, Yale University Press, New Haven CT, 2005.

had been provided with the vocabulary of scansion. In the O-level English literature class, the anthology on our desks, much more time was spent on form and structure than on the melodrama of our historical imagination. We scanned the lines and determined that the iambic tetrameters were insistently regular except for the last lines of most of the stanza, which were trimeters: 'The soldiers coming ... Or perhaps a warning ... Why are you kneeling? ... And now they are running ... But I must be leaving ... And their eyes are burning'. Or maybe we said something like that. We must have been asked about the three four-beat lines followed by a two-beat line at the end of each stanza. We must have been asked for a little bit of reflection on the difference between this form and that of – say – 'The Twa Corbies':

> As I was walking all alane,
> I heard twa corbies makin a mane;
> The tane unto the ither say,
> 'Whar sall we gang and dine the-day?'

what with its perfect tetrameters and the horrible, cold insistence of its regularity. *Well. Girls. And what about the theme of betrayal in both?* (I speak Miss Jean Brodie here. I have no idea if this is what was said.) What about the new slain knight lying dead in a ditch ('His hound is tae the huntin gane,/His hawk tae fetch the wild-fowl hame,/His lady's tain anither mate,/So we may mak oor dinner swate'), compared with the vows he or she had sworn deceiving, deceiving, in Auden's ballad? We were sometimes asked to contemplate character and motivation in these (literally) bloody ballads. Earlier, or perhaps from a cyclostyled sheet to accompany *The Poet's Tale* (for it was not in the anthology), we were invited to observe the capriciousness of kings, as with poor Sir Patrick Spens who in retreat from court life at the seaside is sent over the wintry North Sea to fetch home the King of Norway's daughter simply because the Scots King wants it so.[4] The grim class analysis of the ballad suited well we daughters of post-War social democracy; we liked satire on elites; we were quite pleased that the nobility forced to accompany Sir Patrick got well drowned, that 'mony was the gude lord's son/That never mair cam hame': 'O laith, laith were our gude Scots lords/Tae weet their

---

4 'Sir Patrick Spens', one of the most popular of the Child Ballads (No. 58) is available all over the internet. Francis James Child, *English and Scottish Popular Ballads*, Helen Child Sargent and George Lyman Kittredge (eds), David Nutt, London, 1905.

cork-heelt shuin;/But lang or aw the play wis playd/They wat their hats abuin'. I imagined Sir Patrick to be an old guy, a grizzled sea dog, so I was puzzled – in a detached kind of way; it's a poem! Isn't it? (or *Innit*, though the interrogative tag that isn't interrogative was not to be available for another twenty years. More's the pity)[5] – by the number of Dunfermline ladies playing with their fans and pointlessly combing their hair as they filled in the hours against his return. But the scansion was the best.

Scansion was the loveliest thing, far lovelier to do than clause analysis, into which we had been insistently inducted for two years past in preparation for the English Language O-level exam. Clause analysis provided something of the same sense of orderliness that scansion would afford, but it was materially a messy business if you drew your boxes headed Subject, Object; Article, Main Verb, Preposition, Conjunction; Clause, Subordinate Clause, with a ruler and an ink pen (no ball point pens allowed), for it was very difficult not to smudge the lines; but there was still the joy of neatness as you gently laid out the parts of speech on the page, each in its appointed place. Scansion – tapping out the line of verse and making those dear little marks ˘ and ´ to show the strong and light stress on the syllables – produced in me, at least, a sense of perfect control; of what I thought to be a sophisticated grasp of *how something worked*. The marking of *abba*, or *abab* down the right-hand side of a stanza to show the rhyme scheme, was baby-work compared with scansion. Derek Attridge remembers from his high school years in the US something of the same sense of orderliness and satisfaction when learning to scan Latin verse: 'what looked and sounded like a random arrangement of words into lines could, after mastering a few rules, be shown to be anything but random. A dactylic hexameter could be relied upon to have six feet made up of long and short syllables, according to strict rules governing their disposition across the line. There were no exceptions ...'[6] He was also taught to scan English-language verse, but although the process involved some of the same technical terms, with English poetry there were 'all sorts of uncertainties about stressed and unstressed syllables ... no clear rules about what kind of foot could occur where, elision was a mystery, and different poets ... had different understandings of what constituted a metrical line'.

5 Heike Pichler, 'A Qualitative-quantitative Analysis of Negative Auxiliaries in a Northern English Dialect: I DON'T KNOW and I DON'T THINK, Innit?', PhD thesis, University of Aberdeen, 2008. Personally, I don't think that question mark should be there at the end of the title; but it's an excellent thesis.
6 Derek Attridge, *Moving Words. Forms of English Poetry*, Oxford University Press, Oxford, 2013, p. 1.

Scansion of English verse was a messy affair for him compared with Latin, which he much preferred. He enjoyed the lucid and pleasing patterns that then emerged in Latin verse, including the observation that the pattern did not coincide, at all, with the sound of the lines. For him, 'the pleasure was an intellectual one, not an aural one'. But for me, South London, c.1962, the pleasure of scanning English verse came *with* the untidiness, the exceptions, the blindingly obvious reasons for irregularity when it occurred. You did what you could; there was to be no perfection of analysis. Language was its own, obdurate thing. You could give it enough order to see what was going on in it.

This difference of attitude may be to do with my not being taught Latin. There was a rule, I believe, that said (Why?) that if you did not have competence in maths, you couldn't do Latin. In the summer examinations which determined this (1959? 1960? Can't remember) I got over 95% in every subject except maths, for which I was awarded 3% for writing my own name correctly. (I was, stupidly, rather proud of this: if you're not good at something, there's a lot of satisfaction in defiantly doing it *really badly*. If I'd read *Wuthering Heights* by then I could have claimed my first sisterhood with Nelly Dean: being Latin-less was all you could expect of a poor man's daughter.) Learning scansion without the means to compare Latin and English verse meant that its pleasures in and with English were not so much intellectual *as* aural. We were taught to read the poem out loud, to find its rhythm and beat by tapping on the desk, then to annotate a copied stanza in our notebook. It was visceral, this pleasure: it involved hands and eyes and ears. You, the reader, *worked* at it, to make its meaning by looking at the moving parts of this little engine of language; you took it into yourself along the way. And by this method, a lot of it did end up in you, for you acquired it, fixed it in your brain, to say aloud later on. I had been taught how to learn language (including poetry) by heart at primary school. But this secondary school teaching method embedded (some) verse much deeper in the heart and consciousness than did the technique imbued in 8-year-olds.

As a technology of analysis scansion placed a deal of emphasis on the sound-system of the English language. How this was understood, I cannot quite work out, for we had an extremely limited vocabulary for discussing sounds: just 'hard' and 'soft' and maybe 'strong' and 'silent'. I didn't learn about phonology or know what a phoneme was until my 20s, when I taught children to read by the modified phonetic method then in vogue. But the ideas of sound and the tonal occupied my literary imagination. From 1958 to 1965 my school was a London County Council (the LCC became the Greater London Council in 1965) girls' grammar, run on the Dalton principle. We were told that it was the only secondary school in the country that still operated a system of learning by teacher-prepared syllabi or assignments, with children working individually in study spaces or rooms; there were relatively few class lessons in each subject. '*Modified* Dalton, girls! We operate a modified Dalton system' – which meant rather more lessons than the originators would have thought proper, but far fewer than in other local secondary schools.[7] English literature classes and private study hours spent scanning made me somewhat obsessed with sound and phonology. In the sixth form, studying for English A-level, I had great good fun in the library, or maybe it was at one of the tables in the hall set aside for individual study, with the week's cyclostyled syllabus and the instruction to comment on 'the sound qualities displayed by Miss Tilney' – in some early chapter or other of *Mansfield Park*, which was our Austen set text. I made a happy little analysis of the tonal qualities of the character's discourse, the soft and sibilant, persuasive and plosive sound – whatever – of what she said. In the lesson, I silently drew a line through my page of analysis, hid my notebook beneath my copy of the novel so that no one could see; for five minutes in it became clear that I had been meant to comment on the sound *moral* or *ethical* values of Miss Tilney's speech. You taught me about sound! And my profit on it is that it's often the only thing I do when confronted with a text! I do now understand that it was a not very well-framed question; but still.[8]

The education in poetry I was given resonates with what Maureen Duffy describes in her autobiographical novel *That's How It Was* (1962). Passing the scholarship exam and entering Trowbridge High School for Girls in the closing stages of the Second World War, she experienced 'the most enlightened liberal humanist tradition' which, she says, she took to as if her family had been enjoying it for generations; the pleasures of 'learning, of music and the visual arts took me over. Above all … there

---

7 Helen Parkhurst, *Education on the Dalton Plan*, G. Bell, London, 1922. My school was named after its former headmistress Rosa Bassett, who contributed to the volume by describing her experiment with the plan in 1920. Rosa Bassett, 'A Year's Experiment in an English Secondary School', idem, pp. 125–143. In the 1930s many primary and secondary state schools operated on the Dalton Plan.

8 'A trained speaker, my mother always told me, could recite the London telephone directory and make it interesting … The corollary of this, I noticed in adulthood, is that many actors say their lines as if reciting the London telephone directory, as if the words have no intrinsic meaning at all … I was damaged by my education.' Lynn Barber, *An Education*, Penguin, London, 2009, pp. 18, 56.

was literature in Latin, French and English ... Poetry ... was a source of the intensest pleasure.' Much of her time was spent 'in a dream of verse writing, reading and learning ... impersonating John Keats and imitating his odes'.[9] I recognise the Keats; I can still recite the Keats poems I acquired at 14; 'Ode to a Nightingale' can sometimes work as well as any sleeping pill. But I did not and do not recognise the story of the scholarship girl Duffy also tells: the way in which a grammar school education set her apart from home and family. By the time I was 20 I had read enough sociology of education and class to know that the estrangement she discusses was a dominate theme of the literature, not least by reference to Richard Hoggart's *The Uses of Literacy*, whose 'anxious and uprooted' scholarship boy of the 1930s is still used to account for working-class children's experience of education. I felt grammar school to be just ... normal, as passing the 11-plus exam had been just ... normal, though, of course, statistically it wasn't ordinary at all. Duffy was born in 1933, went to secondary school before the Education Act (1944) came into force; what I remember of the years after 1947 (when I was born) was that we were 'all the same' (as Auden told the readers of *Mademoiselle* that he and his friends, a different wartime generation of boys, were all the same); we all lived in the houses strung along the same endless South London streets; we had all had our due quota of orange juice and cod-liver oil. By 1958 and secondary school, we all looked pretty much alike as well: white to a girl and with the lean, wiry body that comes from spending your first seven years under a beneficent regime of food rationing.[10] We all had fluffy (pre-conditioner days) mousy hair, cut you might have thought, to match that sported by the girls in the infants' reading primers. There were a lot of us (when did we ever stop hearing that we were The Bulge?), but all institutions of the state were there for all of us: sitting around determining the metric structure of 'Edward' was probably what was

---

9 Maureen Duffy, *That's How It Was* (1962), Virago, London, 1983, pp. viii–ix.

10 All rationing in Britain came to an end in July 1954; Ina Zweiniger-Bargielowska, *Austerity in Britain. Rationing, Controls and Consumption, 1939–1955*, Oxford University Press, Oxford 2002. 'I was in London at the time when meat was taken off rationing and price controls', wrote Auden – about 4 July 1954 it must have been, for that's when it did. 'Immediately, as in New York in 1946, the prices soared but within one week they had fallen to a slightly lower level than under rationing because, instinctively and without any organisation, housewives abstained from buying.' W. H. Auden, 'A Self-Policing People', *Prose Volume III. 1949–1955*, Edward Mendelson (ed.), Princeton University Press, Princeton NJ, 2008, pp. 596–608. Review of Geoffrey Gorer, *Exploring English Character*, orig. pub. *The Griffin*, December 1955.

expected of us, and certainly good for us, like school milk and medical inspections.[11]

A schooling in poetry and poetics appears to produce highly individual mental and emotional frameworks in its learners. There is nothing in the Latin language itself that accounts for the very different attitudes towards metre and line legible in the writing of Auden and Attridge, for example. That *I* find Attridge's theory of poetry more legible than Auden's is due to my own education, which – despite its being Latin-less – was closer in time to Attridge's and provided me with the same vocabulary for comprehension as did his. And we have no first-hand account from Auden of his actual experience of being taught to scan verse, Latin or English. These constraints of experience have made it very hard for me to understand Auden's pronouncements on poetics as anything but confusing. He has been brilliantly explained as a collector of poetic forms: he used 'ballad, cabaret song, canzone, Skeltonics, sonnet, villanelle, iambic or syllabic meter, and the rest' because they were interesting in themselves as well as useful to someone entranced by verbal contraptions – little language-machines – in much the same way as he was entranced by mine and farm machinery, pumps and gasometers. I love to read about his 'imperious idiosyncrasy', especially over the question of syllables and syllabic verse.[12] I can be persuaded that even though the syllable has little aural or emotional resonance for most ordinary speakers of a stress-timed language like English, he does somehow, always (Oh! But how?) make it work, as poetry.[13] Is this because, as a once-upon-a-time Latin learner, little syllabo-neural (I've invented the term. Just now) pathways were laid down in St Edmunds' boys brains? A neural pathway that made syllables perceptually salient to them, for the rest of their English-speaking and -reading days? I spent five days a week over seven years with the French language (the Dalton principle became extremely modified when it came to language teaching); by the sixth form I knew French as a syllable-timed language (with that vocabulary) and could scan its syllabic verse structure like billy-oh. Oh so easy! What with the French metric line being determined by the number of syllables it contains. And saying French poetry aloud I could and can

---

11 'The Bulge' ('Baby-boomers' in the US) was the term identifying the massive increase in births following the Second World War.

12 Sean O'Brien, 'Auden and Prosody', Sharpe (ed.), *W. H. Auden in Context*, pp. 359–368; 359–360. For a somewhat sour – enchanting because it *is* sour – account of Auden and the syllable, Bonnie Costello and Rachel Galvin, 'Introduction', Costello and Galvin (eds), *Auden at Work*, Palgrave Macmillan, Basingstoke, 2015, pp. 1–4.

13 O'Brien, 'Auden and Prosody', p. 363.

hear its organisation by syllables. I cannot do this with English verse that is formally arranged by syllables, as much of Auden's later work, including 'Homage to Clio', is. When I say 'Homage' out loud, my voice falls in pattern of stress determined by the deep structure of the language I am speaking. In his many discussions of prosody, Auden said that in English 'the criterion of emphasis [stress] can be (a) the length of the syllable (b) the degree of vocal accentuation, or (c) a mixture of both'. His praise for the syllabic poetry of Marianne Moore was accompanied by the warning that it was very hard 'to grasp at first hearing' because of its disregard for accents (stresses) and its 'rhyming on unaccented syllables', and he speculated, as we have seen, that the technique lay in her childhood, when she may have noticed that on the printed page metrically equivalent lines usually contained the same number of syllables; that she was never educated into recognising that they also contain the same number of metric feet.[14] He repeated these observations, often: 'a syllabic verse, like Miss Moore's, in which accents and feet are ignored and only the number of syllables count, is very difficult for the English ear to grasp'.[15]

If one wonders what this knowledge about syllabic verse is *for*, if you can't see syllables and can't hear them, and are going to English-it anyway (as they would have said in the eighteenth century), then what's with *the line* in Auden's theory of poetry? It is even more of a puzzle, though at first the propositions about *the line* appear simpler than those to do with metrical feet and syllables. He taught poetry – the analysis and appreciation of poetry – for a very long time, to schoolchildren in the 1930s and to university students and other adult learners for thirty years after that. 'In my first reading of a batch of poems,' he said in 1953, 'I look for one thing and one thing only, a few lines which are really lines and not arbitrary choppings. Poetry may be rhymed or unrhymed, metrically strict or free, but what distinguishes it as a medium from prose is that the words organise themselves into lines rather than into sentences.'[16] (These comments

---

14 W. H. Auden, 'Introduction to *Poets of the English Language*', (W. H. Auden and Norman Holmes Pearson (eds), 1950), in *Prose Volume III*, pp. 103–154; 107; 'Miss Marianne Moore, Bless Her!', *Prose Volume IV. 1956–1962*, Edward Mendelson (ed.), Princeton University Press, Princeton NJ, 2010, pp. 226–229 (review of Moore, *How To Be a Dragon*, in *Mid-Century*, Fall 1959); 'A Marianne Moore Reader', *Prose Volume IV*, pp. 392–395 (review of *A Marianne Moore Reader*, in *Mid-Century*, February 1962).

15 W. H. Auden, *The Dyer's Hand and Other Essays*, Faber and Faber, London, 1963, pp. 296–297.

16 W. H. Auden, 'Foreword to *Various Jangling Keys* [1953] by Edgar Boardus', *Prose Volume III*, pp. 344–347.

are as much about reading poetry manuscripts for publishers and literary prizes as they are about teaching.) Six years later he said the same: 'The first time I go through ... [a poem], I try to exclude from my mind any such considerations as originality, style, taste, or even sense, while I look for one thing only, *lines* of poetry. By this I mean a line which speaks for itself, which, as it were, no longer needs its author's help to exist.'[17] Much, much earlier than this, addressing children on the topic of reading and understanding poetry, he had also emphasised *the line*: 'Accents, long and short syllables, are really quite simple. You will always read a line of poetry right if you know its meaning.'[18]

What would we have made of it, we Rosa Bassett girls, 1958–1965, had we ever encountered such an opinion? Auden was writing for younger children than us, but still: to be told that our pursuit should be *meaning* before the effect on us of sound and rhythm? The line is not an arbitrary category of language, but it appears so arbitrarily flashed before us by Auden. You cannot know what a line (of print, or handwriting) *is* unless you can read, and most of the world, down the ages, has heard, recited, invented, thought ... poetry, without benefit of literacy. We, on the other hand (South London, 1962) had learned that the poetry we read *was* the benefit of our literacy: its encapsulation; the measure of what we had been taught and what we had achieved. The achievement was to know enough not to mind that you'd never know who betrayed whom in 'O What is that Sound', or whether or not it had anything to do with the Battle of Culloden. To have been told to focus on *the idea of a line*, in order to decipher meaning would have removed from us the labour (all that marking up; all that getting it by heart, all that *a–b, b–a–ing*) that had made it ours by the processes of our analysis. Not that we could have put it like that; and the remark *is* unfair, for Auden was the last poet to say that a poem he had written was his own, or that his thoughts about it were particularly valuable. I find it deeply admirable that once he'd written something, he didn't care much about it: that done is done, and gone is gone.[19] Or, as

17 W. H. Auden, 'Foreword to *Of the Festivity*, by William Dickey' (1959), *Prose Volume IV*, pp. 179–183.

18 Naomi Mitchison (ed.), *An Outline for Boys and Girls and Their Parents*, Victor Gollancz, London, 1932, pp. 853–868; 862. University of Warwick Modern Records Centre, MSS.318/4/7a: 'An outline for boys and girls' edited by Naomi Mitchison, (1932)'.

19 Auden, *The Dyer's Hand*, pp. 13–27; above, p. 60. And of course, there is a large literature on Auden's revision of his own work, his attempts to change the moral import of 'September 1939', in particular. But those were political, ethical, and theological

Edward Mendelson puts it when writing about Auden's earlier poems, he used language 'to cross an emptiness to a unity that cannot be found. [They] ... report from a condition of absence, speak to no one, and have no place to go.'[20] But there can be no condition of absence, and Auden tells us so: 'It is both the glory and the shame of poetry that its medium is not its private property, that a poet cannot invent his words and that words are products, not of nature, but of human society, which uses them for a thousand different purposes ...'[21]

The teacher 'Teaching Auden' who opens this chapter doesn't want to know 'what exactly Auden meant', any more than I do. And I don't believe that Debbie his student really wants to know either. She wants, as her teacher says, to 'dip her fingers/in the open piano and sing something like/"I don't want to talk about it".' He, the teacher, wants to dip his fingers into Auden's verse and play (with) ' "Consider this and in our time" ' with quotation marks, and 'the fact that it is later/than we think', without them. Auden's poetry is *in* the teacher and poet, as it is in his verse; and it will be in Debbie's head too, like it or not, because she has been made to say, or write, some of his words. And I have learned from this, Sansom's poem, something about Auden's poems, something about *the line*, that has bothered me so much. I have learned that the best way of taking it into your head and your heart is to make your voice pause, by the slightest beat, at the end of each of Sansom's lines, faltering at the end of the written line rather than hesitating at the end of a unit of meaning; this makes it beautiful and not at all like everyday speech. I couldn't do this unless I could read, unless I had *Everything You've Heard Is True* open in front of me. Lines (and their ends; line-poetry) like this cannot be recited from memory like Tennyson's 'Morte d'Arthur' (also in *The Poet's Tale*) can be recited. The line is a function of written language; of the words resting on the page.

It's sad that the (fictional) Debbie has to see her teacher alone, 'in a room that gets no bigger'. The ordinary glory of the English literature and language classes I describe here was that we all did it together. We (including the teacher) worked together on a text that was freely available to all, and literally *there*, on our desks; in this little hour of social democracy, we

---

attempts to change what he had earlier done, not aesthetic ones. However, at the beginning of *W. H. Auden. Selected by the Author*, Penguin, Harmondsworth, 1958, he does mention 'euphony and sense' as a reason for revising already published poems.

20 Edward Mendelson, *Early Auden* (1981), Faber and Faber, London, 1999, p. 26.
21 Auden, *Dyer's Hand*, p. 23.

worked on material freely provided by a beneficent local state, to *make* something. We could see and hear the product of our labour. We worked alone – homework, the tables set up in the hall – to write essays and analyses of novels, poetry, and plays, and stupidly elaborate accounts of a paragraph of *Mansfield Park*; but in the poetry lesson, something was made in common and together. In 'In Memory of Sigmund Freud' Auden turns the joint enterprise, the labour in common of the poetry lesson, into the individualistic work of history. 'He wasn't clever at all,' he wrote of Freud; 'he merely told/the unhappy Present to recite the Past/like a poetry lesson till sooner/or later it faltered at the line where/long ago the accusations had begun,/and suddenly knew by whom it had been judged ...'.[22]

Being in the democratic workshop of the English class was rather unlike being in a history class where, from 1958 to 1962, we were always alone. We took notes from the history teacher's discourse (a lecture, it was, really), and then went away and wrote answers to questions on the sylla-bus, or composed essays on a set topic. I cannot remember a discussion of anything in any history class from first to fourth form, and there were certainly no history textbooks in use, in class or for written assignments. Your arguments about the execution of Charles I, or what on earth the Seven Years' War was about, or why Captain Jenkins' ear mattered, were written artefacts constructed by solitary workers out of material delivered verbally by the teacher. Things changed dramatically for A-level, when we were taught by the brilliant apparition of Miss Radice, fresh from Oxford with a shiny new degree;[23] and before that, wonderfully, in the fifth form and O-level year (after the demise of the not very good history teacher) – by Mrs Naipaul (Yes! South London in the swim of things!) who was living three streets away from me, in the house where V. S. Naipaul had written *A House for Mr Biswas* (1961). We knew all of these things, except the title of the novel he was currently working on. One speech day in 1963 or 1964 he talked to the assembled school, and told us about a writer's life and what we should expect of it in the future: he measured out some days, he said, by putting a sheet of paper in the typewriter first thing in the morning, and taking it out, perfectly blank, at 5 pm. We *loved* that, though the face of the new headmistress sitting on the platform was a picture to see.[24] *Girls! I'm sure Mr Naipaul didn't mean that you should do that!*

22 W. H. Auden, 'In Memory of Sigmund Freud (d. Sept. 1939)', *Collected Shorter Poems, 1927–1957*, Faber and Faber, London, 1966, pp. 166–170.
23 Margaret Drabble, *A Summer Birdcage* (1963), Penguin, Harmondsworth, 1967, p. 7.
24 Patrick French, *The World Is What It Is. The Authorized Biography of V. S. Naipaul*,

Auden wasn't my first love as a poet. I had learned by heart most of
R. L. Stevenson's *A Child's Garden of Verses* by the time I was 9. There
was the perfection of its ending, which is the book's ending, the comfort-
ing knowledge that things will be over – you, the book, the world – in 'To
Any Reader':

As from the house your mother sees
You playing round the garden trees,
So you may see, if you will look
Through the windows of this book,
Another child, far, far away,
And in another garden, play.
But do not think you can at all,
By knocking on the window, call
That child to hear you. He intent
Is all on his play-business bent.
He does not hear; he will not look,
Nor yet be lured out of this book.
For, long ago, the truth to say,
He has grown up and gone away,
And it is but a child of air
That lingers in the garden there.

Depressive? Me? Just a child with a very strong death-drive. That's all.
Every time I walk by or cross a river, I say to myself: 'Dark brown is the
river/Golden is the sand/It flows along forever/With trees on either
hand', observing to myself, as I have done since 1956, that there are no
golden or sandy banks to rivers in this land, or in Scotland; nowadays
I speculate that maybe Stevenson meant to use 'strand', not 'sand', and
maybe the 'golden' comes from the lesser celandine (the gardener's curse),
or marsh marigolds … whatever. Or: that the gold and the sand come
from the demands of the metre and rhyme, not from somewhere outside
the poem, not from any lost land of childhood. It's those spaces, between
meanings, between the world and the words that purport to be about

Picador, London, 2008, pp. 189, 203–204. French's informant for the Naipauls'
Streatham Hill years (via the Naipaul Archive at Tulsa) says that Mrs Naipaul must
have found us 'rather … dispiriting', as 'most of the girls pitched their aspirations so
low'. University of Tulsa, McFarlin Library, Department of Special Collections and
University Archives: Collection 1993–003. Well. Not in my opinion. I think we were
stunningly aspirational.

the world, that you want poetry for; for its 'condition of absence', as Mendelson puts it.[25] But for me, Auden has been the most enduring poetic force. He must have been on a reading list when I was at university, for I have in my possession a Penguin *W. H. Auden. A Selection by the Author* (1958), in which I wrote my name and the address at which I was living in my second year at Sussex. It is old (obviously!) and used, but doesn't fall open at any particular page. I think it may have been bought for the 'Mass Communications and the Modern Novel' module I took in 1966–1967. This was not a significant encounter. The really significant one came in the summer of 1976 when, leaving the school I had been teaching in, a friend and colleague gave me a goodbye gift, Iona and Peter Opie's *The Classic Fairy Tales* (1974). On the first endpaper she had written out as inscription the last stanza of Auden's 'Schoolchildren':

> Yet the tyranny is so easy. An improper word
> scribbled on a fountain, is that all the rebellion?
> A storm of tears wept in a corner, are these
> the seeds of a new life?

We had often talked of these things. The teacher's easy tyranny over her small fiefdom, the way in which, out of love, the children dissented 'so little, so nearly content/with the dumb play of dogs, with licking and rushing'; we knew all about the bars of love ('the bars of love are so strong'), theirs and ours; that all the captivities – every single one of them – were there in the classroom. The storm of tears had been wept so many times, by us teachers in the lavatory, by the children in a corner, and now by me, who was weeping at what I so profoundly wanted to do, which was to leave. Some years later I tried to write about this time, which *went on* beyond 1976: 'I was a teacher. I never wanted to be, and now that I've stopped, I never will be again, but for several years it took my heart. I entered a place of darkness, a long tunnel of days: retreat from the world … a way of becoming Lucy Snowe's dormouse, rolled up in the prison-house, the schoolroom.'[26] When she gave me the book, my friend told me that Auden knew all about the prison house, for he had accompanied his

---

25 Robert Louis Stevenson, 'To Any Reader'; 'Where Go the Boats?', *A Child's Garden of Verses*, Longmans, Green and Co, London, 1885.

26 Carolyn Steedman, 'Prisonhouses', *Feminist Review*, 20 (1985), pp. 7–21. Lucy Snowe is the protagonist of Charlotte Brontë's *Villette* (1853). If you want to know what the prison house is *really like*, read *Villette*.

father, a school doctor or something like that, driving around Yorkshire doing medical inspections in his horse and cart. Auden had seen these things, she said, when he was a child. The county was the wrong one (but correct as to the poet's birthplace); and biographers do not say that little Wystan *didn't* accompany Dr Auden when he went out to inspect sanitary arrangements in Birmingham schools.

Then began my adult encounter with Auden, reading 'Schoolchildren' in conjunction with W. B. Yeats' 'Among Schoolchildren' (1928). Yeats also thinks of grief and rage as he, the poet, walks among the children in a classroom; his poem knows the terrible intimacies of that place as well as Auden's does. I read a lot of Yeats and Auden together in the 1980s, have found the only annotation in my 1966 *Auden ... Selected by the Author* collection to be 'In Memory of W. B. Yeats', with red ink around the lines that begin and end with 'For poetry makes nothing happen ... it survives,/ A way of happening, a mouth'. I didn't underline the beginning of the stanza:'You were silly like us', either in 1966 or later; but have recently been charmed to read Basil Boothby's memory of Auden's 'snorting laughter at Yeats', which had made him, Boothby, 'think of Boswell's hero, that other strange Englishman from the Midlands'.[27] I love Auden being called a strange cove from the Midlands; there is *so much to do* with thinking of Samuel Johnson and Wystan Auden as Midlands Boys. I am very grateful for the fertility of the connection.[28] However, Auden denied the identity of Midlander to a journalist in 1966: 'I more or less left the Midlands, where I was born, at seven, when I went to boarding school', he told her, forgetting the county of his birth.[29] But there were school holidays, and university vacations: apart from a year in Berlin, time in London, and holidays in parts of the UK littered with decayed agricultural machinery and abandoned mines, he was based in Solihull and Birmingham until he left for the US in 1939; he spent quite as much

27 Basil Boothby, 'An Unofficial Visitor', Stephen Spender (ed.), *W. H. Auden. A Tribute*, Weidenfeld and Nicholson, London, 1975, pp. 93–97; 97. Auden did not discuss Johnson (or himself) as a Midlander: W. H. Auden, 'Man before Myth. On James Clifford's *Young Sam Johnson*', Arthur Krystal (ed.), *A Company of Readers. Uncollected Writings of W. H. Auden, Jacques Barzun and Lionel Trilling*, Free Press, New York NY, 2001, pp. 9–13. For Sam, Midland Man, Donald Greene, *The Politics of Samuel Johnson* (1960), University of Georgia Press, Athens GA, 2009, pp. 22–34.

28 Carolyn Steedman, 'Wall in the Head' (Review of Lynsey Hanley, *Respectable*), *London Review of Books*, 38:15 (28 July 2016), pp. 29–30.

29 Polly Platt and W. H. Auden, 'Interview: W. H. Auden', *The American Scholar* 36:2 (1967), pp. 266–270; p. 269.

of his life in Birmingham and its environs as Johnson spent in Lichfield, Staffordshire. Auden may not have minded the connection between him and Johnson too much, for though he thought 'the eighteenth-century novels ... quite boring', and though he liked Defoe, and he wouldn't read Richardson or Fielding – 'Richardson is simply too long. Smollett is about the only eighteenth century novelist I can read'– he approved of Samuel Johnson, with qualifications:

> Who are the people one likes to read in the eighteenth century? Just Pope and Johnson, and Gay. I don't really like Swift at all. The *Directions for Servants* is good. The poetry is all right, but I find *Gulliver's Travels* one long bore. Oh, I can read the minor eighteenth century people with great pleasure. Akenside, Erasmus Darwin, Dyer. Oh yes, Young. Don't you think that's right though, about Johnson being the prince of middlebrows? But not so much his poetry. And those Johnsonians![30]

Auden was in the primary school classrooms I inhabited between 1974 and 1982 because of the long extracts I taped from Geoffrey Summerfield's *Junior Voices 1–4*, an inestimable series of poetry anthologies.[31] There were some Auden poems here – the usual: 'Musée des Beaux Arts', 'Epitaph on a Tyrant', 'Who's Who', and 'O What Is that Sound'. I could plug a child into the tape recorder, and bung on the headphones with the book in front of them. I thought, in an overweening way, of the pleasures of sitting in a lovely warm bath of words, prepared by me.[32] It was also a very fine form of babysitting, and often served to calm a child down after a storm of tears. I taped much Norse verse and other Norse curriculum material not only because teaching 'The Vikings' was required of me, but also because of the extraordinary fertility of the sources available, especially those of BBC Radio for Schools' *Stories and Rhymes*, which all through the summer of 1979 broadcast on the theme of 'The Northlands', 'The Whale Road', 'The Web of Fate', 'To Go A-Viking', and more.[33] I didn't have the

---

30 Alan Ansen, *The Table Talk of W. H. Auden* (1989), Nicholas Jenkins (ed.), Intro Richard Howard, Faber and Faber, London, 1990, p. 52.

31 Geoffrey Summerfield, *Junior Voices 1–4*, Penguin, Harmondsworth, 1970.

32 *A Language for Life. Report of the Committee of Enquiry appointed by the Secretary of State for Education and Science under the Chairmanship of Sir Alan Bullock FBA*, HMSO, London, 1975, had enjoined parents to bathe their children in language, and teachers, too, in the classroom. But I hated the word 'language' in the injunction, thinking it sounded far too much like 'sandwich' for comfort or seriousness.

33 BBC Radio for Schools, *Stories and Rhymes*, British Broadcasting Corporation, 1979.

children listen to the radio, but rather constructed an entire social history of the Scandinavian peoples and their colonisation of the British Isles, in an attempt to insert the domestic into a relentless story told on the radio about wolfbane, heartsbane, cold dark seas, and the clash of swords. (I also much preferred the sound of my own voice over the incantatory *de haut en bas* of the radio actors going on about great warriors given up to the salt estranging sea.) I did a lot with Viking homes and food, and appear to have been particularly keen to explore the economic base of Viking migration and colonisation; there was quite a lot devoted to the topic of 'Poor Land'. This was not because I was against kings and queens and great warriors called Gunar, at least not in the historical–mythological realm. A few years later I produced quite elaborate arguments about the value of the princess with long hair – combing, combing; waiting, waiting; the warrior – slashing, slashing, grieving, dying – for the grand, elemental emotions they embody; the capacity of such figures, drawn in a project book, to link historical knowledge with the child's own experience of the dark sea of adult emotion battering the little ships of their growing up.[34] I was very much influenced by Bruno Bettelheim's theory of the fairytale: traditional fairytales speak of darkness, abandonment, hurt, and death; they allow children to think about their own experience in abstract, remote, symbolic terms, and thus – what? Confront them? *Deal with them?* Just think about them perhaps, and feel a bit more in control.[35] Hot classroom, summer afternoon, hours to go before we can leave: I wanted them to listen to Philip Larkin's 'Days', third poem of the third *Voices*: I'd taped that – nothing to do with Vikings – with its reassurance that it will be over; this day will end too, like all other days, and the last day. In the meantime, 'Where can we live but days?'[36]

On another poetry card to accompany a tape was 'This is how the Vikings/believed the world began':

Ere were ages
when naught was;

34 Carolyn Steedman, 'Battlegrounds. History and primary schools', *History Workshop Journal*, 17 (1984), pp. 102–112; 'Living historically now?', *Arena*, 97 (1991), pp. 48–64.
35 Bruno Bettelheim, *The Uses of Enchantment. The Meaning and Importance of Fairytales* (1976), Penguin, London, 1991.
36 Geoffrey Summerfield (ed.), *Voices: An Anthology of Poetry and Pictures. The Third Book*, Penguin, Harmondsworth, 1968, No. 3; Philip Larkin, 'Days', *The Witsun Weddings*, Faber and Faber, London, 1964; István D. Rácz, 'The experience of reading and writing poetry. Auden and Philip Larkin', *Hungarian Journal of English and American Studies*, 14:1 (2008), pp. 95–103.

neither sand nor sea
nor the cool waves.
Earth was not known
Nor the high heavens;

gaping the gap
and no grass grew.

I *was* enthusiastic about the dark, and not only from reading Auden's 'In
Memory of Sigmund Freud': 'he would have us remember most of all/to
be enthusiastic over the night,/not only for the sense of wonder/it alone
has to offer, but also//because it needs our love ...'.[37]

Anyway, the upshot of all of this was that for a class project on the
Vikings, I taped verse from in and out of the BBC's *Stories and Rhymes*
and prepared reading cards with cheery messages like 'This is what the
Viking thought the end of the world would be like':

Brothers will battle
and be each other's bane;
all the bonds
of kin will be broken.
Cruel that age
and fierce for folk:
axe-age, sword-age;

shields will be split;

Wind-age, wolf-age,
when the world founders.

Where *did* I get that from? I must have done my preparation in a nearby
university library, though nothing I read then told me about the alliterative form of Norse poetry, the marked caesura in the middle of a line, the
line itself divided into two half-lines, the half-lines known as verses – as
the *a-verse* and the *b-verse* – or the 'hemistich'; I learned nothing about the
Norse and Anglo-Saxon forms, or their syllabic and alliterative devices
which shape much of Auden's later poetry.[38] I had nothing then to tell
me *why* the Norse poetry I taped and copied out as reading material was

37 'In Memory of Sigmund Freud', *Collected Shorter Poems*, pp. 166–170.
38 Auden, *Table Talk*, p. 70, where he mentions Nora Kershaw's *Anglo-Saxon and Norse
   Poems*, Cambridge University Press, Cambridge, 1922, as particularly informative.

so haunting. And – so they said – so very much liked by the children. Perhaps, though, the deep structure of Germanic and Nordic verse forms entered my teacherly unconscious: I find from my own records that I laid out reading material and information sheets (and taped them, the recorded voice to be followed whilst reading) in some odd obeisance to line-ending and rhythm. Or maybe I was copying the layout of many reading primers, where the line equates to a unit of meaning:

> ... they tried to grow crops
> and keep animals.

> But the land was very rocky and very stony.
> Sometimes there was only
> a thin layer of earth over the rocks.

> The land was difficult to dig
> and difficult to plough.
> The crops that grew were very poor ...

> Sometimes there was not enough
> for everyone to eat.

> The Vikings went on raids
> to steal food and farm animals.

> Sometimes they liked the places
> where they raided.
> The land was good
> and the coast was not rocky.

> Sometimes they settled down
> In a place where they raided ... .

Do you see what I mean about *the line*? No poetic principle organises these lines – not stress, not metre, not syllables. Each line is – simply – a clause; a unit of thought.

I had all the means for my pursuit of Yeats and Auden in collected editions of their poetry. My volume of Auden's *Collected Shorter Poems* (1966) is very well worn, and falls open at many places. I do not know when I acquired it, but have kept in it for many years a newspaper cutting of a piece from the *Independent on Sunday* by Neal Ascherson ('From Moscow, on the brink of Great Nowheria'), dated late 1991. In it he quotes from Auden's 'The Fall of Rome (for Cyril Connolly)', telling his readers that it is known as 'The Journalists' Poem' to many in the profession. He quoted three verses; the second, he said, is about the suspicions journalists entertain about their own detachment: 'Unendowed with wealth or pity,/ Little birds with scarlet legs,/Sitting on their speckled eggs,/Eye each flu-infected city'. Ascherson wrote of the way in which poems return to you, again and again, always finding a setting in a new place, the place where you are: he himself, at that moment, was writing from a 'vastness … which has the misfortune to have become nameless. The family of giants who were once the Soviet Union have forgotten their surname and lost their identity cards.' I date my obsession with 'Homage to Clio' from 1991, when Ascherson quoted Auden.[39] A year later, Francis Fukuyama was to declare *The End of History and the Last Man*: the certainties of world conflict, the ceaseless struggle between ideologies that had held history in place as a narrative had ended with the fall of the Soviet Empire witnessed by Ascherson. Western liberal democracy had triumphed over Soviet communism: 'What we may be witnessing is not just the end of the Cold War, or the passing of a particular period of post-war history,' he wrote, 'but the end of history as such: that is, the end point of mankind's ideological evolution and the universalization of Western liberal democracy as the final form of human government.'[40]

From 1991 onwards, I used lines from 'Homage to Clio' as an epigraph many, many times. I was a historian again now, teaching no one Auden, or poetry; forcing no one to listen to poetry. I attempted historiographical readings of the poem.[41] I used it in an attempt to understand what kind of thing history was: a Western thing (or at least, the history I had in mind was a Western thing), a form of thinking, a form of writing: a way of telling.[42] But mostly I just chucked in a few lines at the beginning of what I was writing ('You had nothing to say and did not, one could see,/ Observe where you were, Muse of the unique/Historical fact') because they were beautiful and paradoxical. I did not want to know what *Auden*

39 Neal Ascherson, 'From Moscow, on the Brink of Greater Nowheria', *Independent on Sunday*, 15 December 1991, p. 25; W. H Auden 'The Fall of Rome' (1940), *Collected Shorter Poems*, pp. 218–219.

40 Francis Fukuyama, *The End of History and the Last Man*, Free Press, New York NY, 1992. The book was an expanded version of an article written in 1989: Francis Fukuyama, 'The End of History?', *The National Interest*, 16 (1989), pp. 3–18.

41 Carolyn Steedman, 'La Théorie qui n'en est pas une, or, Why Clio doesn't care', *History and Theory*, Beiheft 31 (1992), pp. 33–50.

42 Carolyn Steedman, 'About ends. On how the end is different from an ending', *History of the Human Sciences*, 9:4 (1996), pp. 99–114.

really meant; I wanted to know what the poem told me about *the thing I did*: history; about history's quiddity, its beingness in the world, its social and cultural function; *what it is*. I should have taken more notice than I did of Clio's silence. I certainly did bang on about the silence, but only because I found it charming that the grand pretensions of History to know all and say all were undermined by a dull girl who had nothing to say. I loved the irony of a History that did not speak and did not write and had no pretence to an opinion, about anything. I should have listened more to the silence. 'What mattered most to ... [Auden] in history was that which he could not describe because it was inaccessibly silent and unnameable', said Mendelson in 1999. 'In 1955 he wrote "Homage to Clio" a poem in which he gave that silence a personal voice and a proper name.' 1999 was too late for she who had already littered her work with quotations from it, in order to voice, over and over again, the poetic paradox of history. Nevertheless, the (historical) information provided by Mendelson, that 'the silence at the core of things was a noisily fashionable subject in the period', was very welcome.

6

Caesura: a worker reads history and a historian writes poetry

(*caesura*: *a break or sense pause, usually near the middle of a verse, marked in scansion by a double line: //*)

Who built the seven gates of Thebes?

The books are filled with names of kings.
Was it the kings who hauled the craggy blocks of stone?
... Every ten years a great man,
Who paid the piper?
... So many questions.[1]

Students of history are routinely advised about the uses of literature – not at length; but they *are* advised – as in John Tosh's guide to historical theory and method, *The Pursuit of History*. When treating literature as historical source material, he says, it is obvious that 'novels and plays cannot ... be treated as factual reports ... Nor, needless to say, do historical novels – or Shakespeare's history plays for that matter – carry any authority as historical statements about the periods to which they refer.'[2]

---

1 Bertolt Brecht, 'Fragen eines lesenden Arbeiters' (1935), trans. H. R. Hays, 'A Worker Reads History', *Selected Poems*, Grove Press, New York NY, 1947; *Compact Poets: Bertolt Brecht*, Denys Thompson (ed.), trans. H. R. Hays, Chatto and Windus, London, 1972. The poem is also translated as 'Questions From a Worker Who Reads', Bertolt Brecht, *Poems 1913–1956*, trans. M. Hamburger, Methuen, New York NY and London, 1976. There are minor variations in wording, spacing and the size of indentation between the two translations. The second translation ends with a double space between the last two lines: 'So many reports.//So many questions'. www.marxists.org/subject/art/literature/brecht/ (accessed 16 October 2017).

2 John Tosh, *The Pursuit of History. Aims, Methods and New Directions in the Study of Modern History* (1984), 5th edn, Pearson, Harlow, 2010, p. 98.

Nevertheless, creative literature is valuable for the insight it offers into a writer's intellectual and social context; the popularity of authors in the past and the longevity of their work may be because they successfully articulated 'the values and preoccupations of literary contemporaries'. This knowledge is deemed useful to the young or aspiring historian. There is no account of *form* or *style* as constituting historical evidence in these recommendations, though in the early days of the journal *Literature and History*, inaugurated to explore the relationship between the two disciplines, there were valiant attempts explore 'literature' as a type of documentary evidence. Sometimes these explorations could only tell the story of the historical profession growing suspicious of literature during the nineteenth century. Literary scholars pointed yet again to historians' sad incapacities: we almost always respond to 'a formal discourse which expresses directly or indirectly the values, ideology, or socio-psychological tensions of a given society'; we are 'unable to come to grips with the past as it is embodied in the ... language and structure ... of a piece of literature'; we restrict ourselves to the 'content or surface meaning' of whatever text we use. In short, historians are not very good at using the evidence of form and style.[3]

All of this was a long time ago of course (though in the same country). Search BBIH (Bibliography of British and Irish History On-line) and you will find many historians using poetry, fiction, hybrid-forms, letters, diaries, and autobiography as source material, in inventive and exhilarating ways. Not much attention to the forms of poetry though. The novel is an extraordinarily difficult – impossible – form to recruit for evidence, yet it is widely employed. When the epistolary form of the seventeenth and eighteenth centuries is used, there is perceived to be no problem at all, for the very structure dictated by the exchange of (fictional) letters, is both form and meaning itself. But the nineteenth-century novel is shaped to such a sagging and joyously disjointed scaffolding, that you could spend a lifetime and ten volumes accounting for the tone, rhythm, and organisation of just one of them, if you were to adduce *structure* to historical argument. All of this was the 1980s, when the exhortations of literary theorists (literary historians? literary-historical theorists?) like Raymond Williams and Franco Moretti were heeded. Williams eschewed the term 'literature', what with its high-cultural connotations of aesthetic value and discrimination; he also eschewed 'genre' in favour of 'form'. 'Writing

3 Antoinette Blum, 'The uses of literature in nineteenth and twentieth-century British historiography', *Literature & History*, 11:2 (1985) pp. 176–203.

in society' was his preferred term for 'literature', because it allows us to read, not so much *between* the lines of poetry, novels, and other written forms, but to read the lines *as* social acts of performance and communication.[4] In 1975, he read the metre, rhythm, and the larger structures of pastoral and labouring-class poetry as political and cultural text (though to be sure, most of his examples for his thinking on the transition to industrial modernity in Britain were taken from novels).[5] Franco Moretti has been enduringly insightful – wonderful – in giving answers to questions about why different forms (epic, novel, crime fiction, *bildungsroman*, 'Childhood', murder mystery ...) have been chosen by writers and desired by readers in different historical epochs: he inaugurated a sociology of literary forms.[6]

When Antoinette Blum wrote her dispiriting account of historians' inabilities with literature in 1985, she did have some kind words for Marxist historians. Christopher Hill was 'the first historian we have encountered to have attempted a thorough analysis of a literary text from a historical perspective'. There was 'some subtlety in his approach', she said, for in *Puritanism and Revolution* (1958) he did *not* use Samuel Richardson's *Clarissa* (1748) to acquire historical knowledge of his themes and topics, but rather employed its *structure* to 'acquire factual knowledge that cannot be gathered from more conventional sources'.[7] She praised E. P. Thompson as well, for his vision of literature as a symbolic expression of the values through which a class is both defined and defines itself; as a source for understanding *mentalité* in the past. She mentions Thompson's analysis of images and imagery in *Pilgrim's Progress* and many nineteenth-century novels; she wishes he had brought his analysis of *charivari* to bear on a the actual analysis of an actual literary text; she concludes that 'Thompson displays a keen sensitivity to literature, but unfortunately does not carry

---

4 Raymond Williams, *Writing in Society*, Verso, London, 1983. Also *Marxism and Literature*, Oxford University Press, Oxford, 1977, pp. 145–150, 180–192; *Keywords. A Vocabulary of Culture and Society* (1976), Fontana, London, 1983, entries for 'Culture' and 'Literature'.

5 Raymond Williams, *The Country and the City* (1973), Paladin, St Albans, 1975.

6 Moretti's enormous project is measured out by what came between *Signs Taken for Wonders. Essays in the Sociology of Literary Forms* (1983) and *The Bourgeois. Between History and Literature. Brooklyn* (2013) taking in *The Way of the World. The Bildungsroman in European Culture* (1987), *The Modern Epic. The World-System from Goethe to García Márquez* (1996), and *The Novel* (2006) along the way. His form of historical choice has to be seen as the novel: 'Style, Inc.: Reflections on seven thousand titles (British novels, 1740–1850)', *Critical Inquiry*, 36:1 (2009), pp. 134–158.

7 Blum, 'Uses of Literature', p. 186.

his perceptiveness into detailed analysis of ... literary text'.[8] She did not mention poetry – as a form, or otherwise – in her discussion of historians who did better than others with literature. She does not mention 'poetry' as literature at all. But the case of Edward Thompson and poetry is an interesting one, for even when writing, much later on and extensively and exhilaratingly *about* a poet in his posthumous book about William Blake (*Witness to the Beast*), he does not, on my reading, once discuss Blake's use of verse form, metrical structure, or stress patterns, though he had a lot to say about Blake's imagery, as Blum noted of his work from twenty years before.[9] Blum's was a doubly interesting observation about the opaqueness of the poetic for Thompson, for (though she was not to know this) it has recently been claimed that his primary identity was as poet, not as historian, at least up until 1960.[10] He certainly wrote poetry and published a few of his poems in his lifetime; there are 125 in the *Collected Poems* (1999). Sometimes he 'published' by the device of insertion in his prose writing, as in 'I will cite one crude line of a poem which I find among my own notes of 1956. The poem is "In Praise of Hangmen" ...'[11] His editor has not much to say about his poems *as poetry*: 'the poet, the man, and the style are one'; 'an aesthetics in which poetry is the best ... the sanest, plainest and most affirmative speech of a free citizen ...'; and finally, perhaps a bit desperately: 'there are surely many echoes of T. S. Eliot'.[12]

As is well known, Thompson was *very* hard on Auden. He had taught Auden with a joyous heart at a weekend school for adult learners in 1950; in 1960 he produced a detailed reading of 'Spain', declaring that the excisions and alteration that Auden made in the 1950s compromised not only this

8 Blum, 'Uses of Literature', pp. 187–188.
9 E. P. Thompson, *Witness Against the Beast. William Blake and the Moral Law*, Cambridge University Press, Cambridge, 1993.
10 Scott Hamilton, 'Between Zhdanov and Bloomsbury. The poetry and poetics of E. P. Thompson', *Thesis Eleven*, 95 (2008), pp. 95–112; *The Crisis of Theory. E.P. Thompson, the New Left and Postwar British Politics*, Manchester University Press, Manchester, 2011, pp. 49–52; Terry Eagleton, 'The poetry of E. P. Thompson', *Literature and History*, 5:2 (1979), pp. 142–145; Roland Boer, 'Apocalyptic and apocalypticism in the poetry of E. P. Thompson', *Spaces of Utopia: An Electronic Journal*, 7 (2009), pp. 34–53, http://ler.letras.up.pt/uploads/ficheiros/7488.pdf (accessed 16 October 2017); E. P. Thompson, *Collected Poems*, Fred Inglis (ed.), Bloodaxe, Hexham, 1999.
11 E. P. Thompson, 'An Open Letter to Lesek Kolakowski', *The Poverty of Theory and Other Essays*, Merlin, London, 1976, pp. 93–192; 131. 'Hangman', *Collected Poems*, No. 75.
12 Thompson, *Collected Poems*, pp. 22–23.

one poem, but 'Auden's whole achievement as a poet'.[13] For Thompson, Auden's earlier achievement (whatever it was) had not been an achievement *in verse*; the point he made was not a point of poetics; for Thompson, Auden's poem *was* the play of ideas. But Luke Spencer has pointed out the influences of Auden on Thompson, and his conscious use of an 'audenesque' voice.[14] In his analysis of Thompson's writing, the historian/poet's 'voice' incorporates Auden's tone, mood, and style; but poetic structure and metre are not part of it, no matter where it comes from.

What might we Rosa Bassett girls have made of Thompson's 'Chemical Works, Part II, The Girls' if, in some other universe, we had been presented with it between 1962 and 1965? Parallel and impossible world: designated one of the 'Early Poems: 1940–1947' in the *Collected Poems*, it was not published until 1999. We *could have* mapped it on to Auden's *Night Mail* (1936) which in auditory memory, at least, was one of the heart-beats of a post-War childhood. A short film produced at the GPO Film Unit with Auden's verse as voice commentary, *Night Mail* was relentlessly anthologised. I have always known it – heard on the Home Service? Read at primary school? Learned by heart at primary school? Perhaps the film itself was shown at Saturday Morning Pictures at the Astoria, Streatham Hill: I had *always already seen it*, at least since 1955.[15] We *could* have recognised the rhythm of Auden's verse commentary to 'Night Mail', in Thompson's 'Chemical Works': 'There's Jean in Woolworth's, Sally at the mill,/Trams and cosmetics, the conquest of skill/In setting your hair or minding a machine/'. We might have enjoyed the 16-year-old worker's longing for 'a tall man at the gates, O, with cream in his hair/And a tight two-seater'. We would not have noticed the (unconscious?) joke of the tight two-seater, and anyway, men's bums were not yet erogenous zones, at least not in Streatham Hill; indeed, you'd never seen one, as men almost universally wore loosely hanging high-waisted bags, more like skirts than

13 Hamilton, *Crisis of Theory*, p. 66; Thompson, 'Outside the Whale' (1960), *Poverty of Theory*, pp. 1–33; Luke Spencer, 'The Uses of Literature: Thompson as Writer, Reader and Critic', Roger Fieldhouse and Richard Taylor (eds), *E. P. Thompson and English Radicalism*, Manchester University Press, Manchester, 2013, pp. 96–117; 42–43.
14 Spencer, 'Uses of Literature', pp. 105, 108.
15 Humphrey Carpenter, *W. H. Auden. A Biography*, Faber and Faber, London, 2010, pp. 181–183; Jennifer R. Doctor, 'The Wonders of Industrial Britain, *Coal Face*, *Night Mail* and the British Documentary Film Movement', Christa Brüstle and Guido Heldt (eds), *Music as a Bridge. Musikalische Beziehungen zwischen England und Deutschland 1920–1950*, Georg Olms, Hildesheim, 2005; Scott Anthony and James Mansell, *The Projection of Britain. A History of the GPO Film Unit*, Palgrave Macmillan, Basingstoke, 2011.

trousers. We *could have* found the idea of cream in the seducer's hair irresistibly funny. *What sort of cream? Single or double? Whipped? Top of the milk? Why not 'Brylcreem in his hair', Miss R____? Then at least it would scan.* [16] Could we have thought that the break in the iambic feet was … deliberate?

> Forget about the orange-blossom, never mind the priest
> But give me a chance. They've done for my skin
> But my figure's still OK. O give me at least
> An ordinary fellow with average pay

Here was all we had escaped, though we did not know it; nor that we, too, were set to meet the Last Seducer, despite all our knowledge of prosody:

> O grant me only this, O grant me, heaven,
> Not any unpossible love, no, no unlikely bliss
> But something somehow to get me out of this
> Before the final suitor with his dark proposal comes. [17]

I am more puzzled by the timing of the poem now than I could have possibly been in 1963. With its partner, 'Chemical Works I. The Machines', 'The Girls' is a study of working-class love and labour, which appears, to my historian's tedious little mind, to be a product of the Thompsons' Halifax years (1948–1965). They moved to the city late in 1948 after Edward Thompson had been appointed staff tutor in the Leeds University Extra-Mural Department. [18] The poem is dated no later than 1947, and of course there is no reason for Thompson's *not* visiting a chemical works before the move to Halifax, though the region was particularly crowded with them, supplying the fulling and dying parts of the woollen manufacture. Industrial psychology, which gave access to the mental life of the workers, flourished in the post-War year; Thompson's poem could be read as a contribution to a developing field. [19] 'Chemical Works I' attempts

16 In the sixth form, our history and English teachers both had names beginning with 'R'. They were not one and the same, as p. 136 above might suggest.

17 Thompson, *Collected Poems*, pp. 50–51.

18 Dorothy Thompson, *The Dignity of Chartism. Essays by Dorothy Thompson*, Stephen Roberts (ed.), Verso, London, 2013; Spencer, 'Uses of Literature', pp. 26–27.

19 Brooke Emma Whitelaw, 'Industry and the Interior Life. Industrial "Experts" and the Mental World of Workers in Twentieth Century Britain', PhD, University of Warwick, 2009.

a psychology of labour; it is a song of what happens to men and women's
souls and psyches drowned in a relentless barrage of noise:

> murderers
> > henchmen
> > > hooligans
> > > > howlings
> menacing and pummellings locking interlocking
> hubbub of driving belts grouse of gearing
> pelting
> > cheering
> > > Knocking at nerves
> beyond endurance ...
> > > Pauses
> Settles respectably into the subconscious ...

The voice moves between the stranger from outside walking the floor,
stunned in his observation and – very briefly and only perhaps – the interior
voice of the worker. Thompson did not attempt occupying the heads of the
male workers as he did with The Girls at the chemical plant who, after all,
have other things on their mind and, maybe, space for a poet. Working-class
women were more legible to the poet than were the men, as was the case with
a short story of 1965, which also emerged from Thompson's Halifax period.[20]
We sixth-form girls wouldn't much have minded this assumption about the
transparency of women, for *all of them*, all writers, from Shakespeare to the
most up-to-date poet on our reading lists, assumed to know women's minds
better than they did themselves. *Men* were the impenetrable, dark heart of all
texts. We may, however (and remember, we're dealing with the never-hap-
pened here), have been pretty offended at another Thompson poem of the
same era, 'New Fashions', which just can't help equating the way in which
during the War years the grander of the Paris fashion houses 'designed the
panties, zips and perms/ To re-invade the women's world', with women's
own complicity in – what? Occupation? Capitalism? Fascism? The verse
interpellates its readers (which we were not) as idiot girls:

20 E. P. Thompson, 'The rising cost of righteousness', *Views*, 7 (1965), pp. 76–79; Carolyn
Steedman, 'A weekend with Elektra', *Literature and History*, 6:1 (1997), pp. 17–42. See
also Thompson, *The Poverty of Theory*, pp. 342–344 where the whole of the Althusserian
project is challenged by the woman factory worker (invented by Thompson) who flings
her copy of – what? *For Marx? Reading Capital?* – at the foreman, yells '"I'm not a bloody
THING!"' and calls The Girls out on strike.

Modom must suit this style of hair –
'La Libération du Caen';
This hat, à petites gouttes de sang.

The Mort à Pucheau brassière ...

Any road up, or whatever which way, our critical response to Thompson's poetry would have been as naive and uninformed as that of the Reverend Old Rector, at whom Elizabeth Hands had such a good laugh at in 1789, in her satiric commentary on her own bourgeois readers; at their want of a workable poetics, and their naive critical principles: 'That "Amnon"you can't call it poetry neither,/There's no flights of fancy, nor imagery either;/You may style it prosaic, blank verse at the best;/Some pointed reflections, indeed, are expressed;/The narrative lines are exceedingly poor'.[21]

But a historian who was also a poet is a rare bird, at least in modern times. Could being a poet make you as competent a reader of plebeian poetry as Brecht's worker is of history? Was this the case? In the 1980s, Thompson edited Stephen Duck's *The Thresher's Labour* (1730) and Mary Collier's *The Woman's Labour* (1739). The poems had appeared together in print for the first time only a few years before Thompson's edition, even though Mary Collier had intended hers as a sardonic response to Duck, 'in Answer to his late Poem', 250 years before.[22] It was a 'so-what?' and more to Duck's account of village field hands who were called on at particularly intense times of the agricultural year. Collier's riposte details the female labourer's double burden: the children fed and dressed, the beds made, the clothes mended, the dinner cooked against the thresher's return, for she has left the field early to get the bacon and dumplings on the fire – all of this as well as the reaping and haymaking she undertakes for cash. Thompson recognised that her poem was 'sharper' than Duck's; he was highly sensible of the sheer hard work Collier described, said she showed no resentment of the farmer who called on the village women's labour, and further that, 'one suspects[,] that she rather enjoys the sociable weeks of harvest, despite the heavy work'.[23]

Among worker writers, poetical servants were the most fashionable in

21 See above, p. 46.
22 Stephen Duck and Mary Collier, *The Thresher's Labour by Stephen Duck, The Woman's Labour by Mary Collier. Two Eighteenth-Century Poems*, intro. E. P. Thompson, Merlin Press, London, 1989; *The Thresher's Labour and The Woman's Labour*, Augustan Reprint Society, N. 230, Andrews Clark, Memorial Library, Los Angeles CA, 1985.
23 *Thresher's Labour*, pp. x–xii.

the second half of the eighteenth century, as has been observed; but Duck was an agricultural labourer, not a domestic worker. We have seen some elite voices opining that 'natural poets' like he were splendid additions to a household, able to fawn on their employers in verse. They often had in mind the Thresher-Poet when they made disparaging remarks like this.[24] But Stephen Duck was rather better thought of by his fellow workers than by contemporary poets and modern critics. He had the reputation of being a bit of a wag, with a nice line in the edgy hilarity of class relations.[25] And Thompson has recently been taken to task for his dismissal of Duck's achievements: 'From the moment that he left the thresher's barn it was downhill all the way', said he.[26] William Christmas challenges Thompson's 'narrative of deracination and corrupted authenticity'. He points out that in Thompson's 1980s view, Duck was only 'authentic' – could only *be* 'authentic' – when he wrote about his labour experience. Thompson, it is now said, believed that experience of toil should be valued above all the other things Duck did and thought in his life. This perspective came from 'a post-Romantic definition of what counts as true poetry' – poetry as the authentic expression of lived experience. Christmas does all of this – performs his critique – by placing Duck in a transhistorical context of working-class intellectualism; by reading him *as* a working-class intellectual.[27] He is thus able to discuss Duck's considerable achievements of mind as well as the poetic forms he used – and his thinking about metre.[28] You would not learn from Thompson's much earlier discussion that both Duck and Collier used perfectly regular iambic ('heroick') couplets to structure their poems, in 1730 and 1739; he was thus unable to provide insight into what this form might mean, or might have meant to the poets themselves.

Thompson had more and more interesting things to say about Collier's work because *she* said more about her labour, detailing as she did the travails of a woman with two jobs as well as a house to look after; much of Collier's poem is taken up detailing her charring work. Early on a winter's morning, the village women rise by prior arrangement ('our Work

---

24 Betty Rizzo, 'The patron as poet maker. The politics of benefaction', *Studies in Eighteenth-Century Culture*, 20 (1990), pp. 241–242.

25 Peter Cunningham, *Peter Cunningham's New Jest Book; or, Modern High Life Below Stairs*, Funny Joe, London, 1785, p. 43.

26 *Thresher's Labour*, intro. p. vii.

27 William Christmas, 'From threshing Corn, he turns to thresh his brains". Stephen Duck as Labouring Class Intellectual', Aruna Krishnamurthy (ed.), *The Working-Class Intellectual in Nineteenth-Century Britain*, Ashgate, Farnham, 2009, pp. 25–48.

28 Christmas, ' "From threshing Corn" ', pp. 38–39.

appointed') and go up to the Big House for the wash. It takes all day. The mistress appears at noon, *perhaps* with a mug of ale for the women, but mainly to nag about being gentle with ruffles and lace, sparing with fire and soap, and to complain about items lost in the last wash. The women work until dusk, sometimes having to 'piece the Summer's day with Candle-light'; by now 'Blood runs trickling down/Our wrists and fingers'. Then, as the women sit in the farmhouse back kitchen rubbing away at the pewter (all part of the job of charring), more 'Trumpery' is brought in 'to make complete our Slavery', as Thompson points out. He noted these details because Collier's language 'implies questions as to the humanity of class divisions, and as to the rationality of luxuries which depend upon the degrading labour of others'. Collier's poem is preferable to Duck's because *she* was 'writing irreverently about the oppressions and sensibilities of class'.[29]

Thompson's comparison between Duck and Collier was inflected by his having noted class feelings in kitchens, washhouses, and brew houses, around things and between women. Duck *does* inscribe the capitalist wage relationship in his poem – knows that each sheaf of corn represents the farmer's greater or lesser profit for the year; yet at the same time, as Thompson points out, his view of the labour process – from cutting, through threshing, though storing, to harvest feast – is framed by the master's perspective. The farmer, rent-day looming, inaugurates the harvest and he rejoices in his profit with a feast for the workers. The master's language becomes the threshers' consciousness: 'These words, or words like these, disclose his Mind:/So dry the Corn was carried from the Fields,/ So easily 'twill thresh, so well 'twill yield./Sure large day's Work I may well hope for now;/Come, strip, and try, let's see what you can do'. Nothing marks a boundary between the master's words and the thresher's thoughts. This is a far cry from Collier's brisk assessment of the wage relationship, made in her own voice: 'And after all our Toil and Labour past,/ Sixpence or Eightpence pays us off at last'. She not only mentions cash payment, but also suggests that it isn't enough. That's why Thompson liked Collier more than Duck (as do I; as do I). But for all Thompson's analysis, she might as well have written ... oh, a letter (threatening, or informative), or a little tract, or an essay, not a poem.[30]

29 *Thresher's Labour*, intro. p. xii–xiii.

30 Workers, writing, poetry, and threatening letters are discussed in Carolyn Steedman, 'Threatening letters. E. E. Dodd, E. P. Thompson, and the making of "The Crime of Anonymity"', *History Workshop Journal*, 82 (2016), pp. 50–82.

More recently, questions *have* been asked about the poetic form these worker-poets chose and the class condescension of not asking about it in the first place. Peggy Thompson (no relation) reminds us that even Raymond Williams claimed it 'easy to feel the strain of this labourer's voice as it adapts, slowly, to the available models in verse'.[31] But surely, '[i]f scholars of the couplet can find tension between Dryden's intentions and his poetic form, and between Pope's state of mind and his form, what kind of conflict will we discern between two laborers' most subversive poems and a verse form overwhelmingly favored by the educated elite and allegedly inseparable from "an authoritative and fixed universe"?' she asks, in 'Duck, Collier, and the ideology of verse forms'. Is a verse form ideological? 'What evidence can we find, in short, for or against an ideology of the heroic couplet?' In answer, Peggy Thompson details the 'interrogation, condescension, and ridicule' that both Collier and Duck endured at the very idea that they might write poetry. This, she says wedged a painful 'dissonance between Duck's and Collier's identities as poets and their identities as laborers and, in Collier's case, as a woman'. Her conclusions are that whilst we must remain sceptical about an essential meaning or ideology of form, forms – Duck's and Collier's heroick couplets – can support 'powerful tendencies and patterns'. The meanings of a verse form must be found in actual practice, as in Collier's more consistent success in sustaining the heroick. Duck implies his unhappiness at the socio-economic regime he inhabits at the same time as he confirms it. Yet, in his better moments, she says, 'Duck uses the couplet to convey rather than betray his class-based anguish, to unmask the master's order as a cheat, and to contrast it to the endless sameness of his own life'.

Neither Collier nor Duck appeared to think, any more than Elizabeth Hands thought, that 'heroick' verse was not for them, or an irreducibly elite form.[32] Poetry offers historical evidence, says Roy Harris, that in pre-literate cultures there was awareness of subtle patterns of rhythm, rhyme, and assonance among poets and their audiences.[33] A charwoman's, a field labourer's, and a domestic servant's poetry offers evidence of a related kind: that in a culture in transition to mass literacy, as was the one they inhabited; in a partially literate society in which the oral and the literate had been so long entangled that they could not be divided from each

31 Raymond Williams, *The Country and the City*, Chatto, London, 1973, p. 88.
32 Peggy Thompson, 'Duck, Collier, and the ideology of verse forms', *Studies in English Literature, 1500–1900*, 44:3 (2004), pp. 505–523.
33 Roy Harris, *Rethinking Writing*, Athlone, London, 2000, pp. 210–211.

other – choice of form, its resonances with individual histories and ways of learning to read, allowed these poets and their audiences (or at least this part of an audience, here, now, writing these words) briefly to hear said, and see, *how it was* in Warwickshire in 1789 (Hands), in Hampshire in 1739 (Collier), and in Wiltshire in 1730 (Duck).

Thompson was criticised by some for his inabilities in reading poetry (no one criticised his writing of it, for few can have laid eyes on it before 1999).[34] John Goode thought that he – perhaps – found it difficult to understand what kind of thing literature was, its beingness in the word; its quiddity. And Goode was 'disappointed' at Thompson's hierarchy of the disciplines, his assertion of the virtues of History – that Queen of the Humanities – over all others.[35] Perhaps for Thompson, poetry was merely a way of saying what had already been said, over and over again. 'It is not always clear ... what the passages of poetry in the "Open Letter" and "The Poverty of Theory" achieve', muses Scott Hamilton in 'The Poetry and Poetics of E. P. Thompson'; when Thompson selected lines other than his own, they 'seem merely to embroider meaning already present in the prose passage preceding them'.[36] This is salutary warning to those of us with a tendency to drop a line of Auden's verse into any space that seems big enough to hold it; but it does not solve the mystery of why a historian *wanted* poetry: to *have it*, I think, by writing or quoting it, but blind to the labours of any worker but himself. But then, reading poetry is *hard*, and takes something out of you. Reading history is so much easier, as Brecht's Worker knew, because it raises blindingly obvious questions, which you can labour to answer. Poetry has no answers; it's what Auden said it was: its own self, its own self-containment, clattering away like the threshing machine that was soon to obviate the labour of men like Duck, and its rewards. Which observation must really make us contemplate Auden's preference for broken, rusted, and abandoned agricultural machinery, over anything that actually *worked*, and made someone a living. But in fact, the threshing machine would not affect the labour supplied by men like Stephen Duck or their earnings yet awhile;

---

34 The whole of 'Powers and Names' (*Collected Poems*, pp. 105–125), appeared in the *London Review of Books*, 8:1 (23 January 1986), pp. 9–10. I cannot find any response to it, critical or otherwise.

35 John Goode, 'Thompson and "the Significance of Literature"', Harvey J. Kaye and Keith McClelland (eds), *E. P. Thompson. Critical Perspectives*, Polity, Cambridge, 1990, pp. 183–203; Spencer, 'Thompson as Writer', p. 102.

36 Hamilton, *The Crisis of Theory*, pp. 227–244.

it was an early nineteenth-century problem.[37] And all this waving around of a falsely obtained poetic licence at border control between the land of history and the realm of poesie is what gives any historian invoking a poet a very bad name.

---

37 For an indication of the enormous literature on the technologising of the agricultural sector, N. E. Fox, 'The spread of the threshing machine in central southern England', *Agricultural History Review*, 26 (1978), pp. 26–28. Also E. J. Hobsbawm and George Rudé, 'The Problem of the Threshing Machine', *Captain Swing*, Lawrence and Wishart, London, 1969, pp. 359–365.

PART II

Historiography

7

Makers of History

Serious historians care for coins and weapons,
Not those re-iterations of one self-importance
By whom they date them,
Knowing that clerks could soon compose a model
As manly as any of whom schoolmasters tell
Their yawning pupils,

With might-be maps of might-have-been campaigns,
Showing in colour the obediences
Before and after,
Quotes from four-letter pep-talks to the troops
And polysyllabic reasons to a Senate
For breaking treaties.

Simple to add how Greatness, incognito,
Admired plain-spoken comment on itself
By Honest John,
And simpler still the phobia, the perversion,
Such curiosa as tease humanistic
Unpolitical palates.

How justly legend melts them into one
Composite demi-god, prodigious worker,
Deflecting rivers,
Walling in cities with his two bare hands,
The burly slave of ritual and a martyr
To Numerology.

With twelve twin brothers, three wives, seven sons,
Five weeks a year he puts on petticoats,

Stung mortally
During a nine-day tussle with King Scorpion,
Dies in the thirteenth months, becomes immortal
As a constellation.

Clio loves those who bred them better horses,
Found answers to their questions, made their things,
Even those fulsome
Bards they boarded: but those mere commanders,
Like boys in pimple-time, like girls at awkward ages,
What did they do but wish?

W. H. Auden, 'Makers of History', 1955.

Well they do: historians do care about coins and weapons among many
other things, though we might prefer to say: care about the economies and
conflicts of the past that coins and canons give access to, even though the
modern social historian (professional, card-carrying, academic historian)
is more interested in the living of everyday lives under particular economic
regimes, or in the female munitions workers – for example – who made
the weaponry of conflict during the First World War ('Young Alexander
conquered India./He alone?/Caesar beat the Gauls./Was there not even
a cook in his army?'). Nor can the first stanzas of 'Makers of History' be
read as an ironic or even sarcastic comment on the monovalent obsessions
of amateur collectors, and Auden may not have thought badly of them
anyway, for his father was a member of the British Numismatic Society,
founded in 1903 for the study of all forms of coinage, tokens, and banknotes
of the British Isles and its colonies. George Auden contributed an article
on antiquities, including coins, found in York, to its journal in 1907, the
year of his third son's birth; Auden knew his father to be a serious man.[1]
Moreover, one serious historian of 1958 thought 'Makers of History' *to be*
a comment on historical method, thanked the *London Magazine* in which
it originally appeared for permission to quote its first lines in which, he
said, Auden argued that as far as ancient history was concerned, coins
were a better form of evidence than ancient texts. Unfortunately however,

---

1 G. A. Auden, 'A leaden cross bearing a styca impression and other antiquities found in
   York', *Journal and Proceedings of the British Numismatic Society*, 4 (1907), pp. 235–237.
   Dr Auden had also read much about coins when translating Friedrich Rathgen's *The
   Preservation of Antiquities. A Handbook for Curators*, trans. George A. Auden, M. A.,
   M. D. (Cantab.) and Harold A. Auden, M. Sc. (Vict.), D. Sc. (Tübingen), Cambridge
   University Press, Cambridge, 1905. Harold Auden was his brother.

added the historian, coins were just as unreliable as the literary tradition, albeit in a different way.[2]

I find it very difficult to determine levels of seriousness here, including my own. On the one hand, it is solace to find a historian, sixty years since, treating one of Auden's history-poems as a straightforward historiographical statement – an assertion of historical theory and method – for this is the way I have spent my last thirty years with Auden's poetry. And it's always a pleasure to find a working historian saying *anything at all* about these questions, for the modern academic variety is generally historiographically mute, preferring, in a dogged, artisnal kind of way to *just get on with it* and leave questions of meaning in what they produce to the philosophers of history. In the 1990s, 'robustly practical practising historians' who skirted round theoretical discussion of their own work occasioned a furore of irritation in the other disciplines, and among other kinds of historian.[3] How serious have I been, in taking Auden's historiographical statements at face value? How serious was he, when he wrote of 'serious historians'? I believe (though I may misremember) that I have always read the first five verses of 'Makers of History' as a kind of comic turn on the history of armies and fleets and great men purveyed at school, the inexorable way in which, through tears of boredom on long summer afternoons and double history, the salacious little details of a king's sexual proclivities doled out to wake you up a bit, a hundred years' war melts into myth in the pages of a child's notebook. How acute it was of Auden, in describing such lessons (and he *may* have been doing that as well as anything else), to note how the deep structure of the historical narrative allows teachers and writers to add the little coda about great kings and caesars wandering their realms in disguise to seek the views of the common people. A 14-year-old might briefly recall through her yawning the Story of King Alfred and the Cakes from primary school. Now, having read

---

2 Michael Grant, *Roman History from Coins. Some Uses of the Imperial Coinages to the Historian*, Cambridge University Press, Cambridge, 1958, pp. 10, 16–17; 'Makers of History', *London Magazine*, 2:9 (September 1955). It was reprinted as one of the *Best Poems of 1955, Borestone Poetry Awards for 1956. A Compilation of Original Poetry, published in the Magazines of the English Speaking World in 1955*, Stanford University Press, Stanford CA, 1957.

3 Keith Jenkins, *Re-thinking History* (1991). With a new preface and conversation with the author by Alun Munslow, Routledge, London, 2003, p. 3 and passim. For some of the arguments and objections, Alexander Macfie, 'Review of Keith Jenkins Retrospective' (review no. 1266), www.history.ac.uk/reviews/review/1266 (accessed 16 October 2017).

Charles Cochrane's *Christianity and Classical Culture* (1940) – because Auden said that *he* read it so often – I see here the inclusionary tactics of the later Roman emperors, in allowing at least the facsimile of opinion to those obedient after conquest, across all their vast empire.[4] Coins were a minor though important part of Cochrane's story – and Auden certainly thought Cochrane a serious historian.[5] Now, the poet moves swiftly across a contemporary historiographical terrain: a history of historical production in the twentieth century. This kind of history learned at school and from other media of instruction is the sort that 'makes the past easier to deal with by punctuating the record with great crises and great persons'. It is history made (written) to be remembered, and it is, as Frank Kermode noted, 'in some measure shared by all, learned and simple alike'.[6]

In the year before Auden composed 'Makers', Arnold Toynbee described his own formation as a historian in a turn-of-the century, upper-class English childhood. He evoked the way in which 'history' was pressed on the minds of many children like him by the war memorials, street names, the fields and farmsteads they saw around them.[7] The child also knew about the inaugurations of presidents and the coronations of kings and queens: 'this automatic social milieu in which a human being grows up, and in which he continues to live and work as an adult, is the earliest and most widely radiative of the inspirations of potential historians', he said.[8] Toynbee also provided the outlines of history-as-myth: the way in which the details of campaigns and battles and treaties shade into legends every child knows, or become a fairystory of some battle or other with King Scorpion.[9]

4 Charles Norris Cochrane, *Christianity and Classical Culture. A Study of Thought and Action from Augustus to Augustine*, Clarendon Press, Oxford, 1940. 'I have read this book many times, and my conviction of its importance to the understanding not only of the epoch with which it is concerned, but also of our own, has increased with each rereading.' W. H. Auden, 'Augustus to Augustine', *Prose Volume II. 1939–1948*, Edward Mendelson (ed.), Princeton University Press, Princeton NJ, 2002, pp. 226–231, orig. review of Charles Norris Cochrane, *Christianity and Classical Culture, New Republic*, 25 September 1944.

5 Cochrane, *Christianity*, p. 143.

6 Frank Kermode, *Poetry, Narrative, History*, Basil Blackwell, Oxford, 1990, p. 50.

7 Arnold J. Toynbee, *A Study of History*, Vol. 10 (*The Inspirations of Historians*), Oxford University Press, London, 1954, pp. 3–24.

8 Toynbee, *Study of History*, pp. 5–6.

9 There were two kings or chieftains named Scorpion in Upper Egypt during the Protodynastic Period. They were mentioned by Toynbee in Volume 9 of *The Study of History*, also published in 1954.

Toynbee's *A Study of History* was published in ten volumes between 1934 and 1954, with subsequent volumes of maps and a *Reconsiderations* published in 1958 and 1961. The last was a response to his many critics, who were vituperative and condescending in the UK, and rather more receptive in the US.[10] The hypothesis of Toynbee's massive work was that civilisations follow a pattern of origin, growth, breakdown, and disintegration. There are parallel processes at work in this pattern of rise and fall across all cultures; stages of development can be discerned; when civilisations 'fall', their cultural, religious, and social forms may shape the 'new' civilisation that then arises.[11] Auden read Toynbee, maybe even the 1954 volumes, though the abridgement of volumes I–VI made in 1946 must also be a contender for his attention.[12] Edward Mendelson says that during the 1950s he was still excited by 'the scale and scope' of Toynbee's *Study*, though had longstanding doubts about claims that it had 'tamed' history into a system.[13] It is said that in *The Age of Anxiety* (1947) Auden

---

10 Alexander Hutton, '"A belated return for Christ"? The reception of Arnold J. Toynbee's *A Study of History* in a British context, 1934–1961', *European Review of History – Revue européenne d'histoire*, 21:3 (2014), pp. 405–424, for critical reactions to Toynbee as 'a veritable intellectual history of the midcentury'. Michael Lang, 'Globalization and global history in Toynbee', *Journal of World History*, 22:4 (2011), pp. 747–783. For other comments on the coming of global history, David Christian, 'The return of universal history', *History and Theory*, 49 (2010), pp. 691–716; Matthew Hilton and Rana Mitter, 'Transnationalism and Contemporary Global History', *Past and Present, Supplement*, [ns], 8, Oxford University Press, Oxford, 2013.

11 'It is a careful, voluminous, intelligent endeavor to find a recurrent pattern enabling a better understanding of the whole range of human history. Its focus of interest lies in civilizations, of which events and personalities are regarded as expressions or indices. Six volumes have appeared; about nine more are projected'. A. L. Krober, '*A Study of History*. Arnold J. Toynbee (Vols 1–6. London, 1934–39)', *American Anthropologist*, 45:2 (1943), pp. 294–299.

12 The abridgement was a wild success in the US. Toynbee appeared on the cover of *Time* magazine in March 1947. For sales figures on both sides of the Atlantic, Hutton, '"A belated return"', p. 408. Humphrey Carpenter says that Auden's taste in reading during the Ischian years was for 'large-scale historical works': Dean Stanley's *History of the Eastern Church*, Toynbee's *The Study of History*, and 'a three-volume account of the later Roman Empire'. Humphrey Carpenter, *W. H. Auden. A Biography*, Faber and Faber, London (1981, 1983), 2010, p. 364. Arthur Penrhyn Stanley, *Lectures on the History of the Eastern Church. With an Introduction on the Study of Ecclesiastical History*, John Murray, London, 1861, does not appear to have been reissued after 1907. There was an Everyman edition in 1910. Toynbee referenced Stanley but in regard to his edition of Thomas Arnold's letters, not his *Lectures*. Carpenter does not say why Auden was reading it. Carpenter, *W. H. Auden*, p. 364; 362–388 for 'Ischia'.

13 Edward Mendelson, *Later Auden*, Faber and Faber, London, 1999, pp. 245, 294; also

used the names of historical clans and kinship groups mentioned by Toynbee across the six volumes by then published – his Qaraquorams and Quaromanlics and Krimchaks, with their inchoate cries announcing the Dance of Death – in order to evoke the irrationalism underlying Western civilisation.[14] The names are also funny to any English-speaking child dozing in a classroom: funny to anyone trying to drag one jot of interest out of a history lesson; almost as funny as the petticoated man tussling with King Scorpion.

Frank Kermode said that although the edges between historical myth and historical record are often blurred, most people can distinguish between the two: most of us, quite spontaneously it appears, accept concepts 'such as the decisive battle, the world-historical-individual'. We need mnemonics, he said, 'if we are to hold in our minds a past we can contemplate or use'. The mnemonics come from a common education (in its broadest sense) in a particular society, and bear in this way some relationship to Jorma Kalela's later conceptualisation of history-in-society.[15] But though Toynbee was eloquent on the social and educational factors that had made him a historian, he did not believe that he was describing a universal social and psychological process, because 'for at least three-quarters of the men and women alive on Earth in A. D. 1952, History was virtually non-existent ... [they were] still living in a social milieu that spoke to them, not of History, but of Nature'. It had been the same through the aeons he had described in his ten volumes: 'for the Peasantry since the dawn of Civilization, History, as they had experienced it so far, had been a tale that had signified nothing, in spite of being "full of sound and fury"'.[16] He gave thanks that he had been born in an era when a 'higher religion' clad in its traditional form made '"going to church" (or mosque or synagogue or Hindu or Buddhist temple) ... an automatic education in History'. Being in such a place, looking, and listening, a child was carried 'far afield in Time and Space'. Toynbee gave particular thanks that he had been born 'early enough in the Western Civilization's day to have been taken to church every Sunday', and to have received his formal education at a school and a university in which the study of Greek and Latin were the foundation of the curriculum. The Church of England

Susannah Young-ah Gottlieb, 'Auden in History', Tony Sharpe (ed.), *W. H. Auden in Context*, Cambridge University Press, Cambridge, 2013, pp. 181–192.
14 Hutton, '"A belated return"', p. 415; W. H. Auden, *Collected Poems*, Faber and Faber, London, 1991, p. 518; Mendelson, *Later Auden*, p. 245.
15 See above, p. 20.
16 Toynbee, *Study*, Vol. 10, pp. 6–7.

and its liturgy gave the child the verbal and visual resources to become a historian: 'the apostles, prophets and martyr cited collectively in the *Te Deum* ... the cross, the sword wheel, or other means of death through which the martyr had attained his crown ... these pictures ... told the spectator at a glance, what they stood for'. He was even more grateful *not* to have been taken to worship in the extreme plainness of a 'tabernacle of a Protestant sect'.[17] Later, after childhood, the sights and sounds of the Anglican liturgy would make the great pattern of history plain – or at least provide a partial vision of 'God seen through the diverse fractions of His "inconceivably mighty works"'; then might be seen 'in History a vision of God's creation on the move, from God its source towards God its goal'.[18]

Under the auspices of the new global history, Toynbee's reputation has been revived, though the 'historical angle of vision' by which he saw 'human souls ... raised by the gift of the Spirit, moving, through a fateful exercise of their spiritual freedom, either towards their Creator, or away from Him', is somewhat downplayed by academic historians. Over the question of faith, particularly the Christian faith, Toynbee remains the 'embarrassing uncle at a house party' that he was in the later twentieth century. It is suggested that one of the reasons for our embarrassment is that practitioners today 'are not at all certain what is signified by the concept of "religion."'.[19] But by 1955, Toynbee's insistence on Christ as the culmination of the historical process had receded. He now proposed a global syncretisation of world religions as the historian's working method and philosophy. 'I have not returned to the religious outlook in which I was brought up', he told his readers. 'I was brought up to believe that Christianity was a unique revelation of the whole truth. I have now come to believe that all the historic religions and philosophies are partial revelations of the truth in one or other of its aspects.' But the problem for historians of the modern era has been the remaining Western, and ultimately Christian, inflection of both his earlier and later positions.[20]

We do not know if Auden read the later pronouncements of Toynbee during the Ischian early summer in which he composed 'Makers of History'. We really do not know what kind of history he read, apart from the frequently noted 'big' historians of the 1930s and 1940: de

17 Toynbee, *Study*, Vol. 10, p. 5.
18 Toynbee, *Study*, Vol. 10, pp. 1, 3.
19 Toynbee, *Study*, Vol. 10, p. 2; Lang, 'Globalization', pp. 747, 783.
20 Arnold Toynbee, 'A study of history. What I am trying to do', *International Affairs* 31:1 (1955), pp. 1–4.

Rougement, Cochrane, Rosenstock-Huessy. Mendelson's discussion of their – and Toynbee's – influence on Auden in the 1940s and 1950s is to do with their historiographical or philosophical meaning for Auden rather than their meaning as works of social, cultural or political history.[21] But there are scattered references to what would now be understood as social history.[22] In 1936, Auden had positively loved R. H. Mottram's *Portrait of an Unknown Victorian*. He knew it was 'self-love' that made readers 'peculiarly interested in the lives of the obscure of another historical period'; but he loved it all the same. 'The historian tells us of the monuments of the exalted, the average laws of behaviour, the civic triumphs and catastrophes, but pays little attention to our first question, which is: "What should I have done if I'd been there?" We want to know what kind of job we should have done, how much money we should have made, what we should have eaten, what hobbies we should have taken up, what sort of things would have irritated or amused us.'[23] Mendelson claims that he found the same kind of history of everyday life in Toynbee; that Toynbee provided 'an authoritative sense of geopolitical scale with almost lyrical passages of praise for humane, domestically scaled societies where one could feel at home'. He argues that Auden adopted Toynbee's double focus on large and small scales in 'In Praise of Limestone' (1948) and that he refused, as Toynbee refused, 'to be overawed by the larger while admitting its power to crush the smaller'.[24] But I don't see it myself, in Toynbee. The home life of his Krimchaks and Timurids was not very much like that of the Norwich bank clerk about whom Mottram Jnr had written. Auden enjoyed the English ordinariness of Mottram Snr in the same way that he enjoyed the Reverend Sydney Smith. We all love the Reverend Smith for his self-satiric horror at being exiled in the provinces, and as far away from the Metropolis as the North Riding! We love his complaining, wittily and self-deprecatingly, about being inured in

21 Mendelson, *Later Auden*, pp. 306–407.
22 For the genealogy of social history, Miles Taylor, 'The beginnings of modern British social history', *History Workshop Journal*, 43 (1997), pp. 155–176; Carolyn Steedman, 'Social History Comes to Warwick', Miles Taylor (ed.), *The Utopian Universities*, Oxford University Press, Oxford, forthcoming.
23 W. H. Auden, 'The Average Man', *Prose Volume I. 1926–1938*, Edward Mendelson (ed.), Faber and Faber, London, 1996, pp. 159–160; review of R. H. Mottram, *Portrait of an Unknown Victorian*, Robert Hale, London, 1936, orig. *New Statesman and Nation*, November 1936.
24 Mendelson, *Later Auden*, p. 294.

a North Yorkshire rectory 'twelve miles from a lemon', in 1809.[25] But it is not clear that Auden read the academic social history produced in the 1930s and 1940s, or any works from its post-War efflorescence, shortly to be described. He just didn't 'click' with G. D. H. Coles' history of the labouring classes, he said. Yet in 1936 he had told Lord Byron about the dissonance between the bright new modernity of the South, and Up North, where lay the desolate battlefields of class conflict –

> in the north it simply isn't true.
> To those who live in Warrington or Wigan
> It's not a white lie, it's a whacking big 'un
>
> There on the old historic battlefield,
>   The cold ferocity of human wills,
> The scars of struggle are as yet unhealed;
>   Slattern the tenements on sombre hills
> And gaunt in valleys the square-windowed mills.[26]

– a view as likely to have come from contemporary social surveys and social anthropology as social history. And yet 'Makers' is a fragment of modern social history.

The poem opens with a comedy, or pastiche, of history teaching, which may have been recognisable to many middle- and upper-class schoolchildren, educated in the UK between 1880 and 1940. It is a kind of satire on 'big history', 'great-man history', and grand, large-scale theories of history, and what happens to them in a classroom. And then, without announcement, without enjambment, Clio arrives, silently mirroring the first verse. She does not merely *care* for those within her purview; she *loves* them. She loves the workers, the menials, the labourers, the clerks who, also in a silence like hers, served Roman Senators and Egyptian Kings; the agricultural workers who bred the fleeter horses for their armies, the contracted writers who penned the pep-talks to the troops; all the workers who made, with the labour of their bodies, all the things with which the elite furnished their many mansions. The house-poet too (like Stephen Duck in his day) is a worker, a maker, just churning out the verse

25 W. H. Auden, 'Portrait of a Whig', *Prose Volume III. 1949–1955*, Edward Mendelson (ed.), Princeton University Press, Princeton NJ, 2008, pp. 273–285; orig. *English Miscellany* (1952).

26 For Auden's response to Cole, above, p. 120. Auden, 'Letter to Lord Byron', *Collected Poems*, p. 88.

celebrating victory in exchange for bread and board; a piper unpaid in cash. Here are the makers who *did* built the Seven Towers of Thebes; who conquered India. Clio may enter stage right, but she will leave stage left. Social history enters here, and I do not for the life of me know where she comes from. Nevertheless, the Clio of 'Makers' (*Clio I*, for there is another, to be discussed in the next chapter) is the perfect – and beautiful – encapsulation of the development of social history as a research practice and historical theory in Britain, between about 1930 and 1970. The origins of social history were understood to be multiple; its origins and progress were frequently discussed in the post-War period. 'The "Cinderella of English historical studies" only a few years earlier, it was by the mid-1960s the "in" thing, the queen of the ball; today, more than thirty years later, it is still often regarded as the main innovation of the period', wrote Jim Obelkevich in 2000.[27] The *Annales* school in France has been described as one point of origin, as has the labour history undertaken in university economic history departments, from the 1930s onwards: the kind Auden couldn't be doing with. An Oxbridge axis of social history has been described, in which Sir Lewis Namier's concerns with the psychological as well as economic factors underpinning social structure and social distinction ('what lay beneath', in Miles Taylor's nice depiction) influenced the work of historians far beyond the golden triangle, from the 1930s through to the 1950s.[28] David Feldman and Jon Laurence have described a baggy, protean concept – 'social history' – which for fifty years now has stood in, more or less, for 'everyday life'.[29] After 'everyday life' had been conceptualised as a field of study within the social sciences in general, says Ben Highmore, historians came to use the term in order 'to side with the dominated against those that would dominate … to invoke … those practices and lives that have traditionally been left out of historical accounts, swept aside by the onslaught of events instigated by elites'. The term 'everyday' became a 'shorthand for voices from "below"'.[30]

Most mid-century commentators on the genesis of social history indicated the importance of G. H. Trevelyan's *English Social History: A*

27 Jim, Obelkevich, 'New developments in history in the 1950s and 1960s', *Contemporary British History*, 4:4 (2000), pp. 125–142.

28 Taylor, 'The beginnings of modern British social history', pp. 155–156.

29 David Feldman and Jon Laurence 'Introduction: Structures and Transformations in British Historiography', Feldman and Laurence (eds), *Structures and Transformations in Modern British History*, Cambridge University Press, Cambridge, 2011.

30 Ben Highmore (ed.), *The Everyday Life Reader*, Routledge, London and New York NY, 2002, p. 1.

Survey of Six Centuries: Chaucer to Queen Victoria (1942, 1944) for popular understandings of what kind of history it was; others reminded readers that J. R. Green's *Short History of the English People* (1874) had under-pinned many early twentieth-century histories for children, teaching not 'of English Kings or English Conquests, but of the English People'.[31] Most small children educated in the state system during the first half of the twentieth century learned more about the furnishings of a Viking long-house, the way food was cooked by medieval people, and clothes made 'through the ages' than they did about war and high politics.[32] When Victor Neuberg discussed Edward Thompson's phrase 'history from below' as indicative of a new way of doing history, he actually reviewed eight works of social history for young children, including the emblematic *Life in England* (1968–1970) series, 'a vivid, panoramic view of how men lived'.[33] Thompson's *The Making of the English Working Class* (1963) is the marker of social history's birth for many of these commentators. His work was understood to be symbolic of a movement to challenge the elite and conservative focus of the historical discipline, by recuperating the experiences of those who had been excluded from conventional histories.[34]

Social history for children was targeted at parents as well as schools: in 1962 *Look and Learn* magazine promised 'Art, Literature, Science, People, World, and Social History – These and More are Presented in a Vivid, Authoritative Way'.[35] An elaborate advertisement for vacuum cleaners in 1950 evoked the concepts of everyday life and (the not yet

31 J. R. Green, *A Short History of the English People*, Macmillan, London, 1874, p. v.
32 Jenny Keating, 'Ideas and Advice about History Teaching 1900–1950s', History in Education Project, Institute of Historical Research, University of London April 2011; David Cannadine, Jenny Keating, and Nicola Sheldon, *The Right Kind of History. Teaching the Past in Twentieth-Century England*, Palgrave Macmillan, Basingstoke, 2011. The twentieth-century project of elementary and primary school history teaching is described as imperialist at best and racist at worst, but that did not prevent 7- to 11-year-olds drawing more farthingales and porringers than they did maps of imperialist conquest. Carolyn Steedman, 'Battlegrounds: History in primary schools', *History Workshop Journal*, 17:1 (1984), pp. 102–112.
33 Victor E. Neuberg, '… History from Below', *Times Literary Supplement*, 22 June 1968, p. 20; E. P. Thompson, 'History from Below', *Times Literary Supplement*, 7 April 1966.
34 This story has been so frequently told by historians for students of history that it is useful to see the emblematic *Making* from the perspective of another discipline: Richard Fardon, Olivia Harris, Trevor H. J. Marchand, Mark Nuttall, Cris Shore, Veronica Strang, and Richard A. Wilson, *The Sage Handbook of Social Anthropology*, Volume 1, Sage, London, 2012, p. 122.
35 A British weekly educational magazine for children published by Fleetway Publications Ltd, 1962–1982.

named) women's history by use of the term 'social history'.[36] 'Social history' spelled selling power for publishers who, throughout the 1950s and 1960s, advertised a wide variety of books with descriptors like: 'the piano as the "centre" for writing the social history of the last 300 years' (November 1955); 'a comment on social history' (March 1959); 'a fresco of social history' (March 1960); 'a delectable social history' (March 1961); 'a lighthearted slice of social history' (1963). There were social histories of hunting, of opera, of button collecting; readers were perceived to like it, and to know what kind of read was promised by the term; reviewers used 'social history' to bestow praise, as in 'a delectable social history'. 'Social History in Song' was broadcast on the Home Service (BBC Radio 4) in February 1968. Material objects, events, and groups of people 'had' a social history; social history *was* clothes, the changing shape of babies' bonnets, or the railways; Asa Briggs' first volume of the history of broadcasting 'is often social history', said one reviewer, reassuringly (1961). It was frequently 'our' social history, a national and personal possession. '*The Nottingham Captain*, a bitter account by Mr Arnold Wesker' was reviewed as 'a sorry episode in English social history' in 1962.[37] Readers of the broadsheets and the literary magazines had been prepared for understanding E. P. Thompson's 1966 proclamation that 'social history lives in the language of the commons', reported in *The Times* under the title 'History's Widening Frontiers'; to understand even (or perhaps especially) the freeborn English men and women who haunt the phrase.[38]

36 'The Missing Volume. Hoover Limited', display advertisement, *The Times*, 20 January 1950: 'One of the most important volumes in the Social History of England has – so far as our knowledge goes – yet to be written. It will deal with the Twentieth Century Housewife and the way her life has been transformed by the introduction of scientific labour-saving devices.'

37 'Music for Wesker Text', *The Times* 21 November 1961. The play had been performed by Centre 42 at the Trades Union Festival held in Hayes and Southall. www. arnoldwesker.com/plays.asp?workID=45 (accessed 16 October 2017). This 'Moral for Narrator, Voices and Orchestra' told the story of Jerry Brandreth, Oliver the Spy, and the Nottinghamshire Luddites, also to be told by Thompson in *The Making of the English Working Class*, Gollancz, London, 1963, pp. 711–733, a year later. Also Paul Long, *Only in the Common People. The Aesthetics of Class in Post-War Britain*, Cambridge Scholars, Newcastle, 2008, pp. 197–198.

38 *The Times*, 9 April 1966: 'Mr E. P. Thompson, of Warwick declares that Labour History now feels confident enough to move onwards from the base which Cole and his successors secured.' E. P. Thompson, 'The free-born Englishman', *New Left Review*, 1:15 (May–June 1962); E. P. Thompson, *The Making of the English Working Class*, Part 1, Chapter 4; Cal Winslow (ed.), *E. P. Thompson and the Making of the New Left. Essays Polemics*, Monthly Review Press, New York NY, 2014, pp. 290–306.

The vocabulary of 'social history' was thus made familiar to parents and children of the post-War era. 'Important Decision in Social History' was a subhead announcing the Robbins Report, 'as important as any in the social history of this country'.[39]

The academic origins of social history were related to these common understandings, sometimes in edgy and distancing ways. At the University of Warwick, Edward Thompson did the same work of distancing in one of the many committee papers he wrote in the long run-up to the formal establishment of the Warwick Centre for the Study of Social History: 'The very considerable advances in recent years in this country in the social studies and in sociology has been accompanied only by a piecemeal and disconnected advance in the study of social history. In some places "social history" has scarcely advanced beyond the status of belles lettres …', he wrote in 1965.[40] The task of persuasion was not only to distance university social history from the middlebrow version, but also from the kind 'advanced within the aegis of departments of economic history'. Progress there had been impressive, but 'distorted by the tendency to limit study to quantitative or institutional problems'.[41] Ten years later (Thompson long departed from Warwick), the new director of the Centre for Social History acknowledged the turn from labour history to social history and the special relationship between the two; but academic social history had still not lost the accent of its somewhat philistine origins out in the wider society: social historians must guard against 'a return to the "everyday", the residual and the tedious'.[42] Labour history remained the more respectable endeavour well into the 1970s.[43] Developments in the paradigm of social history after 1955, when 'Makers of History'

---

39 *The Times*, 20 November 1963. For a detailed account of social history remade as 'the history of everyday life' in the first half of the twentieth century, see Laura Carter, 'The Quennells and the "History of Everyday Life" in England, c. 1918–69', *History Workshop Journal*, 81 (2016), pp. 106–134.

40 'Until recently, much social history was a matter of gifted impressionism, while the most disciplined work was advanced within departments of economic history', University of Warwick, Modern Record Centre (MRC), UWA/FICHE/REF/R1724, 9 March 1966, 'For the meeting of the Planning and Executive Committee 9 March 1966', Agendum 3C.

41 'A Centre for the Study of Social History at the University of Warwick. The Scope of the Subject', MRC UWA/ FICHE/REF/R1724 9 July 1965.

42 Royden Harrison, 'From labour history to social history', *History*, 60 (1975), pp. 236–239.

43 Alexander Hutton, ' "Culture and Society" in Conceptions of the Industrial Revolution in Britain, 1930–1965', PhD thesis, University of Cambridge, 2014, pp. 131–173, 207–310, passim.

was written, are not, of course, of much use in determining whence came the Muse of Social History in Auden's poem. The US experience of the new social history *would* be useful were there evidence that Auden read, or was sent for review, any of its works; but retrospectives of the US social history movement locate its arrival in the 1960s, long after the 'Makers' was written.[44]

'Love' – the way Auden's *Clio I* loves the workers – is so apt; it is so perfect; it denotes Clio in her aspect as social history over the last European and Atlantic World 200 years. Under the title 'Mixed Feelings', Frank Kermode discussed the ways in which being *in love* with the working class became a quest for many bourgeois writers of the 1930s. He almost, but not quite, includes Auden in the work of transference that made the proletariat 'beautiful, doomed, unlucky' and because doomed, irresistible to many a bourgeois sympathiser, whether a member of the Communist Party of Great Britain or not. Kermode suggests that many writers transferred their 'sense of what it meant to be outcast, alienated, *maudit*, to the worker'.[45] The poor were also people 'apart', 'possessors of a strange, possibly a splendid alien culture'. The frontier must be crossed to meet them, dead or alive, however dangerous and costly the journey.[46] This motion of the heart and mind could not be but condescending and – Kermode's judgement – ignorant. He recounts Louis MacNeice's exile in Birmingham in the 1930s, teaching classics at the university and despising his unresponsive and malnourished students as they recited Homer in broad Brummagen. When MacNeice and his wife visited Birmingham picture palaces, sometimes five times a week (what else was there to do in Brum?), *they* were not using it as a means of escape; *they* were not forgetting their troubles in a celluloid world. 'You can tell from the tone,' says Kermode, 'that it was all the other people in the cinema who were experiencing ... bogus solace and not the MacNeices.'[47] There is a glass

44 Paul E. Johnson recalls its arrival at UCLA in the late 1960s; it proclaimed 'a "History from the Bottom Up" that ultimately engulfed traditional history and, somehow, helped to make a Better World'. Paul E. Johnson, 'Reflections. Looking back at social history', *Reviews in American History*, 39:2 (2011), pp. 379–388. The US *Journal of Social History* was founded in 1967.

45 Frank Kermode, *History and Value. The Clarendon Lectures and the Northcliffe Lectures 1987*, Clarendon Press, Oxford, 1988, pp. 42–62.

46 Kermode, *History and Value*, p. 21. Writing of his father's generation, Matthew Spender describes this structure of feeling very well: 'My father thought that the working class possessed a secret which had been eradicated from the bourgeoisie ...'. *A House in St John's Wood. In Search of my Parents* (2015), William Collins, London, 2016, pp. 24–27.

47 Kermode, *History and Value*, pp. 48–49.

wall between the anthropologist-poet visiting the land of the poor and the people passing in its greasy streets. MacNeice's poem 'Birmingham' announces itself as the soundscape of a great industrial city, but all the voices in the street are occluded; he cannot hear what the people are saying:

The lunch hour: the shops empty, the shopgirls' faces relax
Diaphanous as green glass, empty as old almanacs
As incoherent with ticketed gewgaws tiered behind their heads
As the Burne-Jones windows in St. Philip's broken by crawling leads …[48]

The new social history that emerged in the academy between 1950 and 1970 had a different kind of problem with loving the workers, but problem it certainly had. No actually-historically-existing eighteenth-century cobbler, or nineteenth-century fustian cutter could possibly live up to the expectations placed upon him (or her; but that's another story) by the post-Marxist eschatology that would have the course of history reach its end by the revolutionary triumph of the workers. Actually-existent spinners and weavers and labourers and miners were as unheroic to the historical imagination as were MacNeice's shopgirls to the poetic. This is a cheap remark, to which I intend to give better value, and I would not like anyone to think that I am not deeply implicated in this history of political sensibility; and I do know I am re-iterating my own self-importance by stating it.

In the late twentieth-century West, the practice of social history was accompanied by the social historian's guilt and anguish at rescuing those who maybe do not want to be rescued, at all, from what Thompson called the vast condescension of posterity.[49] Other kinds of historian have been plain-speaking about our desires: social historians' desire that our historical subjects be the way we want them to be. In 1977, Jacques Rancière addressed a History Workshop held in Oxford on the topic of 'French social historiography … and the real deep gap between French social history as an intellectual product and the organised working-class movements'. He emphasised social history's effacement by Annales-school *longue durée* history in general, and the 'motionless history' of Leroy Ladurie's work in particular; of what we had already come (after Thompson's *Making*) to know as the workers' 'experience'. The French historiography he evoked

48 Louis MacNeice, 'Birmingham', *New Verse*, 7 (February 1934), pp. 3–4.
49 E. P. Thompson, 'Preface', *The Making*, p. 12.

was 'a comeback to earlier history which is nothing to do with the working class'.[50] 'Who needs social history, or working-class history; and who does it?', he asked. French workers had not (did not), for the main part, want their own history as penned by their historians. 'For instance there was an important literary movement among French workers in the mid-nineteenth century, but they wrote poetry rather than history … (they) wanted to gain their identity through other means than history and memory, and even the history of their own struggles, working-class struggles, did not serve their purpose.'[51] Moreover, in early twentieth-century France, it was not academic historians who wrote the history of trade union and labour struggle, but sociologists and anthropologists producing popular ethnological accounts of the habits and manners of the nineteenth-century working class. Sociologists produced the most twentieth-century French working-class history because sociology was 'the official science of the new radical republic'. After 1870, the science of 'social solidarity and reciprocity' wrote the workers and working-class history from the perspective of class harmony and 'solidarism'. Histories of the working class had been inaugurated by the French state. Civil servants writing state-sanctioned history were often themselves veteran militants of the nineteenth-century working-class movement. 'Dismissed and marginalised by the new forces – socialist, collectivist … anarchist', the first books 'representing real research into the history of trades unions and the working class were written by men who had been defeated in their own attempts to reconcile the classes when they were militants in the labour movement … [they] wanted to take their revenge as civil servants, as investigators for the state'. Rancière also told of the underestimation of working-class history in French universities: 'if you write social history, you are taken to be a militant, interested … because of your political involvement'. Raphael Samuel's editorial note to the published talk explained that 'social history' has a double meaning in French, the first much as in English, the second inherited from the nineteenth century as 'social movement' – the popular forces that battled to resolve 'the social question'. 'Social history' was the

---

50 Bishopsgate Institute, London, History Workshop, 7/43, Session Report; History Workshop Audio Collection RS062b; Jacques Rancière, '"Le Social". The Lost Tradition in French Labour History', Raphael Samuel (ed.), *People's History and Socialist Theory*, Routledge and Kegan Paul, London, 1981, pp. 267–272.

51 He described work that would appear in *La Nuit des prolétaires: archives du rêve ouvrier*, Fayard, Paris, 1981; *The Nights of Labor. The Workers' Dream in Nineteenth-Century France*, trans. John Drury, intro. Donald Reid, Temple University Press, Philadelphia PA, 1989.

narrative of that struggle, he explained; 'in other words something much more akin to the [English] term "labour history"'. In Rancière's argument, the latter meaning was predominant.[52] But how lucky the French! How lucky to be a French academic historian in the 1970s: to be an object of suspicion in a university system so clear-eyed about the political purposes of the history you wrote! How much better to be conflated with the workers and their struggle than to be one of those (English) academics waltzing around with yet another paper about nineteenth-century working-class experience of something-or-other in your hand. Reading what Rancière wrote for the 1979 History Workshop now, after all the turns taken by historical studies these thirty years past, his argument becomes a signal that one day, someone will ask not only about who needs and wants the history of working-class experience that social historians write, but about the propriety of writing it in the first place, with all the acts of treachery it involves.

Self-abasement and suffering-envy were deeply imbued in the practice of British social history. In their deep identification with (their love for) their historical subjects, many *engagé* scholarship boy and girl historians of the mid-twentieth century contemplated the betrayal involved in writing about the working-class dead and gone.[53] Whilst attempting to give the lost myriads of the past – all the nameless ones – a voice and a history, social historians sought out the saddest stories ever told, of what the English fiscal-military state, the legal system, industrial capitalism, *did to* people in the past.[54] Historians had – and have – the very great power of making immortal ordinary people whose stories of suffering are a passport to the historical record, in a way that their everyday, ordinary life never would have been.[55] The sympathies and empathies of twentieth-century British social history can be read as part of a longstanding project of modernity (originating in the eighteenth century and given its most elegant

---

52 Rancière, ' "Le Social" ', p. 272.
53 Annie Ernaux, *La place*, Gallimard, Paris, 1993; Carolyn Steedman, 'Reading Rancière', Oliver Davis (ed.), *Rancière Now*, Polity Press, Cambridge, 2013, pp. 69–84.
54 The project of recovery was proclaimed in E. P. Thompson's Preface to *The Making of the English Working Class*: 'I am seeking to rescue the poor stockinger, the Luddite cropper, the "obsolete" hand-loom weaver, the "utopian" artisan ... from the enormous condescension of posterity.'
55 Leora Auslander, 'Archiving a Life: Post-Shoah Paradoxes of Memory Legacies', Sebastian Jobs and Alf Lüdtke (eds), *Unsettling History. Archiving and Narrating in Historiography*, Campus Verlag GmbH, Frankfurt am Main (distributed University of Chicago Press), 2010, pp. 127–148.

exposition by Adam Smith in *The Theory of the Moral Sentiments*) of finding your own soul finer in its ability to apprehend the pain of others. After the eighteenth-century empathetic turn, you do not ask: how does, or did, this person feel? Rather you ask: how would I feel if that happened *to me*? How do *I* feel, looking at the weight of the world, the suffering of others?[56] ('What should I have done if I'd been there?', as Auden put it.) Mark Phillips now suggests that the sentiment which propelled twentieth-century social history originated in the eighteenth century, in its own history-writing, and its concern with the everyday habits and manners of all kinds of people, dead and gone, remote in time and space, or emerging on a city street or in a novel, Somewhere Near You: a way of seeing and thinking the social world.[57] This was the structure of feeling that provided George Henry Lewis's historiography, as early as 1844. He had visited Paris in 1842, had a conversation Jules Michelet, and now reported on 'The State of Historical Science' in France.[58] He discussed Michelet's *Oeuvres Complètes* in comparison with the work of Thierry, Guizot, Hegel, and Michelet's translation of Vico's *Scienza Nuova* into French, reflecting on the charges that might brought against Michelet for want of gravity. Not hard, in this company, for Michelet to be called the most 'captivating' of historians. Lewes' reading also allowed him to speculate on the sources for a history of everyday life. 'History should be grave' he conceded

> but in a deeper sense than our 'classical historians' have understood ... History must be grave, or cannot be written; but this gravity does not *exclude* anything, which throws light upon the subject, whether a ballad, a legend, a custom, a silly fashion, or a secret anecdote; it holds nothing to be derogatory to its dignity, because it *includes* everything, as the greater does the lesser.[59]

Now, beyond the cultural, linguistic, subjective, and archival 'turns' in historical studies, beyond historiographical questions asked from the

---

56 Adam Smith, *The Theory of the Moral Sentiments*, A. Millar, London, A. Kincaid & J. Bell, Edinburgh, 1759, pp. 12–25. For 'social suffering', Pierre Bourdieu, *La Misère du Monde*, Seuil, Paris, 1993, trans. *The Weight of the World. Social Suffering in Contemporary Society*, Polity Press, Cambridge, 1999; Simon J. Charlesworth, *A Phenomenology of Working-Class Experience*, Cambridge University Press, Cambridge, 2000.

57 Mark Salber Phillips, *Society and Sentiment. Genres of Historical Writing in Britain, 1740–1820*, Princeton University Press, Princeton NJ, 2000, passim, but esp. pp. 14–18.

58 (G. H. Lewes), 'State of historical science in France', *British and Foreign Review; or, European Quarterly Journal*, 16 (1844), pp. 72–118.

59 Lewes, 'Historical science', pp. 109–110.

postcolony about the West as the Subject, or 'I', of historical writing, historians have started to interrogate their relationship with all their subjects, asking juridical questions to do with rights, duties, obligation, and ownership.[60] Who owns history? Who has the right to speak for the dead? For particular categories of the dead? New protocols of imagining and writing emerged from Holocaust history and sociology – from the event that 'resisted ... long-standing frameworks of historical reasoning, development, and emplotment ... Who can claim the moral ground to consider the meaning ... of the lives and deaths of others?'[61] Without any right on their side, social historians do it everyday.

Western historical practice is, as Marc Bloch remarked, deeply Christian – eschatological – in its structures of temporality and meaning.[62] And as social history it has operated with a specifically Christian notion of love. *Caritas* accompanies you, whether you want it to or not, as you read the fragmented testimony of the abject child-labourer, child-murdering maidservant in the condemned cell, pauper pleading for relief before a magistrate, for whom you feel the subordinating impulse of sympathy. Its traffic is from high to low, from superior to subordinate; *caritas* involves the pity and tenderness of the superior person (or historian) much more than its conventional translation as 'Christian love of humankind; charity', allows: it is pity, plain and simple. But as you attempt the egalitarian and democratic move of incorporating all the lost ones into a historical narrative, pity is what you most profoundly do not want to feel. It is not a grown-up sentiment; it is not an emotion that pertains between equals in the civil society of the living and the dead; it abandons your historical subjects to the place they are already in, and reaffirms the hierarchies that separate you in the first place. But I do believe that it is *caritas*, dressed as social history, who enters, silently, the stage of Auden's 'Makers of History'.

For readers of 1955, *Clio I* stepped out of the pages of the *London Magazine*, accompanied by the codes and conventions of one particular

60 See the 21st International Congress of the Historical Sciences (Amsterdam, August 2010), Panel on 'Who Owns History? (esp. Anton de Baets, 'Posthumous Privacy'), and Panel on 'The Rights of the Dead', www.ichs2010.org/home.asp (accessed 16 October 2017).

61 Daniel William Cohen, 'Memories of Things Future: Future Effects in "The Production of History"', Jobs and Lüdtke, *Unsettling History*, pp. 29–49; quote p. 43.

62 Marc Bloch, *The Historian's Craft*, Manchester University Press, Manchester, 1992, p. 4, 25–26; *Apologie pour l'histoire; ou, Métier d'historien*, Librairie Armand Colin, Paris, 1949.

'little' magazine.[63] The editorial pages did not mention the poem, concentrated rather on the question of protest in literature, explored by another contributor. Compared with the US, there had been little discussion of the theme since the war, wrote the editor, perhaps because the UK was free of McCarthyism and there had been such enormous advances in social justice in the decade after 1940. But protest *was* needed: 'is there no need, in the tight little Britain of the 'fifties, of artists to "wage contention with their times (sic) decay"?'[64] What alarmed John Lehman was this island's absence of passion. He railed, in a mild kind of way, against a candyfloss world and a never-never culture, in the recognisable tones of a Richard Hoggart (who had not yet published *The Uses of Literacy*) or a Frank Leavis (who had been railing at it for years). Underneath the surface of everyday existence, 'gigantic concentrations of power are forming', not only manifest in colour TV, 'gas turbine sports cars, and Atlantic crossings on the never-never plan'. It was plain that although the Korean War was over, 'The Ministry of Fear has not stopped growing'. This was the herald of Auden's Social-History Clio, or maybe her train, depending on which order readers took in the issue, which contained a review of Auden's selections from Kierkegaard, also published that year.[65]

Here are some points Auden made about social history, for it was in his vocabulary as a critic. In 1936, in a lecture on poetry and film, he provided a history of the Industrial Revolution to chart aesthetic developments across Europe: the Industrial Revolution was formative of class – it made employers and employed and workers and rentiers. A distinct kind of art arose from the outlook of the latter, 'developing through Cezanne, Proust and Joyce'. Co-existent with this, was the 'art of the masses expressing itself in the music-hall'; this had 'been taken over and supplanted by film'.[66] The lecture was an elegant and shorter version of the history he

63 Andrew Thacker, 'Auden and the Little Magazines', Tony Sharpe (ed.), *W. H. Auden in Context*, pp. 337–346; Matthew Philpotts, 'Defining the Thick Journal. Periodical Codes and Common Habitus', https://seeeps.princeton.edu/files/2015/03/mla2013_philpotts.pdf (accessed 16 October 2017); 'The role of the periodical editor. Literary journals and editorial habitus', *Modern Language Review*, 107:1 (2012), pp. 39–337.

64 The quote is from Shelley's 'Adonais: An Elegy on the Death of John Keats' (1821): 'he is gather'd to the kings of thought/Who wag'd contention with their time's decay,/And of the past are all that cannot pass away'.

65 '*Kierkegaard. Selected and Introduced by W. H. Auden*' [Cassell, London, 1955], *London Magazine*, 2:9 (1955), pp. 88–92. This was the UK version of *The Living Thoughts of Kierkegaard*, D. McKay, New York NY, 1952.

66 W. H. Auden, 'Appendix II Reported Lectures. Poetry and Film', *Prose Volume I. 1926–1938*, Edward Mendelson (ed.), Faber and Faber, London, 1996, pp. 712–714. Lecture

related to Lord Byron in *Letters from Iceland*; it moved beyond national borders. He understood the nature of the dual revolution that ushered European modernity into being, writing in 1947 about the political and economic crisis of the later eighteenth century. A society 'weakened from within by the strains of a transition from a mercantile to an industrial economy, and without by the strain of the American and French wars', its political taken-for-granted 'threatened by the ideology of the French Revolution'– in the 1790s 'the social structure of England was nearer collapse than at any time since 1640'.[67] In *The Dyer's Hand* (1963) he reiterated the background to British modernity: 'Between 1533 and 1688 the English went through a succession of revolutions, in which a Church was imposed on them by the engines of the State, one king was executed and another deposed, yet they prefer to forget it and pretend that the social structure of England is the result of organic peaceful growth.'[68] In the year of 'Makers of History' he reviewed a work of US history that pro-voked his antinomian use of 'Nature' as a substitute for 'historical factors': 'Americans think of their society as being made by their own revolution-ary actions', he wrote; 'whilst it was in fact, as a result of Nature', Nature in this case being a large virgin underpopulated territory to appropriate: 'To call their secession from allegiance to the British Crown a Revolution is nonsense'.[69] After 'Makers' had been published, he contemplated the differences between social and literary history, quoting approvingly C. S. Lewis on the literary historian, whose business is not 'the past as it "really" was (whatever "really" means in such a context) but with the past as it seemed to those who lived it: for of course men felt and thought and wrote about what seemed to be happenings to them. The economic or social historian's "appearances" may well be the literary historian's "facts".' Like any other historian, the literary historian had to attempt to see the literary product through 'the eyes of its maker and his contem-poraries'; 'but then, unlike the social historian, he cannot avoid passing

---

delivered 7 February 1936 to North London Film Society at the YMCA Tottenham Court Road; orig. *Janus*, May 1936.

67   W. H. Auden, 'Mystic – and Prophet', *Prose Volume II*, pp. 337–339. Review of J. Bronowski, *A Man Without a Mask*, *New York Times Book Review*, 14 December 1947.

68   'The Americans, on the other hand, like to pretend that what was only a successful war of secession was a genuine revolution.' W. H. Auden, 'American Poetry', *The Dyer's Hand and Other Essays*, Faber and Faber, London, 1963, pp. 354–368.

69   W. H. Auden, 'Authority in America', *Prose Volume III*, pp. 521–527; review of Fiedler, *An End to Innocence*, *The Griffin*, March 1955.

judgement upon it as a work he is now reading'.[70] Editing Goethe's *Italian Journey* the year before, he had made a historiographical statement about the uses of time in various types of history-writing, 'about natural history and ... art history ... the two kinds of history are different. Natural history, like social and political history, is continuous; there is no moment when nothing is happening. But the history of art is discontinuous; the art historian can show the influences and circumstances which made it possible and likely that a certain painter should paint in a certain way, *if he chooses to paint*, but he cannot explain why he paints a picture instead of not paining one,'[71] By now his interest in R. G. Collingwood's philosophy of history – and his history – had, perhaps, faded. But Collingwood's understanding, that the point of history was to discover how and why people managed to believe, feel, and think what they did feel, believe, and think in any specific set of circumstances, *is* present in the thought of his *Homage to Clio* history-poems.[72] Auden had read Collingwood's history of Roman Britain when he worked on his radio play *Hadrian's Wall* in 1937; Collingwood had analysed Auden's play *The Ascent of F6* (1936, 1937) in his *Principles of Art* in 1938 (with a rare sensitivity and perspicacity, says Edward Mendelson). In 1940 appeared the Collingwood book Auden seemed to need the most: *An Essay in Metaphysics*, in which it was argued that metaphysics was not the study of the absolute, as philosophy assumed it to be, but rather the study of 'absolute presuppositions', that is, the unverifiable assumptions about the universe that underlie every society's sum of available knowledge. For Collingwood metaphysics was a means of historical understanding, not a science of timeless truth. Edward Mendelson says that Auden immediately adopted Collingwood's terminology, and his historical analysis as well, which identified Christian orthodoxy with the presuppositions that first enabled modern science. At the same time Auden began his inner debate about whether the same orthodoxy remained the basis of modern science, and thus of political

70 W. H. Auden, 'Stimulating Scholarship', *Prose Volume IV. 1956–1962*, Edward Mendelson (ed.), Princeton University Press, Princeton NJ, 2010, pp. 6–12, 'O Lovely England', review of C.S. Lewis, *English Literature in the Sixteenth Century Excluding Drama*, *The Griffin*, March (1956).

71 W. H. Auden, 'Introduction to *Italian Journey* by Johann Wolfgang von Goethe', *Prose Volume IV*, pp. 324–333; orig. *Encounter*, November (1962).

72 This is the founding thesis of Collingwood's *The Idea of History* (1946), expressed in the idea that 'all history is the history of thought'. But there is no indication that Auden read this book.

practice.[73] We may care to note, as did Mendelson, that Collingwood was Norris Cochrane's tutor at Oxford.

I could – and some will say I ought to – exercise more of the historian's dreary arts in this pursuit of sources and contexts for *Clio I* – for the next five years, or forever: read everything published between the beginning of 1954 and the spring of 1955, find all the works of history produced from 1940 onwards that were not recorded in the ecumenical and international *Annual Bulletin of Historical Literature* (I know what *was* recorded, between 1930 and 1955). I could think hard about the cultural legacy of the Korean War in the US and in Europe. I could note random happenings of the world historical stage of the type that Social History-Clio (*Clio I*) ignores: US McCarthyism; the USSR finally decreeing the end of war with Germany; an EOKA-bomb attack on British government buildings in Cyprus on 1 April 1955; the Soviet Union and its Eastern Bloc allies signing the Warsaw Pact on 14 May 1955, integrating the military, economic, and cultural policy of eight Communist nations; Giovanni Gronchi elected President of Italy (well: Auden was *in* Italy when he wrote *Clio I*); the overthrow of Juan Peron in Argentina (but that happened in September 1955, so scarcely relevant to the composition of 'Makers of History'). I could note the proclamation of Pius X a saint, by Pope Pius XII (he *was* in Italy, after all); and I could go on for a very long time. But none of it would help with my question about where the Clio of 'The Makers' came from, for it is the wrong one. If there is a dark rather than dreary art of historical practice, it is to develop a sense of when you've been asking the wrong questions, looking for the wrong thing (in an archive, in a work of literature, in a timetable of significant events). Social-History Clio does not *come from* anywhere; she is, rather, *there*, as a sign that historiographical change and developments in the philosophy of history emerge outside the academy as well as within it; that they are thought by ordinary people and an extraordinary poet. Of course she's present a little earlier than our conventional works of historiography (history of History) tell us she should be; but then, her earliness is part of my point. Clio may not bless the poets, but she does, sometimes, lob a historian the odd grace.

---

73 Mendelson, *Later Auden*, pp. 141–142; Robert W. Cox, *Universal Foreigner. The Individual and the World*, World Scientific Publishing, London, Singapore and New York NY, 2013, p. 316.

8

Homage to Clio

Our hill has made its submission and the green
    Swept on into the north: around me,
From morning to night, flowers duel incessantly,
    Colour against colour, in combats

Which they all win, and at any hour from some point else
    May come another tribal outcry
Of a new generation of birds who chirp,
    Not for effect but because chirping

Is the thing to do. More lives than I perceive
    Are aware of mine this May morning
As I sit reading a book, sharper senses
    Keep watch on an inedible patch

Of unsatisfactory smell, unsafe as
    So many areas are: to observation
My book is dead, and by observations they live
    In space, as unaware of silence

As Provocative Aphrodite or her twin,
    Virago Artemis, the Tall Sisters
Whose subjects they are. That is why, in their Dual Realm,
    Banalities can be beautiful,

Why nothing is too big or too small or the wrong
    Colour, and the roar of an earthquake
Rearranging the whispers of streams a loud sound
    Not a din: but we, at haphazard

And unseasonably, are brought face to face
    By ones, Clio, with your silence. After that
Nothing is easy. We may dream as we wish
    Of phallic pillar or navel-stone

With twelve nymphs twirling about it, but pictures
    Are no help: your silence already is there
Between us and any magical centre
    Where things are taken in hand. Besides,

Are we sorry? Woken at sun-up to hear
    A cock pronouncing himself himself
Though all his sons had been castrated and eaten,
    I was glad that I could be unhappy: if

I don't know how I shall manage, at least I know
    The beast-with-two backs may be a species
Evenly distributed but mum and dad
    Were not two other people. To visit

The grave of a friend, to make an ugly scene,
    To count the loves one has grown out of,
Is not nice, but to chirp like a tearless bird,
    As though no one dies in particular

And gossip were never true unthinkable:
    If it were, forgiveness would be no use,
One eye for one would be just and the innocent
    Would not have to suffer. Artemis,

Aphrodite, are Major Powers and all wise
    Castellans will mind their p's and q's,
But it is to you, who have never spoken up,
    Madonna of silences, to whom we turn

When we have lost control, your eyes, Clio, into which
    We look for recognition after
We have been found out. How shall I describe you? They
    Can be represented in granite

(One guesses at once from the perfect buttocks
    The flawless mouth too grand to have corners,
What the colossus must be), but what icon
    Have the arts for you, who look like any

Girl one has not noticed and show no special
  Affinity with a beast? I have seen
Your photo, I think, in the papers, nursing
  A baby or mourning a corpse: each time

You had nothing to say and did not, one could see,
  Observe where you were, Muse of the unique
Historical fact, defending with silence
  Some world of your beholding, a silence

No explosion can conquer but a lover's yes
  Has been known to fill. So few of the Big
Ever listen: that is why you have a great host
  Of superfluous screams to care for and

Why, up and down like the Duke of Cumberland,
  Or round and round like the Laxey Wheel,
The Short, The Bald, The Pious, The Stammerer went,
  As the children of Artemis go,

Not yours. Lives that obey you move like music,
  Becoming now what they only can be once,
Making of silence decisive sound: it sounds
  Easy, but one must find the time. Clio,

Muse of Time, but for whose merciful silence
  Only the first step would count and that
Would always be murder, whose kindness never
  Is taken in, forgive us our noises

And teach us our recollections: to throw away
  The tiniest fault of someone we love
Is out of the question, says Aphrodite,
  Who should know, yet one has known people

Who have done just that. Approachable as you seem
  I dare not ask you if you bless the poets,
For you do not look as if you ever read them
  Nor can I see a reason why you should.

                                          1955, 1960.

This is transcribed from the first appearance of the poem, in the journal *Encounter*, in November 1955.[1] The *Encounter*-Clio (*Clio II*) arrives in a silence even more portentous than that of *Clio I*: the poets appearing in this issue have no bylines as do the other contributors; the editors do not mention Auden or his poem. They had much to say about Hugh Gaitskell, about to become leader of the Labour opposition, about the common man having to make up his mind about what he wants from Labour and politics in general, and a plangent sadness that eight years after war, the New Jerusalem has not been built, at least not in architectural terms. This particular issue of *Encounter* has received the most attention over the years for its inclusion of Alan Ross' 'U and non-U. An essay in sociological linguistics'. This was a version of his earlier philological exposition of class-based British speech ('U' stands for 'upper-class') made comprehensible to 'the lay reader', and shortly to be made famous by Nancy Mitford.[2] But only in retrospect does the linguistic company *Clio II* keeps in *Encounter* appear significant.

There are minor variations (of punctuation, capitalisation, and spelling) between *Encounter-Clio* and the version published in the eponymous collection of 1960, and between that and its appearance in the *Collected Shorter Poems, 1927–1957* (1966). Oddly, the version in the volume *Homage to Clio*, published by a UK house, uses US spelling, which the others do not, though Edward's Mendelson's edition of the *Collected Poems* (1971, 1996) which, he says, presents all as Auden would have wished, was also published by Faber but uses US spelling.[3] Clio's second

---

1 *Encounter*, 5:5 (November 1955), pp. 30–31. For recent assessments of the journal's Cold War role: Hugh Wilford, ' "Unwitting assets"? British intellectuals and the Congress for Cultural Freedom', *Twentieth Century British History*, 11:1 (2000), pp. 42–60; *The CIA, the British Left and the Cold War, 1945–1960*, Cass, London, 2003; Sarah Miller Harris, *The CIA and the Congress for Cultural Freedom in the Early Cold War. The Limits of Making Common Cause*, Routledge, Oxford and New York NY, 2016, pp. 111–128. Also, below, p. 192, fn 23.

2 E. G. Stanley, 'Ross, Alan Strode Campbell (1907–1980)', *Oxford Dictionary of National Biography*, Oxford University Press, Oxford, 2004. Nancy Mitford (ed.), *Noblesse Oblige. An Enquiry Into the Identifiable Characteristics of the English Aristocracy*, Hamish Hamilton, London, 1956, contained Ross's and Mitford's essays on the topic and John Betjeman's 'How To Get on in Society', among other light-hearted frolics in the field of socio-linguistics.

3 *Homage to Clio*, Faber and Faber, London, 1960; *Collected Shorter Poems, 1927–1957*, Faber and Faber, London, 1966, pp. 307–310; *Collected Poems* (1976), Edward Mendelson (ed.), 1991, pp. 610–613, noted as composed in June 1955 here. The *Encounter* version is with British spelling.

appearance (after the first, in *Encounter*) was in the US-published *Old Man's Road*, which employs British spelling.[4] There are seven of Auden's 1950s 'history-poems' here, the publishers explaining that the poet has just returned to England to take up the Chair of Poetry at Oxford having completed *The Old Man's Road* 'on the eve of departure' from New York. The pamphlet may be a series of reflections on 'the nature and process of history', but is not at all a valedictory address to New York: the old man's road runs through an entirely English terrain of old cathedrals, new town halls, and housing developments in smart suburbs; a Romano-Briton, on the eve of withdrawal from the British Isles, reflects on the last hot bath to be had for a thousand years.[5] It is a kind of returnee's homage to his own old country, and perhaps particularly a rumination on the hot-water situation in austerity Britain.

The revisions and alterations Auden made to the poems in *Homage to Clio* have been minutely discussed; but there is little account of what the minor changes *meant*; probably not much, beyond the proof-reader's and copy-editor's pen.[6] So it is a real surprise to hear and see Auden read 'Homage to Clio' on YouTube, in a film dated 1960.[7] Here Clio is pronounced Cly-o by Auden (in the correct Greek manner), not Clee-o, as is now common. An extraordinary accent: a discombobulating mixture

4 W. H. Auden, *The Old Man's Road*, Voyager Press, New York NY, 1956; no pagination. 'The Old Man' is God, says the *W. H. Auden Encyclopedia*, David Garrett Izzo (ed.), McFarland, Jefferson NC and London, 2004, with very great authority. Maybe He is; but if so, Auden says that we may walk His road as we wish: He's left it to those who don't know about its purpose and never ask anything at all about its history, or History in general.

5 *The Old Man's Road* includes: the title poem; 'The Epigoni'; 'Makers of History'; 'The History of Science'; 'Merax and Mullin'; 'C. 500 A. D.' (titled 'Bathtub Thoughts' in collections of Auden's poetry); and 'Homage to Clio'.

6 Y. S. Yamada, 'W. H. Auden's Revising Process (VI). Homage To Clio (1960)', Annual Report, Faculty Education, Iwate University, 40:2 (1981–1982), pp. 1–18, available: https://iwateu.repo.nii.ac.jp/?action=pages_view_main&active_action=repository_ view_main_item_detail&item_id=11931&item_no=1&page_id=13&block_id=21 (accessed 16 October 2017). But see the comments on Auden's revisions in Hannah Sullivan, ' "Still Doing It By Hand". Auden and the Typewriter', Bonnie Costello and Rachel Galvin (eds), *Auden at Work*, Palgrave Macmillan, Basingstoke, 2015, pp. 5–23.

7 The YouTube clip is dated 1960; Edward Mendelson, in W. H. Auden, *Prose Volume IV. 1956–1962*, Edward Mendelson (ed.), Princeton University Press, Princeton NJ, 2010, p. 874, says that Auden read 'Homage to Clio' and talked with Anne Fremantle on the CBS television religious series *Look Up and Live* on 1 March 1959; the broadcast was the first of a series of four, entitled 'This Bent World', 'on the problems of Christianity today'.

of public-school classy/mid twentieth-century BBC (*very* 'U', in contemporary English-English terms) and some completely unexpected short vowels: ăfter, not 'arfter' for example, and then another vowel elongated in the ultimate of posh strangulation: 'that' to sound rather like 'thet'. If I didn't know he had spent a quarter of a century in the US, I might detect the West Midlands or even the Pennine ridge, though not North Yorkshire, where baby Auden spent only the first eighteen months of his life.[8] But what do I know? Only as much as the socio-linguists tell me.[9] He also more interestingly, and nowhere else but in this reading, has Clio defend '*each* world of her beholding', rather than the casual, 'some [any-old] world', as if there are now many of them, each individual though unspecified, and known to her. It is very beautifully done; the RP tone of the BBC Home Service newscaster gives it an elegant and stealthy authority, though I should listen to the commentators who have observed the way in which the poet plays syntax against structure: 'as if what the sentences could not possess were far more important than what they could make manifest'.[10] Susan Young ah-Gottlieb puts this point more minutely: 'even in the smallest units, there emerges a difference between the temporal measure that structures the poem and the time of its audible expression. Auden's decision to use only internal rhyme, rather than end-rhymes ... reinforces this divergence, so the resulting metrical pattern remains silent'.[11] Voiced, it moves with suave certainty towards its end. It opens with a very long utterance that works its way through to the first line of the third stanza; sentences are 'driven beyond obvious stopping

8 'Homage to Clio (Recorded in 1960)' by W. H. Auden', 4 January 2016, Uploaded by LPKvideoDesigns: www.youtube.com/watch?v=Gwe2V-mvhgs (accessed 24 May 2016). For Auden's accent, 'Măster/Mãster', 'Letters', *London Review of Books*, 31:24 (17 December 2009).

9 Arthur Hughes, *English Accents and Dialects. An Introduction to Social and Regional Varieties of English in the British Isles* (1996), 4th edn, Hodder Arnold, London, 2005; Suzanne Romaine (ed.), *The Cambridge History of the English Language. Vol.4, 1776–1997*, Cambridge University Press, Cambridge, 1998; David Crystal, *The Stories of English*, Penguin, London, 2005. Meeting Auden in New York in 1958, Edmund White thought that after two years in post as Professor of Poetry, Auden had 'reverted to the Oxford way of speaking to an extent that made him partially unintelligible'. *The Fifties. From Notebooks and Diaries of the Period*, Leon Edel (ed.), Farrar, Strauss and Giroux, New York NY, 1986, p. 528.

10 Charles Altieri, *The Art of Twentieth-Century American Poetry. Modernism and After*, Blackwell, Malden MA and Oxford, 2006, p. 152.

11 Susannah Young-ah Gottlieb, 'Auden in History', Tony Sharpe (ed.), *W. H. Auden in Context*, Cambridge University Press, Cambridge, 2013, pp. 181–192; 186.

points because, in deference to Clio, they are committed to pursuing what has to remain incomplete'.[12] It *does* sound – on YouTube – *driven*, though urbanely so; a voice moves lightly, swiftly to the end. It is said that at the formal level the metrical and thematic patterns of the poem come from a fissure in its perceptual field, in the same way as Clio is seen but not heard. Auden may have modified a Greek verse form as adopted by Horace, but so modified it that its 'classical origins [are] not recognisable'.[13] (The any-old jobbing historian will ask: if it can't be seen and can't be heard, what *is* the point of asking where it comes from?)

What *is* perceptually salient to English-speaking readers with the page in front of them, is the poem's syllabic structure: 'Twenty three quatrains alternate between lines of eleven and nine syllables with remarkable con-sistency.'[14] And yet, as has been observed above, English speakers tend not to *hear* syllabic organisation. Metre is a form of measuring out the time of a verse; Latin measures were formally defined patterns of syllables, which were pronounced long or short, but always lightly stressed.[15] But, however English-language verse is structured, it is heard according to the stress accent of the language itself. I cannot hear the syllables in Auden's reading of 'Homage to Clio', but I can hear the poet moving in measure, to an end that the poem has already predetermined. The effect is uncanny; 'uncanny' as a description of the somatic state in which you say of the unfamiliar and unknown, *I have been here before*.[16] Moreover, syllables used to structure a form of verse organise the language in a linear fashion. The verse moves in one direction, without the pauses that metre and rhyme provide, where the illusion is of brief stops or delays, as words respond to their partners in verse, or even take a step back. In Auden's articulation, however, this poem is already always is at its end. We will

---

12 Altieri, *Art of Twentieth-Century American Poetry*, p. 152. An astute listener to the recorded collection *The Voice of the Poet: W. H. Auden [With Book]* (Audio CD, Audiobook) Random House, 2004 (which does not contain a reading of 'Homage to Clio') says that 'Auden's recitation follows the cadences of the meter, not the sense of the lines. Very old-fashioned.' But wonderful, he hastens to add. And an important fragment of evidence that ordinary readers of poetry do look for lines. See above, pp. 133–134.

13 Gottlieb, 'Auden in History', pp. 186–187.

14 Gottlieb, 'Auden in History', pp. 186–187.

15 Joseph Dane, *The Long and the Short of It. A Practical Guide to European Versification Systems*, Notre Dame Press, Notre Dame IN, 2010; B. W. Fortson, 'Latin Prosody and Metrics', J. Clackson (ed.), *A Companion to the Latin Language*, Wiley-Blackwell, Oxford, 2011.

16 Sigmund Freud, 'The Uncanny' (1919), *Standard Edition of the Complete Psychological Works of Sigmund Freud*, Vol. 17, Hogarth Press, London, 1955, pp. 217–252.

return to Horace, and what Auden appears to have done to his Clio, towards the end of this chapter.

There are illuminating accounts of the composition of 'Homage to Clio', and its relationship to Auden's philosophy (or favourite philosophers) of history. A description of 'Iscia: 1948–57', not only clarifies but moves, in locating all the 'history' poems *on* the island: the first place he ever lived in which he 'acquired a sense of belonging to a community'.[17] Does the poet sit in his garden, early morning, at sun-up perhaps, reading and not reading his book, as he watches the foliage darken as the sun moves across the terrain, up the surrounding hills? Auden gardened in Ischia, as he had done in his Solihull boyhood.[18] Clio does not really *appear* in the poem; but she manifests herself to the poet's mind, *in* a garden. Some have the poem as a summation of his decades-long reflection on nature of history, the role of the poet in history, 'and the proper procedures for the historian'.[19] Or it is read as the summation of Auden's *theories* of history: he offers tribute to ' "the merciful silence" of historical choice'; gives thanks for the ability to make such choices, for 'without the unique historical facts that Clio defends, human life would consist only of an instinctive struggle for survival'. The unique historical 'facts' are, possibly, individual human lives.[20] Unique individuals rather than impersonal structural forces are the proper concern of history.[21] Or should it be 'historians'? Or 'history writing'? It has been and will be a persistent problem that literary scholars and critics will not – cannot – say what History is, or what it was, in the period 1920–1970. For any halfway competent working historian, reading the critics' comments on Auden's 'history' is like trying to grasp mist.

Then, in another perspective on the poem, Clio is the feminine principle of grace: 'her deep, unspeaking attention is a sacred space ... where

17 Edward Callan, 'Ischia: 1948–57. *Nature and History'*, *Auden. A Carnival of Intellect*, Oxford University Press, New York NY, Oxford, 1983, pp. 218–237.

18 Well. He *wrote* about picking soft fruit and turning over the soil in 'The Robin' (1924); W. H. Auden, *Juvenilia. Poems 1922–1928*, Katherine Bucknell (ed.), Faber and Faber, London, 1998, pp. 55–56.

19 Gottlieb, 'Auden in History', pp. 181–192.

20 Edward Mendelson, *Later Auden*, Faber and Faber, London, 1999, pp. 393–404; 'The European Auden', Stan Smith (ed.), *The Cambridge Companion to W. H. Auden*, Cambridge University Press, Cambridge, 2004, pp. 55–67; 62. Humphrey Carpenter, *W. H. Auden. A Biography* (1981, 1983), Faber and Faber, London, 2010, pp. 397–398; John Fuller, *Auden. A Commentary*, London, 1998, p. 464.

21 Edward Mendelson, *Early Auden* (1981), Faber and Faber, London, 1999, pp. 309–314 for Auden's earlier philosophy of History.

maternal love gives being and meaning to a son's existence'.[22] All agree, more or less, that *this* Clio is not the goddess of classical antiquity, nor the replacement for a Marxist (or marxian) view of history that Auden may just possibly have entertained in the 1930s, but rather a Christian theology of time and human existence, inflected by the grand-narrative history he read throughout the 1940s, and by the philosophies of Kierkergaard and Nietzsche.[23] But then, to completely efface the conventional and unconventional Clio, is the poet's view of the matter: he told several contemporaries and friends that she was in fact the Madonna, who 'gave the timeless and bodiless an existence [in Christ], and brought silence to decisive sound'.[24] He discussed the ensuing 'Anglican problem' with one friend, asking her if one 'can … write a hymn to the Blessed Virgin Mary without being "pi"? The Prots don't like her and the Romans want bleeding hearts and sobbing tenors. …'[25] Auden's Christianity – 'a complex of Anglo-Catholic, existential, and neo-orthodox views' – was, by several contemporary accounts, well enough understood for this to be apparent to readers of the 1950s and 1960s – for his problem not to be the mystery it is to later audiences.[26]

22 Janet Montefiore, 'Auden among Women', Sharpe (ed.), *W. H. Auden in Context*, pp. 107–117; 115.

23 Young-ah Gottlieb, 'Auden in History'; Frederick Buell, *W. H. Auden as a Social Poet*, Cornell University Press, Ithac NY, 1973, pp. 77–158; Justin Replogle, 'Auden's Marxism', *PMLA*, 80:5 (1965), pp. 584–595: 'between 1933 and 1938 Marx and Engels contributed to Auden's profoundest ideas about man. They encouraged him to abandon his exclusively psychological view of human behavior … laid the foundation for a conception of human existence, that incorporated into and transformed by Christian theology, became the central theme of his later poetry' (595); Christopher Caudwell, *Illusion and Reality. A Study of the Sources of Poetry* (1937), Lawrence and Wishart, London, 1946, pp. 116, 122, 283; Justin Quinn, 'Auden's Cold War Fame', Costello and Galvin, *Auden at Work*, pp. 231–249.

24 On this point, Robert Bloom, 'W. H. Auden's bestiary of the human', *The Virginia Quarterly Review* 42:1 (966), pp. 207–233; esp. 222–225.

25 Fuller, *Commentary*, p. 465; Mendelson, *Later Auden*, p. 396. He enclosed a typescript in a letter to J. R. R. Tolkien (14 June 1955), telling him that 'it is really, as you will seen, a hymn to Our Lady'. Carpenter, *W. H. Auden*, p. 397, Note 1. It is, of course, possible to discuss the poetics and philosophy of 'Homage to Clio' without focus on the discovery that it is a Christian poem *if* you can find it in yourself to believe it 'based on a conflict between how specific gods represent totally different attitudes towards experience'. Altieri, *Art of Twentieth-Century American Poetry*, p. 149.

26 Frederick P. W. Mcdowell, ' "Subtle, various, ornamental, clever". Auden in his recent poetry', *Wisconsin Studies in Contemporary Literature*, 3:3 (1962), pp. 29–44; Justin Replogle, 'Auden's intellectual development, 1950–1960', *Criticism*, 7:3 (1965), pp. 250–262; Buell, *W. H. Auden as a Social Poet*, pp. 188–189. Buell helpfully remarks

What has entranced me about 'Homage to Clio', over thirty years, are its paradoxes. Above all there was the paradox of the Muse's perfect silence: the very idea of a history that is silent; that has 'nothing to say'. Only much later, when I learned of Clio's classical function as the Proclaimer, did I add irony to paradox. Paradoxical silence allowed me, on many occasions to start something or other (a lecture, a piece of writing) with the observation that with nothing to *say*, Clio has everything to *write*. A quotation from 'Homage'; a few images of Clio, massive in marble with a pen in her hand, and I could discourse upon history as a form of writing. My intention was always to understand 'history' as a form emerging in Western modernity; as a form thinking and feeling (a cognitive form) and as a written form with its own procedures and poetics. I did quite a lot of this in the 1990s, repeating, in a very minor key, some major historiographical statements (history of history-writing) of the period.[27] But all the paradoxes in the world will not help me now, with my Clio-who-never-was.

And now there are some new contradictions about the Madonna-Clio, though they are not of the philosophical kind. '[W]hat icon/Have the arts for you?'. Well, plenty, if the statues and frescos of the Muse pursued across Europe by eighteenth-century gentlemen scholars are anything to go by.[28] But there's no point now in my imagining Auden nipping over on the ferry from Forio to Naples for a good look round the National Archaeological Museum, not least because the last guidebook to detail its ever-changing stock of Clios was published in 1909, and it is not at all clear which statues of her, if any, were there in the 1950s.[29] 'Icon' is a giveaway; this is no classical muse, but a figure from some other system of thought, believed to be worthy of veneration; a devotional representation of a holy

---

that the question of Auden's faith may well lie 'permanently beyond the reach of literary criticism'.

27 Carolyn Steedman, 'La Théorie qui n'en est pas une, or, Why Clio doesn't care', *History and Theory*, Beiheft 31 (1992), pp. 33–50; 'About ends. On how the end is different from an ending', *History of the Human Sciences*, 9:4 (1996), pp. 99–114. Michel de Certeau, *The Writing of History* (1975), Columbia University Press, New York NY, 1988; Philippe Carrard, 'History as a kind of writing. Michel de Certeau and the poetics of historiography', *The South Atlantic Quarterly*, 100:2 (2001), pp. 465–482; Jacques Rancière, *The Names of History. On the Poetics of Knowledge* (1992), University of Minnesota Press, Minneapolis MN, 1994. See also Frank Kermode's remarks on history-as-writing in *History and Value*, Clarendon Press, Oxford, 1988, pp. 108–127.

28 See above, Chapter 3.

29 *Illustrated Guide to the National Museum in Naples. Sanctioned by the Ministry of Education*, Richter, Naples, 1909.

figure. So I haven't had time to be exasperated at Artemis' granite bottom (no time to say triumphantly: *The Greeks didn't work in granite! – though the Egyptians did, it seems …*) for she and her Tall Sister Aphrodite are no more present in the poem than half-sister Clio: they are made of the wrong material. The layers of my assumptions have been peeled away too rapidly to make any jokes.

In June 1955, the BBC Third Programme (Radio 3) broadcast three lectures by Auden under the general title of 'The Dyer's Hand'. Poetry – what it was – and the poetic process would be discussed, and the series would conclude with the problems of writing it in a technological age. Programme notes in the *Radio Times* told listeners that 'Though nearly all poems written in the last nineteen hundred years … are the joint product of the Poet and the Historian, the collaboration is one of uneasy tension'; in the first lecture 'Mr. Auden defines the subject-matter of poetry with the help of two portraits, one of the essential Poet and the other of the essential Historian'.[30] Third Programme listeners were assumed to be highly literate: nowhere was the source of the general title given as Shakespeare's Sonnet 111: 'my nature is subdued/To what it works in, like the dyer's hand'. If you knew that, you would know that the speaker was to appear as craftsman; a working poet; as one of the Makers the other Clio, Social-History Clio, loved.

Mendelson says that 'Historical thought was an essential element of almost every poem Auden wrote in 1955 … and almost all his prose' and that in the BBC lectures he focused on 'the millennia-old debate between poet and historian'.[31] He used two types ('two Theophrastian sort of character sketches'; how erudite you had to be, to listen to Radio 3!),[32] named the Poet and the Historian.[33] The Poet believes that the world of

---

30 'What is Poetry About?', 8 June, repeat 13 June; 'The Poetic Process', 15 June, repeat 20 June; 'On Writing Poetry Today', 22 June, repeat 27 June. Genome BETA Radio Times 1923–2009. Auden, 'The Dyer's Hand', *Listener*, 53, 54, 55 (16, 23, 30 June 1955). The lectures are reproduced in W. H. Auden, *Prose Volume III. 1949–1955*, Edward Mendelson (ed.), Princeton University Press, Princeton NJ, 2008, pp. 536–568 and discussed pp. 768–771. They were written in early April 1955 in New York and recorded at the BBC in the same month. Auden and Kallman were presumably stopping off in London en route to Iscia.

31 Mendelson, *Later Auden*, p. 390.

32 Theophrastus' (371–287 BCE), *Characters* contains thirty brief sketches of character types, thus providing a summary of aspects of human nature.

33 The Poet and the Historian can be thought of as ideal-types: Max Weber, *The Methodology of the Social Sciences*, trans. by E. Schils and H. Finch, Free Press New York NY, 1949, pp. 89–95.

nature, including human beings, is pre-ordained; the Historian, on the other hand, is only interested in human beings because he believes that individual human futures are dependent on the choices people make, for which they are individually responsible. The Poet thinks in terms of a present moment; 'the historian is interested in the present only as it relates the past to the future'.[34] This first lecture proceeds by comparison of the dispositions, beliefs, and writing styles of the two types. This Historian is not one of the actually-existing kind, whose work might be noted in the current issue of the *Annual Bulletin of Historical Literature*, although this actually-existing one is interested in the irony (and Auden does not say that the Historian *can't* deal in irony) that the *Bulletin* reported for 1955 that 'there was no epoch-making contribution to the philosophy of history during the year'.[35] It *did* refer to many journal articles in the field, by Spiegel, Lefebvre, and Wollheim, and singled out one book for praise: 'in the field of historiography Herbert Butterfield's *Man on his Past. The Study of the History of Historical Scholarship* ... is a learned and stimulating exposition of the origins of the notion of a history of historiography'. The 1955 editor may not have listened to the Third Programme, or he may have thought it perfectly obvious that Auden was not talking about historiography, or the philosophy of history, or even history as the ecumenical and broad minded *ABHL* conceived it, but about some kind of moral philosophy of human nature.

In the Third Programme broadcasts, Auden compared the writing of poetry with the writing of history: 'The Historian's method of story telling ... is very different from that of the Poet', he said. The Historian usually tells stories in prose, for he has a 'distrust of formal verse as falsifying the truth'; when he does use verse, it is in 'a homely, not an elevated style'. In comparison with the Poet, he leaves a lot out: 'He rarely tells you where things happened, or describes the landscape. If natural objects play a role in the story, he is not specific; he will say ... "Then Hans came to a tree" ... where the Poet would have said "Then he came to a tall oak" ... Sometimes, indeed, he does not even bother to provide the hero's name, but will begin with ' "A certain man was about to be married".'[36] The Historian knows the ways of comedy; the Poet does not:

34 Auden, *Prose Volume III*, pp. 536–547.
35 'Philosophy of History: Historiography', *Annual Bulletin of Historical Literature*, 41 (publications of the year 1955), George Philip for the Historical Association, London, 1956, p. 5.
36 W. H. Auden, 'The Dyer's Hand', *Prose Volume III*, pp. 536–568, broadcast details Note 30.

'To the Poet comedy is synonymous with satire: only inferiority causes laughter; in the Historian's tales, on the other hand, it is often the comic character who is superior.' For the Poet 'anything which has a history, which changes, contains an element of non-being, which resists poetic expression'. Modern poetry is obscure, he said, because it 'means and cannot help meaning, something more than what it expresses'; the reader is perforce required to play a creative role that 'the reader of ancient poetry is spared'. Edward Mendelson says that Auden's central theme in the 1950s 'was the troubled relations in literature, language, and society, between the Poet and the Historian ... In the collaboration between Poet and Historian that produced his own poems, he evidently believed that he had made himself into a better poet by encouraging the Historian – and by restraining the Poet who had dazzled his early readers.'[37]

Auden had in fact been working with his types 'Poet' and 'Historian' for several years. In 1950, he expressed an aversion to 'absolute systems of historical interpretation' in a review of *The Recollections of Alexis de Tocqueville*. He quoted extensively from the *Recollections* to emphasise that de Tocqueville believed that 'chance does nothing that has not been prepared beforehand. Antecedent facts, the nature of institutions, the cast of minds, and the state of morals are the materials.' He wondered: had de Tocqueville been taught Thucydides as a boy? For his whole approach to the Revolution of 1848 was startlingly similar to that of the great historian of the Peloponnesian War. They both used, said Auden, a 'historical method ... derived from medicine', in which there is a norm: good health; a healthy state of society. Then comes an attack (Auden explored it in a very long analogy); the historian is a physician, watching for symptoms.[38] He thought de Tocqueville's 'extraordinary, perhaps unique, merit as a historian is that he combines in equal measure the philosopher's capacity for drawing general conclusions and the novelist's eye for the particular and grotesque'.

---

37 'In arguing the case for the Historian, he was recommending a future for himself, not prescribing a set of rules for other writers.' *Prose Volume IV*, Introduction, p. xxi.

38 W. H. Auden, 'A Guidebook for All Good Counter-Revolutionaries', *Prose Volume III*, pp. 190–196; orig. pub. *The Nation*, 8 April 1950. Auden's practice of reviewing by extensive quotation, noted by Stefan Collini of the recently published volumes V and VI of *The Complete Works* (1963–1973), was established very early in his writing career. 'He does very little that could be called literary criticism ... Quoting can, of course, be a form of criticism, though Auden rarely comments on the passages he excerpts, and says little about the verbal texture of the writing he discusses,' says Collini. 'Uncle Wiz', *London Review of Books*, 37:4 (16 July 2015), pp. 36–37.

His binary for analysis in an article entitled 'What Is Poetry About?' was Nature and History. These he discussed in 1954 in a review of Marie Bonaparte's edited work *The Origins of Psycho-Analysis*. Freud, said Auden, was the genius who had 'determined that mental events are not natural, but historical, to be approached by the method of the historian'. He explained that in the historical order every event is unique and related to others by the principle of analogy, not, as in the natural order, by the principle of identity, which means that they are not quantitatively measurable: 'to say that A is the cause of B means in the historical order is to say that "A provides B with a motive for occurring" ... A makes B possible or likely but not inevitable'. In the inorganic order, change is reversible; it is cyclical in the organic order: 'in the historical realm, change is irreversible'.[39] He adopted Freud's thesis that imagined events may operate in the unconscious and have effect in the same way as a 'real' ones, by claiming that 'in history a deliberate lie, a mistaken notion, are as real and important as the truth'. In November 1955, after 'Makers of History' and 'Homage to Clio' were in print, he expanded his account of Freud as a historian: 'the life of the mind cannot be studied by the quantitative methods suitable to the study of brain events, for it is a historical life to be studied by the principles which govern historical research'; this individual life contains subjective and objective elements, both of which the historian must pursue. 'The objective or "scientific" side of the historian's work consists in trying to find out what actually happened in the past. In this research he must eliminate so far as possible his personal hopes and fears and never accept second-hand evidence, like the accounts of previous historians, when there is available first-hand evidence, like documents contemporary to his period, by which to check the former.' In assessing the importance of their data, all historians (including Freud) are governed by the same general principle: 'the importance of an historical event is in proportion to its causal effect upon subsequent historical events which includes its influence upon later interpretations of the past'.[40]

He worked hard at providing an alternative vocabulary to the historians' conventional 'cause' (as in 'high food prices and scarcity caused

---

39 W. H. Auden, 'The Freud-Fleiss Letters', *Prose Volume III*, pp. 472–477. Review of Sigmund Freud, *The Origins of Psycho-Analysis. Letters to Wilhelm Fliess. Drafts and Notes, 1887–1902*, Basic Books, New York NY, 1954; orig. *Griffin*, June 1954.

40 W. H. Auden, 'The History of an Historian', *Prose Volume III*, pp. 596–601. Review of Ernest Jones, *Life and Work of Sigmund Freud*, Vol. II; orig. pub. *Griffin*, November 1955.

riots').[41] One of his first analogies for historical method and historical interpretation was music. 'What is music about?', he asked in 1951. It was about choice. 'A succession of two musical notes is an act of choice; the first causes the second not in the scientific sense of making it occur necessarily, but in the historical sense of provoking it, of providing it with a motive for occurring. A successful melody is a self-determined history: it is freely what it intends to be yet is a meaningful whole not an arbitrary succession of notes.'[42] In a 1950 lecture he had laid out the difference between the ideas of cause and motivation: 'Temporal or secular events may be divided into two classes' he said: there are natural events and historical events. The historical are unique, not out of necessity, or according to some law, but 'voluntarily according to provocation'; they may then function as the cause of subsequent events in that 'the former provides them with a motive for occurring'.[43] He said on this occasion that 'the relation of history and nature ... is a problem which has fascinated me for at least ten years'.[44] By the time Auden wrote his history-poems, History was for him neither a strict science nor pure art, says Mendelson. What he spoke and wrote about was what he labelled 'voluntary history', the effect of the free choices of individuals. It was the opposite of 'purposive Hegelian-Marxist History'. Historians were interested in choices people made in the past. History did not merely concern but *was* the subjective, psychological, and moral realm.[45] And he, the poet and person, was *in* History: 'Life, as I experience it in my own person ... is ... a continuous succession of choices between alternatives.' Time, in his experience was 'not ... a cyclical motion outside myself but of an irreversible history of unique moments which are made by my decisions'.[46] History, for this poet, always had somewhere to go, and sailed on, calmly or otherwise.

Auden's use of 'fact', and 'historical fact' is difficult to interpret fifty years after the furore about facts and 'historians and their

---

41 W. H. Walsh, 'Historical causation', *Proceedings of the Aristotelian Society New Series*, 63 (1962–1963), pp. 217–236; Joe Scott (ed.), *Understanding Cause and Effect, Learning and Teaching About Causation and Consequence in History*, Longman, London, 1990.

42 W. H. Auden, 'Some Reflections on Opera as a Medium', *Prose Volume III*, pp. 250–255; orig. *Tempo*, Summer 1951.

43 W. H. Auden, 'Nature, History and Poetry', Appendix III, Public Lectures and Courses, *Prose Volume III*, pp. 636–653.

44 Auden, *Prose Volume III*, p. 648.

45 Mendelson, *Later Auden*, pp. 391–292.

46 Mendelson, *Later Auden*, pp. 392, quoting W. H. Auden, 'At the End of the Quest, Victory', *New York Times*, 22 January 1956, www.nytimes.com/books/01/02/11/specials/tolkien-return.html (acccessed 16 October 2017).

facts'.[47] Historians now prefer to limit themselves to 'event', though may well use the everyday 'fact' for something incontrovertible, like 'it rained in the Waterloo region the night before the battle. That's a fact.' According to Auden, controversy (maybe: how heavily did it rain? Did it soak the battlefield to a sea of mud?) requires prose. 'So does history, as distinct from myth. For the essential point about a historical fact is how and when it actually occurred, not how it ideally might have occurred.' He explored this question with a discussion of the novel: 'The novel differs from the epic or the tale in that it is an imitation of history: however unnaturalistic his technique, the novelist fails if he does not convince us while we are reading that his characters are historical characters, that this is what they actually said and did. The novel as a literary genre could not appear until men had become conscious of the peculiar nature of history.'[48] He contemplated social and cultural history by analogy with the novel. In 1956, he quoted approvingly C. S. Lewis on literary historians, as we have seen: *their* business was not 'the past as it "really" was ... but with the past as it seemed to those who lived it'.[49] The literary historians he spoke of here might well now be designated cultural historians; their problem was 'background' or context, for 'In giving the general historical background, the problem for the ... historian is deciding where to stop. Everything that happens is in some way relevant to what is written.'[50]

47 Inaugurated in 1961 with the publication of E. H. Carr's *What Is History?* the argument about facts has been conducted by philosophers of history rather than by practising academic historians. But see Richard J. Evans, *In Defence of History*, Granta, London, 1997. E. H. Carr, *What is History? With A New Introduction by Richard J. Evans*, Palgrave, Basingstoke, 2001; Martin Bunzl, *Real History. Reflection on Historical Practice*, Routledge, London and New York NY, 1997, pp. 27–43; Beverley Southgate, *History: What and Why? Ancient, Modern and Postmodern Perspectives*, Routledge, London, 1996, pp. 58–85; Joyce Appleby, Lynn Hunt, and Margaret Jacob, *Telling the Truth About History*, Norton, New York NY and London, 1994; Peter Novick, *That Noble Dream: The 'Objectivity Question' and the American Historical Profession*, Cambridge University Press, Cambridge, 1988.

48 W. H. Auden, 'Introduction to *Poets of the English Language*', W. H. Auden and Norman Holmes Pearson (ed.), (1950), Mendelson (ed.), *Prose Volume III*, pp. 103–154. Auden's point about the history of historical consciousness is made at brilliant length by Franco Moretti, *The Way of the World. The Bildungsroman in European Culture*, Verso, London, 1987.

49 Above, pp. 181 W. H. Auden, 'Stimulating Scholarship', *Prose Volume IV*, pp. 6–12; orig. review of Lewis, *English Literature in the Sixteenth Century*, *The Griffin*, March 1956.

50 W. H. Auden, 'Just How I Feel', *Prose Volume IV*, pp. 77–82 orig. review of H. S. Bennett, *Chaucer and the Fifteenth Century*, and E. K. Chambers, *English Literature at the Close of the Middle Ages*, *The Griffin*, April 1957.

In 1963, under the title 'This and That' ('Hic et Ille') he appeared to have historians rather than the Historian in mind as well as the spectrum of kinds of history-writing that did yet have a name: 'History is, strictly speaking, the study of questions; the study of answers belongs to anthropology and sociology.' To ask a question was itself an implied historical act or 'fact': it is 'to declare war, to make some issue a *casus belli*'. Now there was 'history proper' in the definitional melee: proper history was 'the history of battles, physical, intellectual or spiritual'; he thought that 'the more revolutionary the outcome, the greater the historical interest. Culture is history which has become dormant or extinct, a second nature. A good historian is, of course, both a historian in the strict sense and a sociologist.'[51] The idea of 'social history' was available in 1963 (the year in which Thompson's *The Making of the English Working Class* was published); the US publication *Historical Abstracts*, inaugurated in 1955, had 'Social History' as a category heading from its first issue.[52]

But there is little point in looking for traces of the Social-History Clio of 'Maker's of History' in 'Homage'. She is not the same Muse; she has changed, utterly. *Clio II* has nothing but her silence. She does not love, or even care, as does the first. *Clio I* was enthusiastic about workers, artisans, and poets; *this* Clio nurses the pre-sentient and she mourns the dead, whose main attribute is thus, as a condition of their being, a silence to match hers. The poet may say that she must care for the screams – of what? Babies? History's victims? – but they go on and on, or round and round; it really is not clear that Clio cares. Artemis, most famous for her virginity, had no children (though in some variants of the myth, she was protectress of women in childbirth); who then, in this poem, are her children? And *are* there Clio's children present in 'Not yours'? If children she has in this poem, then they are not the Hyacinthus, for example, that some authorities had her bear; they are the unique individuals who came into being by motive, not cause; they come into being like music: they are entities which embody their own 'self-determined history ... [are] freely what ... [they intend] to be'; meaningful in this way, even though dead. But these dead *Clio II* cannot make famous, or proclaim, for they are as silent as she. Clio is not here.

51 W. H. Auden, *The Dyer's Hand and Other Essays*, Faber and Faber, London, 1963, pp. 94–106; 97.

52 *Historical Abstracts, 1775–1945. A Quarterly of Historical Articles Appearing Currently in Periodicals the World Over*, 1:1 (1955). The *ABHL* has never used 'social history' as a category heading.

Her absence is probably best measured by her most likely poetic source, Horace's twelfth Ode:

Quem viram aut heroa lyra vel acri
tibia sumis celebrare, Clio,
quem deum? Cuius recinet iocosa
   nomen imago
aut in umbrosia Heliconis oris
aut super Pino gelidove in Haemo?[53]

In 1742, as we have seen, first lines were translated as 'What man, what hero, wilt thou chuse, to celebrate his rising fame,/And consecrate in verse his name?' and in 1793 as 'What man, what hero, wilt thou chuse,/ Theme of thy lyre, immortal muse?/ What god shall Clio praise?'.[54] The answer to this question was in the dedication to the Ode. In 1830, William Smart did the Odes into prose 'for Students' and, helpfully, his translation of the twelfth is reproduced below.[55] It was dedicated by Horace, the

53 Horace, *Q. Horati Flacci. Carminum Liber I, With Introduction and Notes by James Gow*, Cambridge University Press, Cambridge, 1949, pp. 12–14.

54 Virgil, *The Works of Virgil. Containing His Pastorals, Georgics and Æneis. Translated into English Verse; by Mr. Dryden. In Three Volumes*, J. and R. Tonson and S. Draper, London, 1748; John Dryden, *The Poetical Works of John Dryden, Esq. In Three Volumes. With the Life of the Author*, Apollo Press, Edinburgh, 1794; Virgil, *Virgilii Maronis Opera. Interpretatione et Notis Illustravit Carolus Ruæus, ... Jussu Christianissimi Regis, Ad Usum Serenissimi Delphini. Juxta Editionem Novissimam Parisiensem. Huic Editioni Accessit Index Accuratissimus, Antè Editis Longè Locupletior*, C. Bathurst and twelve others, London, 1777; *The Lyric Repository: A Selection of Original, Ancient, and Modern, Songs, Duets, Catches, Glees, and Cantatas, Distinguished for Poetical and Literary Merit; Many of Which Are Written by Dr. Johnson, Peter Pindar*, J. Johnson, London, 1788; James Brown, *Odes, Elegies, Songs, &c*, for the author, Bristol, 1786; Thomas Broughton, *An Historical Dictionary of All Religions from the Creation of the World to this Present Time. ... Compiled From the Best Authorities ...*, C. Davis and T. Harris, London 1742; Horace, *The Odes, Epodes, and Carmen Seculare of Horace. Translated Into English Verse. By William Boscawen, Esq*, John Stockdale, London, 1793.

55 William Smart, *Horace Literally Translated, for the Use of Students*, Whitaker, Teacher, London, 1830. 'CLIO, what man or hero will you undertake to celebrate on the lyre or shrill pipe? What god? Whose name shall sportive echo repeat, either on the shady borders of Helicon, or upon Pineus, or on cold Haemus. – Whence the woods crowded to follow tuneful Orpheus, retarding the rapid falls of rivers and the swift winds by the craft of his mother Calliope, and so sweet as to draw listening oaks with his tuneful strings. What can I sing before the usual praises of the Father, who governs the affairs of men and gods, who governs sea and land and the world with changing seasons? – Whence nothing is produced greater than he, neither flourishes any thing like him, or second to him; yet

ex-military man now in rural retirement, to Caesar Augustus (c.23–13 BCE) – with whatever degree of irony need not delay us here, except to note that the Emperor was greatly interested in armies and fleets.[56] And that Horace's Clio disappears pretty smartish from Ode XII, for it is Homage to Caesar, not to the Muse, who is absent from Horace's Ode for as long as it takes for her to arrive in Auden's 'Homage'. Indeed, Horace's may not be Clio in the first place, for at least one modern commentator thought that Horace did not know or did not heed the functions assigned to the several Muses (some trouble about that shrill pipe/lyre, or which Muse is responsible for choral odes and which for songs …).[57]

Clio, as historian or as history, has never been in Auden's 'Homage', and I have been finding her there, unseasonably, all these years. But perhaps we should agree with Susannah Young-ah Gottlieb, and take more notice of the other name given her by Auden: Muse of Time. 'The time of historical existence cannot be measured according to the circular movements of clock or calendar but is, instead, given only when it is found,' says Gottlieb. The malaise of historical existence is 'the absence of "the time", understood … as Christological *kairos*'.[58] In the New Testament *kairos* is to do with the time of God's purposes, as in 'the kingdom of God is at hand' (Mark I, 15). Or it is used to signal an opportune moment or

Pallas hath occupied the honours next to him. Neither will I be silent of thee, Bacchus, bold in battles; and of thee virgin Diana, inimical to savage beasts; nor of thee Phoebus, formidable for thy sure dart. I will sing also Hercules, and the sons of Leda [Castor and Pollux] the one distinguished for excelling on horseback, the other on foot; whose benign constellation, as soon as it hath shone forth to sailors the troubled surge flows from the rocks, winds fall and clouds disappear, and the threatening wave subsides on the sea, because they willed it so. I am in doubt whether I shall first commemorate after these Rhamnales, or the peaceful reign of Numa, or the magnificent badges of Tarquin the elder, or the noble death of Cato. Grateful will I celebrate in choicest verse Regulus and the Scauri, and Aemilius Paulus prodigal of his great soul when Hannibal conquered, and Fabricius. Hard poverty, and an inherited farm with a household adapted to it, raised this man useful in war, and Curius with his rough hair, and Camillus. The fame of Marcellus grows, like a tree in stealing-on time. The Julian constellation shines among all, like the moon among smaller stars. Son of Saturn, author and preserver of the human race, to you the protection of great Caesar is committed by the fates; you shall reign, with Caesar as your second. He, whether he shall subdue with a just victory the Parthians hanging over Italy, or render subject the Seres and Indians on the east coast, shall rule the wide world with equity, inferior to you alone – you shall shake Olympus with your mighty car, you shall hurl your hostile thunders at the polluted groves.'

56 W. H. Auden, 'Epitaph on a Tyrant' (1939), *Collected Shorter Poems*, p. 127.
57 Horace, *Q. Horati Flacci* (James Gow), pp. 40–41.
58 Gottlieb, 'Auden in History', p. 187

'season'. The time that Auden says we must find is God's time. In her contribution to the *Tribute* to Auden, Ursula Niebuhr remembered his reading of Kierkergaard and Tillich – 'we lent him *The Interpretation of History*' – in which Tillich made use of ' "the time"/*kairos*: for him *kairoi* were crises in history which demanded an existential decision from human beings'. The coming of Christ was the best example of *kairos*.[59]

There is also much to say about Auden's reading of Nietzsche, particularly, in Gottlieb's account, his 'Use and Disadvantage of History for Life'. In Nietzsche's text, a leaf of memory flutters by. The writer is unhappy in his historical existence, as the animals around him are not. In 'Homage', Auden changes the leaf into the book he is reading as the poem opens. 'If the past were crystallized into a leaf that somehow remains in the present, then the nexus of cause and effect would be unbreakable'; Auden breaks the chain by having Clio as the muse of time itself, in which there will be movement, and an ending. If we can learn from our recollections, we may see that each event could have been otherwise; we can break the (historian's) iron welding of cause to event. The past ceases to be a closed book, but an open one, like the one Auden holds in his hands.[60] Gottlieb concludes her tour de force by remarking on the Nietzsche Auden quoted in *The Viking Book of Aphorisms* (1962): 'By seeking after origins, one becomes a crab. The historian looks backwards; eventually he also *believes* backwards.' Gottlieb claims that Auden's final appeal to Clio ('teach us our recollections') is a plea for this not to happen to him; a plea not to come to *believe* backwards; please God, not to become a historian.[61] Impossible now, after Derrida, not to read into the commentary, and perforce the poem, Derrida's long and convoluted quest to inscribe what the historian's search for beginnings and origins *really means*: Archive Fever, with all its obsessions and compulsions.[62]

59 Ursula Niebuhr, 'Memories of the 1940s', Stephen Spender (ed.), *W. H. Auden. A Tribute*, Weidenfeld and Nicholson, London, 1975, pp. 104–118; 106; Paul Tillich, *The Interpretation of History*, Scribner, New York NY, 1936.

60 Gottlieb, 'Auden in History', pp. 191–192; Friedrich Nietzsche, 'On the Use and Abuse of History for Life' (1874), *Thoughts Out of Season*, Allen and Unwin, London, 1937; *The Untimely Meditations Parts I and II*, Digireads, pp. 96–133.

61 W. H. Auden and Louis Kronenberger, *The Viking Book of Aphorisms. A Personal Selection*, Viking Press, New York NY, 1962, p. 238. Nietzsche is quoted under the heading 'History', which contains 114 aphorisms. Rosenstock-Huessy provides two of these; only sixteen are provided by those who could be considered card-carrying historians. One of the editors was mighty fond of Jacob Burkhardt: he provided nine.

62 Jacques Derrida, 'Archive Fever. A Freudian impression', *Diacritics*, 25:2 (1995), pp. 9–63; *Mal d'archive. Une impression freudienne*, Editions Galilée, Paris, 1995, *Archive*

Thing is, I'm a Vico girl. Auden hinted that he may have been a Vico Boy when, in his farewell to the South, to Ischia – 'Good-Bye to the Mezzogiorno' (1958) – he invoked his 'sacred meridian names, *Vico, Verga, /Pirandello, Bernini, Bellini*'.[63] Pausing not to ask about the company Giambattista Vico keeps here, what on earth could Auden have read of his in 1955, when he wrote his two Clios? The slow translation history of Vico's *New Science* (1744) is notorious. Edmund Wilson had made much of French historian Jules Michelet's astonished reading of Vico in the 1820s, in *To the Finland Station* (1940), and Auden reviewed Wilson's book in the year it was published.[64] Michelet had made Vico's writings available in French, but there was no widely available translation into English until 1961.[65] Auden must have read Vico in Italian. After Michelet, many historians have been as amazed and entranced as he was at his 'oration of rare literary clarity' (above, p. 123), after which – after his observation that the social world had been made by men and women – Vico continued with:

> Whoever reflects on this cannot but marvel that the philosophers should have bent all their energies to the study of the world of nature, which, since God made it, He alone knows; and that they should have neglected the study of the world of nations, or civil world, which, since men had made it, men could come to know.[66]

Fever. A Freudian Impression, trans. Eric Prenowitz, University of Chicago Press, Chicago IL, 1996. For a not entirely serious account of 'real' Archive Fever, see Carolyn Steedman, *Dust*, University of Manchester Press, Manchester, 1992, pp. 17–37.

63 Auden, *Collected Shorter Poems*, pp. 338–341.

64 Edmund Wilson, *To the Finland Station. A Study in the Writing and Acting of History* (1940), Doubleday, New York NY, 1953; W. H. Auden, 'Who Shall Plan the Planners?', *Prose Volume II. 1939–1948*, Edward Mendelson (ed.), Princeton University Press, Princeton NJ, 2002, pp. 88–89. Review of Edmund Wilson, *To the Finland Station*; orig. *Common Sense*, November 1940. Auden may not have read *The New Science* at all; but *The Autobiography of Giambattista Vico*, trans. Max Harold Fisch, Thomas Goddard Bergin, Cornell University Press, Ithaca NY, was published in 1944.

65 Giambattista Vico, *The New Science of Giambattista Vico*, trans. Goddard Bergin and Max Harold Fisch, Doubleday, New York NY, 1961. M. Donzelli, 'La Conception de l'Histoire de J. B. Vico et son Interpretation par J. Michelet', *Annales Historiques de la Révolution Française*, 53:4 (1981) pp. 633–658. For the English-language translation history of Vico's works, Giambattista Vico, *Keys to the New Science. Translations, Commentaries, and Essays*, Thora Ilin Bayer and Donald Phillip Verene (eds), Cornell University Press, Ithaca NY, 2009, pp. 199–204.

66 Joseph Mali, *The Legacy of Vico in Modern Cultural History*, Cambridge University Press, Cambridge, 2012, p. 6; Vico, *New Science* (1961), pp. 52–53; Southgate, *History*,

Adoption of this perspective was made an emblem of the new social history in the 1960s and 1970s.[67] We cared less about *why* Vico sought to restore to historical thinking the traditional distinction between sacred and profane – for if God made all, including civil society, then men cannot have done so. There were arguments, then and now, that Vico attempted to evade censorship by insisting that God had made special interventions, in the Jewish past, for example.[68] But accounts of sacred history and the time of God in Vico no more delayed us than they did Karl Marx, whose equally beautiful and plangent (and so hackneyed that one can scarcely give oneself permission to quote it) 'Men make their own history …' is a companion to Vico's and taken as one of the founding principles of social history.[69]

A prose work allows the reader a certain freedom to take from it what is desired, or needed, whether it be a set of propositions about sacred history or the agency of human beings in making the social world. A poem, an intricate little machine of thought and language, will not let you do that. I have been reading the wrong Clio in 'Homage to Clio' for a very long time; and wilfully so. I had no permission from the text to make my reading. I could have worked these things out for myself, twenty years ago. *Clio II*

p. 119; Hayden White, *Metahistory. The Historical Imagination in Nineteenth Century Europe* (1971), Johns Hopkins University Press, Baltimore MD, 2014, pp. 135–162.

67 'Take Marx and Vico and a few European novelists away, and my most intimate pantheon would be a provincial tea party: a gathering of the English and the Anglo-Irish.' E. P. Thompson, *The Poverty of Theory*, Merlin Press, London, p. 109; Richard Fieldhouse and Richard Taylor, *E. P. Thompson and English Radicalism*, Manchester University Press, Manchester, 2013, p. 2.

68 David Bebbington, *Patterns in History: A Christian Perspective on Historical Thought*, Regent College, Vancouver, 1990, pp. 97–107; M. C. Lemon, *Philosophy of History. A Guide for Students*, Routledge, London, 2003, p. 153.

69 For differences between Vico and Marx over the question of 'making', Terence Ball, 'Vico and Marx on "Making" History', *Reappraising Political Theory. Revisionist Studies in the History of Political Thought*, Oxford University Press, Oxford, 1994, pp. 212–228, esp. 220–225. For 'Men make their own history' (quoting it is just about possible in a footnote), 'The Eighteenth Brumaire of Louis Bonaparte' (1852): 'Men make their own history, but they do not make it as they please; they do not make it under self-selected circumstances, but under circumstances existing already, given and transmitted from the past. The tradition of all dead generations weighs like a nightmare on the brains of the living. And just as they seem to be occupied with revolutionizing themselves and things, creating something that did not exist before … they anxiously conjure up the spirits of the past to their service, borrowing from them names, battle slogans, and costumes in order to present this new scene in world history in time-honored disguise and borrowed language.' www.marxists.org/archive/marx/works/1852/18th-brumaire/ch01.htm (accessed 16 October 2017).

is not History, or *about* history, or about *doing* history. She is about some other form of time that isn't historical time; she is – about – Christian time.[70] And I simply do not have the emotional or devotional ticket that might take me to the end of her line. There are other realms of historical thinking where I can get on with the job of working out how stuff happened. How people decided to do stuff. Made moves. Altered things. A realm in which we all know that what is made out of the past depends on who's doing the observing, and that what we think about it depends on what we're actually doing, which is writing this history (some history or other), right now. I shall ignore Mr Irwin, calling after me that he doesn't know what I'm talking about.

70 John R. Hall, 'The time of history and the history of times', *History and Theory*, 19:2 (1980), pp. 113–131.

9

The Ridiculous Historian's Hopes

Gracious exterior, but the rooms are small and mean
and so papered over with secrets that even their shape
is uncertain, but it is the shape of the past:
no love, no extra credit, not even civility
from these shades. Do they even see you?

They were so anxious for you to be there,
once, in the playground of what was happening to them.
Messages were bright then, hats undoffed,
manners fresh and cool, like a seasonable day
in early spring. The glancing
rivulets in the gutters struck a note that was a trifle flint-like,
though, and the birds were warier, warier than usual.

It took a man with a cane to magnetize
all those invisible and partly visible crosscurrents,
reluctant, downright sullen, or one that hadn't yet had the time
to reflect on what was being set up here: a point,
no more nor less. Instead of trying to kiss you,
I too felt sucked into the ambient animal-revenge scene:
By twos and threes the animals returned, to their cages,
and sat obediently while the trainer barked orders at them.
They, it seemed, had nothing to lose. Nor in all the whitewashed domain
of the present past tense was anyone privy to the secrets
that now make us strong, or tall, or vulnerable
as a bride left waiting at the church, inching backwards
to the cliff's edge as the photographer gets ready to smile.

John Ashbery, 'The Ridiculous Translator's Hopes', 1994.[1]

This, as shall be proposed, is poetry – a poem – for historians, because it describes the emotional situation of 'doing' history; because it tells us a story about what we do, contains propositions about the cultural and intellectual activity called 'history', lets us see ourselves, and have a laugh at our activities. It doesn't set out to do those things; but historians can make them happen: make poetry out of a future that had not happened when the actual poet wrote his actual words. It is particularly illuminating on the grammatical tenses of writing history: the past present tense of the poem itself, and the tenses – future conditional, subjunctive, future perfect – which have been discussed throughout this book. And it provides a good laugh, because although the activity of writing history is no more peculiar than the writing of poetry, there is much more commentary on the latter and remarkably little on the former. There is virtue, then, in laughing up our sleeve, in the back kitchen, at our own prosaic mission impossible.

It is pointless to ask – of course! – what 'Ridiculous' *really means*, as Debbie's teacher just might be doing by setting her an essay on Auden. It is an open poem that allows freedom of use, and this despite the secrets it covers over and the secret it is as a poem. There is very little critical commentary on it, and none of what there is commits the intentionalist fallacy of Debbie and her teacher. Some few critics are interested in the absence of the first person singular in this and other Ashbery poems of the period in which it was written; they are interested in the disappearance of the 'I'.[2] The kind of 'vertigo within [our] recognition' of the arbitrary malevolence of a photographer just about to smile as his or her subject inches back towards her death, is tracked across Ashbery's Romantic Postmodernism of the 1980s and 1990s.[3] In a different reading, the secrets that gay men keep are seen to 'crowd … [this] poem', making it cramped and mean in a way its gracious exterior belies.[4] But these readings are by literary scholars, more predisposed to fly than they are to ask the child's and the historian's questions: *Who is the man with the cane? Why the animals? What is going on here? Is the shape of this past really … History?* Is the 'present

1 First appearance in the UK in *The Times Literary Supplement*, 23 October 1992, p. 4; reproduced here from *And the Stars Were Shining*, Carcanet, Manchester, 1994, p. 16.

2 Rudiger Heinze, *Ethics of Literary Forms in Contemporary American Literature*, Die Deutsche Bibliotek/Transaction, New Brunswick NJ, 2005.

3 Geoff Ward, 'A Being All Alike? Teleotropic Discourse in Ashbery and Wordsworth', Edward Larrissey (ed.), *Romanticism and Postmodernism*, Cambridge University Press, Cambridge, 1999, pp. 86–97; 96.

4 John Emil Vincent, *John Ashbery and You. His Later Books*, University of Georgia Press, Athens GA and London, 2007, pp. 108–109.

past tense' really … the historians' tense, of thinking, and of writing? The 'present past tense' of the poem is not a grammatical category, and therefore cannot be *le présent historique* in which French-speaking historians conventionally write, or the doughty, straightforward historic past tense used by the English speaking. It's something like the tense implied by Auden in his 'Letter to Lord Byron': the tense you use to describe something that is over and gone and yet isn't dead. Nothing goes away.

I spent a lot of time in the 1990s disinterring the obdurate set of beliefs inherited from nineteenth-century researches in physiology, biology, and psychology: that nothing goes away; that nothing is capable of being dispersed. This set of assumptions about the material world shaped historical thinking across the life and social sciences – and the discipline of history. This was a 'scientific' idea translated to many publics by a wide variety of media. It was a commonplace by the beginning of the twentieth century, as Auden's assertion 'that no past dies' attests.[5] Other accounts of the work of history in the modern period allow Ashbery's 'present past' to be read as an encapsulation of R. G. Collingwood's many lyrical descriptions of historical knowledge as the re-enactment of past thought in the historian's mind, thus producing the perpetual presentness of the past.[6] Moreover, I believe that I am allowed to know these shades – do they even see me? – as the historian's ghosts, determined by the sociologist Avery Gordon to be fragments of all that is unsettled, ignored, and repressed, when historians write about the past. Gordon's shades signal what is missing from the story of the present.[7] 'History', she says

is that ghostly … totality that articulates and disarticulates itself and the subjects who inhabit it. It is, in contrast to sociology and other modern retrieval enterprises, never available as a final solution for the difficulties haunting creates for the living. It is always a site of struggle between the living and the ghostly, a struggle whose resolution has to remain partial to the living, even when the living can only partially grasp the source of the ghost's power.[8]

5 Carolyn Steedman, *Strange Dislocations. Childhood and the Idea of Human Interiority, 1780–1930*, Virago, London and Harvard University Press, New Haven CT, 1995, pp. 77–95, and passim.

6 R. G. Collingwood, *The Idea of History* (1946). *Revised Edition with Lectures 1926–1928*, Jan van der Dussen (ed. and intro.), Clarendon Press, Oxford, 1994.

7 Avery F. Gordon (1997) *Ghostly Matters. Haunting and the Sociological Imagination*, University of Minnesota Press, Minneapolis MN, 2008.

8 Gordon, *Ghostly Matters*, p. 184.

For this sociologist, History (the past as it is thought and what gets written of that thinking: the work and works of history) is a 'wavering yet determinate social structure', like a system of socio-economic stratification, or a social institution like law, religion, or education. History wavers, moves in and out of our field of vision and understanding; but it *is* a structure; it is a ghost in the present tense. Gordon also says, optimistically, that the ghost is *something to be done*: 'this something to be done is not a return to the past but a reckoning with its repression in the present, a reckoning with that which we have lost, but never had'.[9]

But historians are much more used to commerce with the dead than they are with ghosts; we may not be able to see Avery's or Ashbery's shades. We spend a lot of time with the dead. Most of the data we use for description and analysis of past phenomena is derived from the written words and material artefacts of the dead and gone. If we work with oral history methods, or with the testimony and documentation of living subjects, what we *write* about them gets incorporated in existing historical argument and narration; we thus make the living speak the many dialogues of the dead. This is an attenuated, unnamed genuflection towards a popular eighteenth-century European literary form. For a wide variety of writers and audiences, classical literature demonstrated many formal models that allowed the dead to speak. There were narratives of descent into the underworld, letters from the dead to the living, and vision-like dreams in which the dead had conversations with each other. In the dialogue of the dead 'the voice of the dead was presented without a framing narrative: the dead speak to each other, the reader overhears'.[10] Readers are not speaking *with* the dead and, in truth, no more over-hearing them speak than was Lucian of Samosata (CE c.125–180), or François Fénelon in the later seventeenth century; *they* – of course! – wrote the invented conversations of the dead and gone. Of an analogous eighteenth-century writerly practice, that is, the attribution of speech, set between inverted commas or in italics, to historical figures, James Beattie thought that readers should *just get over* their worries about authenticity and verisimilitude. 'Everyone' knew that departed kings and senators hadn't really said

---

9 Gordon, *Ghostly Matters*, p. 185; Carolyn Steedman, 'Living with the Dead', Carol Smart and Jennifer Hockley (eds), *The Craft of Knowledge. Experiences of Living with Data*, Palgrave, Basingstoke, 2014, pp. 162–175.

10 Markman Ellis, '"Author in Form". Women writers, print publication, and Elizabeth Montagu's *Dialogues of the Dead*', *ELH*, 79:2 (2012), pp. 417–445; Frederick M. Keener, *English Dialogues of the Dead. A Critical History, An Anthology, and a Check List*, Columbia University Press, New York NY, 1973.

those words. Why did historians do it – 'take the liberty to embellish their works in this manner?' – when 'we know, either from the circumstances that they could not, or from more authentic records that they did not, make any such orations?'.[11] One reason, he thought, was to display 'their talents in oratory and narration'; but it was done chiefly to 'render their composition more agreeable', and readers should be grateful for it. There was evidently 'something more pleasing than real nature, or something which shall add to the pleasing qualities of real nature', to be devised by human fancy. Pleasing people was usually the poet's business, but a historian might be pleasing too, even though it was not his natural tendency: 'an historian is a person who usually assumes a character of great dignity, and addresses himself to a most respectable audience'; historians usually sought a language that would enhance their reputation for high seriousness.[12] But, warned Beattie, should they make the attempt to add to the gaiety of nations, they could go too far into the realms of pleasure, as had Voltaire in his account of the Battle of Fontenoy (1745), lengthening 'a description into a detail of fictitious events'. Doing this 'he loses his credit with us, by raising a suspicion that he is more intent upon a pretty story, than upon the truth'.[13] Whatever which way, fictionalising events was a more dangerous practice than inventing the voices of the dead and gone.

Modern history-writing too makes the already-dead speak, but only when something once said has been recorded in some document or other and may be presented between inverted commas (or, in a mid eighteenth-century transitional practice for representing direct speech, set in italics). Indeed it was an early proclamation of the new, modern, professional, university-based history which emerged in the long European nineteenth century, that the dead could be made to walk and talk. In 1869, Jules Michelet announced the raising of the dead in writing as the proper task of the historian. He was remembering back to his

---

11 James Beattie, *Essays. On Poetry and Music, ... On Laughter, ... On the Utility of Classical Learning*, William Creech, Edinburgh, E. & C. Dilly, London, 1776, pp. 47–49. For example, in the case of 'Volumnia haranguing her son Coriolanus ... from what these historians relate, one would conjecture: that the Roman matron had studied at Athens under some long-winded rhetorician ...'. He had other ludicrous examples. Who says James Beattie couldn't make jokes? Vic Gatrell, *City of Laughter. Sex and Satire in Eighteenth-Century London*, Atlantic, London, 2006, p. 169. Carolyn Steedman, 'Out of Somerset; or, Satire in Metropolis and Province', Paddy Bullard (ed.), *Oxford Handbook to Eighteenth-Century Satire*, Oxford University Press, Oxford, forthcoming.
12 Beattie, *Essays*, pp. 217–218.
13 Beattie, *Essays*, pp. 47–48.

first days in the Archives Nationales in Paris, early in the new century, long before his appointment to a chair at the Collège de France and as Head of the History Section of the Archives Nationales. He remembered himself, a young man, moving through the 'catacombs of manuscripts' and discerning 'a movement and murmur which were not those of death. These papers and parchments, so long deserted, desired no better than to be restored to the light of day.' He did not say that he had *heard* them, exactly; he apprehended them; was conscious of them: 'Toutefois je ne tardai pas à m'apercevoir dans le silence apparent de ces galeries, qu'il y avait un mouvement, un murmure qui n'était pas de la mort.' He told the dead, or the undead, how and in what manner they should emerge from their tombs: 'Softly my dear friends, let us proceed in order if you please ...'. Then, as he 'breathed their dust, I saw them rise up. They rose from the sepulchre ... as in the Last Judgement of Michelangelo or in the Dance of Death. This frenzied dance ... I have tried to reproduce in [my] work ...'[14] Addressing all the nameless ones buried in files and folders, he told them that even though they had never really lived – had never really been – he, the historian, could give them a new life. He did not give them words; this was not a dialogue of or with the dead; he could not hear them because he had not already given them speech.

Many besides me have had a lot of fun with the sheer zaniness, the true weirdness, of these propositions about the relationship between historians and the dead. We've had particular fun with Michelet's assertion that he knew better than the dead themselves what they (had) really wanted. After Michelet, remarked Benedict Anderson drily, 'the silence of the dead was no obstacle to the exhumation of their deepest desires'.[15] Ever willing to mock our own presumptions that we *really know* what happened in the past, or what people really thought and felt about it, we have laughed mer-

14 'Et à mesure que je soufflais sur leur poussière, je les voyais se soulever ...'. J. Michelet, 'Préface de l'Histoire de France' (1869); and 'Examenen des remainments du texte de 1833 par Robert Casanova', *Oeuvres Complètes, Tome IV*, Flammarion, Paris, 1974, pp. 613–614, 727; Francis X. Blouin Jr and William G. Rosenberg, *Processing the Past: Contesting Authority in History and the Archives*, Oxford University Press, New York NY, 2011, pp. 25–27.

15 Benedict Anderson, *Imagined Communities. Reflections on the Origin and Spread of Nationalism* (1983), Verso, London, 1991, p. 92; Edmund Wilson, *To the Finland Station. A Study in the Writing and Acting of History* (1940), Doubleday, New York NY, 1953, p. 8; Roland Barthes, *Michelet par lui-même* (1954), Seuil, Paris 1968, pp. 89–92; Hayden White, *Metahistory. The Historical Imagination in Nineteenth-Century Europe*, Johns Hopkins University Press, Baltimore MD, 1973, pp. 149–162; Carolyn Steedman, *Dust*, Manchester University Press, Manchester, 2001.

rily along with Anderson. Or, if we are historians of the European nine-teenth century, explained (away) Michelet's propositions with a history of romanticism and the romantic movement.[16] Or we have made sane, or normalised, Michelet's disconcerting propositions by treating them as an extraordinary poetics of the archive: as a highly-wrought, Romantically-inflected description of the psychological and somatic states experienced by some historians in some archives.[17]

Michelet conjured up the Dead, not ghosts. His frenzied dancers are the dead and gone, animated by the historian's eye, the working of her imagination, the movement of his pen, later, after the archive.[18] But what Ashbery's 'Ridiculous Translator's Hopes' allows you to make out are Avery Gordon's ghosts; it allows you to wonder if – maybe – you're already among them, or at the very least what the hell you're doing here (or there; making a point, no more nor less. It can only be to make a point). There's nothing in the poem itself, the biography of the poet, or the lit-erary commentary on his work, to say that you, the Ridiculous Historian, *can't* do this. This is not the case with Auden, or his poetry, his life, or his commentators: you have to reckon with books like *Auden and Christianity*, many accounts of his God, his contributions to theology; his enthusiasm for 'big' history and the works of Thucydides, and much, much more, before you can get near his Clio, approachable though she may seem. In fact, and as has been described, to approach her is to see her fade into the past and into what she never was – into nothing – in the first place.[19]

My trouble with Auden's Clio – one of my many troubles with his history-poems – was that I'm not used to the enormity of documentation that entombs her. Commentary on Auden's writing would fill a floor of any library I am used to working in; there is archival material scattered across dozens of repositories on both sides of the Atlantic. A historian is used to reading everything there is on the topic she has chosen to work

---

16 Stephen Bann, *Romanticism and the Rise of History*, Twayne, New York NY, 1995.

17 As does Barthes in *Michelet par lui-même*, and White, in *Metahistory*. For what is felt in archives and in other sites of history's making, by some historians, see Stephanie Downes, Sally Holloway, and Sarah Randles (eds), *Feeling Things. Objects and Emotions through History*, Oxford University Press, Oxford, 2018, forthcoming.

18 Carolyn Steedman, 'After the archive', *Comparative Critical Studies*, 8:2–3 (2011), pp. 321–340.

19 Arthur Kirsch, *Auden and Christianity*, Yale University Press, New Haven CT, 2005; Edward Mendelson, 'Auden and God', *New York Review of Books*, 6 December 2007. Tony Sharpe, *W. H. Auden in Context*, Cambridge University Press, Cambridge, 2013, for the many modern discourses surrounding Auden's life and work.

on. Some topic – some problem, some idea – precipitates itself. It comes out of the work of many other historians, about which you murmur as you read: *no: not quite like that, it wasn't quite like that; there's more to say.* Or, in the course of *something else*, some long afternoon in a stifling hot county record office, you while away the waiting time for the documents you have ordered from the stacks by going through the card catalogue *one more time.* This is how my last project started, in Nottinghamshire Archives sometime in 2008. I'd had to go back to the record office in order to complete a footnote to Chapter 6 of *Labours Lost* (2009). I needed to consult the magistrates' notebooks of JP Sir Gervase Clifton, Bart (1772–1812) yet one more time. I'd spent days – weeks – there reading them and taking notes, over the past decade, though he'd been a minor pursuit of mine. In order to write in detail about his adjudication of domestic service disputes across his estates and the wider South Nottinghamshire region, I needed a date and a name that I'd neglected to note two, or ten, years before. I had not obeyed my own injunction to graduate students, to make a full reference to every bloody thing you lay your eyes on, there and then. In the card catalogue – so much more reliable than the online version – I gave the 'Place' drawers one more go: Clifton was not only the magistrate's name and did not only describe his 600-acre Nottinghamshire estate, but was also the name of the village three miles south west of Nottingham, which clustered at the bottom of the drive up to Clifton Hall. There was a card that read: 'Clifton. DD 311/1–6, Diaries of Joseph Woolley, framework knitter, for 1801, 1803, 1804, 1809, 1813, 1815'. I sent for them (checking the reference I'd come for in Clifton's notebooks took all of five minutes) and on a first, over-excited read through, found justicing room incidents that the magistrate himself did not record, a very great deal about the sex-life of Joseph Woolley's friends and neighbours, and that some Clifton people had dreams about Sir Gervase in his aspect as a landlord. I noticed, there and then, how Joseph Woolley used the language of the law to assess character and to make judgement on the wild stories of drunken nights out and marital infidelity he told. I knew, there and then, what my next project would be. I think I even knew, there and then, that I was going to have to spend seven years reading about Luddism – 'the machine-breaking crisis of Regency England' – and Nottinghamshire Luddism, and stocking-making (framework knitting), and the everyday life of the English working class, in a period of war, trade depression, and food shortages, c.1800–1815. I knew what I had to discover, because of knowing about what was already known, historically speaking. I think I knew, there and then, that it would be a book, and that every word I wrote would be a reflection on, an elaboration of, a kind of waltz with the current historiography of the Luddite rebellion and the making of the English working class. Later, in the summer of 2010, transcribing Woolley's 10,000 words (at home, using the photocopy Nottinghamshire Archives provided), I found how useful his diaries were for tracking Sir Gervase's movements between Nottinghamshire, his London house, and the house he rented in Bath for the season. Woolley recorded Clifton's activities as landowner, landlord, and employer: he wrote about Clifton's swearing in of tenants, his discharging of them, his sacking of his own domestic servants; and as a man with a 'hore but a very fine woman' – the plebeian woman he took up with after his wife's death, sometime after 1779. I thought it my great good fortune to work on a document that reversed the common traffic of most social commentary of the modern period, for here one of the low wrote up an elite person. Sir Gervase played a part in Woolley's narrative – he strode the stage of Woolley's writing – whilst the stockingmaker did not appear in the magistrate's much briefer legal records. Woolley watched the magistrate, and wrote him up. In this relationship Woolley intermittently had the power of the pen, or at least the power of observation; the power of those who watch, and are not watched.

I am a devotee and advocate of full transcription, for by copying some other writer's words in your own hand, you get as close as it is possible to get to the dead and gone: you use pretty much the same kind of materials and implements, and the words pass through your mind onto your page, as they did from Joseph Woolley's mind to the pages of six *Old Moore's Almanacs* interleaved with blank sheets. By transcribing, you slow your reading to the pace at which the words were put on *his* page; you read and write the spaces and absences in his text; the intended ironies, the literary allusions, the jokes. You discard your earlier presumptions and assumptions; a man was revealed not as the misogynist I had thought him to be at first glance, but as a writer who empathised with the difficulties of many women's lives, who noticed violent and deeply unhappy sexual relationships and recorded them, who wrote about women as if they were the same kind of creatures as men. Someone read through the window of transcription becomes – a writer. And transcription provokes more of itself: later, writing *An Everyday Life*, I decided that I had to make a full transcription of Clifton's two justicing notebooks, so that I might exploit to the full the good fortune of finding two men, from opposite ends of the social spectrum, recording the same time and place, and sometimes the same the same incidents. Transcribing both sets of documents produced the central conundrum of the book-to-be: how does the Ridiculous Historian write about a Nottinghamshire stockingmaker who was *not* a Luddite, in the birthplace and epicentre of Luddism? I would devise an argument to say that Woolley was *in Luddism*; that you could not be in Nottinghamshire in 1811–1812 and not be *in Luddism*. But he was not 'a Luddite', in the way that its historians have written the Luddites. If the historian wants to account for Joseph Woolley, she must write against many accreted historical assumptions about men *like him*.

There is reading to do, of other historians and of other documents in different archives. There will arise (always does, in my experience) several crises of *too-much* (too many documents, too much commentary) as so brilliantly described by Gabriel Garcia Márquez in his postscript to *The General in His Labyrinth* (1991), his novel about Simon Bolivar's last and terrible journey to the coast of Nueva Granada in 1830. Márquez described the historical overload he experienced during research for the book: so many historical 'facts'; so many that he did not know the meaning of. He refused to renounce 'the extravagant prerogative of the novel' in recounting 'a tyrannically documented life', and only the last few weeks of that life, to boot. (Auden's life and works are tyrannically documented in the same way.) The vortex of meaningless information (or information to which he had not yet assigned meaning) sent Márquez, as it does us all, into blind panic. Luckily, he had friendly historian-informants at the end of a telephone line to give him 'a first inkling of a method for investigating and ordering facts', which was the brilliantly simple stalwart of the file card system. File cards will do it; so will computer searchable transcription – anything really to get the stuff in order and make it think-able. I have always hoped that Márquez's historian-informants told him how unlucky he was to have so very, very much.[20]

If I had the ability, it would have been better to write a poem or a novel about the Clio made of so much, yet always absent, in Auden's history-poems; she who isn't anywhere. But I do not have that ability. I write in the form called 'history', or more correctly, 'academic history'. This prose form has two characteristics that press upon the consciousness of the writer. The first is that the narrative, as you compose it, *explains* something. It is perfectly possible to write a prolegomenon or paragraph that lays out what you're up to and what you mean in the book or article to follow; but that is usually repetition of what is to come, which is narrative

20 Gabriel Garcia Márquez, *The General in His Labyrinth* (1990), Jonathan Cape, London, 1991, pp. 271–274.

that unfolds its meaning (all its theoretical points, its adjustment of fact, its historiography) as it goes along. You have to assume a reader something like you, possessing something like your general knowledge of the period or topic under discussion, and something like the same model of time and chronology. It is perfectly possible to tell your story backwards; but your reader would still know that things happened in a forward movement. Second, the story you are going to tell, or the story you are telling, is but one narrative chipped out of the great unhewn rock of all the other possible narratives, or ways it could be told.

It is dictated by its end; that is, what you are going to say in the future when it *will have been* written. It is thought in the future perfect tense (will have been). You shape a narrative towards it, though it does not yet exist. And the ending will change as you write: even though it doesn't exist (yet), some version of an end has to be imagined in order to get to it. The ending is a conditional future (though not in the grammatical meaning of 'future conditional tense'). The conclusion, or the end-place, is (will be) littered with all the mewling little bodies of the occluded and discarded endings that never came into existence. Then you go back to the beginning and write an introduction, or revise the one you made just to get going, so that a harmony of linerality may infuse the whole. Or you may rely on your readers to do this for you anyway. This is not a poem or a form of poetics; really, your readers (historian-readers) will not care very much about how you make your words work. Modern readers of history are not very much like James Beattie's eighteenth-century audiences, on the lookout for the agreeable composition which make the historian's narrative 'in that degree poetical'.[21] You may be fortunate enough to have a reader who cares enough to react to your prose style; a reader who will say, as did R. G. Collingwood of Thucydides, 'harsh, artificial, repellent. In reading Thucydides I ask myself, What is the matter with the man, that he writes like that?'[22] (Any reaction is better than none.) But historians have been trained, like fishwives, to gut and fillet the documents, including the new work of history another one of them has just produced, to get to *the stuff*: the argument, the new items of information; what used to be called *the facts*. The work has *to be able* to be treated like this: cut up, unravelled so that it can make one thread of some other historian's story. This is why any modern historical story, told in a book, or an article, or a BBC tele-doc, really does not have an end. There are endings and

21 Beattie, *Essays*, pp. 48–49.
22 Collingwood, *Idea of History*, p. 29.

end-stops, because narratives draw to a close, because an article has to be sent to the journal editors, or because you just can't stand it anymore; but an end is different from an ending. Very soon, your story will be picked up, turned about, made part of some other historian's story. Formally and philosophically, a modern narrative of history is without end. It will never – cannot – exist as the shaped, finite, bordered artefact of language that is a poem. Auden wrote of 'Objects' in the same period as his history-poems, that 'If shapes can so to their own edges keep,/No separation proves being bad'. But the work of history cannot keep its own edges; it is unfinished business.[23] I have always claimed to enjoy this form called 'a history' because of its elegant contradiction of story without an end: the closest I ever get to the dangerous edge of things. But you get weary of it and, really, I think now that its pleasure lies in the comfort of knowing that you can't have the final word, because there isn't one; and because knowing this obviates your responsibility as a writer.

But all of that is the writing of history, only a part of its making. The first making begins with your sources or in the record office (or any place or activity that can stand in for a record office). It looks good at first glance: the document, the diaries, whatever; a gracious exterior for the topic or project you have in mind, but soon you find that this little fragment of the past is so papered over with secrets that even its shape, and the shape of your vague idea, is uncertain. You read their words: an account book, a magistrate conducting a settlement examination and making a truly inadequate record of what a woman said in his justicing notebook, a working man describing a riotous night of ale-house trashing on a blank page of his almanac; and you wonder *if they really want you to be there*, watching them. This anxiety is particularly pressing on the social historian operating, however tenuously, under the injunction of E. P. Thompson, who described his mission, perhaps the mission of social history, as the 'rescue [of] the poor stockinger, the Luddite cropper, the "obsolete" hand-loom weaver, the "utopian" artisan, and even the deluded follower of Joanna Southcott, from the enormous condescension of posterity'.[24] Harder thoughts still if your subject *is* a poor stockinger in the era of Luddism. Does Joseph Woolley want to be rescued? By me? Does he want you to be there, at all, in the playground of what was happening to him? I, myself,

23 W. H. Auden, 'Objects' (1956), *Collected Shorter Poems, 1927–1947*, Faber and Faber, London, 1966, p. 320.
24 E. P. Thompson, *The Making of the English Working Class* (1963), Penguin, London, 1980, p. 12.

would not want the condescension of a social historian 200 years on, finding me a subject of empathy or sympathy – *caritas*, really – and diminishing me yet again. I don't want anyone's pity. For these reasons I wrote a scene set nowhere, half-imagined, at the beginning of *An Everyday Life*, in which I expressed all my reluctance to feel anything at all about Joseph Woolley. Some historians have enjoyed their meeting with the shades of their historical subjects. Thinking of the eighteenth-century British *philosophes* and friends with whom he spent time when working on *Enlightenment*, Roy Porter said that he found their company and their conversation congenial: 'I savour their pithy prose, and feel ... in tune with these warm, witty, clubbable men.'[25] But I never could have looked forward to an evening with Joseph Woolley down the Coach and Horses, Clifton. Nor he me, for that matter. He wouldn't have wanted me to be there. His own stories – his own writing – were so bound up in secrets that even their shape was uncertain. They still aren't known; will never be known.[26] It was only the acknowledgement of Joseph Woolley's silence and secrets that allowed me to get on with it; I had to convince myself, for as long as it would take me to write, that I did not assume a right to speak for working-class men (dead or alive) out of my superior and experiential knowledge; that all of them will *keep their secrets*. But there is always that flint-like refusal of your presence; the birds outside the ale-house are wary; the men at the bar turn away from you, back to their pints, as you walk through the door.

Or: are you the man with the cane? Does the historian magnetise all the 'invisible and partly visible crosscurrents' in the multiple stories you have in your notes, simply so that you can tell one more historical story and make a point? Or are you the photographer, watching, not quite ready to smile, as you think (see and imagine) these fragments of other people's past? You are almost certainly the bride, who all the way through the writing of it, inches backwards towards the cliff's edge; to the ending that won't be an end. What right do you have to be there? To recount other lives and make them part of your purpose?

There have been many 'turns' taken by historical studies over the last quarter century. All of them provoke new questions about the historian's responsibilities to their subjects. Beyond the cultural, linguistic, subjective, and archival 'turns' in history-writing, and beyond historiographical

25 Roy Porter, *Enlightenment. Britain and the Creation of the Modern World*, Allen Lane at the Penguin Press, London, 2000, p. 6.
26 Carolyn Steedman, *Landscape for a Good Woman*, Virago, London, 1986, pp. 48–61.

questions asked from the postcolony about the West as the Subject, or 'I', of historical writing, historians have started to ask juridical questions to do with rights, duties, obligation, and ownership of the past.[27] Who owns history? Who has the right to speak for the dead? For particular categories of the dead? These are ethical considerations of the historian's role as a writer, in relationship to his or her (dead) subjects.[28] Global history calls for a new ethics of historical reconstruction and imagination.

Historians have been asked to exercise their moral responsibilities by moving beyond nationalism and national stories to a global universalism: they should, it is said, undertake an empirically based universal history encompassing the history of the Universe itself.[29] An ecumenical global history is extolled as 'the moral duty of the historical profession of our time'.[30] The reason for this is that both the present and the past are whitewashed, as in a dual meaning of Ashbery's 'whitewashed domain/of the present past tense': covered over by the paper of Western imperialism and colonialism. Orientalism and European self-regard literally 'papered' over the past, in reference to the treaties and covenants and land deeds by which Western powers legitimated conquest. The dream that global history can strip away the layers is an honourable one exactly because it is *not* the 'noble dream' of Peter Novick, who traced the twentieth-century profession's high moral concept of objectivity in historical writing back to Leopold von Ranke and the early nineteenth-century development of modern, academic history.[31] In global history theory and practice, Western 'objectivity' is part of the problem: it is the whitewash of

27 Anton de Baets, *Responsible History*, Berghahn, New York NY, 2009; 'A historian's view on the right to be forgotten', *International Review of Law, Computers & Technology*, 30:1–2 (2016), pp. 57–66; Heather Conway, *The Law and the Dead*, Routledge, Abingdon, 2016.

28 Sebastian Jobs and Alf Lüdtke (eds), *Unsettling History. Archiving and Narrating in Historiography*, Campus Verlag GmbH, Frankfurt am Main (distributed by the University of Chicago Press), 2010.

29 David Christian, 'The return of universal history', *History and Theory*, 49 (2010), pp. 691–716; James Vernon, 'The history of Britain is dead; long live a global history of Britain', *History Australia*, 13:1 (2016), pp. 19–34.

30 Jane Haggis, 'What an "archive rat" reveals to us about storying theory and the nature of history', *Australian Feminist Studies*, 27:73 (2012), pp. 289–295. Haggis suggests that such 'claims to moral verisimilitude are … the most recent case of "Archive Fever" and the dream of making the past speak in verity through the historian's modernist ventriloquism'; this quote p. 291.

31 Peter Novick, *That Noble Dream: The 'Objectivity Question' and the American Historical Profession*, Cambridge University Press, Cambridge, 2007.

Western historiography as it has been conducted over the last century and a half.[32]

At the same time, new protocols of imagining and writing have emerged from Holocaust history and sociology – from the event that 'resisted ... long-standing frameworks of historical reasoning, development, and emplotment ... Who can claim the moral ground to consider the meaning ... of the lives and deaths of others?'[33] Some say that Holocaust history and sociology underpin both the subjective and ethical turns in historical studies. 'I have not always written [personally]', says Leo Spitzer, discussing historical representations of the Holocaust. He explains that academic historians like him tend to avoid the personal voice: 'a seamless narrative and impersonal, omniscient, historical voice' usually masks 'the constructed nature of historical inquiry and writing'. He wanted 'to show how the historian is invested in the construction of a historical account – how he or she shapes and constructs it as an embodied being, with a subjectivity and personal history that need to be taken into account'; he started to resist the conventions of history-writing.[34] He started to write, perhaps, in the way Michelet wrote in his Preface to the *History of France*, when he described the visceral experience of the archival work that underpinned the history he wrote.

The ethical turn in historical studies suggests that our responsibilities are much greater towards those we imagine, or write into being, than they are to the nameless, unconsidered dead whom Michelet imagined raising from their tombs of paper and parchment. Michelet did recognise, opaquely, that his dead were devices of writing, the products of his imagination. He described them as not really wanting to be there (or here), not even in his beautiful words; they wanted to go back to their own dreams, not be part of his:

---

32 J. M. Blaut, *Eight Eurocentric Historians*, Guildford Press, New York NY, 2000; Jack Goody, *The Theft of History*, Cambridge University Press, Cambridge, 2006; Bruce Mazlish, *The New Global History*, Routledge, New York NY, 2006; George Iggers and Q. E. Wang, *A Global History of Modern Historiography*, Pearson, Harlow, 2008; Maxine Berg (ed.), *Writing the History of the Global Challenges for the Twenty-First Century*, Oxford University Press for the British Academy, Oxford, 2013.

33 D. W. Cohen, 'Memories of Things Future: Future Effects in "The Production of History"', in Jobs and Lüdtke (eds), *Unsettling History*, pp. 29–49; this quote p. 43.

34 Julia Baker, 'A Conversation with Marianne Hirsch and Leo Spitzer', Christine Guenther and Beth Griech-Polelle (eds), *Trajectories of Memory: Intergenerational Representations of the Holocaust in History and the Arts*, Cambridge Scholars, Newcastle, 2008, pp. 3–12.

Men of a hundred years, nations of two hundred 2,000 years, infants who died
when nursing, they all say that they hardly lived, that they barely began ...
They say that if they had the time to know themselves and prepare, they might
have accepted their lot; they would have ceased to wander around us, they
would have gently allowed their urns to be closed up, lulled by friendly hands,
going back to sleep and rebinding their dreams.[35]

I used to cry quite a lot in libraries and record offices, at moments like
the one Michelet described; at the feelings *my reading* of documents and
texts attributed to the dead and gone; I cried often for shivering poor
children washing cresses at Farringdon Green Market as they prepared
their goods for sale, winter 1849; at the formulaic, desperate narratives of
the settlement or bastardy examination; at the terrible, enduring weight of
the world of which I am a part.[36] Lately, though, I have laid off the tears,
having finally understood that I was only ever crying for myself.[37] I now
know where I'm coming from, in the ridiculous intensity of my archival
encounters.[38]

Archives are places for feeling things, or at least places in which many
historians feel things. You may feel: anxious (*I'll never get it done!*),
despairing, guilty (about so many things, not least the money you're
spending, by just being fruitlessly *here*); almost certainly you feel tired,
possibly exhausted, and hungry, and dirty. Documents, if you're allowed
to lay your hands on them, are often filthy things; it's quite difficult to get
hold of food in most county record offices, and going out to eat something
is *such a waste of time*, for the doors will close at 5pm. You may feel the
simple, quiet pleasure of finding something, something you're looking
for, and writing it down. You may, sometimes, in a different modality
of perception, feel the decaying leather of a notebook cover, the ever so
slightly dusty surface of the page on which someone (maybe, if you're

---

35 Jules Michelet, 'Préface', p. 281, discussed by Arthur Mitzman, *Michelet, Historian.
     Rebirth and Romanticism in Nineteenth-Century France*, Yale University Press, New
     Haven CT and London, 1990, pp. 42–43.
36 Henry Mayhew, 'Watercress Girl', *London Labour and the London Poor. Volume I. The
     London Street Folk*, Griffin, Bohn and London, 1861, pp. 151–152; Pierre Bourdieu,
     La misère du monde, Seuil, Paris, 1993, trans. *The Weight of the World. Social Suffering
     in Contemporary Society*, Polity Press, Cambridge, 1999; Carolyn Steedman, 'The
     Watercress Seller', Tamsin Spargo (ed.), *Reading the Past. Literature and History*,
     Palgrave, Basingstoke, 2000, pp. 18–25.
37 Steedman, *Landscape for a Good Woman*, p. 30.
38 Emily Robinson, 'Touching the void. Affective history and the impossible', *Rethinking
     History*, 14:4 (2010), pp. 503–520.

lucky, the historical person you are pursuing) wrote a long time ago: the movement of her pen, the pencilled groove of notation in the margin. But most likely not; you will spend a lot of hot and flurried time interfacing with all the slippery surfaces of a microfilm reader. Even at the microfilm reader, you may hear things.

Words are material things, as eighteenth-century sensationalist psychology taught, not simply, or not only, because the human voice may be skewered by a pen to the page of notebook, but because words are a product of the human body and are sensible to other bodies: they are apprehensible to the senses.[39] Magistrates' clerks and court reporters writing down the required testimony of the poor made reference to the language philosophy of John Locke in their mundane acts of recording and writing, however bored, or careless, or inattentive, their transcription may have been.[40] But centuries on, opening their decaying registers, the writing dissolves and you fancy that you hear the witnesses and plaintiffs, the poor young woman seven months gone naming the father of her unborn child, as they speak their material but ephemeral words. But really, you're only listening to the void.[41]

Take this as an example: look up from the page of the 'Overseers' Accounts and Rates, 1813–1822, parish of Hardington Mandeville, Somerset', out through the window of Somerset Archives in Taunton, at a landscape and a sky that is just a bit like that enclosing a village twenty-five miles or so south east of where you are now. I sit in a building provided by the local state – a country record office – on the outskirts of a county town that inscribed the very limits of the administrative world that the poor and paupers of Hardington Mandeville c.1800–1820 knew. I am not alone; I am as much at home as it is possible to be with the state. I believe that the hum of voices I hear around me, as local historians load

39 Thomas Astle, *The Origin and Progress of Writing, as well hieroglyphic as elementary, &c.*, for the author, London, 1784; James Beattie, *The Theory of Language. In Two Parts*, Strahan, Cadell & Creech, Edinburgh, 1788; Raymond Williams, *Marxism and Literature*, Oxford University Press, Oxford, 1977, pp. 21–54; Ann Banfield, *Unspeakable Sentences. Narration and Representation in the Language of Fiction*, Routledge and Kegan Paul, London, 1982; Nicholas Hudson, 'Eighteenth-century language theory', *Eighteenth-Century Life*, 20:3 (1996), pp. 81–91; Hannah Dawson, *Locke, Language and Early-modern Philosophy*, Cambridge University Press, Cambridge, 2007.

40 For the narratives of the poor as required speech and the use of their testimony in the eighteenth-century novel, see Carolyn Steedman, 'Enforced Narratives. Stories of Another Self', Tess Cosslett, Celia Lury, and Penny Summerfield (eds), *Feminism and Autobiography. Texts, Theories, Methods*, Routledge, 2000, pp. 25–39.

41 Robinson, 'Touching the void'.

the microfilm reader machines, and search the microfiche pages for one
of the lost ones, one of their family from 100 years ago, is pretty much
like what I might have heard in the Hardington Mandeville vestry room
in 1814: similar accents; something like the same quality of voice. I like
working in local record offices, enjoy the little space of quiet you can make
for yourself as the busy world of family and local history buzzes around.
They and you provide the only possible place of origin for the voices you
hear. Yet, like many historians of the European eighteenth century, I am
as convinced as Arlette Farge that 'juridical records ... created a space of
captured speech'.[42] The humble, everyday legal records composed by jus-
tices' clerks and poor law officials do this quite as well as the case-notes and
jottings of a Lord Chief Justice.[43] But whose speech? Whose voices? The
words of those entombed in the past? In his very first days in the Archives
Nationales Michelet heard muffled voices; he wrote as if the documents
themselves spoke, out of their own desires: 'these papers and parchments,
so long deserted, desired no better than to be restored to the light of day'.[44]
It's taken me an inordinately long time to understand what Michelet is so
clear about: that the murmuring came from the documents, not from the
city state of the dead and gone.

In *Reflections on Aristotle's Treatise of Poesie* (1674), Thomas Rymer
(translating René Rapin) thought it well 'to conclude with a touch of
Morality', for was not 'the reputation of being modest ... (more) worth
than that of making Verses'? If *he* were to make verses, he 'wou'd never
forsake honesty nor modesty'. All men were ridiculous for 'the kind opinion they conceive of themselves, and of their performances', but 'the Poets
are yet more ridiculous than other Men, when their vanity rises from the
difficulty of succeeding well in their Mystery'. If *he* were to make verses
better than another's, he 'wou'd not force any man to find them good':

> I wou'd not have a greater opinion of my self, though all the world applauded
> them; nor shou'd the success blind me ... and I wou'd impose silence on them,
> who in commending me, spoke further than my Conscience; to save my self
> from that ridiculousness, which some vain spirits fall into, who wou'd have

---

42 Arlette Farge, *Le Goût de l'archive*, Editions du Seuil, Paris, 1989; Arlette Farge, *The
     Allure of the Archive*, trans. Thomas Scott-Railton, foreword by Natalie Zemon Davis,
     Yale University Press, New Haven CT and London, 2013.

43 Carolyn Steedman, 'Lord Mansfield's women', *Past and Present*, 176 (2002), pp. 105–
     143; 'Lord Mansfield's Voices. In the Archive, Hearing Things', Holloway, Downes,
     and Randles (eds), *Feeling Things*, pp. 209–228.

44 Carolyn Steedman, *Dust*, Manchester University Press, Manchester, 2001, pp. 26–27.

praises and admirations eternally for every thing they do. I wou'd employ all my reason, and all my wit, to gain more docility, and more submission, to the advice my Friends shou'd give me; I wou'd borrow their lights, to supply the weakness of mine; and I wou'd listen to all the world, that I might not be ignorant of any of my faults ... Lastly, I wou'd rid myself of all the ridiculous vanities, to which those who make Verse are ordinarily obnoxious ... [45]

He followed the Aristotlean line in thinking 'the portraits of History ... less perfect than the portraits of Poesie ... Sophocles, who in his Tragedies represents men as they ought to be, is, in the opinion of Aristotle, to be prefer'd before Euripides, who represents Men as really they are'. The reason for Aristotle's preference, he explained, was that 'History proposes not virtue but [the] imperfect, as it is found in the particulars; and Poetry proposes it free from all imperfections, and as it ought to be in general, and in the abstract'.[46] He had much to say as well about Ridiculous Poets whose verse was more History than Poesie, dwelling as they did upon the ordinary, and the everyday, on the littleness of what actually happened, as opposed to lessons about 'what may, and what ought to be'. Poor historian! And poor, poor poet, reduced to the level of a brute historian, writing something 'strictly ty'd up to the Truth'. Thus the difficulties with Clio, who was in her own way, and no matter how dull, the sort of poet who proclaimed that which was already there to praise. Once historians had recognised, however obliquely, their own acts of making – the everyday poeisis that creates History out of the past – there was no need for her.

---

45 Thomas Rymer, *Monsieur Rapin's Reflections on Aristotle's Treatise of Poesie, Containing the Necessary, Rational, and Universal Rules for Epick, Dramatick, and the Other Sorts of Poetry. With Reflections on the Works of the Ancient and Modern Poets, and their Faults noted. By R. Rapin*, H. Herringman, London, 1674, pp. 155–156. This was a translation of René Rapin's *Réflexions sur la poétique d'Aristotle et sur les ouvrages des poétes anciens et modernes*, 1674.

46 Rymer, *Reflections*, pp. 35, 75.

Conclusion

If a poet gets into conversation with a stranger in a railway coach and the latter asks him: 'What is your job?', he will think quickly and say: 'A schoolteacher, a bee keeper, a bootlegger', because to tell the truth would cause an incredulous and embarrassing silence.

W. H. Auden, 'Squares and Oblongs', 1948.

I never answer 'writer' ... The most satisfactory ... I have discovered, satisfactory because it withers curiosity, is to say *Medieval Historian*.

W. H. Auden, *The Dyer's Hand*, 1963.[1]

TIMMS: Sir. I don't always understand poetry.
HECTOR: You don't always understand it? Timms, I *never* understand it.
              But learn it now and you'll understand it whenever.

Alan Bennett, *The History Boys*, 2004.

There's no incredulity when you say nowadays, on a train, that you're a historian. If anyone cares enough to ask, they're interested enough to say: *What kind of history?* When you mumble something about eighteenth- and nineteenth-century social history, mainly British ... they ask if you've published anything, and then tell you about the BBC 4 history programmes they like best of all. I suppose that Auden didn't to want engage in conversation in the first place, to be left to read his newspaper

---

1 W. H. Auden, 'Squares and Oblongs', *Prose Volume II. 1939–1948*, Edward Mendelson (ed.), Princeton University Press, Princeton NJ, 2002, pp. 339–350; 346; orig. *Squares and Oblongs. Essays Based on the Modern Poetry Collection at the Lockwood Memorial Library, University of Buffalo*, 1948; W. H. Auden, *The Dyer's Hand and Other Essays*, Faber and Faber, London, 1963, p. 74.

in peace; but he *said* that the potential embarrassment of both parties was the reason, for everyone knew that 'nobody can earn a living simply by writing poetry' (as indeed he didn't, and is the reason for the vast output of reviews and journalism, by which he did).[2] He didn't have trouble with the authorities putting the question about trade or profession, for 'immigration and customs officials know that some kinds of writers make a lot of money'.[3] But that was long ago, and I surmise that he was on a US train ('railway coach' is a giveaway, let alone 'bootlegger'). In the twenty-first century UK, anyone who can afford to travel by train is a full citizen of Jorma Kalela's republic of history – of history-in-society – has an articulate understanding of the role of history in the making of self and identity and can locate you immediately as one of the clerisy. They know exactly how much you earn from your university teaching job, and that what extra you make from your publications will maybe just about enable you to buy a nicer pair of the shoes you have in abundance anyway.[4]

The stranger on a train asks you about the kind of thing you've published, and you say something about eighteenth-century domestic servants. A majority of your interlocutors will then tell you that their granny, or their great grandmother, was a servant. Or that their grandfather was a miner, a steel-worker, a bus-driver; their great-grandmother a weaver, a char, worked in the jam factory: was some kind of manual worker. They know that in the republic of history-in-society it is the working class that carries the historical narrative, explaining who they are, now, asking questions on a train. No one, now, tells the story that my imagined Auden-on-a-train just might just possibly once have told, about 'book-loving, Anglo-Catholic parents of the professional classes'; about the doctor father, the graduate mother, the 'study full of books ... reading aloud in the evenings ...'.[5] Upper middle-class origins don't tell much of a story anymore about the origins of the self and the social; the social history of the working class inscribes the constitution of the modern republic of

---

2 Sean O'Brien, 'Auden in Prose', Tony Sharpe (ed.), *W. H. Auden in Context*, Cambridge University Press, Cambridge, 2013, pp. 329–336.
3 Auden, *Dyer's Hand*, p. 74.
4 See Alan Bennett – who actually studied medieval history and taught it too, at Oxford – on this point: *The History Boys*, Faber and Faber, London, 2004, pp. xxiv–xxv.
5 W. H. Auden, 'Honour [Gresham's School, Holt]', Graham Greene (ed.), *The Old School. Essays by Divers Hands* (1934), Oxford University Press, Oxford, 1984, pp. 1–12; W. H. Auden, *The Prolific and the Devourer* (1976, 1981), Ecco Press, Hopewell NJ, 1994, p. 9, quoted by Richard Davenport-Hines, *Auden*, Heinemann, London, 1995, p. 14.

history. Historians have an easy or – depending on their disposition – irritated ride compared with travelling poets who would probably evade the question of their *métier* just as Auden did, in anticipation of blank incomprehension. Yet both historians and poets are workers: they make something, in writing.

The modern word 'poetry' is derived from the ancient term for 'making' – 'to make' (poeisis), so it was first of all a verb to denote an action that transforms and continues the world: keeps the world going. This is a kind of abstract, a-historical, dictionary rendering of the labour theory of value associated with Marxist thought, but given its profoundest – certainly most resonant – articulation in John Locke's philosophy of labour, in the seventeenth century, *avant la lettre* of Marxism. In all of Locke's writing, and particularly in the *Two Treatises of Government* (1689), man is a maker, and his making makes him a person. People fashion things out of the material of the earth, which is provided by God. Labour transforms His earthly provision into objects of use; those who labour on it have a property in its product. The moment of making, the transfer of property from worker to employer (which will not delay us here for very long), was famously described: 'the grass my horse has bit, the turfs my servant has cut ... become my property ... The labour that was mine removing them out of the common state they were in, has fixed my property in them,' wrote Locke. When Locke wrote about the servant's labour, an image had occurred to his imagination, and hence sprang the horse and the turf-cutter. There is also a more opaque image, of the philosopher, looking up from his writing table (thus eschewing the first metaphor for all manner of philosophers down the ages); he looks out of a window, to see a man and a horse in a lonely field. Dobbin is standing by, the panniers on his back, quietly cropping the grass of the field yet uncut. The pair in the field are the plainest analogy of the appropriation of property and the circulation of labour in an agricultural market economy. We are not to know if the man – the figment of an imagination – was a servant in husbandry on an annual hiring, or a labourer paid by the piece (or the load), or by the day or the week. We do know that in the two centuries and a half to follow, the labourer and the horse will become one and the same in the deep structure of the (English) political and economic imagination.[6] All writers use metaphors (and similes, and other figures), and while academic industries and deep pleasures of the imagination have been made out of

6 Carolyn Steedman, 'The servant's labour. The business of life, England 1760–1820', *Social History*, 29:1 (2004), pp. 1–29, p. 29.

their contemplation, it is always salutary to recognise the contingency of their origin; we need to be reminded, again and again, of the probable lack of intention in the turf-cutting passages of the second *Treatise*.[7] But it *is* worth noting the light a poet shone on them – albeit on the turf, the object of labour, not on the horse or the man. Wordsworth is helpful on turf, ideation, and intentionality: 'Oft on the dappled turf at ease/I sit, and play with similes,/Loose type of things through all degrees', he wrote a century after Locke.[8] He was apostrophising a daisy, not a man or a horse; I do know that. But he draws attention to the slippery, uncontrollable figures used by all writers: philosophers, political scientists, historians, and even on this occasion, a poet, for I presume that he, Wordsworth, had no idea that the merest mention of 'turf' would set some historian or other 200 years on, haring after the labour theory of value, tracking it to its lair in John Locke's poetic imagination.

All writing, including the writing of history, is a form of poeisis. It is the making of something, at the same time as it continues the world of philosophers, turf-cutters, poets, and historians. The making involves changing the material laboured on into something else, something new; but it also sustains something outside itself – the world; a bigger story – in something of the same state. Can I call this thing that I have just made – this book – a history? It is a history in parts, perhaps. It follows the conventions of historical narrative in giving some details about Auden's childhood and education out of a conviction that social background explains something of artistic production (as, indeed, Auden assumed in his historical report to Lord Byron); thus in parts – but only in parts – it is a narrative that explains something. It is historical, perhaps, in its investigation of popular understandings of history and poetry in the long eighteenth century; it has something to say about an education in history and poetry in twentieth-century Britain. These were all long ways round to understanding, not poetry in society, but the question of history in society raised by some of Auden's poems, composed for the main part in the 1950s. Understanding – attempting to understand – the working of those artefacts of written language was subordinated to other questions about the making and workings of history (the written artefact; 'a history'). I do

7 Jeremy Waldron, '"The Turfs My Servant Has Cut"', *Locke Newsletter*, 13 (1982), pp. 1–20; James Tully, *A Discourse on Property. John Locke and His Adversaries*, Cambridge University Press, Cambridge, 1980.
8 William Wordsworth, 'To the Same Flower' (1802, 1807), Paul D. Sheets (ed.), *The Poetical Works of Wordsworth*, Houghton Mifflin, Boston MA, 1982, p. 29.

not think that it can be seen as a *work* of history, for its lack of linerality and chronological cohesion. It is, perhaps, a kind of historiography, particularly in its rather painful discovery that the Clio of Auden's 'Homage', isn't History; and never was, and simply isn't there.

And so the anxious question: what has been made? Anxiety is a vague and unpleasant emotion experienced in anticipation of an uncertainly defined misfortune. But the misfortune that lies in wait for this book is not at all ill-defined. It may be read as something like Alexander McCall Smith's *What W. H. Auden Can Do for You*.[9] Smith is illuminating – canny – on a lifetime of reading Auden and the changing shape of a reader's love over many years. He read Auden's poetry differently when he was in his 20s from the way he reads now. He also provides a straightforward and simply clever explanation of Auden's choice of syllabic metre, always with the reader – or reciter – in mind. He writes about the poems as they are lived – used and remade – in countless individual imaginations. He tells how he found resource in the poetry when facing moral dilemmas and in learning how to come to ethical decisions about the public world, or civil society. There is a lot of McCall Smith in his book: the self-portrait and 'the wisdom and courage he has found in Auden's poems' has been appreciated by the great Auden scholar Edward Mendelson and many others, though some have found it short on historical context.[10] A lot of it is in schoolteacher Hector's voice – or tone of voice – from Alan Bennett's *The History Boys*, as when Timms says in class 'I don't see how we can understand it [poetry]. Most of the stuff poetry's about hasn't happened to us yet', and the schoolmaster replies 'But it will, Timms. It will. And then you will have the antidote ready! Grief. Happiness. Even when you're dying.'[11]

Bennett had left Oxford by the time Auden came to live in The Brewhouse, Christ College, in 1972, but he had seen him in Hall at Exeter College way back in 1955 (uncannily, the year in which Auden made his Clio). A year later he dutifully attended Auden's inaugural lecture as

9 Alexander McCall Smith, *What W. H. Auden Can Do for You*, Princeton University Press, Princeton NJ and Oxford, 2013.
10 Not much space in such a short book 'for nuanced historical contextualisation, or for biographical criticism of Auden's poems', said Chris Jones in *The Times Higher Education Supplement* (5 December 2013); 'yet the reader is sometimes offered gestures towards such a big picture that are just blunt enough to cause puzzlement rather than enlightenment'.
11 Bennett, *History Boys*, p. 30. Also 'Alan Bennett Writes About His New Play', *London Review of Books*, 31:21 (5 November 2009), pp. 15–17.

Professor of Poetry, because he too wanted to be 'A Writer', and out of some impulse of the not-yet-named celebrity culture. 'I don't think I'd read much of his poetry or would have understood it if I had', he wrote in 2009. 'When Auden outlined what he took to be the prerequisites of … a life devoted to poetry, I was properly dismayed. Besides favourite books, essential seemed to be a literary landscape (Leeds?), a knowledge of metre and scansion and (this was the clincher) a passion for the Icelandic sagas. If writing meant passing this kind of kit inspection, I'd better forget it.'[12] Later, for a rather different audience, he wrote that he 'would be hard put to say what a great poet is, but part of it, certainly in Auden's case, is the obscurity … Perhaps he was too clever for the English.'[13]

In *What W. H. Auden Can Do for You*, McCall Smith has a section headed: 'He Reminds Us of Community, and of How Our Life May be Given Meaning through Everyday Things', in which he discusses Auden as a poet in the tradition of Horace, teaching us to give thanks for the quotidian and to be concerned with the personal moral life.[14] Another recent work of poetry-for-self-help is *about* Horace – nothing to do with Auden – and delivers up *Life Lessons from an Ancient Poet*. Poet and journalist Harry Eyres, like McCall Smith, dwells on the domestic, on a life lived in some retreat, country or otherwise. He, a poet, thinks that 'Horace can help us most of all not in leading us to some rural idyll where we can definitely put the city behind us, but in acknowledging the pull in both directions.'[15] The recent efflorescence of work describing a writer's personal and textual experience of another's – 'and Me' books – has some relationship to the development of sickness memoir. The British Library Catalogue suggests that the first UK title in the genre (*Breast Cancer and Me*) appeared in 2005; there were two publications using *Cancer and Me* as a title in the first half of 2016. But the 'and Me' title form is much older, appearing first in 1880s Britain when it was almost invariably used for the children's market and for the parents who bought their books: *Little Nell and Me* (1885); *For Teddy and Me. A Story Book for Little Folk* (1910); *An ABC for Baby and Me* (1919). By the 1920s the form was also being used for love stories, novels, and reminiscences. J. B. Priestley published the pamphlet *You and Me and the War* in 1935, a political tract in a sea of

---

12 Bennett, *History Boys*, p. v.
13 'Alan Bennett on the Poems that Inspire Him', *Daily Telegraph*, 17 June 2015.
14 See above, pp. 201–202; McCall Smith, *What W. H. Auden*, pp. 131–137.
15 Harry Eyres, *Horace and Me. Life Lessons from an Ancient Poet*, Bloomsbury, London, 2013, p. 153.

memoirs about acquaintance with film stars or ghosted for film stars them-selves.[16] The 'and Me' title signalled familiarity with famous people and notorious ideas, as in *Timothy Leary, the Madness of the 60s and Me* (1974), *Elvis and Me* (1985), *Ann Frank and Me* (1997), *Renoir and Me* (2010), *The Man Within My Head. Graham Greene, My Father and Me* (2012). These are not all – not mostly – attempts to attach insignificance to fame, though if I had not used the form myself for the title to Chapter 5 of this book, I might be moved to ponder the childish disingenuousness of the usage 'and Me'. I wouldn't worry about the thousand grammarians who since the early nineteenth century have opined that 'Graham Greene' and 'Me' (for example) *are the subjects of the utterance … therefore the subject pronoun, I, is considered correct … 'me' is acceptable in spoken English … don't use it in writing.* It's the coy playfulness, the evasive flirtatiousness of the term, that I dislike; I very much hope that my usage is ironic; that I was trying to raise a laugh, in a pre-emptive strike like Elizabeth Hands' pre-emptive strike, against sneering at her (my) presumption in doing something with Auden's poetry in the first place.

There is always another way in which it could have been done; a differ-ent book written, a different story told. Reviewing McCall's *What W. H. Auden Can Do for You*, Chris Jones (School of English, University of Aberdeen, exponent of Auden's Anglo-Saxon attitudes and influences) ruminated on the book that wasn't – that *could have been*: 'one that would subsequently narrate McCall Smith's travels *with* Auden', from the time of his first encounter with his poetry in the 1970s when McCall Smith was researching the issue of criminal responsibility, 'rather than chronolog-ically retrac[ing] some of the familiar facts of Auden's biography'.[17] It's true, as Auden said, that no past dies, not even the past of the discarded and half-thought words you might have written; it's not so much that 'what is done is done', as that when you're actually *doing* it is so easy to forget the other possible products, because what you're making is the thing that *will have been*. This is not the 'subjunctive history' that Dakin describes in *The History Boys* (Dakin is the closest to Alan Bennett's historiographical avatar the play has – though not the one the playwright actually claims).[18]

16 J. B. Priestley, *You and Me and War*, National Peace Council, London, 1935.
17 Note 10, above.
18 Bennett, *History Boys*, pp. 89–90; p. xxvii for Bennett's named avatar, Posner. Also Alan Bennett, 'The History Boy', *London Review of Books*, 26:11 (3 June 2004), pp. 20–22. Posner may have an unrequited passion for the very clever Dakin, but Bennett doesn't approve of the big bow-wow school of history Dakin finds so alluring; of 'the new breed of historians [who] … all came to prominence under Mrs Thatcher and share some of her

In the play 'subjunctive history' is Dakin's invention (textually speaking): 'The subjunctive is the mood you use when something might or might not have happened, when it's imagined', he says. 'Subjunctive history' appears to have been first used in the early 2000s as an alternative to 'counterfactual history': 'a recounting of the past that purposely locates itself in the realm of the counter-factual: what didn't actually happen, but rather, what could possibly have happened'. Historians in general dislike it as a form for structuring narrative explanation, though some concede its usefulness in asking historical questions about the past.[19] Indeed, some few think that 'the idea of conjecturing on what did not happen, or what might have happened, in order to understand what did happen' is a fundamental of historical thinking.[20] I interpret Dakin's (or Bennett's) 'subjunctive' grammatically ('a mood' says that I may), as a form of telling or writing. The subjunctive mood is the verb form used to express a wish, a suggestion, a command, or a condition that is contrary to fact; in English, the subjunctive mood is used to explore conditional or imaginary situations. Here, it's the might-have-been, or the could-possibly-have-been book we're talking about; but as you write – make something that has its own shape and form – you very quickly forget all the 'what ifs', the 'could have done it that ways'; they keep getting forgotten as you plod your way through its writing: it is a thing that already has some kind life independent of its maker; it is already that which you have dug out from the material of the past and are making into something new. ('New' is not to bestow praise: millions of dove-tail joints have been made over the ages; each is a new one, but it may not be as well executed as that of the joiner working at the bench next to you.) It is a thing made out of the irreducible stuff of the Past, which does not – cannot – die; you, in the happy or unhappy Present 'recite the Past/like a Poetry lesson till sooner/or later it falter[s] at [a] line …'[21]

characteristics. Having found that taking the contrary view pays dividends, they seem to make this the tone of their customary discourse. A sneer is never far away and there's a persistently jeering note, perhaps bred by the habit of contention.' *History Boys*, p. xxiv. But does Dakin jeer? Really? I think this judgement should be reserved for Irwin, the play's perfectly ghastly teacher. But then: I am *so* seduced by Dakin's cleverness. Also, Alan Bennett, *Keeping On Keeping On*, Faber and Faber, London, 2016, p. 244.
19 Martin Bunzl, 'Counterfactual history. A user's guide', *American Historical Review*, 109:3 (2004), pp. 845–858; Richard Evans, *Altered Pasts. Counterfactuals in History*, Little Brown, London, 2014.
20 Jeremy Black and Donald M. MacRaild, *Studying History*, Palgrave Macmillan, Basingstoke, 2007, p. 125.
21 'Letter to Lord Byron', 'In Memory of Sigmund Freud'.

The line at which you are permitted to falter is Ben Lerner's. His book *The Hatred of Poetry* provides not so much a re-reading, or contemplation, of the might-have-been, as a refashioning of what has already been made and, ultimately, about the making of poetry into prose. In *The Hatred of Poetry*, the poet recommends working with the feeling many have that, like Timms, they 'don't get poetry in general or my poetry in particular and/or believe that poetry is dead'.[22] He says that many poets dislike poetry too; he quotes Marianne Moore's 'Poetry' (the 1967 version, he says, in its entirety) for she was another who hated it well. She doesn't say *why* she hates it, only that reading it with the contempt it deserves, it is possible, grudgingly, to find something genuine – her word – in it. Lerner has a long and darkly hilarious account of the difficulties of remembering the 1967 version of 'Poetry'. And he may forget again – in order to make a point, no less – that in its 1919 incarnation, the poem has five stanzas, and began: 'I, too, dislike it: there are things that are important beyond all this fiddle./Reading it, however, with a perfect contempt for it, one discovers that there is in/it after all, a place for the genuine./Hands that can grasp, eyes/that can dilate, hair that can rise/if it must, these things are important ...'.[23]

Why? And why 'I too'? Why the dislike of poetry among poets and their readers? It is because poetry 'arises from the desire to get beyond the finite and the historical'; it's because poetry wants to reach the transcendent, or the divine; it's because any poem is always a record of failure to do that: 'Poetry isn't hard, it's impossible.'[24] Lerner has extraordinary – revolutionary; frightening – recommendations for *getting over it*; getting over the hatred of poetry. He praises a contemporary US poet who writes only prose. He shows what you may do with poetry if *you* make it more like prose by punctuating it. He is brilliant on punctuation (I had attempted it, in fear and trepidation, with a tiny number of Auden lines before I read Lerner's book, as in the quotation from 'Letter to Lord Byron' that is one of its epigraphs: a comma [in square brackets] makes Auden say something about the historian's perspective from which history gets written: 'That what we see depends on who's observing,/And what we think[,] on our activities ...'. However, I must, and perforce, recognise

22 Ben Lerner, *The Hatred of Poetry*, Fitzcarraldo, London, 2016, p. 9.
23 Marianne Moore, 'Poetry', Alfred Kreymborg (ed.), *Others for 1919. An Anthology of the New Verse*, Nicholas L. Brown, New York NY, 1920, pp. 131–132. Lerner refers to *The Complete Poems of Marianne Moore* (1967).
24 Lerner, *Hatred*, pp. 9–15.

that without the inserted comma, Auden *could have been* expressing the perfectly straightforward Marxist view that material life determines mental life; that 'the mode of production of material life conditions the general process of social, political and intellectual life'; that 'it is not the consciousness of men that determines their existence, but their social existence that determines their consciousness ...'.[25] With the insertion of a comma, I have – possibly – made a general 'think', or thinking, into cogitation about history. Punctuation is a powerful thing.

Lerner is racily enthusiastic about the *virgule*, the '/' which I use all over the place, and not just here and with Auden's poetry. This is the conventional way of indicating a line break when verse is quoted and set as prose: publishers like it, at least when historians do it, for it cuts down on the cost of typesetting; writers who are historians use it all the time. In the margin, Lerner labels it *Virgula Divina*.[26] He says it is the mark for verse that 'is not yet, or no longer, or not merely actual'. Poems are always failing us – readers and poets – 'you can only compose poems that, when read with perfect contempt, clear a place for the genuine Poem that never appears'.[27] By punctuation – by inserting punctuation marks, including the *virgule* – you can make *something* appear. There has not been a discussion of the divinity of punctuation (of English-language texts) like this since the eighteenth century, when daring, excited, rebellious, and inebriated discussion of what could be done for writers and readers by these printers' marks took place all over the shop.[28] So too did the brilliant and daring footnote, which is about to be discussed, come to the party. '[For] the purposes I have in view,/The English eighteenth-century will do', as it has throughout this book.[29]

And yet ... the divine virgule can make some strongly stressed poetry much harder to read, especially when the poetry it proses (as the 1813

25 Karl Marx, 'Preface', *A Contribution to the Critique of Political Economy* (1859), Progress Publishers, Moscow, 1977. www.marxists.org/archive/marx/works/1859/critique-pol-economy/preface.htm (accessed 16 October 2016).
26 Lerner, *Hatred*, p. 95–103. I *know* that this is Latin for a divining rod; even Nelly Dean knows that when Lerner tells her so (p. 99). But the virgule is *just divine!* as in modern US and UK English and Lerner uses it in that way (too).
27 Lerner, *Hatred*, p. 103.
28 Carolyn Steedman, 'Poetical maids and cooks who wrote', *Eighteenth-Century Studies*, 39:1 (2005), pp. 1–27; 'Sights unseen, cries unheard. Writing the eighteenth-century metropolis', *Representations*, 118 (2012), pp. 28–71.
29 W. H. Auden, 'Letter to Lord Byron', *Collected Poems* (1976), Faber and Faber, London, 1991, p. 100. To explain developments in twentieth-century literary culture to the dead Lord Byron, Auden invited him to 'what I'll call the Poet's Party' (102).

Lady's Magazine would put it) is placed between inverted commas and makes its appearance on a page that already consists of densely set prose. This was particularly apparent with all the regular and ridiculous imprecations that the eighteenth-century Clio received in Chapter 3. For the ease of readers, including myself, I went back and restored the original setting (as lines of verse) to any quotations longer than four of them (lines). All this mucking about with and remaking of poetry in the manner recommended by Lerner makes one contemplate, yet again, Auden's opaque pronouncements on *the line* as the fundamental unit of organisation in English-language verse. The line remains irreducibly something you can't know about except as a literate person; that objection to it as a means to poetics remains. Nevertheless, there are depths to *the line* that are yet unplumbed; there will be no end to working on whatever Auden was *doing with it*, ever. The poetics of history teaches that there may be endings, but that there is no end.

It *is* anxiety provoking, all this encouragement to remake, reshape, restructure, another's verse. I wonder if am allowed to do it? What legal and copyright infringements lurk behind the encouragement to remake poetry as prose? What probity, particularly a historian's probity, is undone by the practice? It is an inviolable rule of historical writing that what you put between inverted commas is exactly what has been written in documents, in transcripts of spoken language, and in the work of other scholars you quote. It is the same kind of rule that prescribes footnotes, and what is sometimes seen as historians' sad, pedantic obsession with them.[30] All scholars employ the apparatus of the note or reference in their writing – of course. But footnotes are the particular declaration of the historian's honesty; an open, contract-like invitation to readers to check the sources she has used. Or maybe it's more like the pact that Philippe Lejeune describes in regard to the autobiography and its readers: in opening an autobiography the reader undertakes to believe that the name on the cover of a piece of self-writing is that of the person who wrote it, and that the story found in its pages is the story of that person.[31] The reader is the dominant, legal partner in the autobiographical pact; but historians *force* the contract implied in the footnote on their readers. The footnote says: Look, Reader! I have done *this*: I have taken the train to the distant county

30 Anthony Grafton, *The Footnote. A Curious History* (1997), Harvard University Press, Cambridge MA, 1999, pp. 1–33, 62–93 ('How the Historian Found His Muse').
31 Philippe Lejeune, *Le Pacte autobiographique*, Seuil, Paris 1975; *On Autobiography*, University of Minnesota Press, Minneapolis MN, 1989.

town where lies the record office; I have called up DD/CH Bx 16; I have sat reading and note-taking in the search room. You can do the same; you can check my sources, confirm my probity, acknowledge that I have told a true story, or at least a likely story, out of those documents.

To my mind, though endnotes *will do*, at a pinch, it really should be a footnote. The reader must be able to move swiftly between the text and the single-spaced note at the bottom of the page; must be allowed read with a dual eye, for the story and where the story comes from. I enjoy the very great authority that this appeal to the evidence gives me as a story-teller. I find the printed page of the history I publish aesthetically and rhetorically so very pleasing (though I am *very* taken with Lerner's use of italicised marginalia): there is the deep seabed of the references, citations, call numbers, and classmarks, above which my argument sails, a happy ship on a bright sea. As in a child's crayoned drawing, the printed page of history-with-footnotes shows a clear cross-section through process and product (ocean floor, deep sea, calm surface; little ship sailing on); shows where the historian's been and what she's done in the making of the story you read. I get quite upset when asked to use a social-science citation method: no footnotes and a messy, jumbled appearance to the page, which surely must discombobulate readers. And – coming clean – I really don't like endnotes *at all*, though publishers prefer them, for reasons of cost, as described in the case of the virgule above, and because some of them underestimate the reading capacities of those who buy their books; publishers find footnotes 'unsightly, costly, forbidding'.[32] But reading with endnotes is like reading that satire on British historical 'truth' which is Maria Edgeworth's *Castle Rackrent* (1800) into all eternity. In this novel, everybody has endnotes: the fictional author, the fictional editor, the servant Thady's transcribed and edited words. One of the servant's functions in Western literature is to utter truth to the master's power – in the back kitchen, behind the door, or in her mind, as she silently brings in the tea-tray with murder on her face. But any power of the Irish servant to speak truth to English Ascendancy is quite removed in *Castle Rackrent*, not only by giving him a name that echoes with 'toady', but also by the elaborate forms of citation and reference that occlude it.[33] To say that it is the first novel in English to employ the device of an unreliable narrator who does

---

32 Chuck Zerby, *The Devil's Details. A History of Footnotes*, Simon & Schuster, New York NY, 2003, p. 2.
33 The novel is actually pre-Ascendancy in that it is set in Ireland in 1782, before the Act of Union (1801).

not participate in the action s/he describes, but is its author and editor, doesn't say the half of it. Moreover, the reading of it is quite deliberately made uncomfortable to the point of impossibility: on my count you have to keep a finger between *five* places in the text of *Castle Rackrent* if you read the notes you are (textually) desired to read.[34] There is, of course, much commentary on these matters, but nothing suggests, as I do suggest, that Edgeworth's form subverts the 'history' she purports to tell by preventing everyone from actually reading it.[35] So – I admit it – reading *Rackrent* is worse than reading a work of history which employs endnotes, where you only need three fingers, for text, notes (and where *are* they? At the end of each chapter? Or gathered together at the end? Both are equally impossible), *and* the bibliography.[36]

These are some the things to know if you intend to study the linguistic techniques used in history-writing (if you intend a poetics of it). There is also – in some place between writing and politics – a poetics of democracy, or collectivity, that all scholars, including historians, entertain as their ghostly guest ('ghost' in the meaning that Avery Gordon has determined) when they write (a footnote is an augury of the ghost's good intention). Historian Roger Chartier has surely persuaded us that whatever it is they do, authors don't produce *books*; they produce piles of manuscript pages (or heaps of notes). Typesetters, editors, copy-editors, proofreaders, translators, *make books*.[37] Any printed and published history is the work of many hands. I, for one, enjoy my editors; I would be mortified if any

34 Maria Edgeworth, *Castle Rackrent. An Hibernian Tale Taken from Facts and from the Manners of the Irish Squires before the Year 1782*, J. Johnson, London, 1800.
35 Marilyn Butler, 'Edgeworth's Ireland. History, popular culture, and secret codes', *Novel*, 34:2 (2001), pp. 267–292; Lisa M. Wilson, 'British women writing satirical works in the romantic period. Gendering authorship and narrative voice', *Romantic Textualities*, 17 (2007), pp. 24–46, www.romtext.org.uk/articles/rt17_n02/ (accessed 16 October 2017). Alex Howard, ' "The Pains of Attention". Paratextual reading in *Practical Education* and *Castle Rackrent*', *Nineteenth-Century Literature*, 69:3 (2014), pp. 293–318; 'Speaking Subalterns and Scribbling Colonists. Narrative Voice in Castle Rackrent', nd, http://people.qc.cuny.edu/Faculty/david.Richter/Documents/rackrent.html (accessed 16 October 2017).
36 Chuck Zerby describes well the extreme discomfort of reading with endnotes: *The Devil's Details*, p. 122. Grafton does not mention endnotes at all in his *Footnote*. Neither of them mention the relatively new publishing practice of having no note numbers *at all* in the text, leaving the reader to find page numbers listed at the end with cursory references to the one you're on. If it takes eight hours to read an average historical monograph, I reckon that all this fiddling about adds at least another two to reading time.
37 Roger Chartier, *The Order of Books. Readers, Authors and Libraries in Europe between the 14th and 18th Centuries*, Stanford University Press, Stanford CA, 1992.

editor ever said I wasn't easy to work with. (I am cheerfully compliant with all readers' reports in the hope that I might be able to ignore fifty percent of their suggestions for changing my prose.) Your readers matter to you the historian in a way they may not matter so much to a poet. They are always irreducibly ever-present (though they may not read your work) in the common understanding of *how things work*. Not only could you render Herodotus' *Histories* as verse and your audience still know it's history, as Aristotle pointed out, you could tell it backwards and your readers would still know that it happened forwards. Of course, they may not believe that it happened *at all*, but they know that they are hearing or reading a narrative that happens in one direction, things unfolding until the last moves off stage, out of their field of vision. The story is still there, structured the way it goes. In a poem, the movement is different, even in a narrative poem about history. Nothing leaves the stage; they're all there, in perpetual *tableau*: rhyme, stress, alliteration, etc, nodding at each other, responding to each other's schtick. They are their own summary of the emotional situation of the poem.[38] Time and chronology will not affect *these* shades, forever together in little engine room of their making, the machinery clattering away.

To add to the audience as a factor in the poetics of history, there is the shaping purpose that philosophers have provided for anyone writing it. I have written about this so many times that I have no more to say, and must perforce plagiarise myself: historians make the stuff (or Everything) of the past (no past dies) into a structure or event, a happening or a thing.[39] They do this through the activities of thought and writing. What they write (create; force into being) was never actually *there*, once upon a time, in the first place.[40] There is a double nothingness in the writing of history and in the analysis of it: it is about something that never did happen in the way it was (at the time) represented, or in the way it is represented 300

38 For the *tableau* as the visual summary of stage melodrama, Martin Meisel, *Representations. Narrative, Theatrical and Pictorial Arts in Nineteenth-Century England*, Princeton University Press, Princeton NJ, 1983, pp. 45–51.

39 Or, as Naomi Mitchison had it in 1932, in the encyclopedia to which Auden contributed (above, p. 73) 'just as scientists make science, so historians make history'. Editor's intro. to N. Niemeyer and E. Ashcroft, 'An Outline of World History', *An Outline for Boys and Girls and their Parents*, Gollancz, London, 1932, pp. 395–416.

40 I am well aware of Perry Anderson's criticism of E. P. Thompson's belief in 'history … [as] the record of everything that has happened'. This is 'a notoriously vacant conclusion', he says. But I am not proposing it.' 'History' is the written form and narrative extracted from the Everything of the Past. *Arguments with English Marxism*, NLB and Verso, London, 1980, p. 13.

years on. The happening exists in the telling or the text; it is made out of a Past undead, but that isn't there in an archive, or anywhere else. It lives, or exists (no past dies) because we believe in the irreducibility of matter, that nothing goes away; its not-dying is in our imagination, and our writing out of it. We should be entirely unsurprised that literary deconstruction made no difference to this kind of writing. When Jacques Derrida decried (or maybe just described) the historian's crab-like thinking backwards, he also suggested that her nostalgia for origins and original referents cannot be satisfied, because there is actually *nothing there*: she is not looking for any*thing*: only silence, the space shaped by what once was; and now is no more.[41] What has survived – the ghost – is not the thing itself, but what has already been said and written about it. 'There is history', says Jacques Rancière, 'because there is the past and a specific passion for the past. And there is history because there is an absence ... The status of history depends on the treatment of this twofold absence of the "thing itself" that is *no longer there* – that is in the past; and that never was – because it never was *such as it was told*.'[42] Doing historiography (analysing the principles, theories, methodology, and philosophy of scholarly historical research and presentation) appears, then, to be an activity that falls within the realm of poetics, not the realm of writing history.

I have always wanted to write my own historiography, as I go along. I think the assumption that we should leave the determination of meaning in our writing to the philosophers and social theorists is just a little bit demeaning. But my attempts to do this have made no difference to anyone reading the history I've written, for you can always, like the fishwife that historian-readers are trained to be, gut the text, extract the story (the historical information and argument) from the way it is told, and happily ignore all questions of textuality it may raise. Historians do not pause to ask *what is this particular text up to?* Nothing I do by way of structure, or analogy, or figures of speech – and not all the poetry in the world, not even Auden's – will prevent this book being subjected to the fishwife's knife. It would have been better – really; wouldn't it? – to have invoked Thalia, the Muse of Comedy, rather than Clio in the writing of it. We shouldn't stand on our dignity, as George Trevelyan suggested a century ago we do

---

41 Jacques Derrida, *Mal d'archive. Une impression freudienne*, Editions Galilée, Paris, 1995, trans. *Archive Fever. A Freudian Impression*, University of Chicago Press, Chicago IL, 1996.

42 Jacques Rancière, *The Names of History. On the Poetics of Knowledge* (1992), University of Minnesota Press, Minneapolis MN, 1994, p. 63.

in regard to Thalia.[43] Eighteenth-century writers made fewer references to Thalia than to her silent sister; but when they did, she was a Muse of wider application and more exhilarating use; she is, in the nicest possible way, a bit of a fishwife herself; she turned up in a wider variety of more interesting settings than did Clio.[44] She always has a laugh at what she sees and hears, and often, at herself. She *has* been here as well, though not named: sniggering up her sleeve in the back kitchen; smirking behind a fan when in a drawing room, she has one to hand, at the ridiculousness of what is about to be said; getting ready to smile as she bears with fortitude the puerile observations of her charges, in some schoolroom – fictional 1790s; historical South London 1964; somewhere – deciding before they're uttered that the observations will not be worth either the smile or the making of verse out of them. She is not named either, in two modern novels that relate how the whole crew – her, and Clio's sisters and brothers, cousins thrice removed, uncles, aunts ... are always here – and there – when anyone attempts to account for stuff happening in the world, past and present; attempts to account for people making moves, altering things.[45]

43 'The "dignity of history", whether literary or scientific, is too often afraid of contact with the comic spirit.' George Macaulay Trevelyan, *Clio, A Muse, and Other Essays Literary and Pedestrian*, Longmans Green, London, 1913, p. 11.

44 Gentleman of Fortune, *The Complete Modern London Spy, for the Present Year, 1781. Or, A Real New, and Universal Disclosure, of the Secret, Nocturnal, and Diurnal Transactions of London and Westminster*, Alex. Hogg and T. Lewis, London, 1781, pp. 117–122; *The Pocket Magazine of Classic and Polite Literature. Volume 3*, John Arliss, London, 1819.

45 Kate Thompson, *Down Among the Gods*, Virago, London, 1997 (without which this book could not have been written in the way it has been written). Also John Banville, *The Infinities*, Picador, London, 2009, for their infinite omnipresence.

Permissions

E. P. Thompson, 'New Fashions' and 'Chemical Works I and II', by E. P. Thompson, *Collected Poems* (ed. Fred Inglis), Bloodaxe Books, Newcastle-upon-Tyne, 1999. Used by kind permission of Kate Thompson.

Bibliography

Books and articles etc

Adam, Alexander, *A Summary of Geography and History, both Ancient and Modern ... with an Abridgement of the Fabulous History or Mythology of the Greeks ... the Second Edition, Corrected, to Which is Added, A Geographical Index, Containing the Latin Names of the Principal Countries, Cities, ... Illustrated with Maps*, A. Strahan and T. Cadell jun. and W. Davies, London, W. Creech, Edinburgh, 1797.

Adams, Jaspar, *The Elements of Useful Knowledge ... Short Systems of Astronomy, Mythology, Chronology, and Rhetoric; with a Brief Account of the Trial and Execution of Louis XVI ... by the Rev. J. Adams*, B. Law, London, 1793.

Almon, John, *An Asylum for Fugitives. Published Occasionally*, for the author London, 1776.

Altieri, Charles, *The Art of Twentieth-Century American Poetry. Modernism and After*, Blackwell, Malden MA and Oxford, 2006.

Alves, James, *The Banks of Esk; Or, A Saunter from Roslin to Smeaton. A Poem, Descriptive, Historical, & Moral; with An Introductory Canto, ... to Which is Added, Drummond Castle; A Poem of the Same Kind. With an Address to Impudence*, for the author, Edinburgh, 1800.

Anderson, Benedict, *Imagined Communities. Reflections on the Origin and Spread of Nationalism* (1983), Verso, London, 1991.

Anderson, Perry, *Arguments with English Marxism*, NLB and Verso, London, 1980.

Ansen, Alan, *The Table Talk of W. H. Auden* (1989), Nicholas Jenkins (ed.), intro. Richard Howard, Faber and Faber, London, 1990.

Anthony, Scott and James Mansell, *The Projection of Britain. A History of the GPO Film Unit*, Palgrave Macmillan, Basingstoke, 2011.

The Apollo. Being An Elegant Selection of Approved Modern Songs, Favourite Airs From Celebrated Operas, &C. To Which Are Prefixed, Twelve New and Original Songs (Never Before Published) Written to Beautiful & Familiar Tunes, for the author, Bath, 1791.

Appleby, Joyce, Lynn Hunt and Margaret Jacob, *Telling the Truth About History*, Norton, New York NY and London, 1994.

Aristotle, *Poetics*, trans. and intro. Kenneth McLeish, Nick Hern Books, London, 1998.

The Art of Poetry on a New Plan. Illustrated with a great Variety of Examples from the best English Poets, and of Translations from the Ancients, 2 vols, Newbery, London, 1762.

Ascherson, Neal, 'From Moscow, on the Brink of Greater Nowheria', *Independent on Sunday*, 15 December 1991, p. 25.

Ashbery, John, *And the Stars Were Shining*, Carcanet, Manchester, 1994.

Astle, Thomas, *The Origin and Progress of Writing, as Well Hieroglyphic as Elementary, &c*, for the author, London, 1784.

Attridge, Derek, *Poetic Rhythm. An Introduction*, Cambridge University Press, Cambridge, 1995.

Attridge, Derek, *Moving Words. Forms of English Poetry*, Oxford University Press, Oxford, 2013.

Auden, G. A., 'A leaden cross bearing a styca impression and other antiquities found in York', *Journal and Proceedings of the British Numismatic Society*, 4 (1907), pp. 235–237.

Auden, George Augustus, 'Height and weight of Birmingham school children in relation to infant mortality', *School Hygiene*, 1:5 (1910), pp. 290–299.

Auden, George Augustus, 'Minutes of Evidence given before the Royal Commission on Ancient Monuments in Wales and Monmouthshire', Vol. 1 [Cd. 6549], HMSO, London, 1912.

Auden, George Augustus, 'The Local Authority and the Health of the Child', Charles William Kimmins (ed.), *The Mental and Physical Welfare of the Child*, Partridge, London, 1927, pp. 171–178.

Auden, John, 'A Brother's Viewpoint', Spender (ed.), *W. H. Auden*, pp. 25–26.

Auden, W. H., 'Poem', *New Verse*, 7 (February 1934), pp. 6–7.

Auden, Wystan Hugh and John Garrett, *The Poet's Tongue*, Bell, London, 1935.

Auden, Wystan Hugh and Thomas Cuthbert Worsley, *Education Today and Tomorrow. Day to Day Pamphlets*, Hogarth Press, London, 1939.

Auden, W. H. (ed.), *The Portable Greek Reader*, Viking Penguin, New York NY, 1948.

Auden, W. H., *The Old Man's Road*, Voyager Press, New York NY, 1956.

Auden, W. H., 'W. H. Auden', Dean of New York (ed.), *Modern Canterbury Pilgrims. The Story of Twenty-three Coverts and why they chose the Anglican Communion*, Mowbray, London, 1956, pp. 32–43.

Auden, W. H., *Selected by the Author. The Penguin Poets*, Penguin, Harmondsworth, 1958.

Auden, W. H., *Homage to Clio*, Faber and Faber, London, 1960.

Auden, W. H. and Louis Kronenberger, *The Viking Book of Aphorisms. A Personal Selection*, Viking Press, New York NY, 1962.

Auden, W. H., *The Dyer's Hand and Other Essays*, Faber and Faber, London, 1963.

Auden, W. H., *Collected Shorter Poems, 1927–1957*, Faber and Faber, London, 1966.

Auden, W. H., 'Honour [Gresham's School, Holt]', Graham Greene (ed.), *The Old School. Essays by Divers Hands*, Jonathan Cape (1934), Oxford University Press, Oxford, 1984, pp. 1–12.

Auden, W. H., *Collected Poems*, Faber and Faber, London, 1991.

Auden, W. H., *The Prolific and the Devourer* (1976, 1981), Ecco Press, Hopewell NJ, 1994.

Auden, W. H., *Juvenilia. Poems 1922–1928*, Katherine Bucknell (ed.), Faber and Faber, London, 1994.

Auden, W. H., *Prose Volume I. 1926–1938*, Edward Mendelson (ed.), Faber and Faber, London, 1996.

Auden, W. H., 'Man before Myth. On James Clifford's *Young Sam Johnson*', Arthur Krystal (ed.), *A Company of Readers. Uncollected Writings of W. H. Auden, Jacques Barzun and Lionel Trilling*, Free Press, New York NY, 2001, pp. 9–13.

Auden, W. H., *Prose Volume II. 1939–1948*, Edward Mendelson (ed.), Princeton University Press, Princeton NJ, 2002.

Auden, W. H., *Prose Volume III. 1949–1955*, Edward Mendelson (ed.), Princeton University Press, Princeton NJ, 2008.

Auden, W. H., *Prose Volume IV. 1956–1962*, Edward Mendelson (ed.), Princeton University Press, Princeton NJ, 2010.

Auslander, Leora, 'Archiving a Life. Post-Shoah Paradoxes of Memory Legacies', Jobs and Lüdtke (eds), *Unsettling History*, pp. 127–148.

de Baets, Anton, *Responsible History*, Berghahn, New York NY, 2009.

de Baets, Anton, 'A historian's view on the right to be forgotten', *International Review of Law, Computers & Technology*, 30:1–2 (2016), pp. 57–66.

Bain, Marie, *Chambers's Periodic Histories. Book III. England in the Making (To 1066 AD)*, Chambers, Edinburgh, 1915.

Baker, Julia, 'A Conversation with Marianne Hirsch and Leo Spitzer', Christine Guenther and Beth Griech-Polelle (eds), *Trajectories of Memory. Intergenerational Representations of the Holocaust in History and the Arts*, Cambridge Scholars, Newcastle, 2008, pp. 3–12.

Ball, Terence, *Reappraising Political Theory. Revisionist Studies in the History of Political Thought*, Oxford University Press, Oxford, 1994.

Banfield, Ann, *Unspeakable Sentences. Narration and Representation in the Language of Fiction*, Routledge and Kegan Paul, London, 1982.

Bann, Stephen, *The Clothing of Clio. A Study of the Representation of History in Nineteenth-century Britain and France*, Cambridge University Press, Cambridge, 1984.

Bann, Stephen, *Romanticism and the Rise of History*, Twayne, New York NY, 1995.

Banville, John, *The Infinities*, Picador, London, 2009.

Barber, Lynn, *An Education*, Penguin, London, 2009.

Barrell, John, *Poetry, Language and Politics*, Manchester University Press, Manchester, 1988.

Barthélemy, Jean-Jacques, *The Travels of Anacharsis the Younger, in Greece, during the middle of the fourth century before the Christian æra. Abridged from the original work of the Abbé Barthelemi. Illustrated with plates, designed and engraved by H. Richter*, Vernor and Hood and five others, London, 1800.

Barthes, Roland, *Michelet par lui-même* (1954), Seuil, Paris, 1968.

Bassett, Rosa, 'A Year's Experiment in an English Secondary School', Helen Parkhurst (ed.), *Education on the Dalton Plan*, G. Bell, London, 1922. pp. 125–143.

Bate, Jonathan, *John Clare. A Biography*, Pan Macmillan, Basingstoke, 2004.

BBC Radio for Schools, *Stories and Rhymes*, British Broadcasting Corporation, 1979.

Beattie, James, *Essays. On Poetry and Music, as they affect the Mind. On Laughter, and Ludicrous Composition. On the Utility of Classical Learning*, William Creech, Edinburgh, E. & C. Dilly, London, 1776.

Beattie, James, *The Theory of Language. In Two Parts: Of the Origin and General Nature of Speech*, Strahan, Cadell & Creech, Edinburgh, 1788.

Bebbington, David, *Patterns in History: A Christian Perspective on Historical Thought*, Regent College, Vancouver, 1990.

Beckett, John with Sheila Aley, *Byron and Newstead. The Aristocrat and the Abbey*, University of Delaware Press, Newark NJ and Associated University Presses, London, 2001.

Beckett, John, 'Politician or poet? The 6th Lord Byron in the House of Lords, 1809–13', *Parliamentary History*, 34:2 (2015), pp. 201–217.

Bedford, W. K. Riland, *Three Hundred Years of a Family Living, Being a History of the Rilands of Sutton Coldfield*, Cornish, Birmingham, 1889.

Bennett, Alan, 'The Wrong Blond', *London Review of Books*, 7:9 (23 May 1985), pp. 3–5.

Bennett, Alan, 'The History Boys', *London Review of Books*, 26:11 (3 June 2004), pp. 20–22.

Bennett, Alan, *The History Boys*, Faber and Faber, London, 2004.

Bennett, Alan, 'Alan Bennett Writes About His New Play', *London Review of Books*, 31:21 (5 November 2009), pp. 15–17.

Bennett, Alan, *The Habit of Art*, Faber and Faber, London, 2009.

Bennett, Alan, 'Alan Bennett on the Poems that Inspire Him', *Daily Telegraph*, 17 June 2015.

Bennett, Alan, *Keeping On Keeping On*, Faber and Faber, London, 2016.

Bentley, Samuel, *Poems on Various Occasions. Consisting of Original Pieces and Translations*, for the author, London, 1774.

Berg, Maxine (ed.), *Writing the History of the Global. Challenges for the Twenty-First Century*, Oxford University Press for the British Academy, Oxford, 2013.

Berkhofer, Robert F. Jr, 'The challenge of poetics to (normal) historical practice', *Poetics Today*, 9:2 (1988), pp. 435–452.

Berkeley Hall; Or, the Pupil of Experience. A Novel. In Three Volumes, J. Tindal, London, 1796.

Berryman, John, 'Auden's Prose', *New York Review of Books*, 1 February 1963.

Best Poems of 1955, Borestone Poetry Awards for 1956. A Compilation of Original Poetry, published in the Magazines of the English Speaking World in 1955, Stanford University Press, Stanford CA, 1957.

Bettelheim, Bruno, *The Uses of Enchantment. The Meaning and Importance of Fairytales* (1976), Penguin, London, 1991.

Bird, James Barry, *The Laws Respecting Masters and Servants, Articled Clerks, Apprentices, Manufacturers, Labourers and Journeymen*, W. Clarke, London, 1799.

Black, Jeremy and Donald M. MacRaild, *Studying History*, Palgrave Macmillan, Basingstoke, 2007.

Blacklock, Thomas, *Poems on Several Occasions*, for the author, Edinburgh, 1754.

Blackwell, Thomas, *Memoirs of the Court of Augustus*, A. Millar, London, 1764.

Blau, Robert, *The Accidences of the Parts of Speech; Or, the Rudiments of Etymology. After a New and Easie Method. Containing, 1. The Alphabet with its Division, and the Definitions of the Eight Parts of Speech most Intelligible by Youth; ... 2. The Accidences of Noun and Pronoun with their Examples and all that Relates to Them; ... 3. Verb & its Accidences, with Four Regular Examples & Some Irregular. ... 4. Participle with all that Relates Thereto, Adverbs, Prepositions, Interjections and Conjunctions, with their English*, for the author, Edinburgh, 1710.

Blaut, J. M., *Eight Eurocentric Historians*, Guildford Press, New York NY, 2000.

Bloch, Marc, *Apologie pour l'histoire; ou, Métier d'historien*, Librairie Armand Colin, Paris, 1949.

Bloch, Marc, *The Historian's Craft*, Manchester University Press, Manchester, 1992.

Bloom, Robert, 'W. H. Auden's bestiary of the human', *The Virginia Quarterly Review*, 42:1 (1966), pp. 207–233.

Bloomfield, B. C., 'The publication of *The Farmer's Boy* by Robert Bloomfield', *The Library*, Sixth Series, 15 (1993), pp. 75–94.

Bloomfield, Robert, *The Farmer's Boy. A Rural Poem*, Vernor and Hood, London, 1800.

Bloomfield, Robert, *Selected Poems*, John Goodridge and John Lucas (eds), Nottingham Trent University, Nottingham, 1998.

Blouin Jr., Francis X. and William G. Rosenberg, *Processing the Past. Contesting Authority in History and the Archives*, Oxford University Press, New York NY, 2011.

Blum, Antoinette, 'The uses of literature in nineteenth and twentieth-century British historiography', *Literature & History*, 11:2 (1985) pp. 176–203.

Boer, Roland, 'Apocalyptic and apocalypticism in the poetry of E. P. Thompson', *Spaces of Utopia: An Electronic Journal*, 7 (2009), pp. 34–53; http://ler.letras. up.pt/uploads/ficheiros/7488.pdf (accessed 16 October 2017).

du Bois, Abbé Jean Baptiste, *Critical Reflections on Poetry, Painting and Music. With an Inquiry into the Rise and Progress of the Theatrical Entertainments of the Ancients. Written in French by the Abbé du Bois … Translated Into English by Thomas Nugent, Gent. From the Fifth Edition Revised, Corrected, and Inlarged by the Author*, John Nourse, London, 1748.

Boothby, Basil, 'An Unofficial Visitor', Spender (ed.), *W. H. Auden*, pp. 93–97.

Bosworth, G. F. (ed.), *Cambridge Historical Readers, Intermediate*, Cambridge University Press, Cambridge, 1914.

Botonaki, Effie, 'Seventeenth-century Englishwomen's spiritual diaries. Self-examination, covenanting, and account keeping', *Sixteenth Century Journal*, 30 (1999), pp. 3–21.

Bourdieu, Pierre, *The Weight of the World. Social Suffering in Contemporary Society*, Polity Press, Cambridge, 1999.

Bowra, Maurice, *New Bats in Old Belfries. Some Loose Tiles*, Wolfson College, Oxford, 2005.

Boydell, Thomas, *Medicaster Exenteratus, Or the Quack's Pourtrait. A Poem*, for the author, London, 1714.

Bozorth, Richard R. 'American Homosexuality, 1939–1972', Sharpe (ed.), *W. H. Auden in Context*, pp. 99–106.

Branwell, Eric Benjamin, *The Ludford Journals of Ansley Hall*, privately printed, 1988.

Brecht, Bertolt, *Selected Poems*, trans. H. R. Hays, Grove Press, New York NY, 1947.

Brecht, Bertolt, *Compact Poets. Bertolt Brecht*, Denys Thompson (ed.), trans. H. R. Hays, Chatto and Windus, London, 1972.

Brecht, Bertolt, *Poems 1913–1956*, trans. M. Hamburger, Methuen, New York NY and London, 1976.

Brewer, John, *The Pleasures of the Imagination. English Culture in the Eighteenth Century*, Harper Collins, London, 1997.

British Council, *English Miscellany. A Symposium of History, Literature and the Arts*, Edizioni di Storia e Letteratura for the British Council, Rome, 1952.

Broughton, Thomas, *An Historical Dictionary of All Religions from the Creation of the World to this Present Time. … Compiled from the Best Authorities*, C. Davis and T. Harris, London, 1742.

Brown, James, *Odes, Elegies, Songs, &c*, for the author, Bristol, 1786.

Bru, Teresa, 'Essaying in autobiography: Wystan Hugh Auden's and Walter Benjamin's Faces', *Biography*, 33:2 (2010), pp. 333–349.

Buchanan, Robert, *Poems on Several Occasions*, for the author, Edinburgh, 1797.

Bucknell, Katherine, 'Phantasy and Reality in Poetry', Katherine Bucknell and Nicholas Jenkins (eds), *'In Solitude, for Company'. W. H. Auden after 1940*, Oxford University Press, Oxford, 1995, pp. 177–196.

Buell, Frederick, *W. H. Auden as a Social Poet*, Cornell University Press, Ithaca NY and London, 1973.

Bulley, Rosamira, 'A Prep School Reminiscence', Spender (ed.), *W. H. Auden*, pp. 31–36.

Bunzl, Martin, *Real History. Reflection on Historical Practice*, Routledge, London and New York NY, 1997.

Bunzl, Martin, 'Counterfactual history. A user's guide', *American Historical Review*, 109:3 (2004), pp. 845–858.

Burch, Edward, *A Catalogue of One Hundred Proofs from Gems, Engraved in England, by E. Burch*, for the author, London, 1795.

Burke, Tim (ed.), *Eighteenth-Century Labouring Class Poets, Volume III, 1700–1800*, Pickering and Chatto, London, 2003.

Burman, John, *Solihull and Its Schools*, Cornish, Birmingham, 1939.

Butler, Marilyn, 'Edgeworth's Ireland. History, popular culture, and secret codes', *Novel*, 34:2 (2001), pp. 267–292.

Caesar, Adrian, 'Auden and the Class System', Sharpe (ed.), *W. H. Auden in Context*, pp. 69–78.

Caledoniad. A Collection of Poems, Written Chiefly by Scottish Authors, 3 vols, William Hay, London, 1775.

Callan, Edward, *Auden. A Carnival of Intellect*, Oxford University Press, New York NY, Oxford, 1983.

Callières, François de, *Characters and Criticisms Upon the Ancient and Modern*

Orators, Poets, Painters, Musicians, Statuaries, & Other Arts and Sciences. With An Heroick Poem (In Blank Verse) Intituled the Age of Lewis the Great. Written Originally in French by the Archbishop of Cambray, and made English by J. G., Richard Smith, London, 1714.

Cannadine, David, Jenny Keating and Nicola Sheldon, *The Right Kind of History. Teaching the Past in Twentieth-Century England*, Palgrave Macmillan, Basingstoke, 2011.

Carey, John, *Latin Prosody Made Easy; Or, Rules and Authorities for the Quantity of Final Syllables in General, and of the Increments of Nouns and Verbs*, for the author, London, 1800.

Carpenter, Humphrey, *W. H. Auden. A Biography* (1981, 1983), Faber and Faber, London, 2010.

Carper, Thomas and Derek Attridge, *Meter and Meaning. An Introduction to Rhythm in Poetry*, Routledge, London, 2003.

Carr, David, *Time, Narrative and History*, Indiana University Press, Bloomington IN, 1986.

Carr, David, 'Narrative explanation and its malcontents', *History and Theory*, 47:1 (2008), pp. 19–30.

Carr, E. H., *What is History?* (1961), With a New Introduction by Richard J. Evans, Palgrave, Basingstoke, 2001.

Carrard, Philippe, *Poetics of the New History: French Historical Discourse from Braudel to Chartier*, Johns Hopkins University Press, Maryland MD, 1992.

Carrard, Philippe, 'History as a kind of writing. Michael de Certeau and the poetics of historiography', *South Atlantic Quarterly*, 100:2 (2001), pp. 465–483.

Carter, Laura, 'The Quennells and the "History of Everyday Life" in England, c. 1918–69', *History Workshop Journal*, 81 (2016), pp. 106–134.

Carthy, Charles, *A Translation of the Second Book of Horace's Epistles, Together with Some of the Most Select in the First, with Notes. A Pastoral Courtship, from Theocritus. One Original Poem in English, and a Latin Ode Spoken Before the Government on His Majesty's Birth-day*, for the author, Dublin, 1730.

Caudwell, Christopher, *Illusion and Reality. A Study of the Sources of Poetry* (1937), Lawrence and Wishart, London, 1946.

Cazden, Courtney B., 'Play with language and metalinguistic awareness. One dimension of language experience', *International Journal of Early Childhood*, 6 (1974), pp. 12–23.

de Certeau, Michel, *The Practice of Everyday Life*, University of California Press, Berkeley CA, 1984.

Charlesworth, Simon J., *A Phenomenology of Working-Class Experience*, Cambridge University Press, Cambridge, 2000.

Charmer, The: A Collection of Songs, Chiefly Such As Are Eminent for Poetical Merit ... in Two Volumes, J. Sibbald, Edinburgh, 1782.

Charms of Melody; Or, Siren Medley. Being the Most Extensive Collection of Love ... Political Songs, Old English, Irish, Scotch and German Ballads, Legendaries, &c. Ever Brought Together in a Single Publication, Selected from the Best Poets and Most Admired Writers, for the author, Dublin, 1795.

Chartier, Roger, 'The Practical Impact of Writing', Chartier (ed.), *A History of Private Life. III. Passions of the Renaissance,* Harvard University Press, Cambridge MA and London, 1989, pp. 111–159.

Chartier, Roger, *The Order of Books. Readers, Authors and Libraries in Europe between the 14th and 18th Centuries,* Stanford University Press, Stanford CA, 1992.

Chatterton, Thomas, *The Auction. A Poem: A Familiar Epistle to a Friend,* George Kearsley, London, 1770.

Child, Francis James, *English and Scottish Popular Ballads,* Helen Child Sargent and George Lyman Kittredge (eds), David Nutt, London, 1905.

Christian, David, 'The return of universal history', *History and Theory,* 49 (2010), pp. 691–716.

Christmas, William J., *The Lab'ring Muse: Work, Writing and the Social Order in English Plebeian Poetry, 1730–1830,* University of Delaware Press, Newark NJ, 2001.

Christmas, William, '"From threshing Corn, he turns to thresh his brains". Stephen Duck as Labouring Class Intellectual', Aruna Krishnamurthy (ed.), *The Working-Class Intellectual in Nineteenth-Century Britain,* Ashgate, Farnham, 2009, pp. 25–48.

Chun, Lin, *The British New Left,* Edinburgh University Press, Edinburgh, 1993.

Churchill, William, *October; A Poem. Inscrib'd to the Fox-hunters of Great Britain. In Two Books,* for the author, London, 1717.

Clark, Thekla (intro. James Fenton), *Wystan and Chester. A Personal Memoir of W. H. Auden and Chester Kallman,* Faber and Faber, London, 1995.

Clarke, Martin Lowther, *Classical Education in Britain, 1500–1900,* Cambridge University Press, Cambridge, 1959.

Classical Arrangement of Fugitive Poetry, John Bell London, 1797.

Claxton, William J., *Peeps into the Past, or, History without History Books,* Pitman, London, 1911.

Cochrane, Charles Norris, *Christianity and Classical Culture. A Study of Thought and Action from Augustus to Augustine,* Clarendon Press, Oxford, 1940.

Coe, Richard N., *When the Grass Was Taller. Autobiography and the Experience of Childhood,* Yale University Press, New Haven CT, 1984.

Cohen, Daniel William, 'Memories of Things Future: Future Effects in

"The Production of History"', Jobs and Lüdtke (eds), *Unsettling History*, pp. 29–49.

Collection of the Most Esteemed Farces and Entertainments Performed on the British Stage, W. Thompson, North Shields, 1786–1787.

Collection of Scarce and Interesting Tracts, Tending to Elucidate Detached Parts of the History of Great Britain; Selected From the Sommers-collections, and Arranged in Chronological Order, R. Edwards, London, 1795.

Collingwood, R. G., *Autobiography*, Oxford University Press, London, 1939.

Collingwood, R. G., *The Idea of History* (1946). *Revised Edition with Lectures 1926–1928*, Jan van der Dussen (ed.), Clarendon Press, Oxford, 1994.

Collini, Stefan, 'Uncle Wiz', 37:4 (16 July 2015), pp. 36–37.

Colman, George, *The Connoisseur. By Mr. Town, Critic and Censor-general*, for the author, Dublin, 1756.

Conway, Heather, *The Law and the Dead*, Routledge, Abingdon, 2016.

Coolley, William Desborough (ed.), *Comments on the History of Herodotus ... from the French of P. H. Larcher ... in Two Volumes*, Whitaker and three others, London, 1844.

Costello, Bonnie and Rachel Galvin (eds), *Auden at Work*, Palgrave Macmillan, Basingstoke, 2015.

Costello, Bonnie, 'Setting Out for "Atlantis"', Costello and Galvin (eds), *Auden at Work*, pp. 133–155.

Cox, Robert W., *Universal Foreigner: The Individual and the World*, World Scientific Publishing, London, Singapore, and New York NY, 2013.

Crystal, David, *The Stories of English*, Penguin, London, 2005.

Cumming, Valerie, C. W. and P. E. Cunnington, *The Dictionary of Fashion History*, Berg, Oxford and New York NY, 2010.

Cunningham, Peter, *Peter Cunningham's New Jest Book; or, Modern High Life Below Stairs*, Funny Joe, London, 1785.

Currie, Robert, 'The Arts and Social Studies, 1914–1939', Brian Harrison (ed.), *The History of the University of Oxford, Vol. VIII. The Twentieth Century*, Clarendon Press, Oxford, 1994, pp. 109–138.

Curteis, A. M., 'The Teaching of History in Preparatory Schools', Board of Education, *Special Reports on Educational Subjects Vol. 6. Preparatory Schools for Boys. Their Place in Secondary Education*, HMSO, London, 1900.

Dalporto, Jeannie, 'Landscape, labor and the ideology of improvement in Mary Leapor's "Crumble Hall"', *The Eighteenth Century. Theory and Interpretation*, 42 (2001), pp. 228–244.

Dane, Joseph, *The Long and the Short of It. A Practical Guide to European Versification Systems*, Notre Dame Press, Notre Dame IN, 2010.

Dauberval, Jean Bercher, *Amphion and Thalia; Or, Amphion, the Pupil of the Muses:*

A Pantomimic Ballet, in One Act. Composed by M. d'Auberval, … Represented for the First Time At the King's Theatre in the Pantheon, the Seventeenth of February, MDCCXCI, Reynell, London, 1791.

Davenport-Hines, Richard, *Auden*, Heinemann, London, 1995.

Dawson, Hannah, *Locke, Language and Early-modern Philosophy*, Cambridge University Press, Cambridge, 2007.

Decan, F., *The Quantity; Or, Measure of Latin Syllables, Interspersed with Useful and Familiar Rules, to Assist Young Poets in the Composition of Pentameters and Hexameters*, F. & C. Rivington, London, 1795.

Delaney, Paul, *British Autobiography in the Seventeenth Century*, Routledge and Kegan Paul, London, 1969.

Delap, Lucy, *Knowing their Place. Domestic Service in Twentieth-century Britain*, Oxford University Press, Oxford, 2011.

Dereli, Cynthia, 'In search of a poet: The life and work of Elizabeth Hands', *Women's Writing*, 8 (2001), pp. 169–182.

Derrida, Jacques, *Of Grammatology*, Johns Hopkins University Press, Baltimore MD, 1974.

Derrida, Jacques, 'Archive fever. A Freudian impression', *Diacritics*, 25:2 (1995), pp. 9–63.

Derrida, Jacques, *Mal d'archive. Une impression freudienne*, Galilée, Paris, 1995.

Derrida, Jacques, *Archive Fever. A Freudian Impression*, trans. Eric Prenowitz, University of Chicago Press, Chicago IL, 1996.

Dewey, John, *Experience and Education*, Collier, New York NY, 1938.

Doctor, Jennifer R., 'The Wonders of Industrial Britain, *Coal Face*, *Night Mail* and the British Documentary Film Movement', Christa Brüstle and Guido Heldt (eds), *Music as a Bridge. Musikalische Beziehungen zwischen England und Deutschland 1920–1950*, Georg Olms, Hildesheim, 2005.

Domestic Management; or, the Art of Conducting a Family with Instructions to Servants in General, Addressed to Young Housekeepers, H. D Symonds at the Literary Press, London, 1800.

Donovan, Jeremiah, *Rome, Ancient and Modern, and its Environs*, for the author, Rome, 1842–1844.

Donzelli, M., 'La Conception de l'histoire de J. B. Vico et son interpretation par J. Michelet', *Annales Historiques de la Révolution Française*, 53:4 (1981) pp. 633–658.

Downes, Stephanie, Sally Holloway, and Sarah Randles (eds), *Feeling Things. Objects and Emotions through History*, Oxford University Press, Oxford, 2018, forthcoming.

Downing, George, *The Temple of Taste; Or, A Dish of All Sorts. Consisting of*

Prologues, Epilogues, Songs ... &c. ... to Which is Annex'd a New Farce, Call'd Newmarket; Or, the Humours of the Turf. With A Sketch of One Year's Account of the Life of the Author, for the author, London, 1763.

Drabble, Margaret, *A Summer Birdcage* (1963), Penguin, Harmondsworth, 1967.

Duck, Stephen and Mary Collier, *The Thresher's Labour and The Woman's Labour*, Augustan Reprint Society, No. 230, Andrews Clark, Memorial Library, Los Angeles CA, 1985.

Duck, Stephen and Mary Collier, *The Thresher's Labour by Stephen Duck, The Woman's Labour by Mary Collier. Two Eighteenth-Century Poems*, Intro. E. P. Thompson, Merlin Press, London, 1989.

Duffy, Maureen, *That's How It Was* (1962), Virago, London, 1983.

Dworkin, Dennis, *Cultural Marxism in Postwar Britain. History, the New Left, and the Origins of Cultural Studies*, Duke University Press, Durham SC, 1997.

Dryden, John, *The Poetical Works of John Dryden, Esq. In Three Volumes. With the Life of the Author*, Apollo Press, Edinburgh, 1777.

Duguid, John, 'Mr Auden, Schoolmaster', *The American Scholar*, 69:3 (2000), pp. 81–86.

Duncombe, John, *The Feminiad. A Poem*, M. Cooper, London 1754.

Eagleton, Terry, 'The poetry of E. P. Thompson', *Literature and History*, 5:2 (1979), pp. 142–145.

Edgeworth, Maria, *Castle Rackrent. An Hibernian Tale Taken from Facts and from the Manners of the Irish Squires before the Year 1782*, J. Johnson, London, 1800.

Ellis, Markman, '"An Author in Form". Women writers, print publication, and Elizabeth Montagu's *Dialogues of the Dead*', *ELH*, 79:2 (2012), pp. 417–445.

Ernaux, Annie, *La place*, Gallimard, Paris, 1993.

Ebner, Dean, *Autobiography in the Seventeenth Century*, Mouton, The Hague, 1971.

Elegy on the Much Lamented Death of Ch—les Co—ey, the Poet, Dublin, 1725.

English, Harriet, *Conversations and Amusing Tales. Offered to the Publick for the Youth of Great Britain*, Hatchard, London, 1799.

Eyres, Harry, *Horace and Me. Life Lessons from an Ancient Poet*, Bloomsbury, London, 2013.

Evans, A. A. (ed.), *The Poet's Tale. An Anthology of Narrative Verse (London English Literature)*, London University Press, London, 1957.

Evans, Richard J., *In Defence of History*, Granta, London, 1997.

Evans, Richard, *Altered Pasts. Counterfactuals in History*, Little Brown, London, 2014.

Fardon, Richard, Olivia Harris, Trevor H. J. Marchand, Mark Nuttall, Cris Shore, Veronica Strang, and Richard A. Wilson (eds), *The Sage Handbook of Social Anthropology*, Volume 1, Sage, London, 2012.

Farge, Arlette, *Le Goût de l'archive*, Editions du Seuil, Paris, 1989.

Farge, Arlette, *The Allure of the Archive*, trans., Thomas Scott-Railton, Foreword by Natalie Zemon Davis, Yale University Press, New Haven CT and London, 2013.

Feldman, David and Jon Laurence, 'Introduction: Structures and Transformations in British Historiography', Feldman and Laurence (eds), *Structures and Transformations in Modern British History*, Cambridge University Press, Cambridge, 2011.

Fellows, John, *The Lady & Gentleman's Pocket Magazine of Literary and Polite Amusement*, J. Lyon & Co, New York NY, 1796.

Fergus, Jan, 'Provincial Servants's Reading in the late Eighteenth Century', James Raven, Helen Small, and Naomi Tadmor (eds), *The Practice and Representation of Reading in England*, Cambridge University Press, Cambridge, 1996, pp. 202–225.

Fernandez, Jean, *Victorian Servants, Class, and the Politics of Literacy*, Routledge, London and New York NY, 2010.

Fieldhouse, Richard and Richard Taylor, *E. P. Thompson and English Radicalism*, Manchester University Press, Manchester, 2013.

Finnegan, Ruth, *Oral Poetry. Its Nature, Significance and Social Context*, Cambridge University Press, Cambridge, 1977.

Fisher, Anne, *An Accurate New Spelling Dictionary, and Expositor of the English Language. Containing a Much Larger Collection of Modern Words than Any Book of the Kind and Price Extant*, for the author, London, 1788.

Fletcher, C. R. L. and Rudyard Kipling, *A School History of England*, Clarendon Press, Oxford, 1911.

Foltz, Jonathan, 'Vehicles of the Ordinary. W. H. Auden and Cinematic Address', Costello and Galvin (eds), *Auden at Work*, pp. 49–68.

Foote, Samuel, *The Patron. A Comedy. In Three Acts. As it is Performed at the Theatre in the Hay-market. By Samuel Foote, Esq*, P. Wilson and 4 others, London, 1764.

Ford, Charles Howard, *Hannah More. A Critical Biography*, Peter Lang, New York NY, 1996.

Fortson, B. W., 'Latin Prosody and Metrics', J. Clackson (ed.), *A Companion to the Latin Language*, Wiley-Blackwell, Oxford, 2011.

Fox, N. E.,'The spread of the threshing machine in central southern England', *Agricultural History Review*, 26 (1978), pp. 26–28.

Fox, Orlan, 'Friday Nights', Spender (ed.), *W. H. Auden*, pp. 173–181.

Francis, Anne, *Miscellaneous Poems, by A Lady*, for the author, Norwich, 1790.

Franklin, Caroline (ed.), *The Romantics. Women Poets 1770–1830*, Routledge, London, 1996.

French, Patrick, *The World Is What It Is. The Authorized Biography of V. S. Naipaul*, Picador, London, 2008.

Freud, Sigmund, 'The Uncanny' (1919), *Standard Edition of the Complete Psychological Works of Sigmund Freud*, Vol. 17, Hogarth Press, London, 1955, pp. 217–252.

Freneau, Philip Moron, *The Poems of Philip Freneau. Written Chiefly During the Late War*, for the author, Philadelphia, 1786.

Frost, Chloe (ed.), *Sir Terry Frost R. A. (1915–2003). A Leamington Lad. Catalogue published to accompany the exhibition held at Leamington Spa Art Gallery and Museum, 24 July-11 October 2015*, Warwick District Council, 2015.

Fukuyama, Francis, 'The end of history?', *The National Interest*, 16 (1989), pp. 3–18.

Fukuyama, Francis, *The End of History and the Last Man*, Free Press, New York NY, 1992.

Fuller, John, *Auden. A Commentary*, London, 1998.

Gardiner, Samuel Rawson, *Outline of English History, B. C. 55-A. D. 1880, first published in 1881 and brought up to the current year in 1895 and 1899*, Longman, London, 1901.

Gattrell, Vic, *City of Laughter. Sex and Satire in Eighteenth-Century London*, Atlantic, London, 2006.

Garvey, Catherine, 'Play with Language and Speech', Susan Ervin-Tripp and Claudia Mitchell-Kernan (eds), *Child Discourse*, Academic Press, New York NY, 1977.

Gee, James, *Social Linguistics and Literacies. Ideology in Discourses*, Falmer, Basingstoke, 1998.

Gentleman of Fortune, *The Complete Modern London Spy, for the Present Year, 1781; Or, A Real New, and Universal Disclosure, of the Secret, Nocturnal, and Diurnal Transactions of London and Westminster*, Alex. Hogg and T. Lewis, London, 1781.

Gentleman of the Inner Temple, *Law Concerning Master and Servants, Viz Clerks to Attornies and Solicitors ... Apprentices ... Menial Servants ... Labourers, Journeymen, Artificers, Handicraftmen and other Workmen*, His Majesty's Law Printer, London, 1785.

Gentleman of the University of Oxford, *An Agreeable Companion for a Few Hours, Either on the Road or at Home. In Several Fugitive Pieces*, F. Newbery and two others, London, 1773.

Gerrard, Christine, *Aaron Hill, The Muses' Projector, 1685–1750*, Oxford University Press, Oxford, 2003.

Glossographia Anglicana nova; or, a dictionary, interpreting such hard words of whatever language, as are at present used in the English tongue, with their etymologies, definitions, &c, Daniel Brown and seven others, London, 1707.

Goldsmith, Oliver, *The Bee. A Select Collection of Essays, on the Most*

Interesting and Entertaining Subjects, by Dr. *Goldsmith*, W. Lane, London, 1790.

Goode, John, 'Thompson and "the Significance of Literature"', Harvey J. Kaye and Keith McClelland (eds), *E. P. Thompson. Critical Perspectives*, Polity, Cambridge, 1990, pp. 183–203.

Goody, Jack, *Cooking, Cuisine and Class. A Study in Comparative Sociology*, Cambridge University Press, Cambridge, 1982.

Goody, Jack, *The Interface Between the Written and the Oral*, Cambridge University Press, 1987.

Goody, Jack, *The Theft of History*, Cambridge University Press, Cambridge, 2006.

Gordon, Avery F., *Ghostly Matters. Haunting and the Sociological Imagination*, University of Minnesota Press, Minneapolis MN, 1997.

Gordon, D., *The Young Man's Universal Companion. Containing, among many other Necessary and Entertaining Particulars ... A Geographical Description of the World; the Fourth Edition ... With An Accurate Map of the Whole World*, P. Hill, S. Payne, and D. Davidson, London, 1766.

Gottlieb, Susannah Young-ah, 'Auden in History', Sharpe (ed.), *W. H. Auden in Context*, pp. 181–192.

Gottlieb, Susannah Young-ah, 'The Fallen Empire', Costello and Galvin (eds), *Auden at Work*, pp. 156–178.

Gough, Richard, *British Topography. Or, An Historical Account of What Has Been Done for Illustrating the Topographical Antiquities of Great Britain and Ireland*, T. Payne and J. Nichols, London, 1780.

Graff, Harvey J., *The Legacies of Literacy. Continuities and Contradictions in Western Culture*, Indiana University Press, Bloomington IN, 1987.

Grafton, Anthony, *The Footnote. A Curious History* (1997), Harvard University Press, Cambridge MA, 1999.

Graham, Elspeth, Elaine Hobby, Hilary Hind, and Helen Wilcox, *Her Own Life: Autobiographical Writings by Seventeenth-Century English Women*, Routledge, London, 1989.

Grant, Michael, *Roman History from Coins. Some Uses of the Imperial Coinages to the Historian*, Cambridge University Press, Cambridge, 1958.

Green, J. R., *A Short History of the English People*, Macmillan, London, 1874.

Greene, Donald, *The Politics of Samuel Johnson* (1960), University of Georgia Press, Athens GA, 2009.

Grigson, Geoffrey, 'A Meaning of Auden', Spender (ed.), *W. H. Auden*, pp. 13–25.

Haggis, Jane, 'What an "archive rat" reveals to us about storying theory and the nature of history', *Australian Feminist Studies*, 27:73 (2012), pp. 289–295.

Hall, Catherine, *Macaulay and Son. Architects of Imperial Britain*, Yale University Press, London, 2012.

Hall, John R., 'The time of history and the history of times', *History and Theory*, 19:2 (1980), pp. 113–131.

Hamilton, Scott, 'Between Zhdanov and Bloomsbury. The poetry and poetics of E. P. Thompson', *Thesis Eleven*, 95 (2008), pp. 95–112.

Hamilton, Scott, *The Crisis of Theory. E.P. Thompson, the New Left and Postwar British Politics*, Manchester University Press, Manchester, 2011.

Hands, Elizabeth, *The Death of Amnon. A Poem, with an Appendix, containing Pastorals, and other Poetical Pieces*, N. Rollason, Coventry, 1789.

Hanley, Lynsey, *Respectable. The Experience of Class*, Penguin Random House, London, 2016.

Hannay, Margaret P. (ed.), *Silent But for the Word: Tudor Women as Patrons, Translators and Writers of Religious Works*, Kent State University Press, Ohio OH, 1985.

Harloe, Katherine and Neville Morley (eds), *Thucydides and the Modern World: Reception, Reinterpretation and Influence from the Renaissance to the Present*, Cambridge University Press, Cambridge, 2012.

Harris, Roy, *Rethinking Writing*, Athlone, London, 2000.

Harrison, Royden, 'From labour history to social history', *History*, 60 (1975), pp. 236–239.

Hatch, James V., *Sorrow Is the Only Faithful One. The Life of Owen Dodson*, University of Illinois Press, Urbana and Chicago IL, 1993.

Hawkins, John, *Probationary Odes for the Laureateship: with A Preliminary Discourse, by Sir John Hawkins, Knt*, James Ridgway, London, 1791.

Hay, Doug and Paul Craven (eds), *Masters, Servants, and Magistrates in Britain and the Empire, 1562–1955*, University of North Carolina Press, Chapel Hill NC and London, 2004.

Harington, Sir John, *Nugæ Antiquæ. Being a Miscellaneous Collection of Original Papers in Prose and Verse. Written in the Reigns of Henry VIII ... James I, &c. By Sir John Harington ... with An Original Plate of the Princess Elizabeth*, 2 vols, W. Frederick, Bath, 1775.

Harris, Sarah Miller, *The CIA and the Congress for Cultural Freedom in the Early Cold War. The Limits of Making Common Cause*, Routledge, Oxford and New York NY, 2016, pp. 111–128.

Heinze, Rudiger, *Ethics of Literary Forms in Contemporary American Literature*, Die Deutsche Bibliotek/Transaction, New Brunswick NJ, 2005.

Hederici, Beni. *Lexicon Manuale Graecum, Omnibus Sui Generis Lexicis Longe Locupletius: in Duas Partes Divisum: Quarum Prior Vocum Graecarum Ordine Alphabetico Digestarum ... Interpretationem Latinam Continet. Altera Vocum Phrasiumque Latinarum ... Interpretationem Graecam Exhibet*, H. Woodfall and thirty-one others, London, 1756.

Herodotus, *The Famous Hystory of Herodotus Conteyning the Discourse of Dyvers Countreys, the Succession of Theyr Kyngs, the Actes and Exploytes Atchieved by Them. The Lawes and Customes of Every Nation with the True Description and Antiquitie of the Same. Devided Into Nine Bookes, Entituled with the Names of the Nine Muses*, Thomas Marsh, London, 1584.

Herodotus, *Herodotou Kleio, in Usum Regiæ Scholæ Cantuariensis*, R. Knaplock, London, 1715.

Herondo, F., *The World's Argument; Or, Justice and the Stage. A Dramatic Debate*, Selwyn, London, 1887.

Highmore, Ben (ed.), *The Everyday Life Reader*, Routledge, London and New York NY, 2002.

Hill, Aaron, *The Works of the Late Aaron Hill, Esq; in Four Volumes*, for the author's family, London, 1753.

Hill, Robert, *Poems on Several Occasions, Chiefly Miscellaneous; Calculated to Please the Admirers of Taste, … to Which are Added Some Pastorals*, for the author, London, 1775.

Hilton, Matthew and Rana Mitter, 'Transnationalism and Contemporary Global History', *Past and Present, Supplement*, [ns] 8, Oxford University Press, Oxford, 2013.

Hobsbawm, E. J. and George Rudé, *Captain Swing*, Lawrence and Wishart, London, 1969.

Hoggart, Richard, *Auden. An Introductory Essay*, Chatto and Windus, London, 1950.

Hoggart, Richard, *The Uses of Literacy. Aspects of Working Class Life*, Chatto and Windus, London, 1957.

Hoggart, Simon, 'Foreword', Sue Owen (ed.), *Rereading Richard Hoggart. Life, Literature, Language, Education*, Cambridge Scholars, Newcastle, 2008, pp. xii–xiii.

Homer, Philip Bracebridge, *The Garland; A Collection of Poems*, C. S. Rann, Oxford, n.d. [1783].

Hopkins, Anthony, 'The Real American Empire', James Belich, John Darwin, Margret Frenz, and Chris Wickham (eds), *The Prospect of Global History*, Oxford University Press, Oxford, 2016, pp. 146–159.

Horace, *The Odes, Epodes, and Carmen Seculare of Horace, Translated into English Prose … Together with the Original Latin from the Best Editions*, by David Watson MA, J. Oswald, London, 1712.

Horace, *The Odes, Epodes, and Carmen Seculare of Horace. Translated Into English Versey William Boscawen, Esq*, John Stockdale, London, 1793.

Horace, *Q. Horati Flacci. Carminum Liber I, With Introduction and Notes by James Gow*, Cambridge University Press, Cambridge, 1949.

Howard, Alex, '"The pains of attention". Paratextual reading in *Practical Education* and *Castle Rackrent*', *Nineteenth-Century Literature*, 69:3 (2014), pp. 293–318.

Howlett, John, *Progressive Education. A Critical Introduction*, Bloomsbury, London, 2013.

Hudson, Nicholas, 'Eighteenth-century language theory', *Eighteenth-Century Life*, 20:3 (1996), pp. 81–91.

Hudson, Thomas, of Blakiston, *Poems on Several Occasions. In Two Parts. By Mr Hudson*, Thompson, Newcastle-upon-Tyne, 1752.

Hughes, Arthur, *English Accents and Dialects. An Introduction to Social and Regional Varieties of English in the British Isles* (1996), 4th edn, Hodder Arnold, London, 2005.

Hurst, Isobel, *Victorian Women Writers and the Classics. The Feminine of Homer*, Oxford University Press, London, 2006.

Hutton, Alexander, '"A belated return for Christ"? The Reception of Arnold J. Toynbee's *A Study of History* in a British Context, 1934–1961', *European Review of History – Revue européenne d'histoire*, 21:3 (2014), pp. 405–424.

Iggers, George and Q. E. Wang, *A Global History of Modern Historiography*, Pearson, Harlow, 2008.

Isherwood, Christopher, *Lions and Shadows. An Education in the Twenties* (1938), Vintage, London, 2013.

Illustrated Guide to the National Museum in Naples. Sanctioned by the Ministry of Education, Richter, Naples, 1909.

Ingram, Anders, *Writing the Ottomans. Turkish History in Early Modern England*, Palgrave Macmillan, Basingstoke, 2015.

Izzo, David Garrett (ed.), *W. H. Auden Encyclopedia*, McFarland, Jefferson NC and London, 2004.

Janowitz, Anne, *Lyric and Labour in the Romantic Tradition*, Cambridge University Press, Cambridge, 1998.

Jenkins, Keith, *Re-thinking History* (1991), With a new preface and conversation with the author by Alun Munslow, Routledge, London, 2003.

Jenkyns, Richard, *The Victorians and Ancient Greece*, Basil Blackwell, Oxford, 1980.

Jobs, Sebastian and Alf Lüdtke (eds), *Unsettling History. Archiving and Narrating in Historiography*, Campus Verlag GmbH, Frankfurt am Main (distributed by the University of Chicago Press), 2010.

Johnson, Paul E. 'Reflections. Looking back at social history', *Reviews in American History*, 39:2 (2011), pp. 379–388.

Jones, Charles, *The Miscellaneous Poetic Attempts of C. Jones, An Uneducated Journeyman-Woolcomber*, for the author by R. Trewman, London, 1781.

Jones, Charles, *The History of Charles Jones, the Footman. Written by Himself*, J. Marshall, London, 1796.

Jones, Chris, 'W. H. Auden and "The 'Barbaric' Poetry of the North". Unchaining one's daimon', *The Review of English Studies*, 53 (2002), pp. 167–185.

Jones, Chris, 'Anglo-Saxon Anxieties. Auden and "The Barbaric Poetry of the North"', Jones (ed.) *Strange Likeness: The Use of Old English in Twentieth-Century Poetry*, Oxford University Press, Oxford, 2006, pp. 68–121.

Juvenal, *The Original Text of Juvenal and Persius, Printed for the Most Part, According to Henninius's Edition; Cleared of All the Most Exceptionable Passages; … by Edward Owen, MA*, Rivington and three others, London, 1786.

Juvenal, *A New and Literal Translation of the I, II, IV, VII, VIII, XIII, XIV Satires of Juvenal, with Copious Explanatory Notes … by the Rev. M. Madan*, for the author, Dublin, 1791.

Kahn, Madeleine, 'Hannah More and Ann Yearsley. A collaboration across the class divide', *Studies in Eighteenth-Century Culture*, 25 (1996), pp. 203–223.

Kalela, Jorma, *Making History. The Historian and the Uses of the Past*, Palgrave Macmillan, Basingstoke, 2012.

Keating, Jenny, 'Ideas and Advice about History Teaching 1900–1950s', History in Education Project, Institute of Historical Research, University of London April 2011.

Keegan, Bridget, 'Cobbling verse. Shoemaker poets of the long eighteenth century', *The Eighteenth Century: Theory and Interpretation*, 42 (2001), pp. 195–217.

Keegan, Bridget (ed.), *Eighteenth-Century Laboring Class Poets, 1700–1800. Volume II, 1740–1780*, Pickering and Chatto, London, 2003.

Keener, Frederick M., *English Dialogues of the Dead. A Critical History, An Anthology, and a Check List*, Columbia University Press, New York NY, 1973.

Ker, W. P., *Collected Essays. In Two Volumes*, Macmillan, London, 1925.

Kermode, Frank, *History and Value. The Clarendon Lectures and the Northcliffe Lectures 1987*, Clarendon Press, Oxford, 1988.

Kermode, Frank, *Poetry, Narrative, History*, Basil Blackwell, Oxford, 1990.

Kershaw, Nora, *Anglo-Saxon and Norse Poems*, Cambridge University Press, Cambridge, 1922.

Kilner, Dorothy, *Life and Perambulations of a Mouse*, John Marshall, London, 1781.

Kilner, Dorothy, *Anecdotes of a Boarding-school; Or, An Antidote to the Vices of those Useful Seminaries … in Two Volumes*, for the author, London, 1790.

Kindley, Evan, 'Auden's Preoccupations. Education and *The Orators*', Costello and Galvin (eds), *Auden at Work*, pp. 216–230.

King, Ronald, *All Things Bright and Beautiful? A Sociological Study of Infants' Classrooms*, Wiley, Chichester, 1979.

Kirsch, Arthur, *Auden and Christianity*, Yale University Press, New Haven CT, 2005.

Klauk, Tobias, 'Is there such a thing as narrative explanation?', *JLT*, 10:1 (2016), pp. 110–138.

Knox, Vicesimus, *Essays Moral and Literary*, 13th edn, 2 vols, London, 1793.

Krober, A. L., '*A Study of History*. Arnold J. Toynbee (Vols 1–6. London, 1934–39)', *American Anthropologist*, 45:2 (1943), pp. 294–299.

Lacey, Mr. J. M., 'Invocations, Serious and Comic', *The Lady's Magazine; Or Entertaining Companion for the Fair Sex, Appropriated Solely to Their Use and Amusement*, 44 (1813), pp. 192–193.

Landry, Donna, *The Muses of Resistance. Laboring Class Women's Poetry in Britain, 1739–1796*, Cambridge University Press, Cambridge, 1990.

Landry, Donna, 'The Labouring Class Women Poets. "Hard Labour we most chearfully pursue"', Sarah Prescott and David E. Shuttleton (eds), *Women and Poetry, 1660–1750*, Palgrave Macmillan, Basingstoke, 2003, pp. 223–243.

Lang, Michael, 'Globalization and global history in Toynbee', *Journal of World History*, 22:4 (2011), pp. 747–783.

Language for Life. Report of the Committee of Enquiry appointed by the Secretary of State for Education and Science under the Chairmanship of Sir Alan Bullock FBA, HMSO, London, 1975.

Larkin, Philip, 'Days', *The Witsun Weddings*, Faber and Faber, 1964.

Leapor, Mary, *The Works of Mary Leapor*, Richard Greene and Ann Messenger (eds), Oxford University Press, Oxford, 2003.

Leavis, F. R. and Denys Thompson, *Culture and Environment*, Chatto and Windus, 1933.

Lebow, Richard Ned, 'International Relations and Thucydides', Harloe and Morley (eds), *Thucydides and the Modern World*, pp. 197–213.

Le Goff, Jacques, *History and Memory* (1977), Columbia University Press, New York NY, 1992.

Lejeune, Philippe, *Le Pacte autobiographique*, Seuil, Paris 1975.

Lejeune, Philippe, *On Autobiography*, University of Minnesota Press, Minneapolis MI, 1989.

Lehmann, Gilly, 'Women's cookery in eighteenth-century England: Authors, attitudes, culinary styles', *Studies on Voltaire and the Eighteenth Century*, 305 (1992), pp. 1737–1739.

Lemann, Gilly, *Martha Bradley: The British Housewife; or, the Cook, Housekeeper's and Gardiner's Companion*, Prospect, Totnes, 1996.

Lemon, M. C., *Philosophy of History. A Guide for Students*, Routledge, London, 2003.

Lerner, Ben, *The Hatred of Poetry*, Fitzcarraldo, London, 2016.

Levy, Alan, *W. H. Auden. In the Autumn of the Age of Anxiety*, Permanent Press, Sag Harbor NY, 1983.

Lewes, G. H., 'State of historical science in France', *British and Foreign Review; or, European Quarterly Journal*, 16 (1844), 72–118.

Lloyd, Robert, *The Tears and Triump[hs] of Parnassus. An Ode for Musick, As It is Perform'd at the Theatre-royal in Drury-lane*, Vaillant, London, 1760.

Llwyd, Richard, *Beaumaris Bay. A Poem; with Notes, Descriptive and Explanatory; Particulars of the Druids, Founders of Some of the Fifteen Tribes of North Wales, the Families Descended from Them, … with An Appendix*, for the author, London, 1800.

Locke, John, *Two Treatises of Government* (1689), Cambridge University Press, Cambridge, 1970.

Long, Paul, *Only in the Common People. The Aesthetics of Class in Post-War Britain*, Cambridge Scholars, Newcastle, 2008.

Lonsdale, Roger (ed.), *Eighteenth-Century Women Poets*, Oxford University Press, Oxford, 1990.

Looser, Devoney, *British Women Writers and the Writing of History, 1670–1820*, Johns Hopkins University Press, Baltimore MD, 2000.

Luke, Carmen, *Pedagogy, Printing and Protestantism. The Discourse on Childhood*, SUNY Press, New York NY, 1989.

Lyric Repository. A Selection of Original, Ancient, and Modern, Songs, Duets, Catches, Glees, and Cantatas, Distinguished for Poetical and Literary Merit; Many of Which are Written by Dr. Johnson, Peter Pindar, J. Johnson, London, 1788.

McCann, Phillip and Francis A. Young, *Samuel Wilderspin and the Infant School Movement*, Croom Helm, London, 1982.

MacCarthy, Fiona, *Byron. Life and Legend*, John Murray, London, 2002.

Maccuzzo-Than, Cecile, ' "Easier than a Chimney Pot to Blacken". Catharine Macaulay, "The Celebrated Female Historian" ', Paula R. Backscheider and Timothy Dykstal (eds), *The Intersections of the Public and Private Spheres in Early Modern England* (1996), Routledge, Abingdon, 2013, pp. 78–104.

Mcdowell, Frederick P. W., ' "Subtle, various, ornamental, clever": Auden in his recent poetry', *Wisconsin Studies in Contemporary Literature*, 3:3 (1962), pp. 29–44.

Macfie, Alexander, 'Review of Keith Jenkins Retrospective' (review no. 1266), www.history.ac.uk/reviews/review/1266 (accessed 16 October 2017).

Maclaurin, John, *The Works of the Late John Maclaurin, Esq. of Dreghorn. One of the Senators of the College of Justice, ... in Two Volumes*, for the author, Edinburgh, 1798.

MacNeice, Louis, 'Birmingham', *New Verse*, 7 (February 1934), pp. 3–4.

Mcracken, Marlene and Robert, *Stories, Songs and Poetry to Teach Reading and Writing*, American Library Association, London, 1986.

Madden, Samuel, *Boulter's Monument. A Panegyrical Poem, Sacred to the Memory of That Great and Excellent Prelate and Patriot, the Most Reverend Dr. Hugh Boulter*, for the author, London, 1745.

Mali, Joseph, *The Legacy of Vico in Modern Cultural History. From Jules Michelet to Isaiah Berlin*, Cambridge University Press, Cambridge, 2012.

Mann, Golo, 'A Memoir', Spender (ed.), *W. H. Auden*, pp. 98–103.

Marincola, Jon, 'Herodotus and the Poetry of the Past', Carolyn Dewald and Marincola (eds), *The Cambridge Companion to Herodotus*, Cambridge University Press, Cambridge, 2006, pp. 13–28.

Markovits, Stefanie, *The Crimean War in the British Imagination*, Cambridge University Press, Cambridge, 2009.

Márquez, Gabriel Garcia, *The General in His Labyrinth* (1990), Jonathan Cape, London, 1991, pp. 271–274.

Marriott, Charles, *The New Royal English Dictionary; Or, Complete Library of Grammatical Knowledge. Containing a Full and Copious Explanation of all the Words in the English Language. ... to Which is Prefixed, A Copious Grammar of the English Language*, J. Wenman, London, 1780.

Marsden, William Edward, 'Contradictions in progressive primary school ideologies and curricula in England. Some historical perspectives', *Historical Studies in Education*, 9:2 (1997), pp. 224–236.

Mascuch, Michael, *Origins of the Individualist Self. Autobiography and Self-Identity in England, 1591–1791*, Cambridge University Press, Cambridge, 1997.

Maxwell, Glyn, *On Poetry*, Oberon, London, 2012.

Mayhew, Henry, *London Labour and the London Poor. Volume I. The London Street Folk*, Griffin, Bohn, London, 1861.

Mazlish, Bruce, *The New Global History*, Routledge, New York NY, 2006.

Mead, Rebecca, 'Ink A Home-EC Bible and W. H. Auden', *The New Yorker*, 20 March 2000, p. 46.

Medley, Robert, 'Gresham's School, Holt', Spender (ed.) *W. H. Auden*, pp. 37–43

Meisel, Martin, *Representations. Narrative, Theatrical and Pictorial Arts in Nineteenth-Century England*, Princeton University Press, Princeton NJ, 1983.

Mendelsohn, Daniel, 'Arms and the Man', *New Yorker*, 28 April 2008.

Mendelson, Edward, *Early Auden* (1981), Faber and Faber, London, 1999.

Mendelson, Edward, *Later Auden*, Faber and Faber, London, 1999.

Mendelson, Edward, 'Auden and God', *New York Review of Books*, 6 December 2007.

Michael, Ian, *The Teaching of English from the Sixteenth Century to the Present Day*, Cambridge University Press, Cambridge, 1987.

Michelet, Jules, *Oeuvres Complètes, Tome IV*, Flammarion, Paris, 1974.

Milliken, E. K., *The Teaching of History*, Incorporated Association of Preparatory Schools, Pamphlet No. 3, 1930.

Mills, William, *The Georgics of Virgil, translated into English blank verse by William Mills*, for the author, London, 1780.

Milner, John, *An Abstract of Latin Syntax; Together with Directions for Construing, Parsing; and Making Latin by the Signs of Cases. to Which is added, Prosody ... for the Use of Schools*, John Noon, London, 1743.

Mitford, Nancy (ed.), *Noblesse Oblige. An Enquiry Into the Identifiable Characteristics of the English Aristocracy*, Hamish Hamilton, London, 1956.

Mitchell, Donald, *Britten and Auden in the Thirties. The Year 1936* (1981), Boydell Press, Woodbridge, 2000.

Mitchell, Sally, *Daily Life in Victorian England*, Greenwood Press, Westport CT, 1996.

Mitchison, Naomi, *An Outline for Boys and Girls and Their Parents*, Victor Gollancz, London, 1932.

Mitzman, Arthur, *Michelet, Historian. Rebirth and Romanticism in Nineteenth-Century France*, Yale University Press, New Haven CT and London, 1990.

Mokyr, Joel, *The Gifts of Athena. Historical Origins of the Knowledge Economy*, Princeton University Press, Princeton NJ, 2002.

Montefiore, Janet, 'Auden among Women', Sharpe (ed.), *W. H. Auden in Context*, pp. 107–117.

'Monthly Catalogue for November 1790', *Monthly Review*, 179 (1790), pp. 345–346.

Moore, Marianne, 'Poetry', Alfred Kreymborg (ed.), *Others for 1919. An Anthology of the New Verse*, Nicholas L. Brown, New York NY, 1920.

Moretti, Franco, *The Way of the World. The Bildungsroman in European Culture*, Verso, London, 1987.

Moretti, Franco, 'Style, Inc.: Reflections on seven thousand titles (British novels, 1740–1850)', *Critical Inquiry*, 36:1 (2009), pp. 134–158.

Morris, Ronald, *Success and Failure in Learning to Read*, Penguin, Harmondsworth, 1973.

Murphy, James Jerome (ed.), *A Short History of Writing Instruction. From Ancient Greece to Contemporary America*, Routledge, New York NY, 2012.

Mythology Made Easy; Or, A New History of the Heathen Gods and Goddesses,

Demi-gods, and Other Fabulous Deities of the Ancients, … Designed to Facilitate the Study of History, Poetry … &c., G. Riley, London, 1790.

Nabokov, Nicolas, 'Excerpts from Memories', Spender (ed.), *W. H. Auden*, pp. 133–148.

Nash, Samuel, *Juvenile Epigrams, and Poems, Written by Samuel John Nash, LLD and Addressed to the Gentlemen of the Army, and the Navy*, for the author, London, 1800.

Niebuhr, Ursula, 'Memories of the 1940s', Spender (ed.), *W. H. Auden*, pp. 104–118.

Neuberg, Victor E., '… History from Below', *Times Literary Supplement*, 22 June 1968, p. 20.

New Royal and Universal Dictionary of Arts and Sciences: Or, Complete System of Human Knowledge. Containing … A Very Great Variety of Useful Discoveries, … the Anatomical, Chemical, and Medicinal Parts by M. Hinde, … the Mathematical Parts by W. Squire, … Gardening and Botany by J. Marshall, … Criticism, Grammar, Poetry, Theology, &c. By the Rev. Thomas Cooke … and the Other Parts by Gentlemen of Eminence …, J. Cooke, London, 1772.

Niemeyer, Nancy, *Stories for the History Hour. From Augustus to Rolf*, Harrap, London, 1917.

Nietzsche, Friedrich, 'On the Use and Abuse of History for Life' (1874), *Thoughts Out of Season*, Allen and Unwin, London, 1937.

Nietzsche, Friedrich, *The Untimely Meditations Parts I and II*, Digireads, pp. 96–133.

Nimmo, Richie, *Milk, Modernity and the Making of the Human. Purifying the Social*, Routledge, Abingdon, 2010.

Novick, Peter, *That Noble Dream: The 'Objectivity Question' and the American Historical Profession*, Cambridge University Press, Cambridge, 1988.

Nussbaum, Felicity, *The Autobiographical Subject*, Johns Hopkins University Press, Baltimore MD, 1989.

Obelkevich, Jim, 'New developments in history in the 1950s and 1960s', *Contemporary British History*, 4:4 (2000), pp. 125–142.

O'Brien, Sean, 'Auden in Prose', Sharpe (ed.), *W. H. Auden in Context*, pp. 329–336.

O'Brien, Sean, 'Auden and Prosody', Sharpe (ed.), *W. H. Auden in Context*, pp. 359–368.

Oldmixon, John, *A Funeral-idyll, Sacred to the Glorious Memory of K. William III*, Nicholas Cox, London, 1702.

Olson, David R., *The World on Paper. The Conceptual and Cognitive Implications of Writing and Reading*, Cambridge University Press, Cambridge, 1994.

Olson, David R., 'Literate Mentalities: Literacy, Consciousness of Language, and

Modes of Thought', Olson, Nancy Torrance, and Angela Hilyard (eds), *Modes of Thought: Explorations in Culture and Cognition*, Cambridge University Press, Cambridge, 1996, pp. 141–151.

Olson, Linda, 'Did Medieval English Women Read Augustine's Confessiones? Constructing Feminine Interiority and Literacy in the Eleventh and Twelfth Centuries', Sarah Rees Jones (ed.), *Learning and Literacy in Medieval England and Abroad*, Brepols, Turnhout, 2003, pp. 69–96.

Ong, Walter J., *Orality and Literacy: The Technologising of the Word*, Methuen, London, 1982.

Ong, Walter J., 'Writing is a Technology that Restructures Thought', Gerd Bauman (ed.), *The Written Word: Literacy in Transition*, Clarendon Press, Oxford, 1986.

Ovid, *Ovid's Art of Love. In Three Books. Together with His Remedy of Love. Translated Into English Verse, by Several Eminent Hands. To Which Are Added, the Court of Love and the History of Love. With Copperplates*, for the booksellers, London, 1793.

Owen, Sue (ed.), *Rereading Richard Hoggart. Life, Literature, Language, Education*, Cambridge Scholars, Newcastle, 2008.

Palmer, Bernard, *Willingly to School. A History of St Edmund's, Hindhead*, The Governing Body of the St Edmund's School Trust, Hindhead, 2000.

Parkhurst, Helen, *Education on the Dalton Plan*, G. Bell, London, 1922.

Parson's Genuine Pocket Edition of Hume's History of England, with a Continuation to the Death of George II by Dr Smollett & a further Continuation to the Present Time by J. Barlow Esq. Embellished with Historical Engravings & Delicate Portraits of all the English Monarchs, & most Eminent Characters of the Present Reign, Vol. 5, J. Parsons, London, 1793.

Pearch, G., *A Collection of Poems, in Four Volumes by Several Hands*, for the author, London, 1775.

Peckham, Ann, *The Complete English Cook, or, Prudent Housewife*, Griffith Wright, Leeds, 1773.

Pemberton, Robert, *Solihull and Its Church*, for the author, Exeter, 1905.

Percy, Carol, 'Learning and Virtue. English Grammar and the Eighteenth-Century Girls' School', Mary Hilton and Jill Shefrin (eds), *Educating the Child in Enlightenment Britain. Beliefs, Cultures, Practices*, Ashgate, Farnham, 2009, pp. 77–98.

Phillips, Mark Salber, *Society and Sentiment. Genres of Historical Writing in Britain, 1740–1820*, Princeton University Press, Princeton NJ, 2000.

Philpotts, Matthew, 'Defining the Thick Journal. Periodical Codes and Common Habitus', https://seeeps.princeton.edu/files/2015/03/mla2013_philpotts.pdf (accessed 16 October 2017).

Philpotts, Matthew, 'The role of the periodical editor: Literary journals and editorial habitus', *Modern Language Review*, 107:1 (2012), pp. 39–337.

Platt, Polly and W. H. Auden, 'Interview. W. H. Auden', *The American Scholar*, 36:2 (1967), pp. 266–270.

Pocket Magazine of Classic and Polite Literature, 3:1 (1819), John Arliss, London.

Poetical Justice; or, The Trial of A Noble Lord, in the Court of Parnassus, for An Offence, Lately Found Bailable in the Court of King's Bench, J. Murdoch, London, 1768.

Pomaré, Carla, *Byron and the Discourses of History*, Ashgate, Farnham, 2013.

Pomey, François, *The Pantheon, Representing the Fabulous Histories of the Heathen Gods, and Most Illustrious Heroes; in a Short, Plain, and Familiar Method, by Way of Dialogue. The Sixteenth Edition. Revised, Corrected, Amended, and Illustrated with New Copper Cuts ... for the Use of Schools. By Andrew Tooke*, A. Ward and four others, London, 1747.

Porter, Roy, *Enlightenment. Britain and the Creation of the Modern World*, Allen Lane at the Penguin Press, London, 2000.

Potts, James, *The Historical, Political, and Literary Register. Containing An Account of Every Public Transaction ... of the Year*, printed by the author, London, 1796.

Priestley, J. B., *You and Me and War*, National Peace Council, London, 1935.

Priestley, Jessica, *Herodotus and Hellenistic Culture. Literary Studies in the Reception of the Histories*, Oxford University Press, Oxford, 2014.

'Proposals for printing by Subscription for the Benefit of the Author', *Jopson's Coventry Mercury*, 24 November 1788, p. 3.

Pye, Henry James, *A Commentary Illustrating the Poetics of Aristotle, by Examples taken chiefly from the Modern Poets. To which is prefixed, a new and corrected edition of the translation of the Poetics*, John Stockdale, London, 1792.

Quinn, Justin, 'Auden's Cold War Fame', Costello and Galvin (eds), *Auden at Work*, pp. 231–249.

Rácz, István D., 'The experience of reading and writing poetry. Auden and Philip Larkin', *Hungarian Journal of English and American Studies*, 14:1 (2008), pp. 95–103.

Raga, William G., 'Condescension and critical sympathy. Historians of education on progressive education in the United States and England', *Paedagogica Historica*, 50:1–2 (2014), pp. 59–75.

Rancière, Jacques, '"Le Social". The Lost Tradition in French Labour History', Raphael Samuel (ed.), *People's History and Socialist Theory*, Routledge and Kegan Paul, London, 1981, pp. 267–272.

Rancière, Jacques, *The Nights of Labor. The Workers' Dream in Nineteenth-Century*

France, trans. John Drury, intro. Donald Reid, Temple University Press, Philadelphia PA, 1989.

Rancière, Jacques, *The Names of History. On the Poetics of Knowledge*, University of Minnesota Press MN, 1994.

Rathgen, Frederick, *The Preservation of Antiquities. A Handbook for Curators*, trans. George A. Auden, M. A., M. D. (Cantab.) and Harold A. Auden, M. Sc. (Vict.), D. Sc. (Tübingen), Cambridge University Press, Cambridge, 1905.

Raymond Esq, George Frederick, *A New, Universal and Impartial History of England, From the Earliest Authentic Records, and Most Genuine Historical Evidence, to the Summer of the Year 1786 … Embellished … with Upwards of One Hundred and Twenty Beautiful Copper Plate Engravings … Raymond … assisted by Alexander Gordon and Hugh Owen, Esqrs. and others*, J. Cooke, London, 1787.

Rée, Jonathan, 'Funny voices. Stories, punctuation and personal identity', *New Literary History*, 21:4 (1990), pp. 1039–1060.

Replogle, Justin, 'Auden's intellectual development, 1950–1960', *Criticism*, 7:3 (1965), pp. 250–262.

Replogle, Justin, 'Auden's Marxism', *PMLA*, 80:5 (1965), pp. 584–595.

'Review of New Publications. *The Death of Ammon* [sic] *A Poem; with an Appendix, containing Pastorals and other Poetical Pieces. By Elizabeth Hands*', *Gentleman's Magazine* 60 (1790), p. 540.

Richards, I. A., *Practical Criticism*, Kegan Paul, London, 1929.

Ridsdale, George Twisleton, *An Ode, Congratulatory, Monitory, and Epistolary, on the Ever-memorable Victory Obtained by Lieut. General Johnson, at Ross, Over the Rebels, on the 5th of June, 1798. Composed for the Anniversary Rejoicing on the Ensuing Fifth of June, 1799*, for the author, London, 1799.

Rizzo, Betty, 'The patron as poet maker: the politics of benefaction', *Studies in Eighteenth-Century Culture*, 20 (1990), pp. 241–266.

Robbins, Bruce, *The Servant's Hand. English Fiction from below* (1986), Duke University Press, Durham and London, 1993.

Robinson, Emily, 'Touching the void. Affective history and the impossible', *Rethinking History*, 14:4 (2010), pp. 503–520.

Romaine, Suzanne (ed.), *The Cambridge History of the English Language. Vol.4, 1776–1997*, Cambridge University Press, Cambridge, 1998.

Ross, Alan S. C., 'U and non-U. An essay in sociological linguistics', *Encounter*, 5:5 (November 1955), pp. 11–20.

Roth, Paul A., 'Narrative explanations. The case of history', *History and Theory*, 27 (1988), pp. 1–13.

Rousseau, Jean-Jacques, *On the Origin of Language: Two Essays. Jean Jacques*

Rousseau and Johann Gottfried Herder, University of Chicago Press, Chicago IL, 1966.

Rousseau, Jean-Jacques, *A Discourse on Inequality* (1755), Penguin, Harmondsworth, 1984.

Rymer, Thomas, *Monsieur Rapin's Reflections on Aristotle's Treatise of Poesie, Containing the Necessary, Rational, and Universal Rules for Epick, Dramatick, and the Other Sorts of Poetry. With Reflections on the Works of the Ancient and Modern Poets, and their Faults noted. By R. Rapin*, H. Herringman, London, 1674.

Salmon, William, *Polygraphice: Or, the Arts of Drawing, Engraving, Etching, Limning, Painting, Varnishing, Japaning, Gilding, &c in Two Volumns [Sic]. ... the Eighth Edition. Enlarged*, A. and J. Churchill, J. Nicholson, London, 1701.

Salmon, J., *A Description of the Works of Art of Ancient and Modern Rome, Particularly in Architecture, Sculpture & Painting. To Which is Added, A Tour Through the Cities and Towns in the Environs of That Metropolis*, for the author, London, 1800.

Sanches, Mary and Barbara Kirshenblatt-Gimblett, 'Children's Traditional Speech Play and Child Language', Kirshenblatt-Gimblett (ed.), *Speech Play*, University of Pennsylvania Press, Philadelpha PA, 1976.

Sansom, Peter, *Everything You've Heard is True*, Cancarnet, Manchester 1990.

Sarson, Mary and Mary E. Paine, *Piers Plowman Histories, Junior Book II. Greek, Roman, and Old English History* (1913), 3rd edn, Philip, London, 1937.

Scott, Joe (ed.), *Understanding Cause and Effect, Learning and Teaching About Causation and Consequence in History*, Longman, London, 1990.

Scribner, Sylvia and Michael Cole, *The Psychology of Literacy*, Harvard University Press, Cambridge MA, 1981.

Secondat, Charles de, baron de Montesquieu, *The Spirit of Laws ... With Corrections and Additions Communicated by the Author*, trans. Thomas Nugent, 2 vols, J. Nourse and P. Vaillant, London, 1750.

Sharpe, Tony (ed.), *W. H. Auden in Context*, Cambridge University Press, Cambridge, 2013.

Sharpe, Tony, 'The Church of England: Auden's Anglicanism', Sharpe (ed.), *W. H. Auden in Context*, pp. 69–78.

Shaw, Philip, *Waterloo and the Romantic Imagination*, Palgrave Macmillan, Basingstoke, 2002.

Siskin, Clifford, *The Work of Writing. Literature and Social Change in Britain, 1700–1830*, Johns Hopkins University Press, Baltimore MD and London 1998.

Sketch of the Campaign of 1793. Part I. Letters From an Officer of the Guards, on the Continent, to a Friend in Devonshire, T. Cadell and W. Davies, London, 1795.

Smart, William, *Horace Literally Translated, for the Use of Students*, Whitaker, Teacher, London, 1830.

Smith, Adam, *The Theory of the Moral Sentiments*, A. Millar, London and A. Kincaid & J. Bell, Edinburgh, 1759.

Smith, Alexander McCall, *What W. H. Auden Can Do for You*, Princeton University Press, Princeton NJ and Oxford, 2013.

Smith, Bonnie G., *The Gender of History: Men, Women, and Historical Practice*, Harvard University Press, Harvard MA, 2000.

Smith, Harold Llewellyn, 'At St Edmund's 1915–1920', Spender (ed.), *W. H. Auden*, pp. 34–36.

Smith, Nancy, Hilda Booth, and E. H. Spalding, *Piers Plowman Histories, Junior Book I. Stories of Hebrew, Trojan, Early Teutonic, and Medieval Life*, Philip, London, 1913.

Smith, Stan (ed.), *The Cambridge Companion to W. H. Auden*, Cambridge University Press, Cambridge, 2004.

Southgate, Beverley, *History. What and Why? Ancient, Modern and Postmodern Perspectives*, Routledge, London, 1996.

Spargo, Tamsin (ed.), *Reading the Past. Literature and History*, Palgrave, Basingstoke, 2000.

Spence, Joseph, *A Guide to Classical Learning; Or, Polymetis Abridged. In Three Parts … Being a Work, Necessary, Not Only for Classical Instruction, but for all Those who Wish to Have a True Taste for the Beauties of Poetry, Sculpture and Painting. By N. Tindal, Translator of Rapin*, J. Dodsley and R. Horsfield, London, 1764.

Spencer, Luke, 'The Uses of Literature: Thompson as Writer, Reader and Critic', Roger Fieldhouse and Richard Taylor (eds) *E. P. Thompson and English Radicalism*, Manchester University Press, Manchester, 2013, pp. 96–117.

Spender, Matthew, *A House in St John's Wood. In Search of my Parents* (2015), William Collins, London, 2016.

Spender, Stephen (ed.), *W. H. Auden. A Tribute*, Weidenfeld and Nicholson, London, 1975.

Spender, Stephen, 'Valediction', Spender (ed.), *W. H. Auden*, pp. 224–248.

Stanley, Arthur Penrhyn, *Lectures on the History of the Eastern Church. With an Introduction on the Study of Ecclesiastical History*, London, 1861.

Steedman, Carolyn, 'Battlegrounds. History and primary schools', *History Workshop Journal*, 17 (1984), pp. 102–112.

Steedman, Carolyn, 'Prisonhouses', *Feminist Review*, 20 (1985), pp. 7–21.

Steedman, Carolyn, *Landscape for a Good Woman*, Virago, London, 1986.

Steedman, Carolyn, *Childhood, Culture and Class in Britain. Margaret McMillan, 1860–1931*, Virago, London, 1990.

Steedman, Carolyn, 'Living historically now?', *Arena*, 97 (1991), pp. 48–64.

Steedman, Carolyn, 'La Théorie qui n'en est pas une, or, Why Clio doesn't care', *History and Theory*, Beiheft 31 (1992), pp. 33–50.

Steedman, Carolyn, *Strange Dislocations. Childhood and the Idea of Human Interiority, 1780–1930*, Virago, London and Harvard University Press, New Haven CT, 1995.

Steedman, Carolyn, 'About ends. On how the end is different from an ending', *History of the Human Sciences*, 9:4 (1996), pp. 99–114.

Steedman, Carolyn, 'A weekend with Elektra', *Literature and History*, 6:1 (1997), pp. 17–42.

Steedman, Carolyn, 'Enforced Narratives. Stories of Another Self', Tess Cosslett, Celia Lury, and Penny Summerfield (eds), *Feminism and Autobiography. Texts, Theories, Methods*, Routledge, 2000, pp. 25–39.

Steedman, Carolyn, 'The Watercress Seller', Spargo (ed.), *Reading the Past*, pp. 18–25.

Steedman, Carolyn, *Dust*, Manchester University Press, Manchester, 2001.

Steedman, Carolyn, 'Going to Middlemarch: History and the novel', *Michigan Quarterly Review*, 40:3 (2001), http://hdl.handle.net/2027/spo. act2080.0040.310 (accessed 12 October 2017).

Steedman, Carolyn, 'Lord Mansfield's women', *Past and Present*, 176 (2002), pp. 105–143.

Steedman, Carolyn, 'Servants and their relationship to the unconscious', *Journal of British Studies*, 42 (2003), pp. 316–350.

Steedman, Carolyn, 'The servant's labour. The business of life, England 1760–1820', *Social History*, 29:1 (2004), pp. 1–29.

Steedman, Carolyn, 'Poetical maids and cooks who wrote', *Eighteenth-Century Studies*, 39:1 (2005), pp. 1–27.

Steedman, Carolyn, *Master and Servant. Love and Labour in the English Industrial Age*, Cambridge University Press, Cambridge, 2007.

Steedman, Carolyn, *Labours Lost. Domestic Service and the Making of Modern England*, Cambridge University Press, Cambridge, 2009.

Steedman, Carolyn, 'After the archive', *Comparative Critical Studies*, 8:2–3 (2011), pp. 321–340.

Steedman, Carolyn, 'Sights unseen, cries unheard. Writing the eighteenth-century metropolis', *Representations*, 118 (2012), pp. 28–71.

Steedman, Carolyn, *An Everyday Life of the English Working Class. Work, Self and Sociability in the Early Nineteenth Century*, Cambridge University Press, Cambridge, 2013.

Steedman, Carolyn, 'Reading Rancière', Oliver Davis (ed.), *Rancière Now*, Polity Press, Cambridge, 2013, pp. 69–84.

Steedman, Carolyn, 'Living with the Dead', Carol Smart and Jennifer Hockley (eds), *The Craft of Knowledge. Experiences of Living with Data*, Palgrave, Basingstoke, 2014, pp. 162–175.

Steedman, Carolyn, 'The Poetry of It (Writing History)', Angelika Bammer and Ruth-Ellen Joeres (eds), *The Future of Scholarly Writing. Critical Interventions*, Palgrave Macmillan, New York NY, 2015, pp. 215–226.

Steedman, Carolyn, 'A lawyer's letter. Everyday uses of the law in early nineteenth century England', *History Workshop Journal*, 80 (2016), pp. 62–83.

Steedman, Carolyn, 'Threatening letters. F. F. Dodd, E. P. Thompson, and the making of "The Crime of Anonymity"', *History Workshop Journal*, 82 (2016), pp. 50–82.

Steedman, Carolyn, 'Wall in the Head' (Review of Lynsey Hanley, *Respectable*), *London Review of Books*, 38:15 (28 July 2016), pp. 29–30.

Steedman, Carolyn, 'Lord Mansfield's Voices. In the Archive, Hearing Things', Holloway, Downes and Randles (eds), *Feeling Things*, pp. 209–228.

Steedman, Carolyn, 'Out of Somerset; or, Satire in Metropolis and Province', *Oxford Handbook to Eighteenth-Century Satire*, Paddy Bullard (ed.), Oxford University Press, Oxford, forthcoming.

Steedman, Carolyn, 'Social History Comes to Warwick', *The Utopian Universities*, Miles Taylor (ed.), Oxford University Press, Oxford, forthcoming.

Steinfeld, Robert J., *The Invention of Free Labor. The Employment Relation in English and American Law and Culture, 1350–1870*, University of North Carolina Press, Chapel Hill NC and London, 1991.

Stephens, Chris, *Terry Frost*, Tate Publishing, London, 2004.

Stern, James, 'The Indispensable Presence', Spender (ed.), *W. H. Auden*, pp. 123–127.

Stevenson, Robert Louis, 'To Any Reader'; 'Where Go the Boats?', *A Child's Garden of Verses*, Longmans, Green and Co, London, 1885.

Stott, Anne, *Hannah More. The First Victorian*, Oxford University Press, Oxford, 2003.

Straub, Kristina, *Domestic Affairs. Intimacy, Eroticism, and Violence Between Servants and Masters in Eighteenth-Century Britain*, Johns Hopkins University Press, Baltimore MD, 2008.

Stray, Christopher, *Classics Transformed. Schools, Universities, and Society in England, 1830–1960*, Clarendon Press, Oxford, 1998.

Sullivan, Hannah, '"Still Doing It By Hand". Auden and the Typewriter', Costello and Galvin (eds), *Auden at Work*, 2015, pp. 5–23.

Summer Miscellany: Or, A Present for the Country. Containing The Pin, An Epigram. Physick and Cards, T. Cooper, London, 1742.

Summerfield, Geoffrey, *Voices. An Anthology of Poetry and Pictures. The Third Book*, Penguin, Harmondsworth, 1968.

Summerfield, Geoffrey, *Junior Voices 1–4*, Penguin, Harmondsworth, 1970.

Sweet, Rosemary, *Antiquaries. The Discovery of the Past in Eighteenth-Century Britain*, Hambledon, London, 2004.

Swinney, Sydney, *The Battle of Minden, A Poem. In Three Books … Enriched with Critical Notes by Two Friends, and with Explanatory Notes by the Author*, Dodsley, London, 1769.

Symons, Michael, *A History of Cooks and Cooking*, Prospect Books, Totnes, 2001.

Tappen, E. M., *In Feudal Times. Social Life in the Middle Ages. Told Through the Ages Series*, Harrap, London, 1913.

Taylor, John, *Elements of the Civil Law*, for the author, Cambridge, 1767.

Taylor, Miles, 'The beginnings of modern British social history', *History Workshop Journal*, 43 (1997), pp. 155–176.

Taylor, Mrs, *An Easy Introduction to General Knowledge and Liberal Education … for the Use of the Young Ladies, at Strangeways Hall, Manchester*, for the author, Warrington, 1791.

Thacker, Andrew, 'Auden and the Little Magazines', Sharpe (ed.), *W. H. Auden in Context*, pp. 337–346.

Thompson, Denys, 'The relevance of I. A. Richards', *Use of English*, 23:1 (1971), pp. 3–31.

Thompson, Dorothy, *The Dignity of Chartism. Essays by Dorothy Thompson*, Stephen Roberts (ed.), Verso, London, 2013.

Thompson, E. P., *The Making of the English Working Class*, Gollancz, London, 1963.

Thompson, E. P., 'The rising cost of righteousness', *Views*, 7 (1965), pp. 76–79.

Thompson, E. P., 'History from Below', *Times Literary Supplement*, 7 April 1966.

Thompson, E. P., 'An Open Letter to Lesek Kolakowski', *The Poverty of Theory*, pp. 93–192.

Thompson, E. P., *The Poverty of Theory and Other Essays*, Merlin, London, 1976.

Thompson, E. P., *Witness Against the Beast. William Blake and the Moral Law*, Cambridge University Press, Cambridge, 1993.

Thompson, E. P., *Collected Poems*, Fred Inglis (ed.), Bloodaxe, Hexham, 1999.

Thompson, Kate, *Down Among the Gods*, Virago, London, 1997.

Thompson, Peggy, 'Duck, Collier, and the ideology of verse forms', *Studies in English Literature, 1500–1900*, 44:3 (2004), pp. 505–523.

Thompson, William B. and J. D. Ridge, *Catalogue of Greek and Latin School Text*

Books (1800 onwards). Part One, Dictionaries, Grammars, Vocabularies, Notes and Miscellanea, Composition Manuals (Prose and Verse), Readers, Selections, 1970. *Part Two, Greek Texts, Notes, Vocabularies, Translations,* University of Leeds, School of Education, 1974.

Thomson, Katherine, *Constance. A Novel. In Three Volumes,* Richard Bentley, London, 1833.

Thucydides, *The History of the Peloponnesian War, Translated From the Greek of Thucydides ... by William Smith,* for the author, London, 1753.

Tillich, Paul, *The Interpretation of History,* Scribner, New York NY, 1936.

Todd, Janet, *Mary Wollstonecraft. A Revolutionary Life,* Weidenfeld and Nicholson, London, 2000.

Tompson, Richard S., *Classics or Charity? The Dilemma of the 18th-century Grammar School,* Manchester University Press, Manchester, 1971.

Tosh, John, *The Pursuit of History. Aims, Methods and New Directions in the Study of Modern History* (1984), 5th edn, Pearson, Harlow, 2010.

Toynbee, Arnold J., *A Study of History,* Vol. 10 ('The Inspirations of Historians'), Oxford University Press, London, 1954.

Toynbee, Arnold, 'A study of history: what I am trying to do', *International Affairs,* 31:1 (1955), pp. 1–4.

Tressan, l'Abbé de, *Mythology Compared with History; Or, the Fables of the Ancients Elucidated From Historical Records. ... to Which is Now First Added, An Enquiry into the Religion of the First Inhabitants of Great Britain. Together with Some Account of the Ancient Druids. ... Translated From the French by H. North,* T. Cadell and W. Davies, London, 1797.

Trevelyan, George Macaulay, *Clio, A Muse, and Other Essays Literary and Pedestrian,* Longmans Green, London, 1913.

Trusler, John, *Trusler's Domestic Management, or, the Art of Conducting a Family, with Economy, Frugality and Method,* J. Souter, London, 1819.

Tully, James, *A Discourse on Property. John Locke and His Adversaries,* Cambridge University Press, Cambridge, 1980.

Tumblety, Joan (ed.), *Memory and History. Understanding Memory as Source and Subject,* Routledge, Abingdon, 2013.

Turner, Frank Miller, *The Greek Heritage in Victorian Britain,* Yale University Press, New Haven CT and London, 1981.

Uglow, Jenny, *The Lunar Men. The Friends Who Made the Future,* Faber and Faber, London, 2002.

Universal Pocket-book; Being the Most Comprehensive, Useful, and Compleat Book of the Kind, Ever Yet Publish'd. Containing ... A Map of the World ... A List of Places At Court, with Their Salaries and in Whose Gift ..., T. Cooper, London, 1740.

Utter, Robert Palfrey and Gwendolyn Bridges Needham, *Pamela's Daughters* (1936), Russell and Russell, London, 1972.

Vance, Norman and Jennifer Wallace (eds), *The Oxford History of Classical Reception in English Literature (Volume 4, 1790–1880)*, Oxford University Press, Oxford, 2015.

Vernon, James, 'The history of Britain is dead; long live a global history of Britain', *History Australia*, 13:1 (2016), pp. 19–34.

Verri, Alessandro, *The Adventures of Sappho, Poetess of Mitylene. Translation from the Greek Original, Newly Discovered*, T. Cadell, London, 1789.

Vico, Giambattista, *The Autobiography of Giambattista Vico*, trans. Max Harold Fisch and Thomas Goddard Bergin, Cornell University Press, Ithaca NY, 1944.

Vico, Giambattista, *The New Science of Giambattista Vico* (1744), trans. Thomas Goddard Bergin and Max Harold Fisch, Doubleday, New York NY, 1961.

Vico, Giambattista, *Keys to the New Science. Translations, Commentaries, and Essays*, Thora Ilin Bayer and Donald Phillip Verene (eds), Cornell University Press, Ithaca NY, 2009.

Vincent, David, *The Rise of Mass Literacy. Reading and Writing in Modern Europe*, Polity, Cambridge, 2000.

Vincent, John Emil, *John Ashbery and You. His Later Books*, University of Georgia Press, Athens GA and London, 2007.

Virgil, *The Works of Virgil. Containing His Pastorals, Georgics and Æneis. Translated into English Verse; by Mr. Dryden. In Three Volumes*, J. and R. Tonson and S. Draper, London, 1748.

Virgil, *The Works of Virgil, in Latin and English … The Æneid Translated by … Christopher Pitt, the Eclogues and Georgics, with Notes … by … Joseph Warton. With Several New Observations by Mr. Holdsworth, Mr. Spence, and Others. Also, A Dissertation on the Sixth Book of the Æneid, by Mr. Warburton. On the Shield of Æneas, by Mr. W. Whitehead. On the Character of Japis, by … Dr. Atterbury, … And, Three Essays … by the Editor. In Four Volumes*, Dodsley, London, 1753.

Virgil, *Virgilii Maronis Opera. Interpretatione et Notis Illustravit Carolus Ruæus, … Jussu Christianissimi Regis, Ad Usum Serenissimi Delphini. Juxta Editionem Novissimam Parisiensem. Huic Editioni Accessit Index Accuratissimus, Antè Editis Longè Locupletior*, C. Bathurst and twelve others, London, 1777.

Vocal Melody; Or, the Songster's Magazine in Three Parts. Being A Collection of Two Thousand of the Most Celebrated English and Scotch Songs, R. Baldwin, London, 1751.

Waldron, Jeremy, ' "The Turfs My Servant Has Cut" ', *Locke Newsletter*, 13 (1982), pp. 1–20.

Walker, Ann, *A Complete Guide for a Servant Maid; or, the Sure Means of Gaining Love and Esteem*, T. Sabine, London, 1787.

Waller, Edmund, *Ballads and Songs chiefly taken from Dr Percy's Reliques of Ancient Poetry ... with Prolegomena Notes and a Glossary. The Whole collected and published by Theophilis Miller*, Kuemmel, Halle, 1793.

Walsh, J., 'Auden. The Lost Poems', *Independent*, 4 September 2007, www.independent.co.uk/arts-entertainment/books/features/auden-the-lost-poems-463874.html (accessed 12 October 2017).

Walsh, W. H., 'Historical causation', *Proceedings of the Aristotelian Society New Series*, 63 (1962–1963), pp. 217–236.

Ward, Geoff, 'A Being All Alike? Teleotropic Discourse in Ashbery and Wordsworth', Edward Larrissey (ed.), *Romanticism and Postmodernism*, Cambridge University Press, Cambridge, 1999, pp. 86–97.

Warner, Lionel, 'Teaching Poetry to Teenagers', Michael Lockwood (ed.), *Bringing Poetry Alive. A Guide to Classroom Practice*, Sage, London, 2011, pp. 99–112.

Watson, Fiona, 'Interview: Chris Smout (Historiographer Royal)', *History Scotland*, 1 (2001), pp. 61–66.

Weaver, Gail Cohen, 'Using the cloze procedure as a teaching technique', *The Reading Teacher*, 32:5 (1979), pp. 632–636.

Weber, Max, *The Methodology of the Social Sciences*, trans. by E. Schils and H. Finch, Free Press, New York NY, 1949.

West, Jane, *Poems and Plays*, Longman and Rees, London, 1799.

White, Hayden, 'The Historical Text as Literary Artifact', Robert H. Canary and Henry Kozicki (eds), *The Writing of History. Literary Form and Historical Understanding*, University of Wisconsin Press, Madison WI, 1978, pp. 41–62.

White, Hayden, *Metahistory. The Historical Imagination in Nineteenth Century Europe* (1971), Johns Hopkins University Press, Baltimore MD, 2014.

Whitehorne, Katharine, *Cooking in a Bedsitter* (1961), Penguin, Harmondsworth, 1963.

Whyte, Samuel, *Poems on Various Subjects, Ornamented with Plates, and Illustrated with Notes, Original Letters and Curious Incidental Anecdotes ...*, for the author, Dublin, 1795.

Wilderspin, Samuel, *The Importance of Educating the Infant Poor From the Age of Eighteen Months to Seven Years. Containing An Account of the Spitalfields Infant School, and of the New System of Instruction There Adopted ... Second edition, with considerable additions*, for the author, London, 1824.

Wilford, Hugh, ' "Unwitting assets"? British intellectuals and the Congress for Cultural Freedom', *Twentieth Century British History* 11:1 (2000), pp. 42–60.

Wilford, Hugh, *The CIA, the British Left and the Cold War, 1945–1960*, Cass, London, 2003.

Williams, Raymond, *The Country and the City* (1973), Paladin, St Albans, 1975.

Williams, Raymond, *Marxism and Literature*, Oxford University Press, Oxford, 1977.

Williams, Raymond, *Keywords. A Vocabulary of Culture and Society* (1976), Fontana, London, 1983.

Williams, Raymond, *Writing in Society*, Verso, London, 1983.

Wilson, Edmund, *To the Finland Station. A Study in the Writing and Acting of History* (1940), Doubleday, New York NY, 1953.

Wilson, Edmund, *The Fifties. From Notebooks and Diaries of the Period Edited and With an Introduction by Leon Edel*, Farrar, Straus and Giroux, New York NY, 1986.

Wilson, Lisa M., 'British women writing satirical works in the romantic period. Gendering authorship and narrative voice', *Romantic Textualities*, 17 (2007), www.romtext.org.uk/articles/rt17_n02/ (accessed 16 October 2017).

Winslow, Cal (ed.), *E. P. Thompson and the Making of the New Left. Essays Polemics*, Monthly Review Press, New York NY, 2014.

Winter, John, *Bury, and its Environs, A Poem, Written in the Year MDCCXLVI*, W. Owen, London, 1747.

Wollstonecraft, Mary, *The Works of Mary Wollstonecraft. Vol. 7. On Poetry. Contributions to the Analytical Review, 1788–1797*, Janet Todd and Marilyn Butler (eds) Pickering, London, 1989.

Worden, Blair, 'Historians and poets', *Huntingdon Library Quarterly*, 68:1–2 (2005), pp. 71–93.

Wordsworth, William, *The Poetical Works of Wordsworth*, Paul D. Sheets (ed.), Houghton Mifflin, Boston MA, 1982.

Yearsley, Ann, *Poems on Various Subjects. A Second Book of Poems … by Ann Yearsley*, G. G. J. & J. Robinson, London, 1787.

York, Powell and T. F. Tout, *History of England*, Longman, Green, London, 1910.

Yorke, Philip Earl of Hardwicke, *Athenian Letters; Or, the Epistolary Correspondence of an Agent of the King of Persia, Residing at Athens during the Peloponnesian War. Containing the History of the Times, in Dispatches to the Ministers of State at the Persian Court …*, J. Walker, London, 1792.

Young, Arthur, *A Six Months Tour Through the North of England. Containing, An Account of the Present State of Agriculture, Manufactures and Population, … in Four Volumes*, W. Strahan and three others, London, J. Balfour, Edinburgh, 1774.

Young, Edward, *Love of Fame, the Universal Passion. In Seven Characteristical Satires*, for the author, London, 1753.

Zerby, Chuck, *The Devil's Details. A History of Footnotes*, Simon & Schuster, New York NY, 2003.

Zweiniger-Bargielowska, Ina, *Austerity in Britain. Rationing, Controls and Consumption, 1939–1955*, Oxford University Press, Oxford 2002.

Newspapers, journals and magazines
Annual Bulletin of Historical Literature
British and Foreign Review; or, European Quarterly Journal
Critical Review, or Annals of Literature
Encounter
Freemasons' Magazine: or, General and Complete Library
Gentleman's Magazine
Historical Abstracts, 1775–1945. A Quarterly of Historical Articles appearing Currently in Periodicals the World Over
Independent
Jopson's Coventry Mercury
Lady's Magazine; Or Entertaining Companion for the Fair Sex, Appropriated Solely to Their Use and Amusement
Listener
London Magazine
London Review of Books
Monthly Review
New Left Review
New Verse
Solihull Parish Magazine
The Times
Times Literary Supplement

Internet sources
Aristotle, *The Poetics*, trans. S. H. Butcher, Section 1, Part I; The Internet Classics Archive, classics@classics.mit.edu (accessed 12 October 2017).

Aristotle, *The Poetics of Aristotle*, trans. Ingram Bywater, with a preface by Gilbert Murray, www.authorama.com/the-poetics-10.html (accessed 12 October 2017).

Burt, Stephen, 'Wake all the dead!', *LRB* Blog, 19 July 2010, www.lrb.co.uk/blog/2010/07/19/stephen-burt/wake-all-the-dead (accessed 12 October 2017).

Crockford's Clerical Directory, 1888–1932; www.crockford.org.uk/ (accessed 12 October 2017).

English Emblem Book Project, Penn State University Libraries, https://libraries.psu.edu/about/collections/english-emblem-book-project/ripa-toc (accessed 12 October 2017).

Genome Beta Radio Times 1923–2009, http://genome.ch.bbc.co.uk/ (accessed 12 October 2017).

Magna Carta, www.magnacharta.com/bomc/king-john-the-genesis-of-a-sinis ter-reputation (accessed 16 October 2017).

Marxists, www.marxists.org/archive/marx/works (accessed 16 October 2017).

Royal College of Physicians, *Lives of the Fellows*, http://munksroll.rcplondon. ac.uk/Biography/Details/155 (accessed 12 October 2017).

Shelley, Percy Bysshe, *Political Essay on the Existing State of Things* (1811), http:// poeticalessay.bodleian.ox.ac.uk/# (accessed 12 October 2017).

Twenty First International Congress of the Historical Sciences (Amsterdam, August 2010), www.ichs2010.org/home.asp (accessed 16 October 2017).

University of Oxford, Nuffield College Library, MSS.GDHC, Papers of G. D. H. Cole in Nuffield College Library, www.nuffield.ox.ac.uk/media/2016/ gdhcole.pdf (accessed 12 October 2017).

Wesker, Arnold, www.arnoldwesker.com/plays.asp?workID=45 (accessed 16 October 2017).

YouTube, 'Homage to Clio (Recorded in 1960)' by W. H. Auden', 4 January 2016, Uploaded by LPKvideoDesigns, www.youtube.com/watch?v=Gwe 2V-mvhgs (accessed 24 May 2016).

Archival sources

Birmingham Central Library, Birmingham Archives Heritage and Photography, BCC/1/BH/1/1/1, Education Committee and Its Related Sub-committees, 1903–1937, Annual Reports to the City of Birmingham Education Committee of the School Medical Officer.

Birmingham Central Library, Birmingham Archives Heritage and Photography, Homer425; 'Accounts of the Births, Deaths and Other Circumstances of the Children of the Rd. Henry Secheverell Homer, Rector of Birdingbury, & Vicar of Willoughby, Warwickshire'.

Birmingham University Library, Special Collections, 1956/V27–27A. Philip Bracebridge Homer, Letters, Papers, Copy of *The Garland* &c.

Bishopsgate Institute, London, History Workshop, 7/43, Session Report; History Workshop Audio Collection RS062b.

Somerset Archives, DD/GB, 148–149, Gore Family Papers. Volume 1, DD/ GB/148: 264.

Somerset Archives, SA, DD/SF, Bishop Lydeard Farming Accounts and Household Accounts, Mrs. Frances Hamilton.

University of London, Senate House Library, 'University of London, General Certificate of Education. Summer. 1963. Ordinary Level English Literature (Syllabus A)'.

University of Tulsa, McFarlin Library, Department of Special Collections and University Archives: Collection 1993–003.

University of Warwick Modern Records Centre, MSS.318/4/7a: 'An outline for boys and girls' edited by Naomi Mitchison, [1932]'.

University of Warwick Modern Record Centre, UWA (University of Warwick Administration).

Warwickshire County Record Office, CR1707, Heber-Percy of Guys Cliffe, 1759–1826. Diaries of Bertie Greatheed.

Warwickshire County Record Office, CR 136/A [565], Newdigate of Arbury, Notebook of books received and sent out from Arbury; CR 136/A [621] Appointment and Memorandum Diaries.

Wiltshire Country Record Office, 776/922A. Household Account Book, kept by Christian Tousey of Salisbury, a cook or housekeeper.

PhD theses and other unpublished work

Elodie Marie Duché, 'A Passage to Imprisonment. The British Prisoners of War in Verdun under the First French Empire', PhD thesis, University of Warwick, 2014.

Alexander Hutton, ' "Culture and Society" in Conceptions of the Industrial Revolution in Britain, 1930–1965', PhD thesis, University of Cambridge, 2014.

Heike Pichler, 'A Qualitative-quantitative Analysis of Negative Auxiliaries in a Northern English Dialect: I DON'T KNOW and I DON'T THINK, Innit?', PhD thesis, University of Aberdeen, 2008.

Michael John Protheroe, 'The Development of Elementary Education in a Voluntary School, 1862–1992. A Study of Change and Continuity in the National Elementary School, Solihull, between the Revised Code and the Geddes Axe', thesis submitted for the Diploma in Education, University College, 1974.

Brooke Emma Whitelaw, 'Industry and the Interior Life. Industrial "Experts" and the Mental World of Workers in Twentieth Century Britain', PhD, University of Warwick, 2009.

Y. S. Yamada, 'W. H. Auden's Revising Process (VI). Homage To Clio (1960)', Annual Report, Faculty Education, Iwate University, 40:2 (1981–2), pp. 1–18, available at https://iwateu.repo.nii.ac.jp/?action=pages_view_main&active _action=repository_view_main_item_detail&item_id=11931&item_no=1&p age_id=13&block_id=21 (accessed 16 October 2017).

Index

Made in the USA
Middletown, DE
26 September 2023

39390334R00056